Photoshop 7®

Tips & Techniques

About the Author

Wendy Willard offers design, illustration, marketing, and consulting services to businesses for both print and web campaigns. She also teaches and writes on these topics, and is the author of *HTML: A Beginner's Guide* and *Web Design: A Beginner's Guide* (both published by McGraw-Hill/Osborne). She holds a degree in Illustration from Art Center College of Design in Pasadena, California, where she first learned how to use Adobe Photoshop.

Wendy's passions include all aspects of digital design, drawing, painting, and photographing Maine, Chop Point School & Camp, and anything related to the Web. She lives and works in the midcoast area of Maine with her husband Wyeth and their two young daughters.

Photoshop 7®

Tips & Techniques

Wendy Willard

McGraw-Hill/Osborne

New York / Chicago / San Francisco
Lisbon / London / Madrid / Mexico City / Milan
New Delhi / San Juan / Seoul / Singapore / Sydney / Toronto

McGraw-Hill/Osborne
2600 Tenth Street
Berkeley, California 94710
U.S.A.

To arrange bulk purchase discounts for sales promotions, premiums, or fund-raisers, please contact **McGraw-Hill**/Osborne at the above address. For information on translations or book distributors outside the U.S.A., please see the International Contact Information page immediately following the index of this book.

Photoshop 7® Tips & Techniques

1234567890 FGR FGR 0198765432

ISBN 0-07-222446-0

Publisher	Brandon A. Nordin
Vice President & Associate Publisher	Scott Rogers
Acquisitions Editor	Megg Morin
Acquisitions Coordinator	Tana Allen
Technical Editor	Sam Wilson
Copy Editor	Bill McManus
Proofreader	John Gildersleeve
Indexer	Irv Hershman
Computer Designers	Tara A. Davis, Melinda Moore Lytle, John Patrus
Illustrators	Lyssa Wald, Michael Mueller
Series Design	Roberta Steele
Cover Series Design	Greg Scott

This book was composed with Corel VENTURA™ Publisher.

To my daughter, Caeli Renee,
who was born during the writing of this book.

Contents at a Glance

Contents

Acknowledgments

Given that this is my third book, I thought things would go pretty smoothly and I'd have the book out in no time. Boy was I wrong! I forgot to account for those unplanned events that inevitably sidetrack you during an important project. You know, little things like flu season, childbirth, and the unavailability of the software you're writing about. Because of those things, I have quite a lengthy list of people to thank.

To start, my unending gratitude and love goes to my husband Wyeth for (among other things) giving up his spring vacation as a teacher to take the girls and just let me write 24/7. This book would not have been possible without your unselfish love and support.

To my editors, Megg, Tana, Katie, and Lyssa—you all were so supportive throughout the craziness of writing this book, and for that a simple "thank you" just doesn't seem to cut it. This book's excellent quality is definitely attributed to all your hard work and dedication. A special thanks goes to Sam Wilson, my technical editor, who went above and beyond the call of duty and added significantly to the book's clarity and quality.

Thanks to designer and friend Tanja Cesh for selflessly jumping in to help out with three chapters when my daughter made her appearance in this world smack dab in the middle of writing this book. Tanja's expertise and whole-hearted love of Photoshop are evident in every paragraph she contributed.

Thanks to the entire Photoshop product team at Adobe for producing such a top-notch product—one that is as much a part of my life as chocolate chip cookies and iced tea. Also, thanks to Diana Helander at Adobe for all her help figuring out how to best reference and discuss Adobe's suite of fantastic products. Thanks to Nicole Andergard at Extensis for the valuable information she provided relating to several of my favorite Extensis plug-ins for Photoshop.

Finally, I thank God for enabling me to write such an excellent book in the middle of such personal stress. Finishing this book on time was nothing short of a miracle—one I attribute to Him alone.

Introduction

Photoshop 7: Tips & Techniques was written with value for the reader in mind. It is structured as both a reference manual and a learning tool. Information and step-by-step tips are written in everyday terms, and the topics covered feature complete cross-referencing to related techniques.

Throughout the development of this book, the objective was always to provide you with a cohesive, easy-to-understand guide for getting the most out of the latest version of Photoshop. With the wide variety of books available on this topic, I strove to give you the most well-rounded, real-world set of tips and techniques possible.

I hate to sound like a broken record or a commercial, but the possibilities Photoshop 7 allows truly are limitless. I find digital design with Photoshop to be a fun and extremely creative activity, and I hope you will as well—whether you plan to make it a career or a hobby.

Who Should Read This Book

Photoshop 7: Tips & Techniques is a book for all levels of users who are using (or considering using) Photoshop 7. The program and each of the tips are explained using simple, everyday language suitable for readers of all ages and backgrounds.

Those who will likely get the most out of this book include:

- Beginning users who are new to Photoshop in version 7
- Beginning to intermediate users who worked with a previous version of Photoshop and are now upgrading to Photoshop 7
- Intermediate to advanced users who typically work with a limited set of features and now wish to expand their knowledge of the product and increase their efficiency using it

What This Book Covers

The book is separated into three distinct parts: preparing for web design, design and production, and integration and testing.

Part I: Using Photoshop to Prepare for Web and Print Design

Part I helps you prepare for the typical design development process by first explaining the ways to customize Photoshop according to your workflow. Chapter 1 discusses customizing the program specifically for web designers, while Chapter 2 discusses the same ideas, but as they relate to print designers.

Chapter 3 focuses on ways to bring content into Photoshop, whether you're working from a digital camera, scanner, or other digital files. This chapter is applicable to both web and print designers.

Chapter 4 rounds out Part I by addressing proper ways to use Photoshop as a web page layout tool, from screen area to page size and structure, as well as web color issues.

Part II: Using Photoshop to Design Web and Print Graphics

Part II moves on from preparing to actually designing in Photoshop by covering the nuts and bolts of the product in four important categories:

- Chapter 5: Using Selections and Masks
- Chapter 6: Using Layers
- Chapter 7: Using Text
- Chapter 8: Drawing and Painting

Finally, I included many of my favorite creative effects in a single chapter (Chapter 9) to inspire you to experiment with the large number of filters in Photoshop 7.

Part III: Using Photoshop to Produce Web and Print Graphics

Part III is included because few designs end in Photoshop. At some point you typically want to save your designs to use them on the Web, or perhaps print them. For either case, tips and techniques for producing both web and print graphics are included in this section of the book.

Specifically, Chapter 10 covers slicing and optimizing web graphics, while Chapter 11 focuses on the more interactive type of web graphics, such as rollovers and animation. When your graphics need to be printed, turn to Chapter 12 for advice on optimizing graphics for output.

Color Insert

A 16-page color insert displays full-color examples of those tips and techniques that wouldn't be demonstrated as well in black and white.

How to Read This Book

Although the book's chapters build on the information presented in preceding chapters, I structured the book so that you can turn to any tip and find the information you need.

To help you quickly locate the information you need, the start of each chapter provides a list of the specific tips included in that chapter. If you need more information on a topic, each chapter provides introductory text that gives you a solid foundation.

 As you scan through the book's pages, watch for the Try It icon, which highlights specific steps within each tip that you can perform immediately to accomplish a task.

Identify Your Platform

I include keyboard commands for both Macintosh and Windows users throughout the tips because there are slight differences in keyboard and shortcut identification across Mac and Windows platforms.

For example, the CMD (short for Command) and OPTION keys pertain to Macintosh users, while the CTRL (short for Control) and ALT (short for Alternate) keys pertain mostly to Windows users. In all instances, Windows key commands are specified first, followed by Mac key commands.

Where multiple keys are pressed simultaneously to accomplish a command, a hyphen (-) joins the key presses (for example, CTRL-S). Where menu and submenu access is referred to, commands are separated by pipe symbols in this way: File | Open.

Getting to Know the Work Area

If you're new to Photoshop, it's important to spend some time getting to know the work area before you jump into a project. While all of the program's windows, menus, and palettes may seem confusing at first, I think you'll be moving around the program comfortably in no time if you keep a few things in mind, such as the names of each main component in Photoshop.

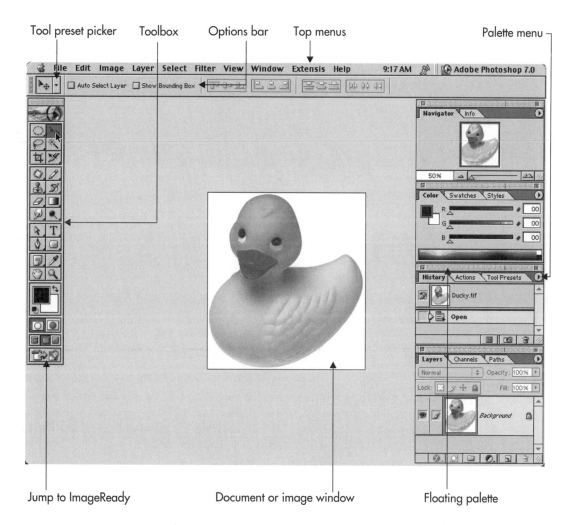

Tool preset picker   Toolbox   Options bar   Top menus   Palette menu

Jump to ImageReady   Document or image window   Floating palette

In addition to the key components of Photoshop, if you plan to use the program to perform web-related tasks, it's important to know your way around ImageReady as well.

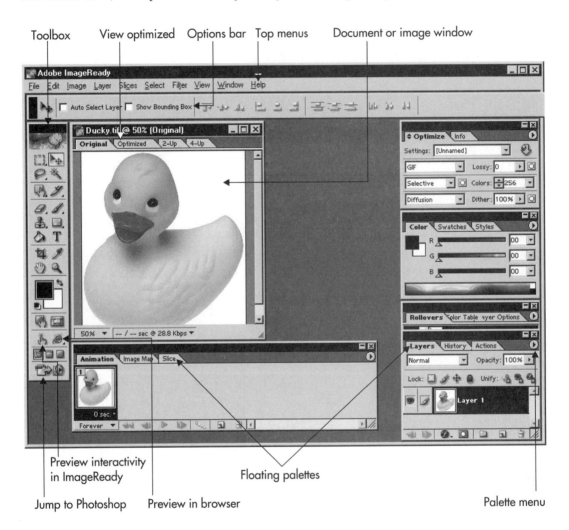

Toolbox

Photoshop and ImageReady both contain a toolbox that typically displays on the far-left side of the screen when you start the program. Clicking any of the buttons in the toolbox activates one of the program's many tools, such as those for drawing, painting, making selections, creating type, and moving elements.

A tiny triangle in the bottom-right corner of a particular tool button indicates there are additional variations on that tool available. To access these, click and hold the tool button.

> ► **QUICK TIP**
>
> *In ImageReady, you can make these tool menus "float" so that each variation of the tool is available at all times. To do so, click and hold the tool button in the ImageReady toolbox and release it when you move the cursor over the small rectangular button at the bottom of the list of tool variations.*

You can also change the foreground and background colors by clicking their respective color swatches in the toolbox; the default foreground and background colors are white and black, respectively.

Finally, you can use the button at the very bottom of the toolbox to jump to Photoshop or ImageReady, depending on which application you're currently using.

► **NOTE**

If you close the toolbox, you can make it visible again by choosing Window | Tools.

Options Bar

The Options bar is docked at the top of the screen by default, but as with the toolbox and floating palettes, it can be moved wherever you need it to be. (To move the Options bar, click and hold the far-left edge and drag it to its new location.)

When you choose a particular tool from the toolbox, its options appear in this Options bar. For example, when you choose the Brush tool from the toolbox, the Options bar changes to display choices for brush tips, painting mode, opacity, and so on.

► **NOTE**

If you disable the Options bar, you can make it visible again by choosing Window | Options.

Tool Presets

On the left of the Options bar is a button that gives you access to the Tool Preset picker. A tool preset is basically your customized version of any tool in Photoshop. For example, if you find that you use 12-pt Verdana type more often than not, you could save those settings as a tool preset for the Type tool. Then, when you select this tool preset from the Tool preset picker in the Options bar, you have quick and easy access to that tool with those particular settings already selected.

► **NOTE**

Tool presets are available in Photoshop only (not ImageReady).

Floating Palettes

The majority of the most commonly used options in Photoshop are displayed in floating palettes. Palettes are essentially sets of options organized according to use. Palettes are considered to be "floating" because you can move and rearrange them as needed on the screen.

When you first launch Photoshop or ImageReady, the palettes are grouped into sets of two or three along the right side of the screen. (In ImageReady, a few palettes are also located along the bottom edge.)

▶ | **QUICK TIP**

To drag a palette away from others in its grouping, click and drag the palette's title tab to its new location. To group a palette with another, click and drag the palette's title tab next to another palette's title tab.

You can also click the Close button in the top of a palette to hide it if you no longer need it visible on the screen. At any time, you can open or close palettes from the Window menu at the top of the screen. Photoshop contains the following palettes:

- Navigator
- Info
- Color
- Swatches
- Styles
- History
- Actions
- Tool Presets
- Channels
- Layers
- Paths
- Character[1]
- Paragraph[1]
- Brushes[2]
- File Browser[2]

ImageReady contains the following palettes:

- Optimize
- Info

- Color
- Swatches
- Styles
- Rollovers
- Color Table
- Layer Options/Style
- Layers
- History
- Actions
- Animation
- Image Map
- Slice
- Character[1]
- Paragraph[1]

Each palette also has a small triangle in the upper-right corner, which is used to access the palette menu. I reference this palette menu countless times in the book because it's frequently used to further refine selections and options related to the particular palette.

Top Menus

The menus at the top of the screen give access to many other options and commands available in Photoshop and ImageReady. You can also access some of these by pressing the appropriate keys on your keyboard. To identify a key command for a command in a menu, look to the right of that command's name.

Context Menus

Photoshop and ImageReady also contain what are referred to as context menus. These extra menus are typically accessed by right-clicking (Windows) or CTRL-clicking (Mac) within an image with a particular tool or over an item in a palette. Whenever you're looking for an option relevant to the active aspects of the program (such as the active tool, selection, or palette), try accessing the context menu first.

---

[1] The Character and Paragraph palettes are the only two not visible on the screen by default when the program first launches.

[2] If your screen resolution is set to larger than 832×768, the Brushes and File Browser palettes are docked by default in an area to the right of the Options bar called the Palette Well.

What's Changed in Version 7

Here's a list of the key changes to Photoshop and ImageReady in version 7, as well as the chapter in which each element is discussed:

- File Browser (Chapter 3)
- Healing Brush (Chapter 9)
- Dithered (web) transparency (Chapter 10)
- Weighted optimization during web output (Chapter 10)
- WBMP file support (Chapter 10)
- Rollovers palette (Chapter 11)
- Tool presets (Chapter 8)
- Auto Color command (Chapter 9)
- Data-driven graphics (Chapter 11)
- New brushes (Chapter 8)
- Pattern Maker (Chapter 8)
- Updated Liquify command (Chapter 11)
- Web photo gallery enhancements (Chapter 11)
- Spell checker (Chapter 7)
- Tighter integration with Adobe InDesign (Chapter 12), Adobe GoLive (Chapter 10), Adobe LiveMotion (Chapter 11), and many other Adobe products

Where to Go for More Information

This book is by no means meant to be an exhaustive resource on Photoshop 7. For additional information regarding Photoshop 7, I recommend you become familiar with the Help files that come with the program, as well as Adobe's web site, which contains communities of users who discuss each product.

For updates to this book and its tips, check my web site: www.willardesigns.com. Finally, for an in-depth look at Photoshop 7, take a look at Laurie Ann Ulrich's *Photoshop 7: The Complete Reference* (McGraw-Hill/Osborne).

PART I

Using Photoshop to Prepare for Web and Print Design

CHAPTER 1

Customizing Photoshop for Web Design

TIPS IN THIS CHAPTER

Just about every program you work with on your computer contains some set of preferences you can customize to suit your specific needs, and Photoshop is no different.

This chapter opens with a discussion on how the Photoshop preferences can affect your work as a web designer, and continues with essential tips on customizing your version of Photoshop for the design of web graphics.

Why Customize Photoshop?

When you use a program like Photoshop frequently, you undoubtedly find yourself performing the same or similar tasks over and over again. For web designers, this might mean changing the unit of measurement for each Photoshop file from inches to pixels—the unit of measurement used on computer monitors. Typically, the developers of the program know this and find ways to minimize the time it takes for you to perform tasks such as this one.

By customizing Photoshop for tasks commonly associated with web design, you not only can save yourself time but also make it easier for the program itself to produce your desired results. For example, by changing your *default* unit of measurement to pixels—a tip included in this chapter—the program will use pixels as its unit of measurement by default, for every file you open. That way, you'll more easily be able to recognize the screen measurements of web graphics than if you had to first translate the measurements from inches or centimeters to pixels.

▶ **NOTE**

The majority of the tips in this chapter refer specifically to Photoshop and not ImageReady. The reason is that while Photoshop is a tool used by both web and print designers, ImageReady was designed specifically for web design. As such, the program is already customized for web designers.

Before I move on to the tips in this chapter, let's look at how the following characteristics of web design affect the creation of graphics in Photoshop:

- Computer operating system
- Monitor settings
- Color

Computer Operating System

The operating system you use affects not only which version of Photoshop you purchase but also some of the preferences you define as a web designer. Specifically, your operating system affects the following items:

- **Image previews and thumbnails**   Pint-size versions of images used to help identify them within file directories

- **File naming conventions**   How you decide to name a file, including how many characters you use and which characters those are
- **Memory allocated to Photoshop**   The amount of RAM given to Photoshop as well as the amount of available overflow memory, referred to as the "scratch disk"

Tips in the following sections specify exactly how to deal with these issues when customizing Photoshop for web use.

Monitor Settings

If you've ever looked at Photoshop on a 15-inch monitor and then on a 21-inch monitor, you're well aware of how monitors and their settings can affect the program. Photoshop's work area includes several palettes that are typically visible in addition to the file you're working on, as shown in Figures 1-1 and 1-2. If you're using a small monitor, or even if you're using a large monitor but have the resolution set to emulate that of a small monitor, all these palettes can quickly take over the screen.

In addition to the monitor's size and resolution, its calibration can affect how your web graphics display on your screen. This is particularly important to web designers, because you want your

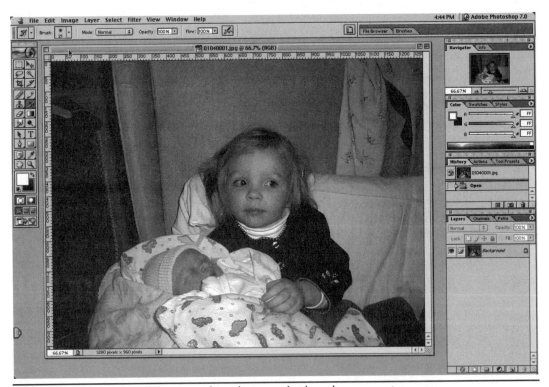

Figure 1-1   A typical workspace in Photoshop, as displayed on a monitor set to a 1280×960 screen resolution

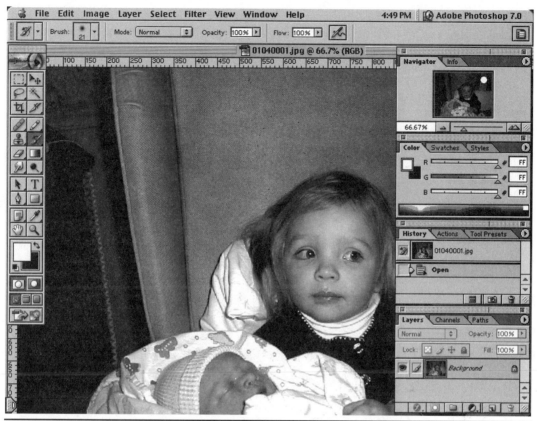

Figure 1-2   A typical workspace in Photoshop, as displayed on a monitor set to an 800×600 screen resolution

images to display as close to "normal" as possible in order to get an idea of how they'll look on other users' monitors.

Tips in the following sections specify exactly how to deal with issues related to a monitor's size, resolution, and calibration when customizing Photoshop for web use.

Color

Color in Photoshop has become quite a large issue in recent versions of the program. While the software developers have given users more control, they've also created more room for confusion in the minds of many users. By and large, however, there are two key color issues for web designers to deal with in Photoshop (note that both of these issues are addressed in the tips throughout the rest of this chapter):

- Color profiles
- Color swatches/palettes

The reason these two issues are particularly important for web designers is that the end result of web graphics is open to interpretation by the viewer's monitor and screen settings. In fact, because no two computer monitors display web graphics exactly the same, much of a web designer's work in Photoshop will center around trying to compensate for this variation in color.

How Computer Monitors Display Color

Computer monitors display color in RGB mode, where R = Red, G = Green, and B = Blue. Each letter (R, G, and B) is represented by a value between 0 and 255, with 0 as the darkest and 255 as the lightest in the spectrum. In RGB, white and black have the following values:

- **White** 255,255,255
- **Black** 0,0,0

The RGB color mode is decimal, or based on the number 10. This means we have 10 units (0–9) to use before we have to repeat a unit (as with the number 10, which uses the 0 and 1). You can see the RGB values for colors in Photoshop by looking at either the Color palette, shown here

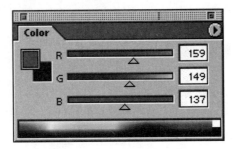

or the Info palette, as shown in the following illustration:

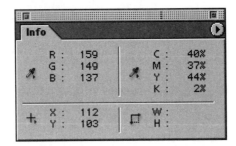

How Web Pages Identify Color

Although web pages are typically displayed on RGB computer monitors, HTML doesn't understand the RGB color values.

The hexadecimal system (hex) uses the same concepts as the decimal system, except it's based on 16 units (see Table 1-1). Because HTML cannot handle decimal color values, the hexadecimal system is used to specify color values. Instead of making up new characters to represent the remaining units after 9, the hexadecimal system uses the first six letters of the English alphabet (A–F).

Decimal	0	1	2	3	4	5	6	7	8	9	10	11	12	13	14	15
Hex	0	1	2	3	4	5	6	7	8	9	A	B	C	D	E	F

Table 1-1   A Comparison of Decimal and Hexadecimal

Whenever you want to use a color in an HTML page, you typically translate that color from decimal (RGB) to hexadecimal. Each red, green, or blue value translates into a two-digit hexadecimal value. You then combine all three of those two-unit hexadecimal values into a single string, preceded by a hash mark, as in: #ffcc00.

▶ **NOTE**

If you're using Cascading Style Sheets to specify your colors instead of HTML, you actually have the option of using the RGB values or the hexadecimal values as needed.

How Monitors and Web Pages Work Together to Display Color

Have you ever looked at your favorite web site on someone else's monitor and noticed the colors seemed a bit different? This may have been because of the different monitor settings. For example, most newer computer systems and monitors are capable of displaying millions of colors (also called 24-bit color), but that wasn't the case only a few years ago, when most DOS-based PCs were set up to display 256 colors or less (also called 8-bit color). This reduced color palette means you can't always be assured the color you choose for your web page is going to be available on the viewer's system.

To compound the problem, Macintosh systems display a different set of 256 colors than their DOS-based PC counterparts. Only 216 colors between the two computer systems (Mac and PC) are the same. Those 216 colors have come to be known as the web-safe color palette.

You can easily recognize web-safe colors by their hexadecimal values. Each of the web-safe colors has RGB values that are multiples of 51, as shown in Table 1-2.

▶ **QUICK TIP**

For a color representation of the web-safe palette, see the Color Swatches section of the color insert.

RGB	Hex
0	00
51	33
102	66
153	99
204	CC
255	FF

Table 1-2   Web-Safe RGB and Hex Color Values

Not all web pages require or benefit from the use of web-safe colors. In fact, while the primary benefit of web-safe colors is that they will display uniformly across monitors set to 8- and 24-bit color modes, they will not necessarily display exactly the same across monitors set to 15- or 16-bit color modes (also called *high color* or *thousands of colors*).

▶ **NOTE**

For more information about the web-safe palette's lack of "safeness" under the 15- and 16-bit color modes, access an article in WebMonkey online, written by David Lehn and Hadley Stern: http://hotwired.lycos.com/webmonkey/00/37/index2a.html.

If you use a color outside of the web-safe palette and your page is viewed on a computer running 256 colors or less, your color will be changed to one that is within the available system palette. So, if you want to guarantee that a particular color is going to remain constant under the largest number of situations, it's best to use a web-safe color.

On the other hand, if you use a color outside the web-safe palette and your page is viewed on a computer running 24-bit color, you don't have to worry because systems running in 24-bit color mode can handle millions of colors.

▶ **QUICK TIP**

It's best to design for the largest possible audience, because it's very likely that your site will be viewed by people using a wide variety of color modes—everything from two-color, hand-held computers to high-end computers with beautiful, large-screen monitors.

While this chapter describes how to load the web-safe palette in Photoshop, Chapter 10 discusses when to use the web-safe palette for a particular image.

Check Your Screen Resolution

Many people don't realize that the physical size of a computer monitor is independent of the amount of space available for the computer desktop—referred to as the monitor resolution. For example, you could run both a 14- and a 21-inch monitor in the 640×480 resolution if you wanted to. Likewise, you could set your 17-inch monitor to run anything from a low 640×480 resolution to a high 1920×1440 resolution. Figures 1-1 and 1-2 at the beginning of the chapter show how changing your monitor's resolution from one resolution to another affects the amount of space on your computer desktop. These figures demonstrate how the monitor's resolution most affects Photoshop—the higher your resolution, the more space you have for all those palettes and windows!

TRY IT   To check your screen resolution, follow the steps outlined next for your operating system. Once you have identified your current screen resolution, you can use the same menu to change it to a larger one as needed.

- **Mac O/S**   From the Apple menu, select Controls Panels | Monitors, and then identify your current screen resolution setting by reading the size from the Resolution menu.
- **Windows 98, ME, 2000, NT, XP**   Right-click your desktop and choose Properties. Click the Settings tab and identify your current screen resolution setting by reading the size from the Screen Area menu.

Change Your Default Unit of Measurement to Pixels

When you work in Photoshop, your files are given dimensions according to the default unit of measurement. For example, if the default unit of measurement for the program is set to inches, any time you display the rulers they will use inches.

Because web files display on computer monitors instead of the printed page, they use the unit of measurement for screens—the pixel. So, when customizing Photoshop for web design, you should use pixels instead of any other print-based method of measurement for all files.

TRY IT   To change the default unit of measurement in Photoshop, choose Edit | Preferences | Units & Rulers. Then, from the Rulers menu, select Pixels (as shown in the following illustration). Note that you can also get to the Rulers menu by double-clicking the rulers surrounding any of your images. If the rulers aren't visible around your image, you can make them appear by choosing View | Rulers or pressing CTRL-R (Windows) or CMD-R (Mac).

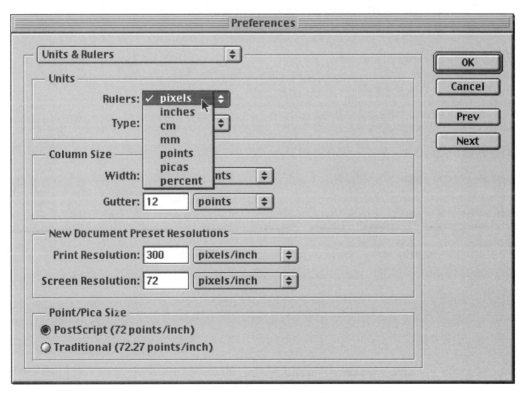

▶ *QUICK TIP*

You can also switch the current unit of measurement on the fly by right-clicking (Windows) or CTRL-clicking (Mac OS) on the rulers around an image and selecting a new unit of measurement from the pop-up menu.

Customize the Color and Style of Your Ruler Guides

Photoshop lets you draw guidelines horizontally and vertically across an image. These guides are especially useful for web designers because they can later be used as the foundation for slicing images apart into web graphics (as discussed in Chapter 10). Figure 1-3 shows how guides can be helpful in laying out web designs.

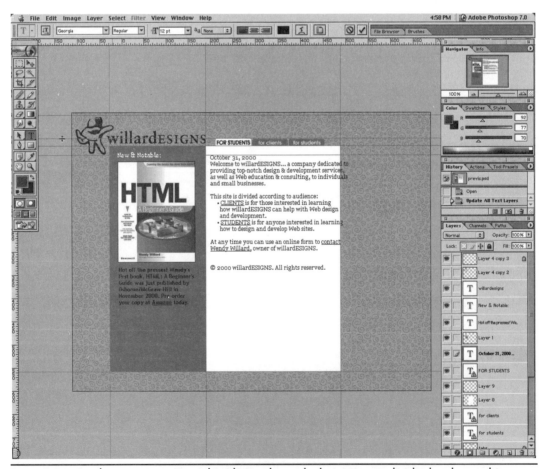

Figure 1-3   Guides were instrumental in slicing this web design into individual web graphics.

▶ **QUICK TIP**

To turn on the display of guides for a particular image that already has guides set up, choose View | Show | Guides or press CTRL-; *(Windows) or* CMD-; *(Mac).*

The guides default to displaying in a light-blue color and as complete lines. You can change the color and style of these guides according to the needs of your graphics. For example, if the background color of your web design is similar to the default light-blue of your guides, you can change the color of those guides in Photoshop's Preferences dialog box.

TRY IT To customize the color and style of your ruler guides, choose Edit | Preferences | Guides, Grid & Slices. Then, specify the desired color and style of your guides in the drop-down list boxes, as shown in the following illustration.

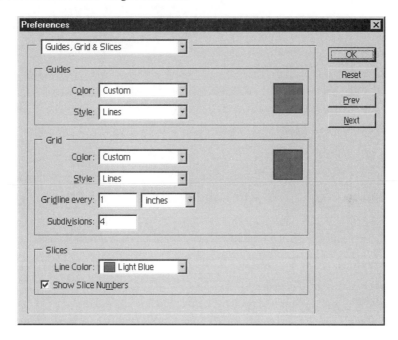

Check Your Color Picker

One of the options you can customize in Photoshop's preferences is the default color picker. The color picker is invoked whenever you click a color swatch in Photoshop's foreground and background selectors, as shown here:

 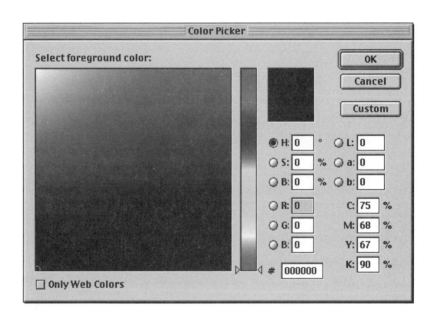

The default color picker that ships with each version of Photoshop, as shown in the previous illustration, is created by Adobe.

► **QUICK TIP**

Click the Only Web Colors check box in the lower-left corner to force all colors selected from this color picker to be within the web-safe palette.

Depending on which operating system you use, you may also have another choice of color pickers. For example, Mac users can choose to use the Apple Color Picker, which gives you the option of selecting colors either according to their hexadecimal values or from an easy-to-use slider of web-safe colors (see Figure 1-4).

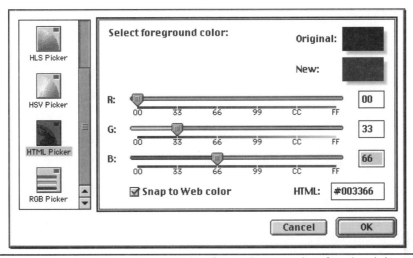

Figure 1-4   The Apple Color Picker comes with a fun and easy web-safe color slider.

TRY IT   To check which default color picker your program is set to use, do the following:

1. Choose Edit | Preferences | General.
2. Click the Color Picker drop-down arrow to identify your available options.

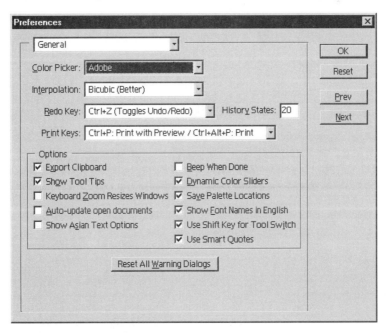

After identifying your options, you can change the color picker as needed. To invoke the color picker after making a change, click OK to return to the main window. Then, click on a color swatch in the foreground or background selector.

 NOTE

You can also load other color pickers from third-party companies using this method.

Use Web Color Sliders

Photoshop's floating Color palette (shown in the following illustration) defaults to showing RGB color sliders. While this is suitable for most web design, there are times when you may prefer to have this palette display only web-safe colors in the sliders. This can easily be accomplished by switching the display from RGB sliders to web-safe color sliders.

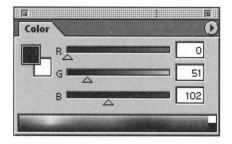

Another customizable aspect of the Color palette is the color ramp along the bottom edge of the palette. While the sliders default to RGB, the ramp defaults to using the CMYK color spectrum. Web designers are better served by changing this to the RGB spectrum. You can then further customize the spectrum by forcing it to display only web-safe colors.

 To switch the slider display to web-safe color sliders, click the triangle in the upper-right corner of the Color palette. From the pop-up menu that displays, choose Web Color Sliders.

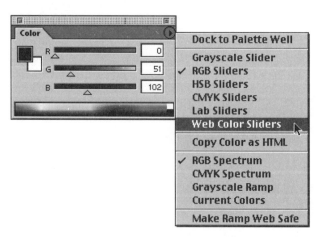

To switch the ramp display to RGB, click the triangle in the upper-right corner of the Color palette. From the pop-up menu that displays, choose RGB Spectrum. Then, to force the ramp to use only web-safe colors, click once more on the triangle in the upper-right corner of the Color palette and select Make Ramp Web Safe.

Use Web-Safe Color Swatches

Photoshop has several ways for you to select colors. The Swatches palette (shown in the following illustration) houses predefined blocks of colors, arranged in libraries according to color mode, use, or style. The default library that loads the first time you launch Photoshop contains 122 colors from across the CMYK color spectrum, but it may not be the most useable palette for many designers.

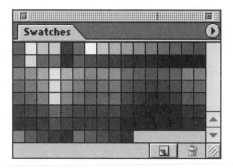

Photoshop ships with several other options that are probably more appropriate, including the following options, which are of particular interest to web designers:

- **Mac OS**   The Mac OS system palette
- **VisiBone**   The web-safe palette as organized by the VisiBone company
- **VisiBone2**   Another representation of the web-safe palette organized by VisiBone
- **Web Hues**   The web-safe palette organized according to hue
- **Web Safe Colors**   The web-safe palette organized by hexadecimal value
- **Web Spectrum**   The web-safe palette organized from lightest to darkest
- **Windows**   The Windows system palette

When you customize the look of your Swatches palette, you have the option to replace the existing swatch library in the palette with a new library or append the current library to the existing swatch library. By grouping several libraries together, you can actually create your own libraries, which you can then save and load as needed.

TRY IT   To customize the Swatches palette for Web use, first make sure the palette is visible by selecting Window | Swatches. Then, click the triangle in the upper-right corner of the palette and choose from any of the web-safe palettes listed in the flyout menu. When prompted, specify whether you want to replace the current swatch library with the new library or add (append) the new library to the current library.

> **QUICK TIP**
>
> *You can even create your own swatches and swatch libraries, as discussed in the following tip, "Create Your Own Swatch Libraries."*

Create Your Own Swatch Libraries

In addition to using predefined swatch libraries as described in the preceding tip, you can also create your own swatches and swatch libraries. This technique is especially useful when you want to create a custom palette, for example, housing all the colors used in a particular web design project, such as the library shown in Figure 1-5.

TRY IT You create your own swatches using the color in the foreground swatch by placing the pointer over a blank space in the Swatches palette and clicking. You'll notice that the pointer changes to a paint bucket when it's over a blank space, indicating you can "fill" the blank space with the current foreground color.

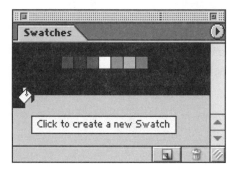

After clicking in the Swatches palette, you're given an opportunity to name your swatch. Keep in mind that the name is the text that appears when you hold the mouse over the swatch for a few seconds (as shown in Figure 1-5). To rename a swatch, simply double-click it and give it a new name.

> **QUICK TIP**
>
> *To create a brand new set of swatches, as I did in Figure 1-5, pick any existing swatch library, and delete all of those swatches before adding your own.*

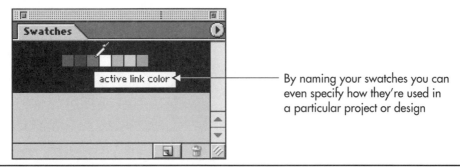

By naming your swatches you can even specify how they're used in a particular project or design

Figure 1-5   This custom library was created for a web design project and identifies all the link and page colors.

To delete a swatch, hold the mouse over the swatch and hold down the ALT key (Windows) or OPTION key (Mac) until a small pair of scissors appears before clicking. Alternatively, you can right-click (Windows) or CTRL-click (Mac) any swatch and choose Delete from the pop-up menu.

When you're finished with a library, click the triangle in the upper-right corner of the Swatches palette and choose Save Swatches to save your new swatch library for later use.

▶ *NOTE*

Although you can delete swatches from the middle of a library, you can only add a swatch at the end of the library in a blank space.

Customize the Info Palette

Photoshop's Info palette has the ability to put a variety of different types of information right at your fingertips. By default, it is set up to display the current color mode and CMYK values of the color beneath the pointer or color sample, as shown in the following illustration. (Note that in this case the current color mode of the file is RGB, so that is what is displayed in the upper-left quadrant of the Info palette.)

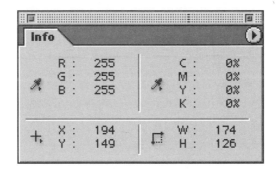

In addition, it also displays the X and Y coordinates of the pointer and even the change in location (X,Y coordinates, angle, and distance) when you move an element. Finally, when you use a tool such as the marquee to move or rotate a selection, the Info palette also displays the width (W) and height (H) of the marquee.

TRY IT   To customize the Info palette, first choose Window I Info to display the palette. After the palette is visible, click the triangle in the upper-right corner of the palette to view the palette menu. Choose Palette Options to bring up several customizable options for the Info palette, as shown here.

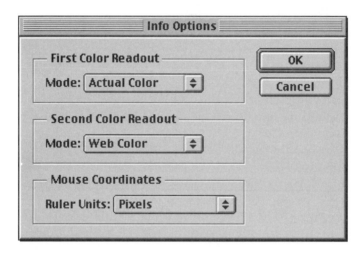

Web designers will find it most useful to change the Second Color Readout option to Web Color, as opposed to the default CMYK Color. This causes Photoshop to print out the hexadecimal color value of any color beneath the pointer or color sample, making it easy to use the color in an HTML page. Furthermore, web designers should confirm that the Ruler Units option is set to Pixels—the unit of measurement for screen design.

▶ **NOTE**

While you can also customize the Info palette in ImageReady, web designers don't need to. Because ImageReady was designed specifically for web designers, the Info palette defaults to displaying the hexadecimal color values in the upper-right quadrant and using pixels as the default unit of measurement.

Make the Color Management Settings Web-Specific

Photoshop has the ability to manage color information within each file it saves by tagging it with a *color profile*. In Photoshop, a color profile tells how to translate color numbers from one color space to another. For example, a designer working on a magazine ad might use a color profile to ensure the colors in the file are geared toward the printing specifications of a certain printer.

Because web designers cannot currently control the color settings on the computers of their users, color profiles are not used. In fact, because the addition of a color profile to a file can increase the file size and download time, it's best to turn off the use of color profiles in Photoshop if you're only producing web- or screen-based graphics.

▶ *NOTE*

I say that web designers cannot currently control the color settings on the computers of their users because there is work to change this. In fact, the specifications for the PNG file format do allow for embedded color profiles. Eventually, when browsers are able to download and interpret these color profiles, it may be possible for web designers to more effectively identify how their files should display on the viewer's screen.

When color profiles are not used, images are displayed using the *working color space,* as defined in Photoshop's color settings. Given that web graphics primarily use the RGB color mode, web designers typically are only concerned with the RGB color space.

TRY IT   To make it easier, Photoshop has automated the process of selecting the appropriate color settings. To adjust the color settings specifically for web files (as shown in Figure 1-6), follow these steps:

1. Choose Edit | Color Settings.
2. In the Settings list box, select Web Graphics Defaults.

By selecting Web Graphics Defaults, Photoshop turns off the use of color profiles and sets the RGB working color space to sRGB—the color space that most closely matches the characteristics of an average PC monitor.

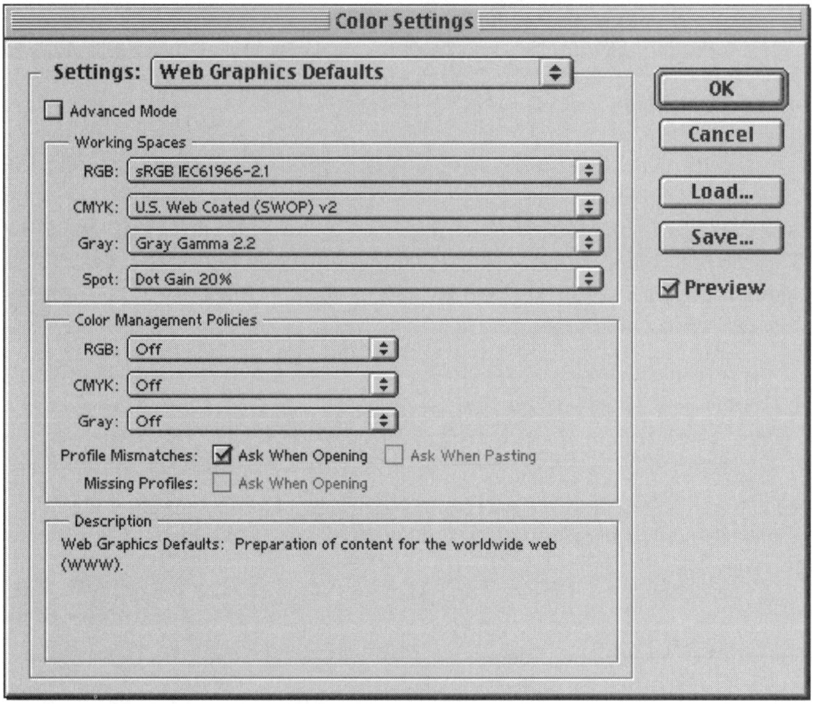

Figure 1-6 Web designers should use Photoshop's Web Graphics Defaults option for color management.

Use RGB for the Default Proof Setup

Photoshop gives you the ability to preview how a file looks under different color modes. This process is called *proofing* a file and is especially important to print designers, for example, looking to proof how colors may change from RGB to CMYK during the printing process.

The default proof setup in Photoshop is called Working CMYK. If you're a web designer, you definitely want to change this default from the CMYK color mode to RGB—the color mode of computer monitors. In fact, designers working on a Mac will likely want to use Windows RGB as their default proof setup, to get an idea of how their web graphics will display on Windows computers. Likewise, Windows users can select Macintosh RGB to preview how their graphics might display on Macintosh computers.

> **QUICK TIP**
>
> *You tell Photoshop to show you a proof of a file by selecting View | Proof Colors or by pressing* CTRL-Y *(Windows) or* CMD-Y *(Mac).*

▶ *NOTE*

Choosing Monitor RGB will cause there to be no color correction on the file. Instead, it is proofed using the current setup of your monitor.

TRY IT   To change the default proof setup in Photoshop, first close any files you have open. Then, select View | Proof Setup and choose the appropriate setting from the pop-up menu. Note that you can further customize the proof setup by selecting Custom from the pop-up menu.

▶ *CAUTION*

If you change the proof setup when a file is open, Photoshop considers the change to be important for that file only. To change the default proof setup, make your change when no files are open in Photoshop.

Make File Extensions Web-Friendly

Because web graphics are housed and displayed on computers that may be different than the one on which they're created, they need to be named in a universally understandable way. There are a few key points to keep in mind when naming web files:

- Filenames are typically case-sensitive.
- Filenames cannot contain any spaces.
- Filenames are best limited to using the alphabet, numbers, and underscores (_) or dashes (-).
- Filenames must end with the appropriate three-letter file extension.

So while "my favorite page" is not a good filename, you could use myfavoritepage.html or my-favorite-page.html. Another common option is to capitalize the first letter of each word in the filename, as in MyFavoritePage.html. When using capitalization, it's important to always refer to the file exactly as you named it, because many web servers are case-sensitive. (This means that if you named your file MyFavoritePage.html but then later referred to it as myfavoritepage.html, a case-sensitive server would show a broken link.)

Depending on which operating system you use, you can customize Photoshop to save your file extensions in a web-friendly way, which saves you time in the long run. For example, Windows users can tell Photoshop to always make the file extensions of its files lowercase, while Mac OS users can specify that Photoshop should always save files with a file extension. This is important because the Mac OS itself doesn't require file extensions, even though web files do.

TRY IT   To make your file extensions web-friendly, first choose Edit | Preferences | File Handling. To force Photoshop to save files with a lowercase file extension, Windows users should then select Use Lower Case from the File Extension menu.

To force Photoshop to automatically save all files with the appropriate three-letter file extension, Mac OS users should select Always from the Append File Extension menu. Then, place a check in the box next to Use Lower Case below that menu.

Determine Whether to Use Image Previews or Thumbnails

When you view files on your computer, you typically have the option to view them in several different formats, such as lists:

or icons:

Files viewed in the icon format appear with a small image next to or above the filename. Typically, this image is a clue to what format the file was saved in or what application was used to create it.

When you save image files in Photoshop, you have the option of saving those files with a customized preview, as opposed to a generic application or file format icon. In fact, Photoshop defaults to saving all image files with a small preview of the image as the file's icon.

Image previews are beneficial for several reasons, the most notable of which is that they enable you to easily identify a file visually without having to open it. It should be noted, however, that image previews do add to the size of a file. This is important when creating web graphics, where file size—and download time—significantly affects an image's success on a web page.

 Within Photoshop's preferences (choose Edit | Preferences | File Handling), you can specify that the program do one of the following with regard to image previews:

- Never Save
- Always Save (default)
- Ask When Saving

If you always work with web graphics, consider choosing Never Save to tell Photoshop never to save image previews for your files. If, on the other hand, you create many different types of files, the Ask When Saving option is probably preferable.

While Windows users can save only one type of preview (viewable on a Windows system), Mac OS users can choose to save four different types of previews:

- **Icon**   Creates a preview to be used as an icon on the desktop.
- **Full Size**   Creates a 72-ppi (pixels per inch) version of the file to be used in applications that only support low-resolution files. (This is most useful for high-resolution EPS files.)
- **Macintosh Thumbnail**   Creates a preview to be used in the Open dialog box.
- **Windows Thumbnail**   Creates a preview displayable on Windows systems.

▶ *CAUTION*

Because each of these previews and thumbnails adds to an image's overall file size, choose only those that are truly necessary for your use.

Save Copyright Information for Files

Photoshop gives you the ability to add copyright information to your graphics files, using the standard format developed by the Newspaper Association of America (NAA) and the International Telecommunications Council (IPTC) for identifying text and images.

The captions and keywords associated with copyrighted files are especially beneficial to web designers, whose files are commonly transmitted all over the world. While this copyright information doesn't display in the web browser, it will be available if the file is opened in Photoshop and some other third-party image browsers. As more browsers are able to interpret this information, it will become even more important to add it to every file.

▶ *CAUTION*

While you can add the copyright information to any file format on the Mac, you can currently only add it to files saved in the Photoshop, TIFF, JPEG, EPS, and PDF formats on Windows computers.

Another way this information is used is in categorizing and searching images, such as with Photoshop's file browser.

TRY IT   To add copyright information to a file, first choose File | File Info. You will then see a File Info dialog box similar to the one shown in Figure 1-7, wherein you can choose from the Section drop-down list to enter the following types of information:

- **General**   Lets you enter information such as the title, author, caption, copyright status, and owner URL.

- **Keywords** Lets you add a list of keywords to be used in categorizing and searching the image.
- **Categories** Lets you place the image in primary and supplemental categories for categorizing and searching.
- **Origin** Lets you specify the history of the image, and gives you a place to credit a source and specify an editorial urgency.

The EXIF option doesn't permit you to add information, but does display certain details about the image, such as the resolution, creation software, and compression type.

▶ **NOTE**

To conform to the NAA and IPTC standards, the categories used should be the three-letter Associated Press codes. You can access a list of these codes by visiting www.ap.org/apserver/userguide/ codes.htm.

To save yourself some time in the future, you can save a copy of commonly used copyright information, and then load it for future files. For example, you could save the author, copyright status, copyright notice, and owner URL information if it's likely to remain constant for all the files you

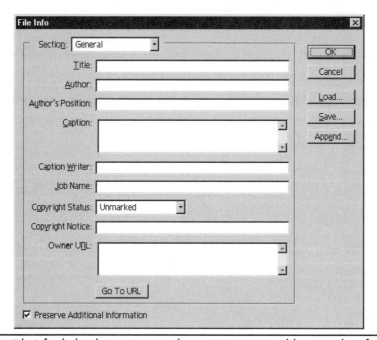

Figure 1-7 The File Info dialog box gives you the opportunity to add copyright information about a file.

create. Then, you can load this information for other files created in Photoshop. You save and load copyright information by clicking the corresponding buttons in the File Info dialog box.

Define and Save Your Preferred Workspace

The first time you opened Photoshop, you likely noticed a large number of windows and palettes filling up the screen (see Figure 1-8). These items can be opened, closed, minimized, and maximized to your heart's content, all to make your workspace easier to deal with and more personalized.

> ### ▶ QUICK TIP
>
> *To temporarily turn off all the windows and palettes, press the* TAB *key on your keyboard. Press* TAB *again to turn them back on.*

Depending on how you typically use Photoshop, you may be able to "hide" some of the windows and palettes by default to save time. For example, I use the Swatches palette significantly more than I use the Color palette, so it makes sense for me to have the Color palette invisible by default.

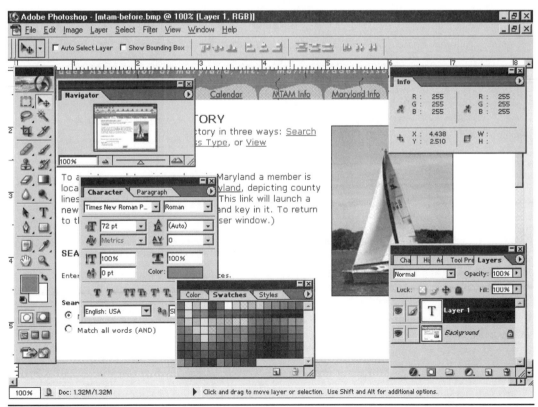

Figure 1-8   After spending some time on this web design, the workspace has become cluttered.

▶ *NOTE*

Before you can best use this tip, play around with all the windows and palettes to decide which ones you need available at all times and which ones you can leave hidden until you need them.

 To define your preferred workspace in Photoshop, you must first identify which windows you need visible and which you can turn off by selecting the palettes from the Window menu.

After you have the windows visible that you need, you can move them around the screen. In addition, you can minimize and maximize certain windows until everything is in place. Once you have all the windows and palettes in the order most suitable to your working style, choose Window | Workspace | Save Workspace and give your workspace a name to save it.

▶ | **QUICK TIP**

If you frequently work on different types of projects, such as some web design and some print design, you can save different workspaces for each one and load them as needed.

To test that your workspace was properly saved, simply move one of your windows around on the screen and then select Window | Workspace and choose the name of your workspace from the bottom of the menu.

Learn the Keyboard Shortcuts

If I were asked to identify the single most important way to make a person more efficient in Photoshop, I'd have to say, "Learn the keyboard shortcuts." Regardless of whether you're a print designer, a web designer, or any other person using Photoshop on a regular basis, the keyboard shortcuts can significantly speed up your use of this powerful program.

For example, suppose you were creating a pattern in Photoshop using the colors in the foreground and background swatches. Without the keyboard shortcuts, you'd have to move your mouse over to the toolbox each time you wanted to switch between the foreground and background colors. However, once you know that the keyboard shortcut for switching between the foreground and background swatches is the letter *X*, you've cut your production time on the pattern in half.

TRY IT   Every version of Photoshop ships with a Quick Reference Card customized for your platform (Mac OS or Windows). This card lists all the keyboard shortcuts for the tools and menus in both Photoshop and ImageReady. Some shortcuts require a single keystroke (such as pressing the B key to select the Paintbrush tool), while others use a combination of keys (such as CTRL-P or CMD-P for printing).

You can also see a shortcut in Photoshop by letting your mouse hover over a particular tool for a few seconds until the tool name and shortcut (shown in parentheses after the name) appear.

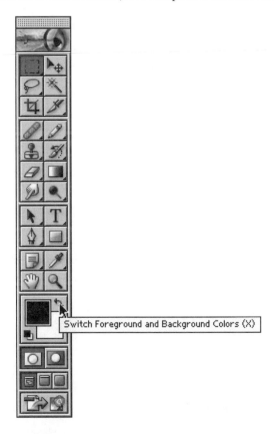

Keyboard shortcuts for menu items are listed (sometimes in parentheses) after the option name.

Some of the most commonly used keyboard shortcuts are listed in Table 1-3.

Tool/Option	Keyboard Shortcut
Arrow	A
Paintbrush	B
Crop	C
Return to default foreground/ background colors	D
Eraser	E
Gradient	G
Hand	H
Eyedropper	I
Healing Brush	J
Slice	K
Lasso	L
Marquee	M
Notes	N
Dodge	O
Pen	P
Blur	R
Rubber Stamp	S
Type	T

Table 1-3   Commonly Used Photoshop Keyboard Shortcuts

Tool/Option	Keyboard Shortcut
Shape tools	U
Move	V
Magic Wand	W
Switch foreground/background colors	X
History Brush	Y
Zoom	Z
Zoom in or out	CTRL-+ or CTRL-- (Windows) CMD-+ or CMD-- (Mac)
Return to 100 percent magnification	Double-click the Zoom tool
Add to any selection	Any selection tool-SHIFT-drag
Subtract from any selection	Any selection tool-ALT-drag (Windows) Any selection tool-OPTION-drag (Mac)
Constrain the proportions of the marquee to a perfect circle or square	SHIFT-drag
Switch between the normal Lasso and the Polygonal Lasso	ALT-drag (Windows) OPTION-drag (Mac)
Toggle between the Paintbrush and Pencil	SHIFT-B
Toggle between multiple versions of a tool	SHIFT-tool shortcut
Toggle rulers on or off	CTRL-R (Windows) CMD-R (Mac)
Toggle guides on or off	CTRL-; (Windows) CMD-; (Mac)
Create a new file	CTRL-N (Windows) CMD-N (Mac)
Open a file	CTRL-O (Windows) CMD-O (Mac)
Close a file	CTRL-W (Windows) CMD-W (Mac)
Save	CTRL-S (Windows) CMD-S (Mac)
Save As	SHIFT-CTRL-S (Windows) SHIFT-CMD-S (Mac)
Save for Web	ALT-SHIFT-CTRL-S (Windows) OPTION-SHIFT-CMD-S (Mac)
Print (with preview)	CTRL-P (Windows) CMD-P (Mac)

Table 1-3   Commonly Used Photoshop Keyboard Shortcuts (continued)

Tool/Option	Keyboard Shortcut
Print (without preview)	ALT-CTRL-P (Windows) OPTION-SHIFT-CMD-P (Mac)
Quit	CTRL-Q (Windows) CMD-Q (Mac)
Undo	CTRL-Z (Windows) CMD-Z (Mac)
Cut	CTRL-X (Windows) CMD-X (Mac)
Copy	CTRL-C (Windows) CMD-C (Mac)
Paste	CTRL-V (Windows) CMD-V (Mac)
Copy Merged	SHIFT-CTRL-C (Windows) SHIFT-CMD-C (Mac)
Free Transform	CTRL-T (Windows) CMD-T (Mac)
New Layer	CTRL-SHIFT-N (Windows) CMD-SHIFT-N (Mac)
Group with Previous	CTRL-G (Windows) CMD-G (Mac)
Ungroup	SHIFT-CTRL-G (Windows) SHIFT-CMD-G (Mac)
Merge Layers	CTRL-E (Windows) CMD-E (Mac)
Create a clipping group	ALT-click on the line between the two layers (Windows) OPTION-click on the line between the two layers (Mac)
Bring up the options for a particular layer	Right-click on the layer (Windows) CTRL-click on the layer (Mac)
Select All	CTRL-A (Windows) CMD-A (Mac)
Deselect	CTRL-D (Windows) CMD-D (Mac)
Photoshop Help	F1 (Windows) CMD-? (Mac)

Table 1-3   Commonly Used Photoshop Keyboard Shortcuts *(continued)*

Enable Workgroup Functionality

If you're a web designer working on a project with a team of designers, it may be beneficial for you to enable workgroup functionality within Photoshop. This feature allows multiple users to share files that are located on a special type of server, called a WebDAV server (WebDAV stands for Web-based Distributed Authoring and Versioning).

The benefits of using workgroup functionality like this include the following:

- Users must *check out* a file before using it and *check in* a file before anyone else can use it, which means that only one person can be using a file at any given time. This prohibits one designer from overwriting another designer's work on a file.
- Traffic on a file is typically logged. This helps keep track of who made changes when.
- One master copy of a file is kept in a central location.

As with any new feature, there are always a few drawbacks as well. For example, while it might be easy to share small GIF and JPEG files over the Internet, can you imagine having to download a 20MB Photoshop file from the Internet every time you want to work on it? Of course, if you're using a high-speed connection, this would not be a problem, but for anyone connecting over a telephone modem, this might be a bit of an inconvenience.

▶ *NOTE*

The workgroup functionality in Photoshop is only available to users of the WebDAV server. For more information on this system, visit www.webdav.org.

 To enable workgroup functionality, you need to do several things:

1. Specify a workgroup server by choosing File | Workgroup | Workgroup Servers.
2. Identify the folder where Photoshop should store local copies of files by clicking Choose and locating the folder on your hard drive you wish to use.
3. Identify the WebDAV server where Photoshop should access the remote copies of files under the Workgroup Servers option box.

To open and check out files from the WebDAV server, choose File | Workgroup | Open, locate the file, and click Check Out. When you're finished working with the file and wish to make it available to other team members, choose File | Workgroup | Check In.

If you want to check a file back into the server without making any changes, choose File | Workgroup | Cancel Check Out.

CHAPTER 2

Customizing Photoshop
for Print Design

TIPS IN THIS CHAPTER

This chapter begins with two large disclaimers. An obvious statement to some, a gentle reminder to all: *Photoshop is a tool, in the same way colored pencils might be a tool for a fine artist*. It is a wonderful, powerful tool that is increasingly capable of producing extravagant, intensely creative images and graphics, but you (the designer) are in charge of how this tool is used.

The second disclaimer is targeted at the print designer: *Photoshop is not a final page-layout program*. I state this early on because with each version update, print designers tend to spend more "creation" time in Photoshop due to the increased possibilities, including positioning type (previously visually risky in this program). Because of this, when it's time to import the created images or graphics into the final page-layout program, often very little time is spent considering the impact Photoshop "creations" will have when the ink actually hits the printed page.

Having stated those two disclaimers, I'd like to move past the sternness of that introduction and say: *Photoshop is fun!* Photoshop 7.0 can create graphics never before dreamed of. It's a visual field trip for graphic designers, a "laboratory" for limitlessly experimenting with effects upon effects. You will impress yourself with very little effort. Think of what your clients will say.

This chapter focuses on the continually cool things Photoshop 7.0 allows you to bring to your print documents. It is ridiculous to say that within these pages you will find all the instruction you need to exhaust the limitless opportunities Photoshop 7.0 presents to you. Let me reiterate the word *limitless*.

You are the designer. In other words, you are the user of the tools, the creator of the yet uncreated. As limitless as the opportunities are, so are your design projects, problems, and solutions. As a designer, do what you do best—design! Let these pages serve merely as a compass as you set out to design the unknown. Let these tips and tricks serve as guidelines to help you out along the way and reminders of how to best reach your final destination (the printed page).

▶ **NOTE**

Before you proceed, back up! If you have turned to this chapter as a resource for applying Photoshop knowledge to print graphics, don't forget to read the section in Chapter 1 "Learn the Keyboard Shortcuts"—an invaluable set of time-saving tips.

Picking a Place to Start

Let's begin by taking a look at your specific project. Ask yourself the question, "Why am I using Photoshop for this project?" Chances are the answer to that question will be, "To create visually appealing, innovative graphics." Another answer might be, "To manipulate photos." Photoshop can be a designer's "playground," but most often your imaging has a reason for existing. In other words, somewhere, somehow your creation will be put to use, either as digital media or as hardcopy output.

This chapter is particularly meant to provide tips and tricks for setting up Photoshop for maximum performance for hardcopy output; simply stated, for print. While Chapter 1 focused on personalizing Photoshop for Web use, this chapter aims at providing specific ways to help your graphics look just as fantastic on paper as they do onscreen.

Just as web media and print media are two completely different communication vehicles, so are their processes of creation. These differences should always be kept in mind while you are creating in Photoshop.

A Quick Review of Important File-Building Basics

This section reviews several basic issues that a print designer should consider as they begin their Photoshop work. Because this first section is an overview, actual techniques are discussed in detail later in the chapter. Issues discussed in this section are as follows:

- File size, dimension, and resolution
- Color
- Layers
- Saving a layered Photoshop (PSD) file

File Size, Dimension, and Resolution

A major difference in the creation of graphics for the printed piece versus the Web is size and resolution. Typically, web graphics are to be kept small not only in physical dimension (inches or pixels) but also in resolution (dpi/ppi—dots per inch/pixels per inch). The reason for this is for downloading purposes. The smaller the file, the quicker the download. For print, file size is generally not an issue. Graphics for printed pieces can be dimensionally enormous if the environment they are being created for calls for grandness. Whether large or small, size in print is important simply because you must prepare your document and graphics accordingly.

For print, you are using Photoshop to create a graphic that will be imported or placed into a page-layout program such as Adobe InDesign or QuarkXPress. Within your page-layout program, you have most likely established the dimensions for the final piece (for example, 8.5×11 inches or 20×30 inches). Knowing your "live" workspace will help you create appropriately sized graphics.

Depending on the method of final print output—this will often be prespecified alongside your client and printer—you should set up your document accordingly. The reason I am emphasizing this is that it is imperative that you set up your Photoshop file to reflect these requirements. Nothing is more frustrating than to have to go back in and re-create your graphic because the dimension or resolution is incorrect. You will save yourself a lot of time and frustration by creating your original Photoshop file based upon your final page-layout specification.

Color

The process of printing a piece is just as important as the process of creating it. Once a file is released from the designer to the printer, it is largely the printer's responsibility to align the color specifications with what rolls off the press. However, what the designer delivers to the printer as final files will play a huge part in how the final piece looks.

Producing accurate color is a careful science. These days, many graphics programs are advertised with the slogan WYSIWYG (What You See Is What You Get). Although technology has reached

Proofing Terms Defined

- **Color key**   A type of color proof where each of the four colors (cyan, magenta, yellow, and black) are printed on separate sheets of acetate, in preparation for printing the composite image.
- **Blue line**   A type of page proof that only shows layout, not color.
- **Color chip**   A sample of how a particular color prints on a certain type of paper. (Visit www.pantone.com to see examples of color chips.)

epic milestones, we all know that we still cannot be truly guaranteed to get on paper what we see onscreen. Yes, proofing on the designer's end is essential—hence the need for rounds of color keys, blue lines, and so forth. Printers are usually highly committed to working through color issues even before ink begins hitting the paper, but what can we do as designers to offer our files to printers as foolproof and print-ready as possible?

Full-color graphics created in Photoshop are typically highly complex and color-rich. Usually, the "punch" of a piece rests on the ability of the graphics and images to tell a story. Therefore, accurate depiction of color is essential.

Setting up your Photoshop files to print as color-correct as possible can sometimes be an intricate process of trial and error. Photoshop 7 now more than ever is tailored to allowing detailed color callouts. Notice the extensive Color palette options shown in Figure 2-1. Knowing what Photoshop offers when it comes to Color palettes allows the designer to use this technology most effectively. For more information, see the section later in this chapter titled "Pick a Color Mode."

▶ *NOTE*

The color-related tips and techniques presented in this chapter are merely recommendations of what I think works the best for altering color. As you become more and more familiar with Photoshop, you will find what works best with your imaging needs. You will find that for specific needs, certain methods will provide more accurate results. Again, color is a science—always have color proofs provided by your prepress professional. Although the color may seem perfect on your screen or even on your desktop printer proof, it is always in your best interest (and in the interest of your client) to see a professional proof before releasing the project to final print.

Know your project and its color specifications. Build your graphic from the beginning, always keeping these specifications in mind. Try not to toggle back and forth between color systems (RGB, CMYK, and so forth). Make sure your client is also aware of the inevitability of color-shift. Calibrate your monitor to display color as it will most likely be seen when output. For details on how to do this, see the section later in this chapter titled "Calibrate Your Monitor."

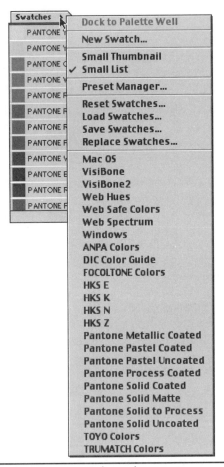

Figure 2-1 Photoshop 7 provides extensive Color palette options

---

> **QUICK TIP**
>
> *If possible, present sample color matching "chips" (Pantone, TOYO, and so on) to your client during the proofing process so that the client doesn't expect a different color on the printed piece. Also include these "chips" when releasing your files to a printer.*

Layers

Part of what makes Photoshop so much fun to work with is the ability to watch the digital magic of what happens when different effects are combined or manipulated. The possibilities of what a designer can do with Photoshop are almost mind-boggling. You could easily spend hundreds of hours just playing around with different effects and exploring how some effects play off other effects. Effects, effects, effects.

When Photoshop introduced the History palette, I think designers around the world breathed a collective sigh of relief. Utilizing the History palette is basically like back-tracking through applied effects. As depicted in Figure 2-2, you are able to go forward and backward, like moving up and down stairs.

Before this palette was added, a new layer had to be added for every effect you wanted to try out (which was time-consuming and memory-absorbing, to say the least). Your other options were to use a one-time "Undo"—only operative for the previously completed command—or, if all else failed, simply to "Revert" to the last saved version of your file.

However, once you save your file (which should be done often), you will notice that the History palette clears or empties itself. No longer do you have the option of walking backward or forward through your "effects experimentation." That's why it is so important for designers to constantly use the Layers palette.

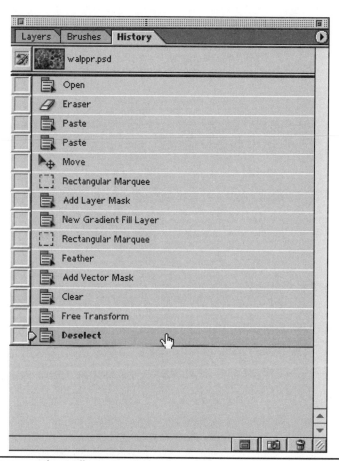

Figure 2-2 The History palette allows you to backtrack through actions applied to your image without committing to a final outcome.

Although utilizing the Layers palette takes up a lot of memory space on your hard drive (Photoshop files are proportionately larger for each added layer), it is the only way to carefully manipulate the fine details of your image without committing to a final outcome before you are ready to. Utilizing layers, as shown in Figures 2-3 and 2-4, allows you to quickly toggle between layers or applied effects by simply clicking the eye icon on the layer.

▶ **NOTE**

See Chapter 6 for more information on utilizing layers.

Save a Layered Photoshop (PSD) File

Our discussion on utilizing the Layers palette correlates directly to the importance of saving at least one nonflattened Photoshop (PSD) file while you are creating your graphic. I think all designers at one time or another have accidentally flattened their multilayered file and, much to their dismay, have been left with the daunting task of completely re-creating their file. From the get-go, save your work as a PSD file so that you will never be tempted to flatten out all of your hours of working on that image.

Photoshop gives you a multitude of format options when saving your file for the first time. Preferred file formats are discussed throughout this book according to the media environment in which they

Figure 2-3   When you select the eye icon, the layer becomes visible.

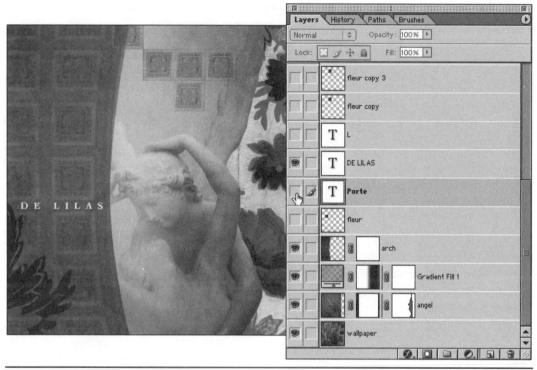

Figure 2-4   When you deselect the eye icon, the layer becomes invisible.

will ultimately be used. Print graphics are usually saved as a TIFF (.tif extension) or EPS (.eps extension) file and imported for placement into a page-layout program. A further discussion on the suggested format for saving specific files can be found in Chapter 12.

We've just spent a bit of time reviewing some important basics that will help you as you begin creating Photoshop graphics for print design. The remainder of this chapter examines these subjects in detail. This chapter is not meant to walk you through building a file from start to finish—please use it for reference only, because the subjects are not always discussed in the order in which you might build a file.

▶ **NOTE**

In addition to the tips in this chapter, there are several tips in Chapter 1 that will prove useful to print designers as well as web designers.

Pick a Color Mode

When working in Photoshop, you will be either opening an existing file or creating a new one. If you are opening a file, it will already be in a specified color mode; most likely it will open in RGB (red, green, blue) mode. This mode is common for viewing images onscreen. It is also the preferred color mode for web graphics, because monitors are calibrated in RGB mode. RGB files are generally smaller in size, which is another reason they are often provided in this mode.

Although you can work in RGB mode, I recommend switching your color mode to CMYK if you are designing for full-color output. Full-color printing is based on the combination of the four colors: cyan (C), magenta (M), yellow (Y), and black (K). All images will separate according to specified ink measurement based on these four color breakdowns. This is a very elementary explanation of a very complex process—however, I use it simply to reiterate the importance of saving your Photoshop files in CMYK mode if your final document will be output on a full-color press.

If you are working on a print piece and have opted to have a color house (prepress specialists used for setting up files for print) provide final placement high-resolution scans or color-altered digital images, you will want to discuss with them their preferred mode for handling files. Most often, they will request original artwork (slides, transparencies, or photographs) and will return a digital file on disk or transfer the file via the Web. The image will likely be set up in CMYK mode unless otherwise requested.

> ### QUICK TIP
>
> *To use soft proofing in Photoshop, first select the mode for your proof by choosing View | Proof Setup and picking one from the flyout menu. Then, choose View | Proof Colors.*

Photoshop is also equipped with a soft proofing feature—Proof Colors—which allows you to view on your screen how your image will appear in its final output. Although not 100 percent accurate (as not all variables can be controlled), soft proofing does attempt to depict a more accurate representation and should therefore be utilized.

TRY IT   To change an existing file's color mode, select Image | Mode and pick the desired color mode from the flyout menu.

To select a color mode when creating a new Photoshop file, choose File | New or press CTRL-N (Windows) or CMD-N (Mac). In the Document dialog box, click the Mode button, select your desired mode, and then click OK.

> ### QUICK TIP
>
> *You can verify what color mode you are in by viewing the top of the image window. The title of the file will be followed by the percentage you are viewing the image at (for example, 33%), followed by the color mode within parentheses as shown in the following illustration.*

Use Grayscale and Bitmap Modes for Black and White Images

If you are working with black and white photography, using 1-Color printing, or designing for a publication such as newsprint, you will want to take advantage of both the grayscale and bitmap modes. If you are scanning original artwork into Photoshop, your scanner software should ask you what mode you would like to scan in. If you select grayscale, then Photoshop will automatically open the file in grayscale mode. If you select Line Art when scanning an image such as a logo, Photoshop will automatically open the image in bitmap file mode. You can also convert any color files you have to grayscale mode and then convert grayscale images to bitmapped images, and vice versa.

If you are preparing your image for newsprint, make sure you talk with the printer or the person that will be taking your files through prepress. Sometimes a grayscale image must be prepared with a specific halftone screen. Halftone screens consist of dots that control how much ink is deposited at a specific location on-press. Varying their size and density creates the illusion of variations of gray. Before creating your halftone screens, check with your print shop for preferred frequency, angle, and dot settings.

You cannot directly convert a color image to a bitmapped image. It must first be converted to a grayscale image, and then to a bitmap image. You should definitely exercise caution when converting your images to bitmaps. I cannot overemphasize how important it is to know what prepress specifications the publication you are designing for requests. Each publication is different—make sure they provide you with all the necessary file preparation information. If it is not provided, ask!

> **QUICK TIP**
>
> *Use Photoshop's default settings for halftone screens unless your print shop specifies changes. Refer to Chapter 12 for more tips on outputting print graphics.*

▶ **NOTE**

Even if you are not using the bitmap mode feature for printing reasons, you can experiment with bitmap mode to create interesting effects. These are discussed in Chapter 9.

TRY IT To convert a color file to grayscale, choose Image | Mode and select Grayscale in the flyout menu. Click OK when the dialog box automatically asks "Discard Color Information?"

TRY IT To convert a grayscale image to a halftone bitmap, choose Image | Mode and select Bitmap in the flyout menu. In the dialog box, type in your requested output resolution. (Unless otherwise specified by printer or publication, I recommend an output resolution of 300 dpi or higher.) Choose Halftone in the Method option box and click OK. The Halftone dialog box automatically pops up, requesting frequency, angle, and pattern—unless otherwise specified by printer or publication, I recommend staying with the default settings, including Round for the pattern.

TRY IT   To convert a grayscale image to a diffusion-dither bitmap, choose Image | Mode and select Bitmap in the flyout menu. In the dialog box, type in your requested output resolution. (Unless otherwise specified by printer or publication, I recommend an output resolution of 300 dpi or higher.) Choose Diffusion Dither in the Method option box and click OK. To compare halftones and diffusion-dither bitmaps, compare the following two illustrations—the one at left is a close-up of a halftone bitmap, whereas the one on the right is a diffusion-dither bitmap.

Set Up Your Swatches Palettes to Be Job-Specific

It seems that every time you turn around, your computer is no longer the newest, your operating system was just upgraded, and there's a new version of Photoshop. Technology has a wonderful way of keeping us on our toes. We have no choice but to keep learning. I admit, sometimes this can be a bit overwhelming, but usually it's a good thing, and zippier technology equips us with tools that allow us to create better designs.

Another constantly changing story in the print business is the introduction of increasingly innovative color palettes. Not too long ago, we were excited by the metallic Swatch book that Pantone produced. At the beginning of this chapter, Figure 2-1 displayed the 24 color libraries to choose from when picking swatches in Photoshop—only eight of those are Pantone libraries.

So let's talk about Photoshop and your swatches. Obviously, all 24 of these libraries will not be utilized at once and certainly not all of them are for print. The web color palettes speak for themselves, as they are usually labeled with the word "Web." The following is a brief description found in Photoshop's Help of the most common inks used in print:

▶ **NOTE**

Because I find PANTONE and TOYO colors to be the most common, my tips focus mostly on these palettes.

- **PANTONE**   Used for printing inks. Each PANTONE color has a specified CMYK equivalent. To select a PANTONE color, first determine the ink color you want, using either the *PANTONE Color Formula Guide 747XR* or an ink chart obtained from your printer. You can select from PANTONE Metallic Coated, PANTONE Pastel Coated, PANTONE Pastel

Uncoated, PANTONE Process Coated, PANTONE Solid Coated, PANTONE Solid Matte, PANTONE Solid to Process, and PANTONE Solid Uncoated.

- **TOYO Color Finder 1050**   Consists of more than 1,000 colors based on the most common printing inks used in Japan. The *TOYO Color Finder 1050 Book* contains printed samples of TOYO colors and is available from printers and graphic arts supply stores.

- **TRUMATCH**   Provides predictable CMYK color matching with more than 2,000 achievable, computer-generated colors. TRUMATCH colors cover the visible spectrum of the CMYK gamut in even steps. The TRUMATCHCOLORFINDER displays up to 40 tints and shades of each hue, each originally created in four-color process and each reproducible in four colors on electronic image setters. In addition, four-color grays using different hues are included.

- **FOCOLTONE**   Consists of 763 CMYK colors. FOCOLTONE colors help avoid prepress trapping and registration problems by showing the overprints that make up the colors. A Swatch book with specifications for process and spot colors, overprint charts, and a chip book for marking up layouts are available from FOCOLTONE.

▶ *NOTE*

Always have a Swatch book for the color system you are working with, always show your client the actual color in the Swatch books, and always provide your printer with color chips of the swatches you are using in your project.

Once you have determined what type of media or paper your project will be printed on, you can often determine which color palette will be most useful to you for that piece. For example, if you are using an uncoated stock, you will want to specify ink from an uncoated palette.

The science of color is further complicated by the science of ink. Inks act differently on every paper they hit. Although this is very much part of a printer's job (to alert you to paper and ink characteristics), this will definitely be an issue you should discuss with your printer before you promise your client that a certain color will look a certain way on a certain paper.

Paper manufacturers and printers will often provide what are called "samples" or "draw-downs" (how ink looks on a specified paper). Reviewing color samples is an important bridge to cross before you are too deep into building your final Photoshop files. Inks specified in the Photoshop palettes will also appear in your page-layout document.

▶ *CAUTION*

If an ink is incorrectly specified, it will not separate correctly when sent to prepress.

TRY IT   To choose a Swatches palette, select Window | Show Swatches. Click the triangle and a flyout menu will appear. Select the palette you wish to work with. Color swatches will then appear within the Swatches Palette.

Customize the Display of Your Swatches for Print Design

Under Palette Options, you can select how you wish to view your ink palette. When working as a print designer, I prefer working with the Small List. That way, I know the name of the color I am working with—which is particularly helpful when I know what ink colors I can or can't use if I have a limited color palette. You can also choose to view them as Small Thumbnails, which are simply small squares of color.

TRY IT To customize the display of your swatches, first choose Window | Swatches to make sure your Swatches palette is visible. Then, click the triangle in the upper-right corner of the Swatches palette and a flyout menu will appear. Select Small List and inks will appear with their names, or select Small Thumbnail and inks will appear as small squares without names.

> ### QUICK TIP
>
> *Is your Swatches palette bogging you down? Too many choices a bad thing? Sometimes. Cut it out—literally. If you hold down the OPTION key (Mac) or ALT key (Windows) while your cursor is over a specific color, a little scissors icon will pop up. Click that color and away it goes. You can eliminate as many colors as you want, and this works with any color palette.*

Create a New Swatch in the Swatches Palette

Perhaps you have negotiated with your printer to use a custom ink mix. For example, you need to match a beige perfectly, and not one of the thousands of premixed inks out there seems to match, so you and your printer have come up with your own mix.

TRY IT Have the printer give you a CMYK color breakdown and then follow these steps:

1. Make sure the color you want to add is currently visible in the foreground color swatch. If it isn't, click once on the foreground color swatch from within the toolbox and specify the color coordinates in the color picker.

2. In the Swatches palette, click the triangle and select New Swatch. A dialog box will appear with a small color box and a text bar for you to name your new special mix.

3. Name your special ink mix.

► NOTE

Photoshop saves colors added to the Swatches palette in the preferences for the program. To permanently save the color, click the triangle in the upper corner of the palette and choose "Save Swatches."

Use the Foreground and Background Colors for Quick Color Changes

The foreground and background colors are found at the very bottom of the Tools palette; they are the two overlapping boxes. The foreground color is the box on top. The background color is the box on the bottom. Photoshop automatically defaults to using a foreground of black and a background of white. You can switch these by clicking the arrow immediately to the upper right of those boxes. Photoshop calls this the "toggle arrow." There are several ways to change the foreground and background colors.

TRY IT   To change the foreground color, click the top color box in the Tools palette and the Color Picker dialog box will pop up. Select a color or enter in specific values, or click Custom to select a preexisting mix. Click OK when you are satisfied with your selected color. Repeat the same steps to change the background color.

TRY IT   Another way to change the foreground or Background color is by using the Eyedropper tool in the Tools palette. Make sure the color you wish to change is active and select the Eyedropper tool from the Tools palette. Click anywhere on your image, and the color will appear in the foreground or background color box, depending on which one you are selecting for.

> ### QUICK TIP
>
> *You can choose a color from anywhere on your desktop—even outside of Photoshop—with the Eyedropper tool. First click anywhere within your Photoshop file. Then drag the cursor to the place on your desktop that contains the color you want to select. Release the mouse button when the color you're looking for appears in the foreground color swatch.*

TRY IT   You can also change the foreground/background color by "mixing" a color in the Color palette. Choose Window | Color and click the triangle in the menu bar. Select the mode you are working in (CMYK sliders, RGB sliders, and so forth). Insert values (from a Swatch book or preexisting mix) or use sliders to achieve your desired color. The selected Foreground or Background color box will reflect the color you are mixing in the Color palette.

> ### QUICK TIP
>
> *To toggle between the foreground and background colors without selecting the "toggle" arrow on the Tools palette, press X on your keyboard, and your foreground and background palette will switch places. Foreground becomes background and vice versa. To return the foreground and background colors to their default settings of black and white, simply press the D key on your keyboard.*

Calibrate Your Monitor

Chances are, your computer monitor is different from mine, different from your prepress professional's, and different from your printer's. This means we are all seeing things just a little differently. And even if all our monitors were universally calibrated to display exactly the same thing, there would still be variables such as inside lighting that would affect how things appear on my screen versus yours. The trick is to set up *your* screen for *your* environment. Let your prepress professional and your printer deal with their monitors. What's most important is how you are seeing color based on hard-proofs (paper printouts). Many times, your printer will have a portable color box or an on-location color-corrected environment for viewing final color before your document goes to print. Let this be your ultimate judge of color.

Most monitors come with a few control buttons on the actual screen. Usually, they allow you to play around with the brightness and contrast (how white your whites are), the horizontal and vertical space, and so forth. Your monitor should come with a user's manual; it's a good idea to read about features that might enhance your work.

▶ *NOTE*

For more information on this subject, refer to the section "How Computer Monitors Display Color" in Chapter 1.

 The way in which you profile and/or calibrate your monitor for your specific working conditions depends on which operating system you are using.

Photoshop for Windows ships with a utility called Adobe Gamma. This utility lets you calibrate and customize your monitor to a certain standard and then saves the settings as a color profile, which can be used by programs like Photoshop to accurately display color. To access Adobe Gamma, choose Settings | Control Panels from the Start menu. Then locate and click the Adobe Gamma control panel. Choose Step By Step to have the utility walk you through the process, or choose Control Panel to calibrate the monitor on your own (as shown in Figure 2-5) if you already have experience doing so.

For more information about Adobe Gamma, click Help | Photoshop Help in Photoshop to access Adobe's online help.

Macintosh operating systems come with a preloaded program called ColorSync, which Adobe describes as "Apple's industry-standard architecture for managing color across input, display, and out-devices. This software is supported by leading applications and works with scanners, digital cameras, monitors, printers, and presses."

You can actually select how your digital information is coming into your computer (scanner, digital camera, and so on), how it is being displayed (monitor), what sort of output device it is being viewed at (Web, desktop printer, prepress proofing device), and press details. Your operating system will communicate "behind the scenes" between applications to display color consistently between applications and output.

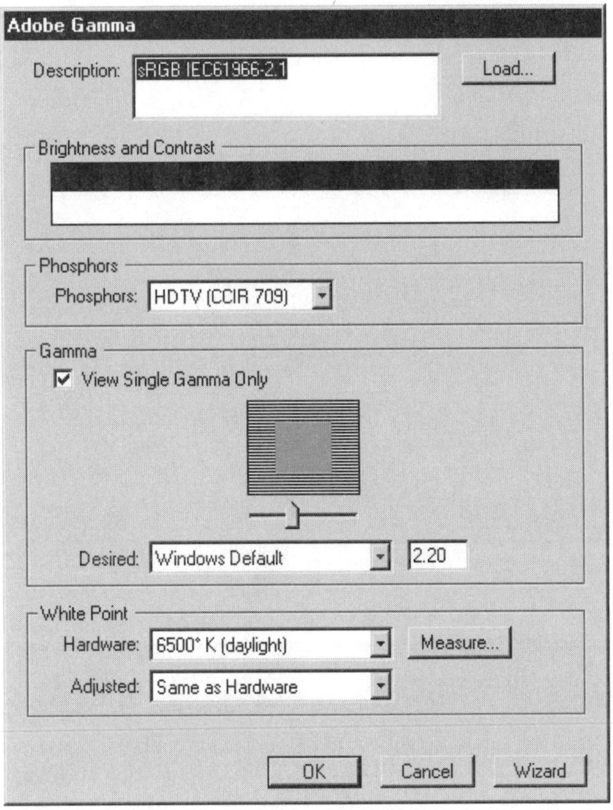

Figure 2-5   The Adobe Gamma Control Panel for Windows

To access ColorSync on your computer, select Control Panels | ColorSync from the Apple menu. You'll be presented with a control panel similar to the one shown in Figure 2-6, where you can make selections based on your system setup and color needs.

For more information about ColorSync, see www.apple.com/colorsync.

▶ **NOTE**

While previous versions of Photoshop for the Mac also shipped with Adobe Gamma, it no longer comes with Photoshop 7 for the Mac. In addition, ColorSync does not operate with Windows. However, the ICC color profiles created by these utilities are universal and can be read on either system.

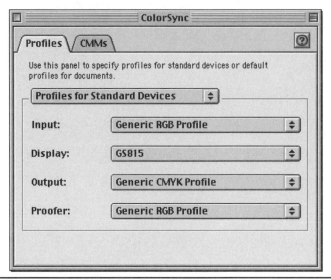

Figure 2-6   The ColorSync Control Panel for Macintosh

Make the Color Management Settings Print-Specific

Photoshop has the ability to manage color information within each file it saves, by tagging it with a *color profile.* In Photoshop, a color profile tells how to translate color numbers from one color space to another. For example, a designer working on a magazine ad might use a color profile to ensure the colors in the file are geared toward the printing specifications of a certain printer.

▶ *NOTE*

Color management is recommended if you anticipate reusing color graphics for print and online media, if you manage multiple workstations, or if you plan to print to different domestic and international presses. If you decide to use color management, consult with your production partners—such as graphic artists and prepress service providers—to ensure that all aspects of your color management workflow integrate seamlessly with theirs.

TRY IT   To make it easier, Photoshop has automated the process of selecting the appropriate color settings. To adjust the color settings specifically for web files (as shown in Figure 2-7), follow these steps:

1. Choose Edit | Color Settings.
2. In the Settings box, select U.S. Prepress Defaults.

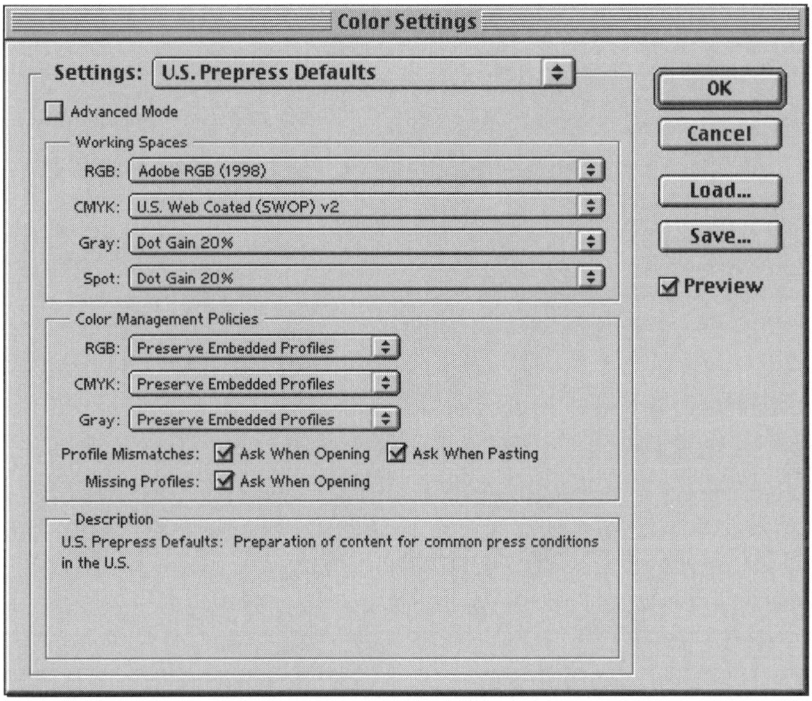

Figure 2-7   Print designers most commonly use the U.S. Prepress Defaults and then further customize these settings as needed

Although the predefined settings should provide sufficient color management for your publishing needs, you may sometimes want to customize individual options in a configuration. For example, you might want to change the CMYK working space to a profile that matches the proofing system used by your service bureau.

> ► | ### QUICK TIP
>
> *You can save custom configurations so that you can reuse or share them with other users and Adobe applications that use the same color management workflows. The color management settings that you customize in the Color Settings dialog box have an associated preferences file called Color Settings.csf, found in the Adobe Photoshop 7.0 Settings folder.*

Allocate More Memory to Photoshop

I'll go ahead and say it—Photoshop is a memory hog. Photoshop 7 requires 250MB just to take up space on your system and a minimum of 12MB of memory to run, although Photoshop recommends using 32MB. For a swiftly moving Photoshop, I recommend bumping that up to at least 50MB.

Still acting sluggish? It is not uncommon for print graphic files to get quite large, and require even more memory.

 To allocate more memory to Photoshop, follow these steps if your operating system is Windows:

1. Choose Edit | Preferences | Memory & Image Cache.

2. Under Physical Memory Usage, specify the amount of memory you'd like to allocate to Photoshop (see Figure 2-8). Note that the number you specify is a percentage of the total amount of RAM available on your computer.

3. Click OK.

4. Choose File | Quit to close Photoshop.

5. The next time you launch Photoshop, your new memory settings will take effect.

To allocate more memory if you are using a Mac:

1. Make sure Photoshop is not running; if it is, exit the program.

2. Find the Photoshop application icon in the Photoshop folder. (Don't double-click to open the program; simply click once on the icon so that it is selected.)

3. Hold down the CTRL key and click once on the Photoshop application icon to reveal a pop-up menu.

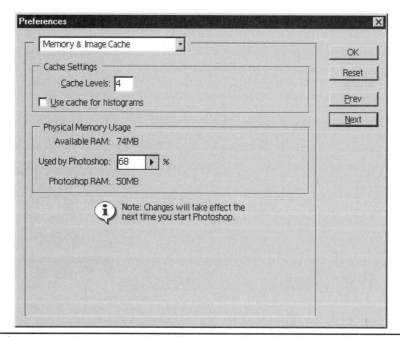

Figure 2-8   The Memory & Image Cache Preferences in Photoshop for Windows

4. From the pop-up window, choose Get Info I Memory.

5. Under Memory Requirements (see Figure 2-9), you will see Suggested Size: 32768K; Minimum Size: 12288K; and Preferred Size: 50000K (this number will vary based on your preference). Enter a larger number in the Preferred Size box to allocate more memory to Photoshop 7.

6. Close the dialog box by clicking the box in the upper-left corner and then launch Photoshop.

▶ *NOTE*

If you know from the beginning of a project that your file will be graphically dense and multilayered, increase the allocated memory. Your system and Photoshop will operate much more efficiently.

Create a New Print Design File in Photoshop

When you begin your work in Photoshop, usually you will have document dimensions already established (8.5×11 inches). You can set up your Photoshop document with these dimensions or estimate the approximate size of the graphic space you will be using within the document layout (for example, 3×5 inches). If you do not know how big to build your graphic, *always* build it larger than you need it. You can always reduce the size without losing digital quality. However, if you have built the file too small, the image will become pixelated and fuzzy if you attempt to increase the image dimensions.

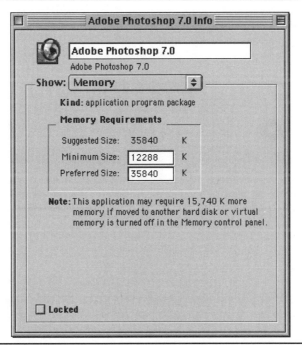

Figure 2-9 The Memory Requirements options for Photoshop on the Mac O/S

I also recommend establishing a larger canvas size than your actual image size. A larger canvas gives you space to move things around and shove things off to the side, plus it gives you the added bonus of being able to see all the "handles" of a selected image if you are transforming it, and so forth. If your page layout calls for a full-bleed image, having a larger canvas allows you to calculate in that additional .25 inch necessary for a full-bleed image. For example, let's say your document is 8.5×11 inches, full-bleed. You have two individual images that, when placed, bleed off the side and are approximately 3×5 inches. I recommend making your Photoshop document size 5×7 inches for those individual images.

TRY IT To set up a new document, select File | New or press CTRL-N (Windows)/CMD-N (Mac). In the dialog box, enter a filename in the title box (if desired). Click Size and select a preset size from the pop-up menu, or select Custom and enter your own specifications. If you are entering Custom measurements, also select desired increments (inches, pixels, and so on). Enter desired resolution into the Resolution box (for example, 300 dpi).

▶ *CAUTION*

Because this chapter is print-specific, I recommend always creating your images at least at 300 dpi. This is an industry standard minimum for high-resolution output. Sometimes, particularly if you are working with line art, you will want to create the file at an even higher resolution (600 or 1,200 dpi). You will notice that your files become proportionately larger as you increase the resolution and the dimensions.

Select the color mode in which you will be working (CMYK, RGB, or Grayscale), and click a Content button (White, Background Color, or Transparent). Click OK when you are finished, and your new document window will pop open.

Customize Preferences for Print Design

Most of the default preferences in Photoshop are sufficient for typical print files, but there are a few you might consider changing, depending on your needs.

TRY IT To adjust your preferences, select Edit | Preferences. A flyout menu will slide out; select General to walk through all the preference options, or select exactly which preference you would like to adjust. If you choose General, you can then click Previous or Next to take you back and forth between preferences. Table 2-1 identifies which preferences I change most often when working on print graphics.

▶ *QUICK TIP*

If your document is open and you want to adjust the units you are working with (in other words, you want to change from inches to picas), you can simply double-click the ruler and the Units & Rulers dialog box will pop up. You can then adjust the measurements from there.

Preference Type	Description of Customization
File Handling	To adjust how Photoshop handles your files, select File Handling in the preferences pop-up menu. Next to Image Previews, select Always Save (this saves a picture preview that allows you to view thumbnails of your images). Mac users need to make sure check marks appear in the following boxes: Select Icon, Mac Thumbnail, Windows Thumbnail. (For more information about previews, refer to the tip titled "Determine Whether to Use Image Previews or Thumbnails" in Chapter 1.) Next to Append File Extension, select Always—this enables Photoshop to automatically tack on the correct file extension (.psd, .tif, .eps, and so forth).
Displays & Cursors	To adjust how Photoshop displays your cursors, select Display & Cursors in the preferences pop-up menu. Underneath Painting Cursors, select Brush Size to show the actual tip size when you are using tools such as the Pen tool or any of the Paint Brushes. Under Other Cursors, select Precise.
Units & Rulers	To adjust how Photoshop displays your units and rulers, select Units & Rulers in the preferences pop-up menu. Next to Rulers, select Inches (or preferred unit). Next to Type, select Points (or preferred unit).

Table 2-1   A Few Ways to Further Customize Photoshop for Print Design

Maximize Your Screen Space, Minimize Palette Clutter

Once you have set up your document and are working in Photoshop, you will notice how quickly your screen fills up with "stuff" that is not even part of your image. There are palettes galore in Photoshop. Conveniently, Photoshop has a Palette Well (see Figure 2-10) where active yet unused palettes can be docked. While you can also double-click the top of a palette to minimize it, the minimized menu bar doesn't indicate which palette it is. The Palette Well is a more efficient way of avoiding clutter without losing sight of the palettes you are working with.

You can also group palettes. For instance, let's say you are working on a multilayered image, using the Layers palette, the Brush palette, the History palette, and the Swatches palette. Suppose you are mostly using the Layers palette and the Brush palette; those two palettes would be "live," the other two palettes you are using would be docked or grouped behind them—just a click away. Because all of Photoshop's palettes are floating, you can drag them around the screen as you see fit, grouping and ungrouping palettes by moving them close together and taking them apart again.

TRY IT   To activate a palette that is grouped or docked behind a currently "live" palette, simply click on the tab and the palette you selected will move forward. You can also give that palette its own environment by simply clicking and holding on the tab and moving it onto the screen. To move a palette to the docking well, click and hold on the top of the palette tab and move it up to the Palette Well and release—it will then be docked.

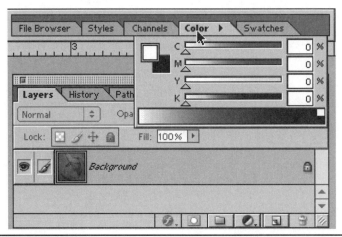

Figure 2-10   The Palette Well allows you to avoid clutter without losing sight of the palettes you are working with.

▶ | **QUICK TIP**

Another way to clean up palette clutter is by simply pressing the TAB *key. All the palettes will disappear. If you want them to reappear, press the* TAB *key again, and they will all reappear exactly in the same location they were before.*

There are three little boxes at the bottom of the Tools palette (see Figures 2-11, 2-12, and 2-13). These are window controls that let you change the screen display mode, including menu bar, title bar, and scroll bar options. The left button displays the default window with a menu bar at the top and scroll bars on the sides. The center button displays a full-screen window with a menu bar and a 50 percent gray background, but no title bar or scroll bars. This mode is helpful when you want to block out everything on your desktop or files that are open in other programs. You still have complete access to all of your palettes, and so forth. The right button displays a full-screen window with a black background, but no title bar, menu bar, or scroll bars. It is difficult to work in this mode because your menu bar is out of sight, but when you really want to see what your image looks like without any other visual distractions, this is the way to go.

▼ Use the Rulers, Guides, and Grids

It's a good idea to get comfortable with your rulers, guides, and grids, particularly when you are working on graphics that will ultimately be placed into a page-layout program. Web designers swear by these things—print designers could certainly stand to learn a thing or two about the precision that rulers, guides, and grids offer. Rulers serve to remind you of the actual image size, as Photoshop files often appear larger than life. Grids provide a parameter for visual alignment and symmetry. Also, if

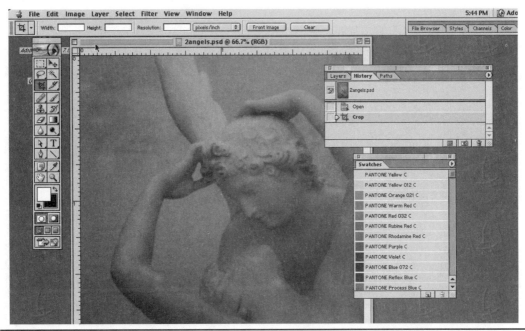

Figure 2-11 The left button displays the default window with a menu bar at the top and scroll bars on the sides.

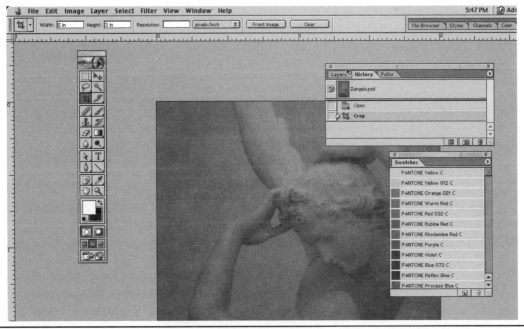

Figure 2-12 The center button displays a full-screen window with a menu bar and a 50 percent gray background, but no title bar or scroll bars.

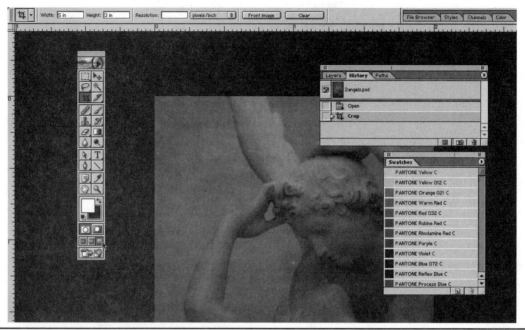

Figure 2-13   The right button displays a full-screen window with a black background, but no title bar, menu bar, or scroll bars.

you are working on a document that is following an established grid, you can replicate that grid in Photoshop and build your image along the same parameters.

 To view your file with the rulers turned on, select View I Rulers or press CTRL-R (Windows)/ CMD-R (Mac). To hide rulers, simply repeat the command and they will disappear.

▶ | **QUICK TIP**

Your zero/zero points or X,Y coordinates are set from the upper-left corner of your image. You can change the location of these by clicking the small box in the upper-left corner and pulling them out to wherever you wish their origin to be. The zero/zero points on your ruler will begin where you released. This is helpful particularly if you need to crop a certain portion of your image and you know that it needs to be an exact measurement. To return the X,Y coordinates to their original starting point, just double-click the little box in the upper-left corner.

Guides are exactly what they say they are, "guides." Not every project requires the use of guides, but many do. Guides appear as lines that float over an image and do not print. You can move, remove, or lock a guide to avoid accidentally moving it. Often, you must grid off a section of your image to create a visual idea of where another element will be or to create an area of specific measurement.

You can also set your guides so that your cursor will "snap to" them or hide guides quickly if they become a distraction to your imaging.

TRY IT To create a guide, click and hold on the ruler. (Click the vertical ruler on the left if you want a vertical guide; click the horizontal ruler at the top if you want a horizontal guide.) Drag the guide to where you want it placed on the image and release. You can also create a guide by selecting View | New Guide. In the dialog box, enter coordinates for horizontal and vertical positioning. Click OK and guides will appear over your image.

To lock your guides, select View | Lock Guides or press CTRL-ALT-; (Windows)/CMD-OPTION-; (Mac). To unlock your guides, repeat the command.

▶ | **QUICK TIP**

To temporarily hide guides, press CTRL-;
*(Windows)/*CMD-; *(Mac)*

Unless a guide is locked, you can remove it by selecting it and sliding it over to the ruler, where it will disappear. (Make sure you use the Move tool when selecting the guide.) You can also remove a guide by selecting View | Clear Guides—however, this removes all the guides.

TRY IT To establish a grid over your image, select View | Show and then select Show Grid from the flyout menu or press CTRL-SHIFT-' (Windows)/CMD-SHIFT-' (Mac).

To alter the increments of a grid, select Edit | Preferences | Guides & Grid. Enter a value for grid spacing in the Gridline Every box (for example, 1) and select the type of units (for example, inches). For Subdivisions, enter a value to subdivide the grid (for example, 4). This example set of specifications would set up a grid that utilized four gridlines within an inch. Your grid can be altered to accommodate your layout.

▶ | **QUICK TIP**

If you frequently work on different types of projects that require the same or similar workspace, you can save different workspaces for each project type and load them as needed. Choose Window | Workspace | Save Workspace and name that workspace to save it.

Improve Performance by Freeing Memory

Sometimes, when you are working with large, multilayered, graphically intense images, you will find that even though you have all the gigabytes in the world, Photoshop is still asking for more memory or it's acting a bit sluggish. Why does this happen? Photoshop utilizes memory for every action completed (you will see this noted in the History palette). Photoshop also utilizes memory to enable users to use the Undo command. Each time you copy an item, memory is also used up. Here are some tips for streamlining your memory.

TRY IT ▶ To free memory used by the Undo command, the History palette, or the Clipboard, select Edit | Purge and choose the item type or buffer you want to clear. If already empty, the item type or buffer is dimmed.

▶ **CAUTION**

The Purge command permanently clears from memory the operation stored by the command or buffer; it cannot be undone.

You can also free memory used by Photoshop by deleting unused layers in the Layers palette. If you notice that you have hidden a layer and are no longer using it, why not throw it out? To delete a layer, select the layer and click the trash can icon at the bottom of the palette. Click Yes when the dialog box asks if you want to delete the selected layer. You can also delete a layer by selecting it and clicking the triangle at the top of the Layers palette. A flyout menu will provide options for the selected layer; select Delete Layer.

CHAPTER 3

Getting Content into Photoshop

TIPS IN THIS CHAPTER

This chapter opens with a discussion of ways to use external content in Photoshop (such as scans and digital photos) and moves on to describe how to actually go about bringing external content into Photoshop and what settings to use.

Ways to Bring Content into Photoshop

While Photoshop is often used to create digital art from scratch, it is also commonly used to edit existing graphics or perhaps to merge existing graphics with new designs. In either case, the existing graphics must be brought into Photoshop in some way.

Perhaps the most popular ways of bringing content into Photoshop involve the use of scanners and digital cameras. In addition, you can open existing digital files in Photoshop, such as JPEGs you downloaded from the Internet or received via e-mail.

Scanners

There are a large variety of scanners available, ranging from sheet-fed scanners to flatbed scanners and film scanners. The type of scanner you use depends primarily on the items you plan to scan. For example, if you only plan to scan business documents and are looking for a scanner that will automatically scan large stacks of single-sheet documents, then the sheet-fed scanner is good for you.

On the other hand, if you're a professional photographer looking to scan not only prints but also film, then you need to invest in a good film scanner. For everyone else, a flatbed scanner is the most popular scanner on the market. Table 3-1 gives a brief synopsis of these three basic types of scanners.

Type of Scanner	Description	Price Range
Flatbed	Flat "box" with a glass window where item to be scanned is placed; sensors behind the glass "read" the image. Can scan virtually anything that can lie flat on the glass.	$50–$150 for the lower-resolution scanners (approx. 600 dpi) $150+ for the higher-resolution scanners (approx. 1,200 dpi)
Sheet-fed	Often bundled with a fax and printer in multipurpose machines. Can scan items no thicker than a single sheet of paper.	$50–$150 for individual sheet-fed scanners $400+ for the multipurpose machines with fax, print, and scan capabilities
Film	Can scan film, often in addition to paper-based items. Capable of scanning at very high resolutions, such as 2,400 dpi.	$400+

Table 3-1   Brief Synopsis of Most Common Types of Scanners

▶ *CAUTION*

Don't get caught up with buying more scanning power than you need. Unless you need to scan a lot of high-quality graphics on a regular basis, the 600 dpi (dots per inch) flatbed scanners are perfectly acceptable for the average user. In addition, many new scanners offer the opportunity to scan at bit depths (color depths) of 36- or even 42-bit. If you keep in mind that a 24-bit depth equals millions of colors, you'll realize that you probably don't need to pay more for anything higher.

After determining the type of scanner you need, also consider the software used to help translate the image being scanned into a digital file. Some popular scanners are even bundled with a version of Photoshop or a utility that allows you to scan right into Photoshop, while others ship with proprietary applications that may or may not be capable of working with Photoshop. I discuss how to actually perform a typical scan in tips later on in this chapter.

Digital Cameras

Like scanners, digital cameras come in all shapes and sizes, from budget and compact cameras to digital camcorders and high-end professional cameras. Also like scanners, the type of camera you use depends primarily on how you intend to use the pictures you'll take with it.

When determining which camera to use, consider the following:

- **Format**   In what file format does the camera save pictures? If you're looking for a digital camcorder, is it capable of saving video as well as still photos?

- **Lens**   How close up or far away do you plan to take pictures? Also, do you need to be able to change lenses? (While some newer cameras offer the option of changeable lenses, many still restrict you to a single, fixed lens.)

- **Resolution**   Do you plan to view the pictures onscreen only or will you also print them? (Printing requires that the pictures be taken at a significantly higher resolution than is necessary for screen viewing.)

- **Storage**   How will your pictures be stored? Common options include mini-CDs, floppy disks, and internal memory cards.

- **Viewfinder/LCD**   How will you view your pictures? Do you want a camera with a screen capable of displaying your pictures immediately after they're taken?

- **Power**   What makes the camera run? What type of batteries does it use? How often will you need to replace them? Is there also an AC adapter you can use?

- **Flash**   Does the camera come with a flash? If not, is it capable of using an external flash?

▶ *NOTE*

For more information about these and other characteristics of digital cameras, check out CNET's Digital Camera Buyer's Guide: http://computers.cnet.com/hardware/0-1078.html.

For digital cameras, the storage method ultimately determines how the images will be transferred to the computer and to Photoshop. For example, if your camera uses an internal memory card, you'll likely use a cable to connect the camera to your computer and then use software on the computer to transfer the images. However, if your camera saves the images in a universal file format (such as JPEG) onto a floppy disk, you typically put the disk into your computer and simply open or copy them as needed. I discuss these storage methods more thoroughly in the tips and techniques presented in this chapter.

What to Consider When Bringing Content into Photoshop

Before I dive into the tips and techniques used to bring content into Photoshop, I need to discuss a few items of consideration when doing so:

- File type
- File resolution
- Color mode

File Type

Many different types of graphics file types exist, but the two most important for our purposes are the following:

- **Bitmap or raster graphics**   Render the image in pixels, whereby information about each individual pixel is stored within the file. Examples of bitmap files include the Photoshop native file format (PSD), TIFF, GIF, and JPEG.
- **Vector graphics**   Are made up of mathematical operations used to draw the lines of an image instead of individual pixels. Common examples include Adobe Illustrator and Macromedia Freehand files.

To see the difference between bitmap and vector files, consider the following illustration, which shows an example of a vector drawing on the left and a bitmap drawing on the right. In addition, Table 3-2 lists the primary differences between the two file types.

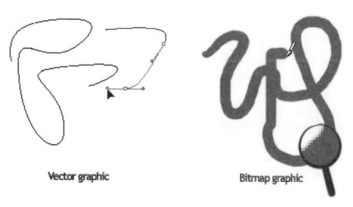

Vector graphic   Bitmap graphic

Vector Files	Bitmap Files
Based on mathematically calculated lines and curves	Pixel-based
Resolution-independent	Resolution-dependent
Memory needs remain constant regardless of the image scale	Memory needs increase according to the image scale
Work best with illustrations using lines and curves	Work well with continuous tone images, such as photographs

Table 3-2   Brief Comparison of Bitmap and Vector Files

Whenever you work with graphics in Photoshop, you're working with bitmap files. In recent years, Photoshop has added support for some vector-type graphics within the program (such as vector-based type, paths, and shapes, which are discussed in later chapters), but ultimately, when you save a file, it is saved as a bitmap graphic.

You can bring vector-based graphics into Photoshop from other programs like Adobe Illustrator, but once they are brought into Photoshop, the graphics are *rasterized,* or turned into pixels. For more information about rasterizing a file, see the tip "Use the Open Command to Open an Existing Vector File in Photoshop."

File Resolution

Another item of consideration is file resolution. So many different uses of the word "resolution" are floating around, it's easy to become confused. Don't worry—this is a difficult concept for many people to understand completely. (I think I must have spent a whole semester in college before I really understood why a 2×2-inch file that was 150 dpi was 4×4 inches on my computer screen.)

Three types of resolutions exist:

- **File resolution**   When you scan an image, you must give it a resolution that stays with the file, regardless of which monitor or output resolution is used to view or print it.

- **Monitor resolution**   This refers to the dots per inch (also called pixels per inch—ppi) displayed on your computer monitor. Most Macintosh monitors default to 72 dpi, while most Windows monitors use 96 dpi. In theory, if you were to take a ruler and hold it up to your Mac's monitor, you could count 72 dots per inch across your screen. (I say *in theory* because many monitors actually vary slightly in resolution.)

- **Output resolution**   Printers also have their own resolutions that determine how many dots they print within each inch on the page. The more dots per inch a printer uses, the smoother the gradations appear within your printed pages.

It is the monitor resolution that determines how large an image appears when displayed on the monitor's screen. Suppose you have a file that will print 3 inches wide by 3 inches high whose file resolution is 144 dpi. Because only 72 dots per inch are available on your Macintosh's monitor, that same 3×3-inch file needs 6×6 inches of space on the screen (144 ÷ 2 = 72 dpi). In other words, for your monitor to display a file with 432 pixels across (144 dpi × 3 inches = 432 total pixels), it needs 6 "inches" of monitor space (432 ÷ 72 = 6).

Color Mode

Whether you scan an image or create a new document in Photoshop, you also have the option to select a color mode. The mode you select will ultimately depend on how you intend to use the image. In other words, will you incorporate it into a page layout that will be printed, or perhaps use it in a web design? While the RGB color mode is best for most web graphics, it is not the standard color mode used for graphics that will be printed. Table 3-3 gives a brief explanation of each of your options in Photoshop, and also specifies each one's most common use.

▶ *CAUTION*

CMYK should never be used for web graphics. Many browsers render an image in CMYK color mode as black-and-white lines horizontally only, similar to how a TV screen looks when a station isn't tuned in correctly.

Color Mode	Description	Common Use
Bitmap	Uses only black and white (without any shades of gray) to represent color values.	Black-and-white line art or single-color graphics to be printed or displayed on screen
Grayscale	Uses only black and white, and combinations of the two in up to 256 shades of gray, to represent color values.	Black-and-white continuous tone graphics to be printed or displayed onscreen
CMYK	Stands for cyan-magenta-yellow-black, and is used in printing where these four pigments are combined to create all colors. Also called an additive color mode; the combination of all color is black, while the absence of all color is white. CMYK images can contain millions of colors.	Color graphics that will be printed
RGB	Stands for red-green-blue, and is used by light, video, and monitors to represent color. Also called an additive color mode; the combination of all colors is white. RGB images can contain millions of colors.	Color graphics that will be displayed onscreen
Lab	Combines three aspects of the color to represent its value: luminance (or lightness), green to red component, and blue to yellow component; is device independent, because it emulates neither a printer nor a monitor.	Comparing and editing graphics before switching to another color mode

Table 3-3   Photoshop Color Modes

Use the Open Command to Bring an Existing Bitmap File into Photoshop

When you want to open an existing digital file in Photoshop, you have to first consider the file's format. Photoshop and ImageReady are capable of opening the file formats listed in Table 3-4.

File Format (extensions)	Photoshop	ImageReady
Photoshop (.psd, .pdd)	X	X
Acrobat TouchUp Image (.pdf, .ai, .pdh)	X	X
AVI (.avi)		X
BMP (.bmp, .rle, .dib)	X	X
Photoshop EPS (.eps)	X	X
Photoshop DCS 1.0 (.eps)	X	
Photoshop DCS 2.0 (.eps)	X	
EPS TIFF Preview (.eps)	X	
EPS PICT Preview (.eps)	X	
Filmstrip (.flm)	X	X
GIF (.gif)	X	X
JPEG (.jpg, .jpeg, .jpe)	X	X
PCX (.pcx)	X	X
Generic PDF (.pdf, .pdp, .ai)	X	X
Photoshop PDF (.pdf, .pdp)	X	X
Photo CD (.pcd)	X	X
PICT File (.pct, .pict)	X	X
PICT Resource (Mac OS only)	X	X
PIXAR (.pxr)	X	X
PNG (.png)	X	X
QuickTime Movie (.mov, .qt)		X
Raw (.raw)	X	
Scitex CT (.sct)	X	
Targa (.tga, .vda, .icb, .vst)	X	X
TIFF (.tif, .tiff)	X	X
Wireless Bitmap (.wbmp)	X	X

Table 3-4   File Formats Supported by Photoshop and ImageReady

▶ *NOTE*

If you wish to open a particular file format not listed here, that doesn't necessarily mean it can't be opened in Photoshop, because Photoshop does support other file formats if you have the necessary plug-in. For more information, check Photoshop's Help files or contact Adobe.

TRY IT   To open a file in any of the formats listed in Table 3-4, choose File | Open to reveal a dialog box similar to Figure 3-1 (Mac) or Figure 3-2 (Windows).

Locate the file you want to open and double-click its name to open it, or click once on the file's name and then click the Open button in the dialog box to open the file in Photoshop.

▶ *CAUTION*

Depending on the format of the file you wish to open, you may be presented with an additional dialog box before the file actually opens. For example, if you attempt to open an EPS file, you'll be asked how you'd like to "rasterize" it. See the tip "Use the Open Command to Open an Existing Vector File in Photoshop" for tips on how to deal with this situation. Other times, you might also be presented with a warning regarding the file's color profile. See the tip "Dealing with Mismatching Color Profiles When Opening Images" for more information.

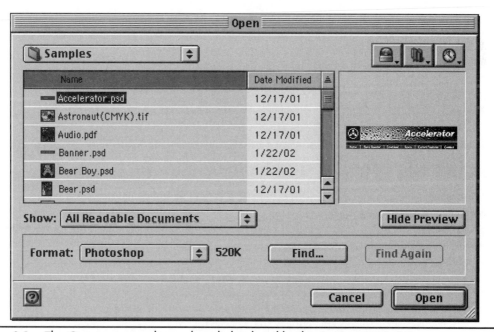

Figure 3-1   The Open command reveals a dialog box like this in Mac OS 9.2.2.

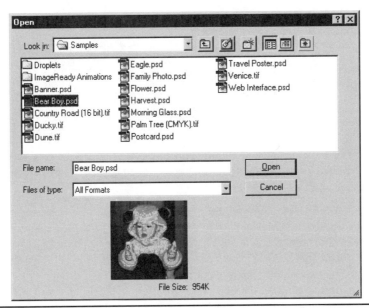

Figure 3-2   The Open command reveals a dialog box like this in Windows 98.

If the filename doesn't include an extension (such as .jpg for JPEG files) and Photoshop doesn't recognize the file, you may need to also specify the file's format from the File Format menu at the bottom of the dialog box.

▶ **NOTE**

If you're working on a Windows computer and Photoshop doesn't recognize your file, choose File | Open As instead of the normal File | Open to specify the file format in which to open the file.

Use the File Browser to Preview and Sort Images

Photoshop ships with a tool that makes previewing and sorting multiple images at once quick and easy. You can even perform simple tasks such as renaming or rotating on several files at once before actually opening them in Photoshop. This is particularly useful when you need to sort through a large library of files—such as stock photos—for a project, because Photoshop shows previews for all files, even if some of those files don't have thumbnails or previews embedded into them. In other words, Photoshop creates those previews on the fly and stores them in the application's cache folder.

In addition to displaying thumbnails, Photoshop generates and displays details about a file, such as its creation date, modification date, format, height, width, color mode, and size. This information—called metadata—is also saved in the application's cache folder.

▶ *CAUTION*

Be forewarned that because Photoshop has to create all these thumbnails and gather all the details about the files viewed in the File Browser, using it can be a slow process if you're pressed for memory. In addition, because Photoshop saves all the file information in a cache folder on your computer, you can free up some of the memory used here by purging the cache file. Know that doing so removes any ranking you've assigned and causes Photoshop to "forget" any thumbnails or metadata it's generated so far.

TRY IT To access the File Browser in Photoshop, choose Window | File Browser. Depending on the size of your screen, the File Browser may appear either as a floating palette (such as in Figure 3-3) or docked in the palette well (at the top or bottom edge of your screen).

Once you've opened the File Browser, you can navigate to the folder of images you're interested in viewing in the directory structure view (in the upper-left corner of the window). After opening a folder in the directory structure view, the images within that folder will be displayed and listed in the preview panel on the right side of the File Browser.

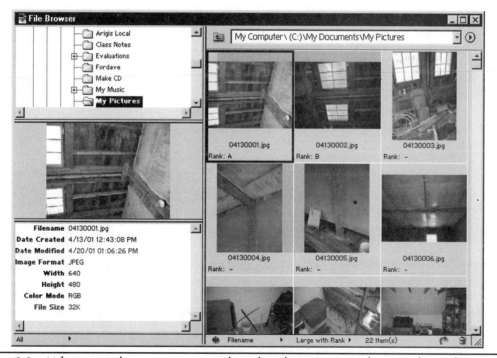

Figure 3-3 When viewed as a separate window, the File Browser can be moved anywhere on your screen.

> ▶ **QUICK TIP**
>
> *To change the size of the thumbnails, click the little triangle in the upper-right corner and choose a different thumbnail size from the list of options in the flyout menu.*

Photoshop defaults to sorting the contents of the preview pane in the File Browser by filename. You can change how the files are sorted by clicking Filename in the options bar along the bottom edge of the File Browser. A single click reveals a pop-up menu of the following ways to sort files:

- Filename
- Rank
- Width
- Height
- File Size
- Resolution
- File Type
- Color Profile
- Date Created
- Date Modified
- Copyright

To view the metadata for a file, click once on the image in the preview pane. The details and a larger thumbnail will be displayed below the directory structure view on the left side of the File Browser.

To open a file from within the File Browser, simply double-click the file from within the preview pane. Alternatively, you can right-click (Windows) or CTRL-click (Mac) and select Open from the pop-up menu.

Rank Images in the File Browser for Customized Sorting

You can use the "Rank" feature of the File Browser as a way to customize your sort method. For example, suppose you have a folder of employee pictures used on a web site, where a third of the pictures are head shots, a third are group shots, and the final third are pictures of "employees at work." You could assign one of three different ranks to the images and then sort the folder according to rank to easily group the image types.

TRY IT First, make sure you have the File Browser open by selecting Window | File Browser. Then, navigate to the folder of images you want to assign ranks to, within the directory structure view on the left side of the File Browser.

▶ **NOTE**

To see an image's rank within the preview page, click the triangle in the upper-right corner of the File Browser and select Large Thumbnail With Rank.

Then, to assign a rank to an image, you have two options. You can either use one of the five default ranks provided by Photoshop (A-E) or type your own.

- To use one of the ranks provided by Photoshop, right-click (Windows) or CTRL-click (Mac) the image to reveal a pop-up menu of options. Select from the five rank options at the bottom of the pop-up menu to assign a rank to the image.

- To enter your own ranking, click the image in the preview page and then click in the space just to the right of the word "Rank:" to reveal a text box. After entering the text string you'd like to assign as a ranking, click the RETURN or ENTER key on your keyboard.

To clear a rank for an image, again right-click (Windows) or CTRL-click (Mac) the image and select Clear Ranking from the pop-up menu.

▶ **QUICK TIP**

To assign the same ranking to several images at once, SHIFT-click each of the images you want to rank the same and then right-click (Windows) or CTRL-click (Mac) and select the appropriate rank from the pop-up menu. (Unfortunately, you can't use this technique to assign custom ranks to multiple files at the same time.)

To change a rank for an image, right-click (Windows) or CTRL-click (Mac) the image and select a different rank from the pop-up menu.

Photoshop defaults to sorting the contents of the preview pane in the File Browser by filename. You can sort the preview pane by rank instead, by clicking Filename in the options bar along the bottom edge of the File Browser and selecting Rank from the pop-up menu that appears.

▶ **NOTE**

Custom rankings are first sorted numerically, then alphabetically. This means that "1A" comes before "A1".

Export Cache from the File Browser for Speedy Image Previews

When you view a folder of images in the File Browser, Photoshop creates thumbnail previews for those images (even if they weren't saved with the original file). These previews are then saved in the cache file for the File Browser. Unfortunately, if the cache file is deleted for whatever reason (perhaps you purge it to free up memory or you view the folder from a different computer), Photoshop has to re-create these previews, causing the process to become quite slow.

Luckily, you can export a copy of that cache file into the folder with the images. This is particularly beneficial if you plan to burn a CD of the images, for example, because the exported cache file will enable anyone viewing the CD to benefit from speedy image previews.

TRY IT To export the cache from the File Browser, first choose View | File Browser or click the File Browser in the Palette Well to make the File Browser visible. Then, navigate through the directory structure until you're viewing the folder of images for which you want to export the cache.

Click the triangle in the upper-right corner of the File Browser and select Export Cache from the flyout menu. (If you're viewing the File Browser while it's docked in the Palette Well, the triangle appears just to the right of the File Browser title.)

▶ *NOTE*

The option to Export Cache will be grayed out and can't be selected if you're viewing a folder that is locked and/or write-protected, because Photoshop is not able to write the cache to that folder.

After choosing Export Cache, Photoshop copies two files into the folder you're currently viewing—one contains the thumbnails for the folder, and the other contains any metadata (details about a file, such as its creation date, modification date, format, height, width, color mode, and size). When copying the images contained in the folder to another disk, copy the entire folder to make sure you get those two cache files as well.

Dealing with Mismatching Color Profiles When Opening Images

When you use the Open command (choose File | Open) to open a file in Photoshop, the program checks to see whether there is a color profile embedded with the file. If a color profile is embedded, Photoshop compares it to the current color profile in use on your computer. If those two profiles don't match, you may see an error message, such as the one shown in Figure 3-4, before the file opens.

The program defaults to asking you every time it encounters a mismatched profile, but you can turn off that setting by choosing Edit | Color Settings and then unchecking the box labeled Ask When Opening next to Profile Mismatches. (Even though you can turn this off, I don't recommend it.)

Once presented with a warning about mismatched profiles, you have three options:

- Use the embedded profile instead of the working color space.

- Convert the document's colors to the working color space.

- Discard the embedded profile and don't color manage.

TRY IT   While the options themselves are fairly self-explanatory, it is nonetheless frustrating to encounter a mismatched profile in the first place. To determine which option to select, consider the following:

- **What is the difference between the two profiles?**   In the example shown in Figure 3-3, the two profiles are both grayscale, one with a gamma of 1.8 and the other with a gamma of 2.2. The reason for the difference is that the file was created with a typical Mac OS gamma (1.8) while the current working gamma is set to a Windows gamma (2.2).

- **Who created the file?**   Consider asking that person whether the profile is required in order to view the file properly. It is not uncommon for color profiles to be attached to files without the designer's knowledge, and if that happens, you likely can discard the embedded profile without suffering any damage.

- **What is the ultimate destination for the file?**   If it's intended to be displayed on a web page, and yet the embedded profile is in the CMYK color space, you can safely covert the document's colors to the working color space (assuming you're working in the RGB color space). On the other hand, if you're a print designer and your current working space is CMYK, but you open a web graphic with an RGB color profile, you likely should use the embedded profile instead of the working color space.

After making a selection, click OK.

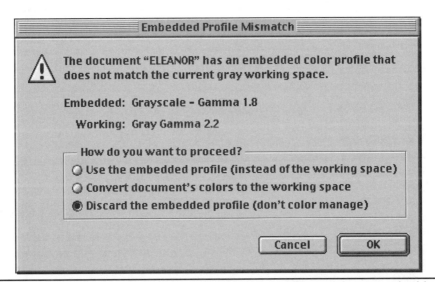

Figure 3-4   A mismatch between the current working color profile and the one embedded in a file produces a dialog box like this one.

Create a New File in Photoshop

Often, when you want to merge several different files together—or whenever you want to start from scratch—you'll need to create a new file in Photoshop. Because of the many options Photoshop gives you, this is not necessarily a one-click task.

 To create a new file in Photoshop, you need to first choose File | New, at which point you'll be presented a window similar to the following:

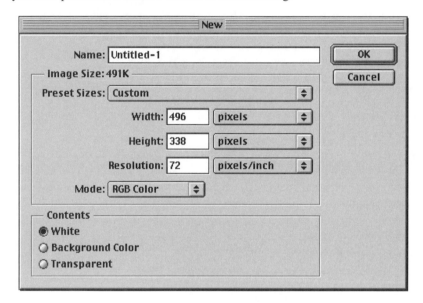

▶ *NOTE*

If you have recently copied an image to your computer's clipboard, Photoshop will automatically fill in the height, width, and resolution of that image when you select File | New.

If you already know the name you want to give your file, enter it in the first text box at the top of the window. If you don't enter a name, Photoshop names your file using a generic "Untitled" and a number. (You can always rename it when you save the file.)

▶ *CAUTION*

Giving a file a name when you first open it does not save it. You must choose File | Save, File | Save As, or File | Save For Web to actually save your file.

For the image size, you can select one of Photoshop's preset sizes (as shown in Figure 3-5) or enter your own size. Photoshop defaults to using inches as its unit of measurement. To enter your image dimensions using another unit of measurement, click the word "inches" and select another method from the pop-up menu. (You can always change an image's dimensions later.)

For resolution, enter the file resolution you plan to work at in Photoshop, even if it's different from the ultimate print resolution. If you're a web designer, this means you'll typically work at 72 dpi, and if you're a print designer, the most common resolution is 300 dpi. For more tips on selecting a file resolution, see the tip "Capture Images Larger than You Plan to Use in Photoshop."

▶ **NOTE**

It's extremely important that you accurately set the image resolution when you create a new file, because trying to change an image's resolution later—particularly if you're trying to increase the resolution—will significantly affect the quality of your image. If you aren't sure which resolution to use, err on the higher side to avoid loss of image quality later.

Assign the color mode of the image by selecting between Bitmap, Grayscale, RGB, CMYK, and Lab Color in the pop-up menu next to Mode. (Again, you can always change this later.) For more information about these color modes, refer to the section "Color Mode" earlier in this chapter.

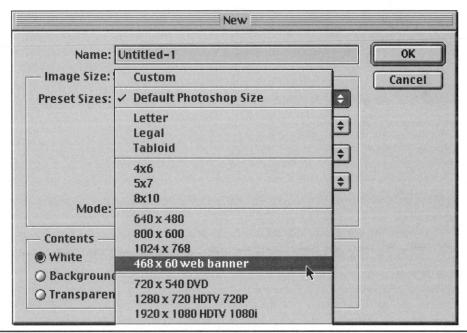

Figure 3-5   Photoshop offers you a short list of preset image sizes.

Finally, specify how Photoshop should fill the background of the file when you first open it. For example, should the background be a solid white, a solid black, or transparent? (In most cases, the default of White is sufficient.) Make the appropriate selection and click OK.

Import a File into Photoshop Using the TWAIN Interface

Most scanners come with a utility or plug-in that allows you to scan your images right into Photoshop. The utility or plug-in uses the industry-standard TWAIN interface to import the scan.

Before you can scan an image, you must make sure the utility or plug-in is installed properly and is working with Photoshop. Consult the documentation that came with your scanner if you're unsure about how to install the software. If you can't find your documentation, check the company's web site for an updated plug-in (some companies may call the scanner plug-in a "driver").

▶ *NOTE*

If your scanning software doesn't work with Photoshop, don't worry, because you can still scan onto your computer and then open the newly digitized file into Photoshop.

Once your scanner is properly set up and the appropriate plug-in is installed, you should be able to access it from Photoshop's Import menu.

TRY IT To scan a file into Photoshop using the TWAIN interface, choose File | Import and select the name of your scanning software from the menu. For example, I have a UMAX scanner that uses the VistaScan software. When I installed this software, it placed a plug-in in the Import/ Export folder, in my Plug-Ins folder, within the Photoshop 7 folder on my hard drive (Hard Drive | Applications | Adobe Photoshop 7.0 | Plug-Ins | Import/Export). Now, whenever I choose File | Import on my computer, I am presented with an option for VistaScan v2.4.3 that invokes the scanning software, as shown in the following illustration.

▶ *NOTE*

After you first install your scanner software and any associated plug-ins, be sure to restart Adobe Photoshop to gain access to the new plug-in from within the program.

▶ | *QUICK TIP*

You can add your own preset page sizes to the menu shown in Figure 3-5 by editing the file "New Doc Sizes.txt" found in the Presets folder of your Adobe Photoshop 7 folder.

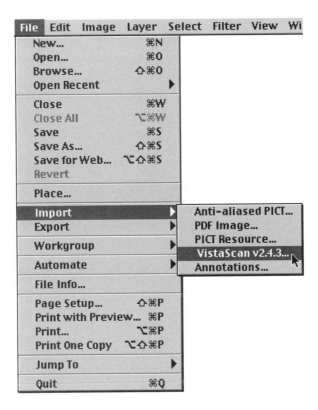

After selecting that option, a new window is displayed offering several options for customizing how the file is scanned, such as the following:

- Color mode
- Scan type (reflective, transparency, and so forth)
- Resolution
- Scan size (usually presented in the form of a percentage—scanning at 100% captures a photo with the same width and height as the printed version)

However, the way in which these options are presented will vary according to your specific scanner software.

QUICK TIP

Always scan from the original document. Just as you lose quality when you make a copy of a copy on a photocopier, so too do you lose quality when scanning from something other than an original file.

Capture Images Larger than You Plan to Use in Photoshop

Whenever you import an image into Photoshop, regardless of whether you captured it from a digital camera or a scanner, it's important to assign an accurate file resolution, as discussed in the section "File Resolution" earlier in this chapter. The reason is that it is very difficult to increase a file's resolution at a later date and retain the same quality.

For example, suppose you scan an image at 72 dpi—the common resolution for web graphics— and later decide to also use the image in your company's printed brochure. If you've ever tried to print a web page that has images on it, you've likely realized that web graphics don't print that well. This is because web graphics are typically created at a very low file resolution—72 dpi—while today's printers are capable of printing at much higher resolutions. When you print a file with a low resolution, you can actually see the dots on the page, causing the image to appear "dotty" or speckled.

In order to have that image print well in your company's brochure, you'd need a file resolution that is ideally closer to 300 dpi. So at this point, you have two options: rescan the image (as long as you still have it!) at a higher resolution, or attempt to "resample" the image in Photoshop.

▶ *NOTE*

Resampling is discussed in the next tip, "Adjust an Image's Resolution in Photoshop."

 To determine the appropriate resolution at which you should capture images, consider the following tips:

- If you're a designer working with images that will ultimately be displayed on the printed page using a halftone printer (such as one that produces color separations for four-color process printing), scan at 1.5 to 2 times larger than the printer's screen frequency or line screen (lines per inch = lpi). (See Table 3-5 for common screen frequencies, but check with your printer to be sure.)

- If you're working with images that will be printed using an ink-jet printer, you don't have to use as high a resolution, because ink-jet printers tend to "bleed" the color across the page. This causes those tiny dots to blend together and reduce the speckled appearance of low-resolution images. In fact, scanning at 150 dpi is usually sufficient when a file will only be printed on an ink-jet printer.

- If you're working with images that you plan to use only on a web site, I recommend you capture them at 150 dpi, even though you'll probably downsample them to 72 dpi for the final web page. The reason I recommend this is that it offers you a higher-quality file with larger pixel dimensions—meaning you can use it at a larger size in your design if needed, and you can also downsample it later to actually increase the quality of the image.

- If you're using a digital camera to capture images, consider using the highest quality setting on the camera if your storage method allows you to. Even though you may not think you'll need to use the file at such a high resolution, you're better off having a copy at the higher resolution if you need it later, given that you can't "rescan" a picture taken with a digital camera.

Printing Method	Screen Frequency
Coarse, low-end screen used for newsletters and other bulk commercial printing	65 lpi
Medium- to average-level screen typically used by newspapers	85 lpi
High-quality screen used for magazines and typical business papers printed with four colors	133 lpi
Very high-end and refined screen used for art prints and high-quality business papers printed with four colors	177 lpi

Table 3-5   Common Screen Frequencies for Typical Printing Methods

- If you're not sure how you will use a certain image, it's a good idea to scan at a resolution of 300 dpi. This is usually high enough for the higher-end printing methods, and is not so high that it produces a file so large that it hogs all of your available system memory. In addition, keeping a copy of a file at 300 dpi typically ensures you won't have to scan the image again later.

Adjust an Image's Resolution in Photoshop

Resampling refers to the process of changing a file's pixel dimensions to affect its display size and ultimately the file's resolution. When you resample down—called *downsampling*—you move from a higher file resolution to a lower one and typically gain quality in the process. However, when you resample up, you move from a lower file resolution to a higher one, and Photoshop is forced to "make up" the contents of those added pixels.

How Photoshop creates those new pixels (and for that matter, how it deletes them as well) is referred to as the *interpolation method.* Photoshop allows you to specify the default interpolation method in its preferences (choose Edit | Preferences | General), and also enables you to adjust that interpolation method for specific files from within the options for changing an image's size.

 To adjust an image's resolution after you've brought it into Photoshop, make sure the file is open and choose Image | Image Size to bring up the following window of options:

![Image Size dialog box showing Pixel Dimensions: 900K, Width: 640 pixels, Height: 480 pixels; Document Size: Width: 2.133 inches, Height: 1.6 inches, Resolution: 300 pixels/inch; Constrain Proportions checked; Resample Image: Bicubic checked. Buttons: OK, Reset, Auto...]

Under Document Size, you are given the opportunity to increase or decrease a file's resolution. As you change that image, you should see the Width and Height of the image also change under Pixel Dimensions. Photoshop adjusts those sizes according to the file resolution you specify.

To change the interpolation method for this particular image, click the pop-up menu next to Resample Image at the bottom of the options window to select one of the following methods:

- **Bicubic**   Photoshop uses this as its default interpolation method. Although this method is the slowest in terms of processing time, it is the most accurate and produces the smoothest gradations.

- **Bilinear**   This method is your average, middle-of-the-road interpolation method, offering midgrade quality and processing time.

- **Nearest Neighbor**   This method is the fastest to process but may produce jagged edges. Adobe recommends using this method for files with non-anti-aliased edges as it helps preserve those hard edges and makes a smaller file size.

After making your adjustments, click OK to see how they affect your file. If you're unsatisfied with the changes, choose Edit | Undo before doing anything else in Photoshop.

▶ | **QUICK TIP**

To preview how resampling up might affect a file, you can first create a duplicate of your file by selecting Image | Duplicate. Then, apply the resampling to the duplicate file instead of your original.

Use the Clipboard to Transfer Files Between Applications

Oftentimes, you want to transfer files quickly between applications without having to first save a file to the hard drive and then reopen it in another application. For example, suppose you want to capture an image from a web page, such as a sample image, used for creating comps, from a stock photography web site. You can copy to the clipboard and paste into Photoshop to quickly gain access to the file.

▶ **NOTE**

You can only have one image file on your clipboard at any given time. This means that if you copy one image and forget to paste it into Photoshop, and then copy another image, that first image is lost.

TRY IT   To copy an image from a web page (or other application), make sure the file you want to copy is visible in your web browser. Right-click (Windows) or CTRL-click (Mac) the image once to reveal a pop-up menu. Although the exact wording varies according to the browser or application, you should see an option to Copy Image.

After selecting Copy or Copy Image, open or return to Photoshop. Choose File | New and click OK. Photoshop will automatically create a new file the exact size of the image you just copied. Next, choose Edit | Paste to paste the image from the clipboard into the new file.

▶ *NOTE*

If the Paste command is not available in Photoshop, first check to make sure you have a new file available for pasting into. If you do and the Paste command is still not available, return to your web browser or other application and attempt to recopy the image.

Use the Open Command to Open an Existing Vector File in Photoshop

When you attempt to open a vector file—such as one created in Adobe Illustrator or Adobe Acrobat—in Photoshop, the program needs to first determine how to *rasterize* the file. Rasterizing refers to the process of translating vector-based file information into pixels. (For more information about these two file types—vector and bitmap—refer to the section "File Type" earlier in this chapter.)

To rasterize a file, Photoshop needs to give it absolute pixel dimensions and a file resolution because, although vector files are resolution- and size-independent, bitmap files require these sizes to display properly. Therefore, it's wise not to rasterize a file until you're sure of the size at which you intend to use it.

Along with being resolution-independent, vector files don't rely on anti-aliasing to create the appearance of smooth edges on curves. Anti-aliasing is a technique used by bitmap applications like Photoshop to add extra pixels of color around curved edges to give the appearance of smooth gradations from one color to another. Therefore, when you rasterize a vector file with lots of curves, I recommend you check Anti-aliased in the options window.

TRY IT To use the Open command to open an existing vector file in Photoshop, first choose File | Open and locate the file in the directory structure before clicking OK. As long as the file is indeed a vector file, you'll be presented with an options window similar to the following:

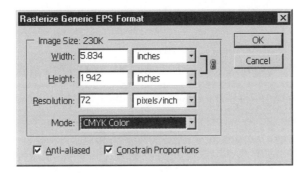

At this point, you must specify the size at which Photoshop should build the file, both in physical height and width and in resolution. In addition, also specify the color mode. Finally, at the bottom of the options window, you can choose whether the file should be anti-aliased and whether Photoshop should constrain the proportions when sizing the image.

▶ *CAUTION*

If you're unsure about what size you'll be using for a vector file within Photoshop, consider using the Place command instead of the Open command to import the vector file, because it offers more flexibility in determining size. See the next tip for the exact technique.

Use the Place Command to Import an Existing Vector File into Another File in Photoshop

Besides using the Open command to bring an existing vector file into Photoshop, you can also use the Place command. This command is more useful than the Open command in two distinct situations:

- When you want to add an existing vector image to another file already open in Photoshop
- When you are unsure as to the ultimate size you'll use for the vector file in Photoshop

TRY IT   To use the Place command to import an existing vector file into Photoshop, you must first have another file open in the program in which to place the file. Then, choose File | Place and locate the file from within the directory structure before clicking OK.

▶ *NOTE*

If you're importing a PDF file that has multiple pages into Photoshop, you'll also be prompted to enter the page number of the page you want to place in the current file.

Photoshop then displays a thumbnail view of the vector file within a bounding box, symbolizing the ultimate size of the file once it is placed within Photoshop. You can edit the file in several ways:

- To move the placed file to a different location on the page, click inside the bounding box and drag it to the desired location.
- To resize the placed file on the page, click one of the four corners of the box and drag it in to shrink the image or drag it out to enlarge the image. Hold down the SHIFT key while resizing the file to retain the original proportions.
- To rotate the placed file on the page, move the pointer just outside one of the four corners of the bounding box until the pointer changes from a straight arrow to a curved arrow. Then, click and drag to determine the angle of the rotation. When rotating a placed file, Photoshop rotates it around the file's center point. You can move that center point by clicking and dragging it to another location.

- To skew a single side of the image, click one of the corners of the bounding box and drag it to the desired location.

▶ *NOTE*

You can also edit all of these characteristics from the Options bar under the Menu bar at the top of the screen. See Figure 3-6 for a visual example.

Just as when using the Open command to import a vector file, you can specify whether the placed image should have smooth (using anti-aliasing) or hard (not using anti-aliasing) edges when rasterized by Photoshop. To do so, check or uncheck the box next to Anti-alias in the Options bar under the Menu bar at the top of the screen (see Figure 3-6).

Figure 3-6　When placing a vector file into another file in Photoshop, the Options bar at the top of the screen contains several ways to edit the file before it's rasterized.

Trim Away White Space Around an Image

Sometimes, a file is created with a canvas—or background—that is too large for the actual image. For example, consider the following illustration, which shows a new file I created in Photoshop that is 400×400 pixels in size.

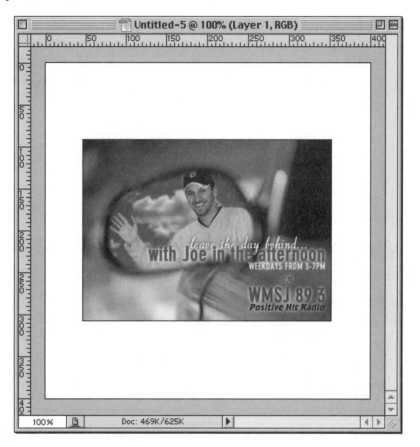

After I pasted in an image that I downloaded from a web site, I realized I had created the new file at the wrong size and now had a lot of extra white space around the image. It's not a problem with Photoshop, though, because I can quickly and easily eliminate the extra white space around the image using the Trim command.

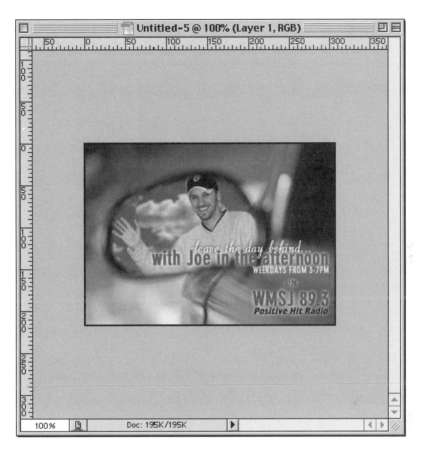

The Trim command (choose Image | Trim) allows you to delete extra space like this because it can actually shrink the file's canvas to match the size of its contents. In other words, it removes blank or white space from around the top, bottom, right, and left sides of an image.

▶ **NOTE**

You can also use the Crop tool (located in Photoshop's toolbox) or the Crop command (choose Image | Crop) to trim away white space around an image. However, when you want to shrink the canvas to match the actual contents of the file, the Trim command is a much quicker and easier way to do so because the Crop tool and command require you to make a selection first.

TRY IT To trim away white space around an image in an open file, choose Image | Trim from the top menu in Photoshop. After doing so, you will be presented with a dialog box similar to this:

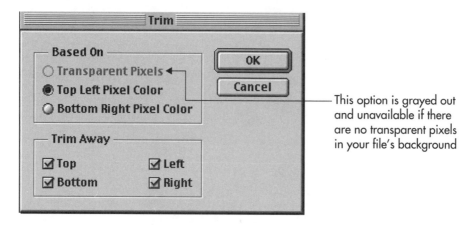

This option is grayed out and unavailable if there are no transparent pixels in your file's background

In the Based On area, select which pixel Photoshop should use as its reference when removing color. This will most commonly be the Top Left Pixel Color if you have a solid color background—such as white or black.

In the Trim Away area, select where Photoshop should trim away the color selected in the Based On section. For example, specify whether you want to remove the white background from around all four sides of the image or only on the top and bottom.

CHAPTER 4

Using Photoshop as a Web Page Layout Tool

TIPS IN THIS CHAPTER

W hereas print designers use programs like Adobe InDesign or QuarkXPress to lay out their pages, web designs typically create their entire layouts first in Photoshop before transferring to another program. This process is often referred to as mockup or comp development, because you're developing a mockup design of how the page will look when it is ultimately displayed as a web page by a browser.

If you're working for a client, this mockup will likely be used to obtain the client's approval before moving on to the coding of the site. For example, in my web development projects, I typically create two possible versions of the home page of the site. I find that quickly creating two designs in Photoshop is much easier than designing them first in Photoshop, and then fully executing them in code—especially since one of those is likely to be rejected by the client anyway. In other words, why bother coding something that may never get used?

The other reason working in Photoshop tends to be better for web design mockups is that clients will undoubtedly request several changes to the pages before you enter the coding phase. Most designers are more comfortable in programs like Photoshop than in HTML editors and can, therefore, make such changes more quickly. This speeds up not only the time it takes to gain client approval, but also the entire development process.

▶ **NOTE**

You may have noticed that there is not a chapter titled "Using Photoshop as a Printed Page Layout Tool." That is because Photoshop is not typically used as a page layout tool for printed design. Instead, Photoshop is most commonly used to prepare and optimize print graphics for placement in a print design (using a page layout tool such as Adobe InDesign or Quark Xpress). Chapter 16 discusses the issues involved in optimizing print graphics.

Diagramming a Web Page

Just as in a theatrical play, where you have actors in the foreground and scenery in the background, two levels of design also exist in a web page—the foreground and background. It is important to define which aspects of your page will be in the background and which will be in the foreground early on, because each piece will be produced a bit differently.

▶ **NOTE**

If you use dynamic HTML (DHTML) to code your web pages, you can also have multiple layers within the foreground of a page. However, HTML can only have a single file in the background of a web page, so it's still important to distinguish between the foreground and background for that reason.

Background Elements

A background can be quite helpful in setting the mood or theme for the whole web page. Background can be as simple as solid colors or as detailed as a mosaic style pattern and everything in between.

HTML enables you to add a single image to be used as the "scenery" in the background of your web page. Several benefits exist to using an image in the background as opposed to the foreground:

- You can achieve a quick and easy layered look in your designs this way because an image in the foreground can actually be placed over the top of an image in the background.

- Background images begin at the top of the page and run all the way to each of the four sides by default. By contrast, elements in the foreground are subject to borders on the top and left, similar to those that occur when you print something.

When you use a background image, you need to remember a few other things:

- All background images tile. *Tiling* means background images repeat in the browser window as many times as needed to cover the entire width and height of the browser window.

- You can only include one image in the background if you use regular HTML. (You can further layer pages by using DHTML, but it is not supported by all browsers.) So, if you want to use two different patterns in your background, they need to be included in a single image file.

- Background images should be small in file size to avoid a long download. Take advantage of the fact that the browser repeats a background image, and cut your image down as much as possible.

Foreground Elements

Aside from the background image, all other aspects of a web page typically fall into the foreground category. This means each individual graphic and text element will be coded into the page using HTML or some other web coding technology.

▶ | **QUICK TIP**

When you design in Photoshop, it's best to keep these different aspects of your page on their own layers (as discussed more in depth in Chapter 5).

When creating mockups in Photoshop that will be presented to a client for approval, every element of the final web page, whether it's an image or text element rendered by the browser, is shown in the mockup page. Take a look at Figure 4-1 to see what I mean. For example, text links are underlined, as they will be in the browser, and are given an appropriate link color; any text itself is shown in a font face and size capable of being rendered by a web browser.

In addition, form elements are rendered as they might appear within a typical web browser. Note, form elements like the text boxes and button shown in Figure 4-1 are rendered differently in various browsers and platforms. For example, Netscape Navigator 4 on Windows renders a text box as 24 pixels in height, while the same text box shown in Netscape Navigator 4 on the Mac is only 16 pixels high.

▶ **NOTE**

Unless otherwise specified, each time I tell you to create a new file in this chapter, you should use 72 dpi as your file resolution and RGB as the color mode, because these are both the default settings for web graphics.

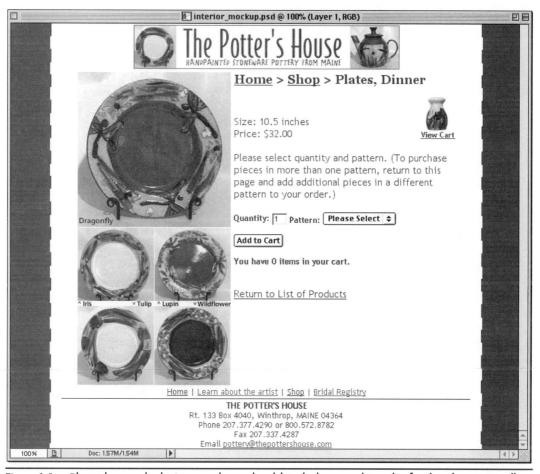

Figure 4-1   Photoshop web design mockups should include everything the final web pages will include, especially if they're being presented to a client for approval.

> ▶ **QUICK TIP**
>
> *This information is important when designing mockups, because you want to design pages flexible enough to handle the smallest and largest of form elements. So if you're planning to have your site's search box fit perfectly into a box 100 pixels wide but 20 pixels high—think twice—and be sure to test the design thoroughly before telling a client it's possible. For all the numbers on how form elements measure up across the various platforms and browsers, visit http://hotwired.lycos.com/webmonkey/99/41/index3a_page5.html.*

Create Sketches with Accurate Proportions

To get those creative juices flowing, I typically do small thumbnail sketches before working in Photoshop, such as those shown in the following illustration. I find that when I'm going to create electronic documents, paper and pencil can sometimes be the best way to help plan a page's structure.

Once you focus in on one or two thumbnails, it might be useful to redraw them within the boundaries of an actual browser window. This way, you can produce sketches like the following, with the proper page proportions.

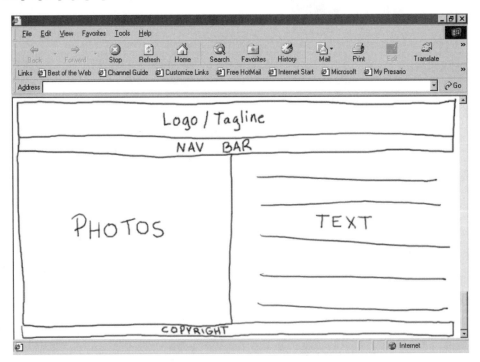

TRY IT To create sketches with accurate proportions, first open a web browser such as Internet Explorer or Netscape Navigator. Then, follow the steps provided next for your operating system.

If you are using a Mac:

1. Make sure CAPS LOCK is on.

2. Press CMD-SHIFT-4 (after you let go, your cursor should look like a little record).

3. Click the window you want to take a picture of (in this case, the browser window).

4. Open Photoshop.

5. Choose File | Open and look within your hard drive folder for a TIFF file beginning with the word "Picture" (if there are more than one, select the last one).

6. Click OK.

7. Use the Marquee tool to select the center area where the web page appears.

8. Choose Edit | Fill.

9. From the dialog box that appears, select White from the pop-up menu next to Use to fill the center area of the page with white.

10. Click OK.

11. Choose Select | Deselect.

12. To redraw your thumbnail design within this web page using pencil or pen on paper, choose File | Print.

13. To redraw your thumbnail design within this web page using the tools available in Photoshop, begin designing now.

If you are using Windows:

1. Press ALT-PRINT SCREEN to take a picture of the browser window.

2. Open Photoshop.

3. Choose File | New and click OK (because there is something on the clipboard, Photoshop will automatically fill in the appropriate sizes).

4. Choose Edit | Paste to paste the picture of the browser window into the current file.

5. Use the Marquee tool to select the center area where the web page appears.

6. Choose Edit | Fill.

7. From the dialog box that appears, select White from the pop-up menu next to Use to fill the center area of the page with white.

8. Click OK.

9. Choose Select | Deselect.

10. To redraw your thumbnail design within this web page using pencil or pen on paper, choose File | Print.

11. To redraw your thumbnail design within this web page using the tools available in Photoshop, begin designing now.

Begin Designing with the Appropriate Page Size

When you begin designing a web page in Photoshop, one of your first tasks is usually to create a new file with the appropriate page size. While this may be a fairly easy task for print designers who know exactly the size of their final printed page, web designers must grapple with the variability of screen size when their web designs are viewed on different monitors.

On the Web, a "page" refers to the information displayed within a single (sometimes scrollable) web browser window. When you create your web graphics in Photoshop, you must specify a size (in pixel dimensions) that will determine how much of the image (and your page) is visible without scrolling.

So, exactly how do you decide which numbers to input into the Height and Width boxes in Photoshop's New dialog box? You first need to determine your target screen resolution. The most popular are the following, listed from most popular to least popular, according to recent surveys from WebSideStory and BrowserNews (www.netmechanic.com/news/vol4/accessibility_no24.htm):

- 800×600
- 1024×768
- 640×480

▶ **NOTE**

Unsure of which screen resolution you're using? See the tip "Check Your Screen Resolution" in Chapter 1.

The difficulty in determining which of these screen resolutions to target is caused by the fact that depending on how you build it, your pages can look drastically different on the screens not targeted. To work around this, many designers choose to develop their pages to grow and shrink on whichever screen size they're being viewed. This process is often referred to as creating "liquid" pages.

Creating images larger than the width of the available space on the screen will cause a horizontal scroll bar to appear. If this is not intended, you need to create your web graphics to fit within the available space on the user's screen. Unfortunately, targeting a 640×480 resolution doesn't mean you can create graphics that are 640 pixels in width. Why? Because the following screen elements also take up space:

- Operating system menus, such as the Windows Start menu and the Apple menu
- Browser menus, toolbars, and other aspects of the browser that display onscreen

- Web page offset, the "buffer space" around the web page that most browsers add by default; this can be overridden with certain HTML codes

- Web page frames, the additional edges of the browser that appear in between some pages that use the HTML coding technique called "frames"

After this space is taken into consideration, you're left with significantly less space to work with when designing web pages in Photoshop. Table 4-1 shows rough estimates on available page widths for the most popular screen resolutions. You can use any of these widths when creating your new "page" in Photoshop.

▶ **NOTE**

These are average widths. Some users have their screens set up in different ways that may reduce the available width for web pages.

▶ | **QUICK TIP**

An article in a recent issue of Evolt does a good job of describing how to create liquid pages: www.evolt.org/article/Liquid_Design_for _the_Web/20/15177/.

If you're planning to create "liquid" pages that grow and shrink according to the user's screen size, you still need to pick one of these sizes to target. The reason is that you want to make sure none of your graphics force a horizontal scroll bar when you didn't intend them to. (In other words, to make sure your liquid pages don't force a horizontal scroll bar even on 640×480 resolutions, make sure none of your graphics extend beyond 600 pixels.)

The height of your web page is less important, because web pages can extend down as far as you'd like them to. This means you should use a value for the height of your file in Photoshop that will ensure there is room for all the content you need to fit on that page. Keep in mind that users tend to prefer shorter pages over longer ones that require extensive scrolling.

TRY IT To create a new file in Photoshop with the appropriate page size, select File | New and input the size into the available boxes in the dialog box or choose from one of the Preset Sizes.

If you've already created a file in Photoshop and you now want to check and perhaps edit the file size, choose Image | Canvas Size. If you plan to change the size of your file to be smaller than the current file, Photoshop may have to crop some of your existing page content. To prevent that from

Resolution	Width
640×480	600 pixels
800×600	760 pixels
1024×768	980 pixels

Table 4-1   Approximate Available Width for Most Common Screen Resolutions

happening, move all page content to the upper-left corner of the image, making sure it doesn't extend beyond the size to which you're about to shrink the image. Then, choose Image | Canvas Size and make the appropriate changes to the sizes. Before clicking OK, click the first box next to Anchor to tell Photoshop to anchor the page in the upper-left corner of the existing file and only crop along the right and bottom edges.

Use Guides to Plan Page Layout

Once you have a page opened in Photoshop and you've begun to design, you'll want to use the guides to help plan your page layout. For example, you can use guides to symbolize:

- Which part of the page some users will have to scroll to see
- Where images might need to be broken in pieces when translated into HTML
- Where HTML table cells, rows, and columns begin and end

When targeting 640×480 screens (as discussed in the preceding tip, "Begin Designing with the Appropriate Page Size"), I tend to begin with pages approximately 600×400 pixels in size. I then drag a guide to 275 pixels (as shown in the following illustration) to signify the fold, or the point at which many people using this screen resolution must begin scrolling. This helps remind me to keep the most important information above that point on the page.

When targeting 800×600 screens, I typically set my page size to 750×500, drawing my guide for the fold at 395. Of course, if you plan to use flexible page sizes (as discussed in the preceding tip, "Begin Designing with the Appropriate Page Size"), these beginning numbers are less important.

> **QUICK TIP**
>
> *You can also use the guides to remind yourself how much of the page will be visible without scrolling for the majority of your visitors.*

TRY IT To create a guide in Photoshop, first make sure your rulers are visible by choosing View | Rulers or pressing CTRL-R (Windows) or CMD-R (Mac). Then, click and hold one of the rulers, and drag away from the ruler toward the inside of your document, letting go wherever you want the guide to rest.

Alternatively, you can create a new guide by choosing View | New Guide. Then, select either horizontal or vertical and enter the location of the guide in the text box before clicking OK.

> **QUICK TIP**
>
> *Guides automatically "snap" to the edges of any content on the current layer. This may make it difficult to draw some of your guides. If you run into a problem like this when drawing guides, choose View | Snap To and select None from the flyout menu.*

To change a vertical guide to a horizontal guide, or vice versa, hold down the ALT key (Windows) or OPTION key (Mac) while dragging the guide.

To move a guide after you've created it, click the Move tool in the toolbox or press V on your keyboard. Then, position the pointer over the ruler you want to move and drag it to the desired location.

▶ **NOTE**

If you can't move a guide, check to make sure it's not locked. Look under the View menu to see if Unlock Guides is an option. If it is, select it to unlock the guides and make them moveable again.

Customize Your Page for MSN TV and Other Set-Top Devices

Most web designers don't need to customize their pages for viewing on MSN TV (previously called WebTV) or other set-top devices, because these systems haven't yet gained enough of a following to warrant it. However, if you've determined that a fair amount of your users do indeed view your site through MSN TV or other such systems, there are certain tips you need to keep in mind.

The most important thing to remember is that the screen size is completely fixed at 544×372 pixels for the systems in North America and Japan using the NTSC television standard, and 768×576 pixels for European systems using the PAL standard. This screen size can't be changed by the user or the web designer, and in fact, the MSN TV system actually compresses all web pages to fit horizontally within that space.

▶ **QUICK TIP**

You can download a free viewer for your Mac or PC that simulates the MSN TV system and enables you to see how your pages will look when viewed on MSN TV (http:// developer.msntv.com/Tools/WebTVVwr.asp).

 To customize your page for MSN TV and other set-top devices, consider the following:

- Avoid critical information in small images, because text isn't as crisp on TV screens.

- Use flexible page layouts whenever possible, so content can rearrange itself to fit within the smaller size.

- Choose Image | Image Size to temporarily shrink your page down to 544 pixels wide and preview how your content looks at that size. After previewing the image, choose Edit | Undo to return to the previous page size.

- Avoid creating page titles over 35 characters in length, because additional characters are cut off anyway.

- Be concise, because the default font for MSN TV is 18 points—significantly larger than that of Netscape or Internet Explorer, meaning users must scroll much more to read content.

- While dark colors on light backgrounds typically work best for most web pages, the opposite is true for pages viewed on MSN TV systems.

- Avoid HTML frames, because MSN TV changes them to tables.

- Avoid image maps. All links become outlined with a selection box when viewed on MSN TV; this means image maps with irregularly shaped hot spots may become unusable.

▶ **NOTE**

For more information, visit developer.msntv.com.

Create a Seamless Photographic Background Tile

A seamless photographic background tile is typically a small photographic image that, when tiled by the browser, appears as one large photograph filling the entire window.

Photographs are not as easy as graphical backgrounds to tile. The reason is that by default photographs typically bleed to the edges on all four sides. So when a photograph such as the one shown in Figure 4-2 is tiled by the browser, those four edges don't match up and look a bit odd.

Suppose I wanted to use an image like this one to spruce up a page on my personal web site that talks about the birth of my second daughter. In order to use a photograph like this in the background of a web page, and still achieve a seamless look, I'd have to blend the edges out to match those opposite them when the image is tiled. Unfortunately, this can be quite a cumbersome task if done by hand, and doesn't always offer the desired results. Luckily, ImageReady has a prefab tool that's just right for the job.

▶ **QUICK TIP**

Using a photograph like this one in the background of a web page may make it difficult to read any text placed directly on top of it. To work around that problem, consider reducing the opacity of the photograph before using it as a tile by choosing Layer | Layer Options. Alternatively, you could place the text of your web page on a solid-colored background using HTML tables or Cascading Style Sheets.

TRY IT To use a photograph as a repeating background tile for a web page, launch Adobe ImageReady and choose File | Open to open the photograph in ImageReady. Then, choose Filter | Other | Tile Maker to launch the Tile Maker tool and bring up a dialog box similar to this one:

Tile Maker

● Blend Edges
    Width: [10] percent
    ☑ Resize Tile to Fill Image
○ Kaleidoscope Tile

[OK]
[Cancel]

Enter a value between 1 and 20 in the box next to Width, to specify how much of the photograph is blended. The default, 10, is usually a good place to start. Also, put a check in the box next to Resize Tile To Fill Image, if you want your tile to be the size of the current image, and click OK to complete the operation. (If you don't care what size your tile is, you can leave that box unchecked, but you'll have to crop the photo after the Tile Maker tool is finished.)

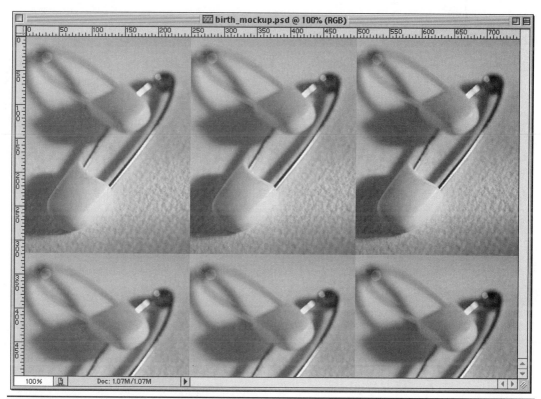

Figure 4-2   Because of their "full-bleed" nature, most photographs don't lend themselves easily to becoming background tiles.

▶ **NOTE**

For tips regarding Photoshop's Pattern Maker filter, see Chapter 9.

The result should look something like Figure 4-3, where the edges of the photo appear to have been blurred with the opposite parts of the image. You can then save the photo as a JPEG and use it in the background of your web page. For tips on saving JPEGs, see Chapter 10.

▶ **NOTE**

To preview how this photo will look when tiled by the browser, see the tip "Preview a Browser Tile in Photoshop," later in the chapter.

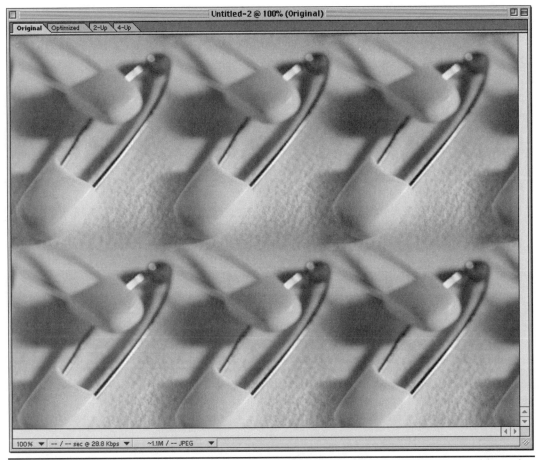

Figure 4-3   After running the Tile Maker tool on this photo, the edges are no longer visible and the image appears "seamless."

Create a Nonrepeating Photographic Background Tile

The earlier tip "Create a Seamless Photographic Background Tile" used a photograph that repeated many times across the background of a web page. Suppose you wanted to use a photograph in the background of your page, but you didn't want it to repeat. You could cut the image out and place it on a solid color large enough so the image wouldn't tile in most cases. The following steps tell how I did this with the photograph from the seamless photographic background tip.

▶ *NOTE*

Avon uses nonrepeating photographic imagery like this in the background of its web pages—a cut-out photograph is pasted on a white background that is so large it restricts the browser from tiling. Visit www.avon.com to see what I mean.

TRY IT To create a nonrepeating photographic background tile like the one shown at the end of this tip in Figure 4-6, begin by opening a photographic image in Photoshop using the File | Open command. In addition, make sure you also have your mockup file open in Photoshop. If you don't, either open it or create a new one with the appropriate page size. (For help with this, see the earlier tip "Begin Designing with the Appropriate Page Size.") Then follow the steps listed here:

▶ *CAUTION*

This works best if you use a photograph whose content is not cut off on the bottom and right edges of the image. If any aspect of the image is cut off on the bottom or right sides, you may have to make up the missing content.

1. Copy the entire photograph (choose Select | All and then Edit | Copy) and paste it into your mockup file (choose Edit | Paste).

2. Using the Move tool, move the photograph to the upper-left corner of the mockup file.

3. Click the Background layer in your Layers palette and fill the layer with whichever color you want to use for the solid part of the background. (Figure 4-4 shows my progress thus far.)

▶ *QUICK TIP*

To fill with a color from the background of your photograph, select the Paint Bucket tool from the toolbox—it is behind the Gradient tool. Then, hold down the ALT *key (Windows) or* OPTION *key (Mac) and click the color in the background of your photograph that you want to fill with, to place that color in your foreground swatch. Make sure the Background layer is selected in the Layers palette and click with the Paint Bucket tool anywhere in the blank space to fill with that color.*

4. Click the layer in the Layers palette with your photograph and select the Smudge tool from the toolbox—it's behind the Blur tool.

Figure 4-4   I used the Paint Bucket to fill my Background layer with a color selected from the background of my photograph.

5. Use the Smudge tool to smudge the bottom and right edges of the photograph, so when you eventually erase some of the photo, you aren't left with any hard edges. I like to pick a fairly large, round brush for smudging edges like this and I usually use the soft, round 65-pixel brush, as shown in Figure 4-5.

6. Click the second button from the left in the bottom of the Layers palette to add a layer mask to the layer containing your photograph. (Another way to add a layer mask is to choose Layer | Add Layer Mask | Reveal All from the top menu.) After adding the layer mask, your Layers palette should look like the following:

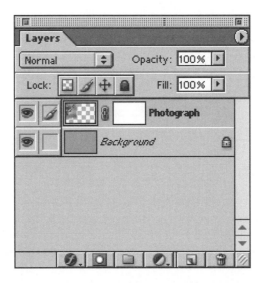

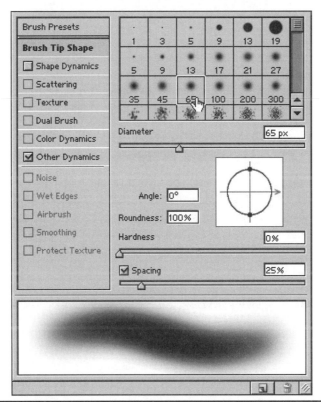

Figure 4-5   I typically select a large, round brush from the Brushes palette when smudging edges of a photograph.

7. Now that you have a layer mask, you can begin "erasing" some of the edges of the photograph, to give it a softer edge. To do this, first make sure your foreground color swatch is filled with black:

8. Select a large, soft, round brush and begin "painting" away the bottom and right edges of the photograph.

▶ **NOTE**

When you paint with black on a layer mask, you are telling Photoshop to hide the contents of that layer in that area. Conversely, painting with white has the opposite effect and tells Photoshop to reveal the contents of that layer in the area. The benefit of using a layer mask to "erase" in this way is that you can easily gain back any areas that you accidentally "erase."

▶ **CAUTION**

Make sure you're painting on the layer mask, by checking in your Layers palette to see which of the two preview images on that layer is selected. To paint on the layer mask, you must click inside the layer mask preview box to select that box. Once selected, the outline around the box is doubled.

9. Erase (and paint back as necessary) until you're satisfied with the appearance of your photo, particularly how it blends with the background color. Figure 4-6 shows how my image looks now.

At this point, you could save a copy of this file as a JPEG or a GIF and use it in your web page's background. However, the small width and height of the file will cause it to be repeated—tiled—by the browser. For example, my mockup file was 750 pixels wide by 500 pixels high. After the browser displays the image once, it'll repeat it after the user scrolls beyond those 750×500 pixels. To combat that situation, I need to do one of the following:

- Use Photoshop to enlarge the canvas of my file to one that is less likely to scroll
- Use Cascading Style Sheets when coding my web page to tell the browser never to scroll the background

Given that this is a book about Photoshop, I'll tell you how to do it the first way. So, to enlarge the canvas in Photoshop, choose Image | Canvas Size. Because many people view the Web on computers with monitors set to a screen resolution of 1,024×768, I typically enlarge my canvas size to 1,100 pixels wide. This helps make sure it doesn't repeat even when people have their resolutions set that high.

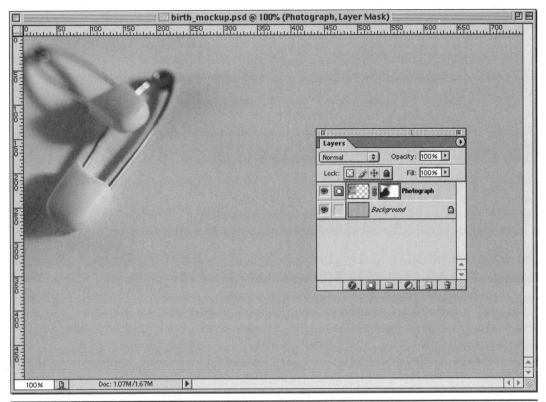

Figure 4-6   After "erasing" part of my photograph using the layer mask, I'm satisfied with how the photo blends into the background color.

▶ *NOTE*

To use Cascading Style Sheets to force the background image never to scroll, add style= *"*background-attachment: fixed;*" to your opening* body *tag. This only works in the most recent versions of Netscape and Internet Explorer.*

For height, I select a number based on how much content is on the page, because the file will repeat only as long as there is content in the foreground to make it repeat. For average page lengths, 800 pixels is usually sufficient, but you may need to increase that if your page is longer.

▶ *NOTE*

When you increase the canvas size, be sure to click in the upper-left corner of the boxes next to Anchor in the Canvas Size options window. This ensures the background you've already created stays in the upper-left corner of the canvas. You'll then need to fill the new part of the background with the existing background color.

After changing the canvas size and filling the new part of the background with the existing background color, you're ready to save the file for Web readability. Be cautious when doing so, as a file this large in height and width can quickly become way too large in file size to use on a web page. I was able to save my diaper pin background as a very low-quality JPEG (10 percent image quality) and get it down to just around 7Kb in file size—not too bad given that the rest of the page this background was intended for is all text. For more tips on saving GIFs and JPEGs, see Chapter 10.

Create a Seamless Graphical Background Tile

A seamless graphical background tile is typically a small graphical image that, when tiled by the browser, appears as one large texture filling the entire window. Graphical backgrounds are a bit easier to make seamless than the photographic images discussed in previous tips.

For example, suppose instead of the photographic image of the diaper pins used in the earlier tip "Create a Seamless Photographic Background Tile," I wanted to use a graphical representation of diaper pins. I could vary the size and angle of the diaper pins to create a wallpaper-like texture for the background of my page, such as the texture shown in Figure 4-7.

TRY IT　To begin, create a new file (choose File | New) measuring 200 pixels in width and height. Then, use the Paint Bucket tool to fill the background of the file with the color of your choosing. In this case, I chose a pale yellow from the web-safe color palette.

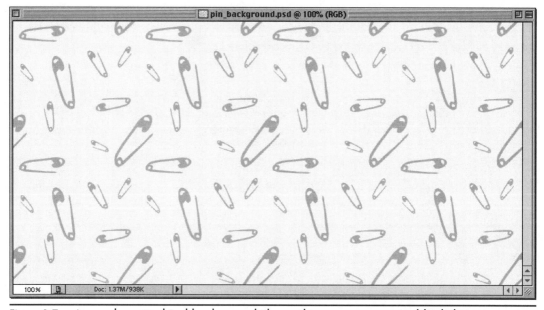

Figure 4-7　A seamless graphical background tile can be a great way to add a little texture to a web page without drawing attention away from the main content of the page.

▶ *NOTE*

You can change the file size if you wish, but for best results use a size that's square and not less than 50 pixels in height and width.

Then, add your graphics or icons in a slightly different color. To do so, first place the color you wish to use for your icons in the foreground color swatch by either clicking the swatch to display the Color Picker or selecting a color from your Swatches or Color palettes. I like to choose colors that are similar in value for the background and graphics, because if I were to use colors with a high amount of contrast, I would risk making any text placed on top unreadable.

After selecting a color, draw, paint, paste, or otherwise put your graphics on the page. For the diaper pin, I use a special type of font called a dingbat that is really a set of pictures instead of letters. For instance, when you type the letter *b* using the font called Baby's Blocks from fraternet.com, you get this diaper pin:

You can also draw your own graphics, or paint with one of the many new brushes in Photoshop.

▶ *NOTE*

For specific tips on using Photoshop's brushes or other dingbats like this one in your web graphics, see Chapter 8.

After I have one diaper pin on my tile, I duplicate that layer to add another one, using the following steps:

1. Click once on the layer with your single graphic in the Layers palette.

2. Click again and drag the layer down to the second-to-last icon at the bottom of the palette window, as shown in the following illustration. Doing so causes Photoshop to create a new

layer using the contents of the layer you dragged on top of the button. (This is a shortcut for choosing Layer | Duplicate Layer from the top menu.)

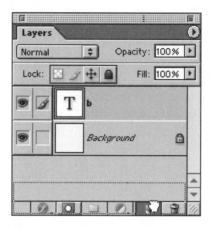

3. Click once on the new layer with a copy of your graphic on it in the Layers palette.

4. Use the Move tool to move the contents of that layer to a new location slightly away from the other graphic.

5. Choose Edit | Free Transform—or press CTRL-T (Windows) or CMD-T (Mac)—and drag on the corners of the bounding box to rotate, scale, or skew the image as shown in the following illustration. Press the RETURN or ENTER key on your keyboard to accept your transformation, or press CTRL-. (Windows) or CMD-. (Mac) to cancel the transformation.

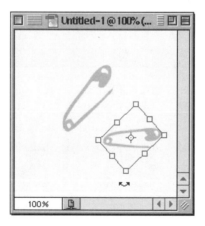

▶ *CAUTION*

When adding your graphics to the tile, it's important to start from the center and never touch any of the edges. The reason is once you touch an edge, that part of the graphic will look cut off when it is placed against another edge during the browser's tiling process.

Continue copying layers and transforming the graphics until you are satisfied with the current view of the tile. However, don't touch the edges with any of your graphics. Instead of placing graphics on the edges, use the Offset filter in Photoshop to move the file around a bit and re-create it in a different format showing how the edges match up when tiled. If you have several different layers and perhaps used type like I did, then there are several steps to take before using the Offset filter (which only works on a single, rasterized layer):

1. Link all the layers with graphics on them together by clicking once in the second box next to the layer name. After clicking, a small chain icon appears to indicate the layer is linked to whichever layer is currently selected (in other words, whichever layer has the paintbrush icon next to it).

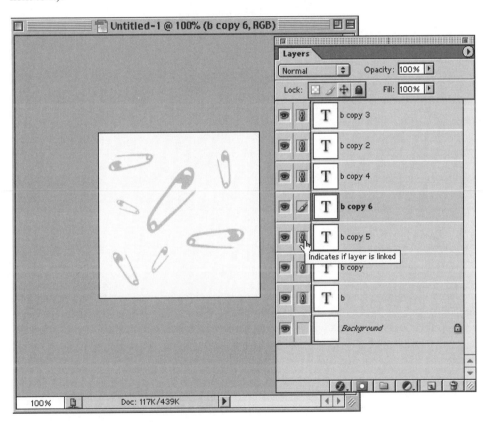

2. Choose Layer | Merged Linked or press CTRL-E (Windows) or CMD-E (Mac) to merge those linked layers together. This process also rasterizes the layers, meaning if they contained type, that type will no longer be editable.

3. Choose Filter | Other | Offset to start the Offset filter.

The dialog box that appears allows you to move the current layer's contents a certain number of pixels down and to the right. If you created a 200×200-pixel file like I did, use 100 and 100 in those boxes to move the file halfway across and halfway down, as shown here:

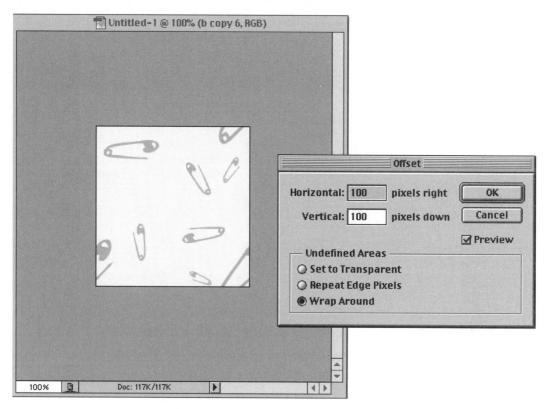

Then, click the button labeled Wrap Around from the options for Undefined Areas at the bottom of the dialog box. This tells Photoshop to add copies of that layer's contents to the spaces left over after the design was offset. In effect, this shows you the edges created when the design is tiled by the browser.

Now that you can see your "edges," continue adding more graphics in the blank spaces. As with before, don't touch any of the edges. Instead, repeat the preceding steps to link and merge your layers before re-offsetting the design.

Once you are satisfied with your design, save it in a web-friendly format such as GIF or JPEG and add it to your HTML body tag to use it as a web page background. For tips on how to save JPEGs and GIFs, see Chapter 10.

▶ NOTE

If you want to preview how this tile will look when tiled in a web page, see the upcoming tip "Preview a Browser Tile in Photoshop."

Create Your Own (Hybrid) Web-Safe Colors

From time to time, I come across a client whose main logo color is not part of the web-safe palette. Although I don't force *all* colors in my web designs to be web-safe, a logo is usually the one thing a client wants to make sure looks as uniform as possible across all users' systems. So what do you do when a client's logo color isn't web-safe?

By mixing two or more existing web-safe colors in a checkerboard fashion, you can actually create what's commonly referred to as a *hybrid* web-safe color. As long as you use colors that are similar in value, the checkerboard pattern will be virtually unnoticeable when viewed in a web page, because our eyes mix the colors and make them appear as one. See Figure 4-8 for an example.

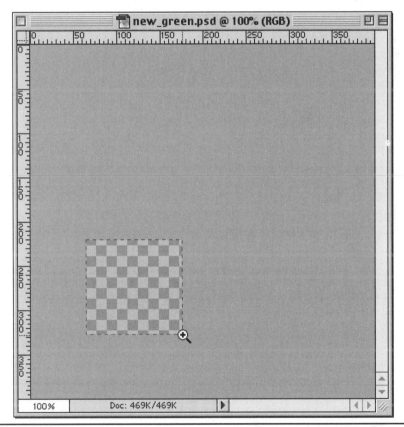

Figure 4-8   When viewed at 100%, the fact that this is really two colors is virtually unnoticeable; when a portion of the image is enlarged the pattern is revealed.

To create your own hybrid web-safe color in Photoshop, choose File | New and create a new file that is only 2×2 pixels in size. Then follow these steps:

1. Use the Zoom tool to zoom in to 1600% (the most you can zoom) or type 1600% in the lower-left corner of the image window as shown here:

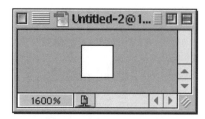

2. Place the two colors you wish to blend together in the foreground and background color swatches. You can do so by either clicking on the swatch to display the Color Picker or selecting colors from your Swatches or Color palettes.

3. Use the Pencil tool (which is hidden behind the Paintbrush tool in the toolbox) and the smallest brush—1 pixel in diameter—to color in the upper-left and lower-right pixels of your 4-pixel file with the foreground color.

4. Press X on your keyboard to switch the foreground and background color swatches.

5. Again use the Pencil tool and the smallest brush to paint the upper-right and lower-left pixels of your file, this time with the other color.

At this point, you have a very tiny file with a small checkerboard of color. You can use the steps outlined in the following tip to preview how this new color will look when used.

Preview a Browser Tile in Photoshop

When you create your own background tiles in Photoshop, it's nice to be able to preview how they'll display when tiled by the browser in a web page. Luckily, you can do so by saving it as a pattern in Photoshop.

 To preview a browser tile in Photoshop, follow these steps:

1. Launch Photoshop and use the File | Open command to open your background tile if it isn't already open.

2. Choose Edit | Define Pattern and give your pattern a name before clicking OK.

3. Switch over to your web page mockup file, or choose File | New to create one. (If you create a new file, remember to use the available screen size of your target audience, or if you're using the file purely for testing purposes, try making a file 750×500 pixels in size.)

4. In the mockup file, choose Edit I Fill. Select Pattern from the pop-up menu next to Use and choose the pattern you just defined by clicking in the box next to Custom Pattern, as shown here:

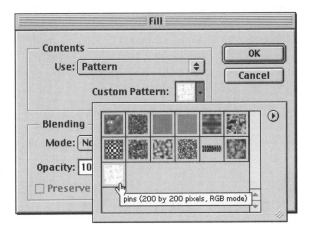

▶ **QUICK TIP**

To rename, save, or delete existing patterns, choose Edit I Preset Manager and select Patterns from the pop-up window.

Use Annotations to Ease Maintenance

It is common for web designers and developers to work in teams, and often the members of the team are in different buildings or perhaps even different parts of the country or world. It is also common for a variety of people to be involved in the various aspects of the process, from the design and development to the production and maintenance. In such cases, it is essential for all persons involved to accurately and efficiently record their work in a way that eases future maintenance.

The process of documenting work begins at the very start of a project, and web designers aren't exempt. In fact, Photoshop's Annotations make it very easy for designers to document mockups right within the Photoshop files. Annotations can be added, for example, to specify when a color change might be appropriate, or why a particular design element needs to be docked along the left side of the page.

▶ **QUICK TIP**

You can use the Audio Annotation tool (hidden behind the Notes tool in the toolbox) to turn your Photoshop files into minitutorials by adding spoken instructions to the viewer.

TRY IT To add an annotation to a file, click the Notes tool from the toolbox. Then, click anywhere within your design file to add a note in that location. When you're finished typing, click the small square in the upper-right corner of the note to close it.

All notes automatically carry the name of the owner of the version of Photoshop currently being used. You can change the name that appears at the top of each note in the options bar at the top of the screen. You can also change the font name, size, and note color in that options bar.

To temporarily hide all annotations, choose View | Show and uncheck Annotations. To delete an annotation, right-click (Windows) or OPTION-click (Mac) the note and select Delete Note from the pop-up menu. To permanently delete *all* annotations, right-click (Windows) or OPTION-click (Mac) one of the notes, and select Delete All Annotations from the pop-up menu. Or, make sure the Notes tool is selected from the toolbox and choose Clear All from the top menu bar.

▶ *CAUTION*

Annotations are only supported by file formats that can handle extras like layers and channels.

Save a Copy as a High-Quality JPEG for Client Approval

When you finish a comp or mockup for a client and need to gain the necessary sign-off to begin developing the site, it's common to prepare a fairly good-quality, flattened version of the file to show the client. In other words, you don't want to show the client a Photoshop file, so you need to show something that can be easily viewed from almost anywhere.

A good option is usually a mid- to high-quality JPEG file, because it can be viewed in a variety of system tools, as well as in a web browser—both of which are usually available on your client's computer.

▶ *NOTE*

If you use the Notes tool to add annotations to your file, they will be stripped off when you save as a JPEG.

To save a copy of your mockup as a JPEG, make sure your mockup is open in Photoshop, and choose File | Save As to open the Save As dialog box.

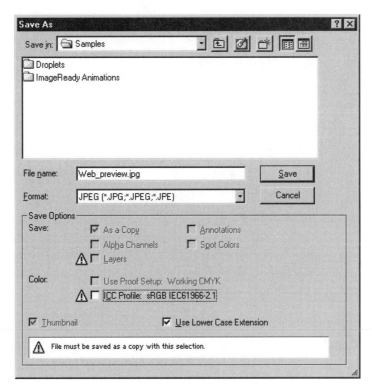

Under Format, select JPEG. Because the JPEG file format compresses a file, Photoshop knows to automatically dim the options for saving Layers, Channels, and so on. It also tells you in the message space at the bottom: File must be saved as a copy with this selection.

Give your file a name—be sure to leave out any spaces and use .jpg as the extension—before clicking the Save button to continue. After doing so, you'll see a few more options related to saving JPEG files.

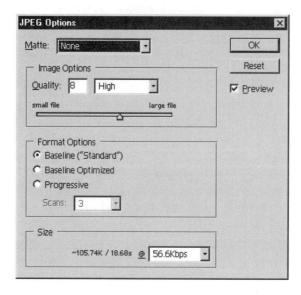

▶ *NOTE*

Unless you want to attach a color profile to the file—which probably can't be read by your client unless they have Photoshop—uncheck the box labeled ICC Profile under Color in the Save As dialog box.

When saving a copy as a high-quality JPEG for client review, you aren't concerned so much with file size as you might be when saving final JPEGs for a web site. So, you can feel safe creating a fairly large file by using a Quality setting of 8 (High) or above (Maximum). You can leave the rest of the options at their defaults—Matte: None, Format Options: Baseline ("Standard")—and click OK.

At this point, you can e-mail the file to your client, or post it to a web site for review. When doing so, it's a good idea to add a note that this file is displayed for "comping" purposes only and is not indicative of the final file size or exact colors.

Use Actions to Automate Common Processes

Web designers commonly perform the same series of tasks over and over again on different files. For example, suppose you were working on a web site for a large accounting firm, and you needed to reformat photos of the company's 50 employees as web-ready JPEGs. Doing this by hand would take significantly longer than doing it once while Photoshop "watches" you and records your actions. Then, you can tell Photoshop to replay those actions on the other 49 files while you take a coffee break. Sound appealing? I thought so.

NOTE

Photoshop ships with many prefab actions that are quite useful. Choose Window | Actions and expand the Default Actions folder to see what I mean. You can also click the small triangle in the upper-right corner of the Actions palette and choose to load additional sets of default actions from the flyout menu.

TRY IT To create an action in Photoshop, you must first have a series of steps in mind that you'd like to record. Then, do the following:

1. From the Window menu, choose Actions to bring the Actions palette up front.

2. When you're ready to have Photoshop start recording your steps, either click the Create New Action button at the bottom of the Actions palette (as shown in the following illustration) or choose New Action from the flyout menu made accessible by clicking the triangle in the upper-right corner of the Actions palette.

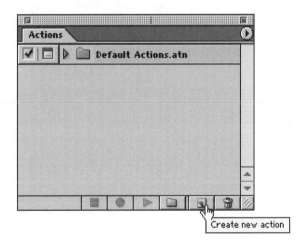

3. Creating a new action prompts you to give it a name and specify which set of actions, or folder, it should be housed in. You can also assign a function key to the action, making it accessible from your keyboard. Finally, give it a color to help it stand out in your Actions palette.

4. After making any changing in the New Action options window, click OK to begin the recording process. From this point on, *almost all*—see the sidebar entitled "Guidelines for Recording Actions"— tasks you perform in Photoshop will now be recording into the action you just created. (You can watch to see the actions being recorded in the Actions palette.)

5. After you're finished recording the action, click the Stop button (the first button) at the bottom of the Actions palette, or choose Stop Recording from the flyout menu accessible from the top triangle in the Actions palette.

▶ **QUICK TIP**

To quickly test your action, open the History palette (choose Window | History) and go back in the history to the point before you started recording your action. Then, click the action you just saved in the Actions palette and choose Play from the buttons at the bottom of the palette.

6. To start recording again at a certain point in your action after you've clicked the Stop button, simply move to that point in the Actions palette and choose Start Recording from the flyout menu accessible from the top triangle in the Actions palette.

7. If you need to add a point in your action where you can perform additional steps not recorded into the action, you need to add what's called a "Stop" in Photoshop. You can do so by moving to that point in the Actions palette and choosing Insert Stop from the flyout menu accessible from the top triangle.

To play your action back on a series of files (as opposed to a single file), choose File | Automate | Batch. From the Play section, choose the action you want to play back on the series of files. Then, specify where that series of files is located in the Source section.

Under Destination, specify what the program should do with the files after it's finished running the action. If you included a Save step within your action, choose None. If you didn't include a Save

Guidelines for Recording Actions

When recording actions in Photoshop, keep the following guidelines in mind:

- You can record tasks performed in the History, Swatches, Color, Paths, Channels, Layers, Styles, and Actions palettes.

- You can record tasks performed with the Marquee, Move, Polygon, Lasso, Magic Wand, Crop, Slice, Magic Eraser, Gradient, Paint Bucket, Type, Shape, Notes, Eyedropper, and Color Sampler tools.

- You can nest actions, meaning you can play one action while recording another.

- Action results will be different when played back on files with different settings, such as color modes or resolutions.

- Photoshop only records changes made in options, palettes, and dialog boxes. So if you want the program to record a default setting (or just one that's already been made), you actually have to change the setting and then change it back to what you want it to be in order for Photoshop to record the setting.

- Tools that record the current position do so using the current units specified for the ruler (pixels, inches, and so on). Note, Adobe recommends setting the ruler units to percent before recording an action that will be played back on files of different sizes.

step and wish to have Photoshop save and close the files to a different location, choose Folder and then specify where the program should save them (including filename information). Choosing Save And Close tells Photoshop to save the files—overwriting the originals—and close them.

Finally, specify how the program should handle any errors it encounters when batch-processing the files. Click OK and take that much-needed coffee break while Photoshop does all the work.

QUICK TIP

If you perform a key command and Photoshop doesn't record it, try accessing the command from the menu (instead of using a key command).

PART II

Using Photoshop to Design Web and Print Graphics

CHAPTER 5

Using Selections and Masks

TIPS IN THIS CHAPTER

Selections are an integral part of using Photoshop. Unless you want to perform an action on an entire image or an entire layer, you typically must first select the area of the canvas on which you want to perform an action.

Each selection tool in Photoshop is classified as making one of the following:

- Bitmap selections
- Vector paths

▶ **QUICK TIP**

You can easily recognize selections in Photoshop because they are surrounded by the famous "dancing ants"—a dotted line that appears to move or dance around a section of the canvas. By contrast, paths are solid lines that don't move.

Making Bitmap Selections

Tools that make bitmap selections are resolution-dependent—just like bitmap graphics—because the selections themselves are tied to actual pixels in the image. (Adobe also calls these *pixel selections*.) The following tools in the toolbox make bitmap selections:

- Marquee
- Magic Wand
- Lasso

In addition, the following commands allow you to make bitmap selections:

- Select | All
- Select | Color Range

▶ *NOTE*

*In ImageReady, you can also create a bitmap selection from an existing slice by choosing Select |
Create Selection From Slices.*

Marquee

The Marquee tool is the most commonly used selection tool. It is located in the first spot in the
toolbox, as shown in the following illustration, and (in Photoshop) has four variations. (ImageReady
also allows you to select rounded rectangles, with the Rounded Rectangle Marquee.)

- Rectangular Marquee
- Elliptical Marquee
- Single Row Marquee
- Single Column Marquee

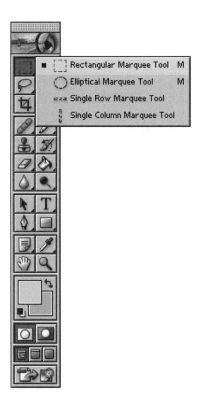

▶ *NOTE*

To access different variations of tools in the toolbox, click and hold on the tool icon.

Each of these tools has an additional set of options available in the Options bar. For example, clicking the Rectangular Marquee Tool reveals the following options in the Options bar:

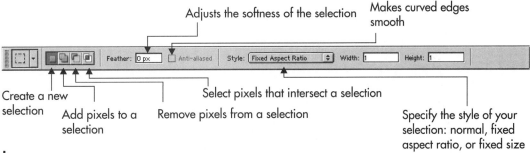

Lasso

The Lasso tool (located just below the Marquee in the toolbox) lets you freehand draw the edges of your selections, in three different variations, as shown in the following illustration:

- Lasso (normal)
- Polygonal Lasso
- Magnetic Lasso

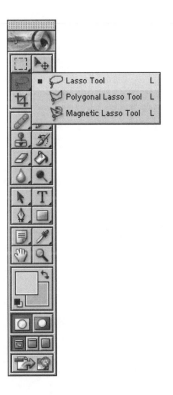

The Lasso tools are capable of drawing both straight-edged and curved selections. In addition, you can specify in the Options bar (as shown in the following illustration) whether your lasso selection should have soft edges and smooth curves using the Feather and Anti-aliased options, respectively.

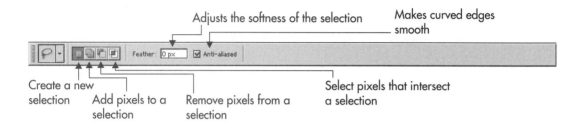

QUICK TIP

If you're using the normal Lasso or Polygonal Lasso tool, you can toggle between drawing straight or curved edges while making a selection by using the ALT *key (Windows) or* OPTION *key (Mac).*

The Magnetic Lasso tool is also capable of drawing straight-edged and curved selections, but it does so by following around the edges of areas within an image. Because of this, it has an additional set of options available in the Options bar:

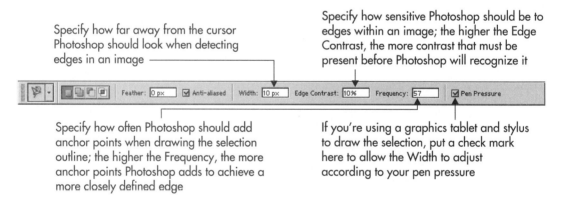

Magic Wand

The Magic Wand tool (located to the right of the Lasso in the toolbox) makes selections based on a color range. This can be particularly useful if the area you need to select is mostly the same color, because you can select it without having to trace its outline.

▶ *CAUTION*

Photoshop will not allow you to use the Magic Wand tool on an image that is in Bitmap mode.

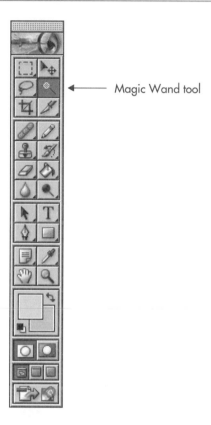

Magic Wand tool

Unlike the other tools discussed so far, the Magic Wand tool doesn't have any variations (see the previous illustration). It does, however, have several options in the Options bar that affect how it makes selections. The most notable of these is the Tolerance option.

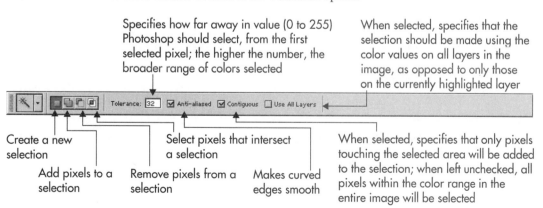

Specifies how far away in value (0 to 255) Photoshop should select, from the first selected pixel; the higher the number, the broader range of colors selected

When selected, specifies that the selection should be made using the color values on all layers in the image, as opposed to only those on the currently highlighted layer

Create a new selection

Add pixels to a selection

Select pixels that intersect a selection

Remove pixels from a selection

Makes curved edges smooth

When selected, specifies that only pixels touching the selected area will be added to the selection; when left unchecked, all pixels within the color range in the entire image will be selected

Making Vector Paths

By contrast to bitmap selections, vector paths are resolution-independent. Instead of being tied to certain pixels, vectors are based on mathematical calculations that can be changed without affecting the pixels of an image. Vector paths are made with the Pen and Shape tools in Photoshop. Figure 5-1 shows a comparison of a bitmap selection and a vector path.

When you draw a path with the Pen or Shape tools, Photoshop stores the information in the Paths palette (choose Window | Paths). In addition, paths drawn with the Shape tool can be seen in the Layers palette (choose Window | Layers).

The Pen and Shape tools in Photoshop are similar to the drawing tools in vector-based programs like Adobe Illustrator. When you draw lines with these tools, the program creates anchor points that can then be edited to alter the shape of the lines.

> ### QUICK TIP
>
> *At any time, you can turn a vector path into a bitmap selection by clicking in the upper-right corner of the Paths palette and choosing Make Selection from the flyout menu.*

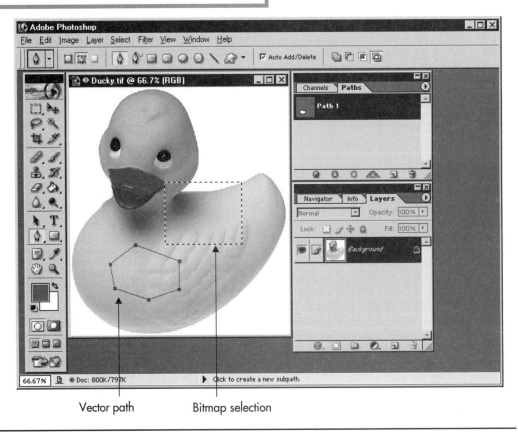

Vector path   Bitmap selection

Figure 5-1   While bitmap selections are indicated by the dancing ants on the screen, vector paths are solid lines with anchor points.

Clicking the Pen tool in the toolbox (as shown in the following illustration) reveals five variations of the tool:

- **Pen Tool (normal)**   Used to draw a selection one point at a time
- **Freeform Pen Tool**   Used to draw a selection freehand, as you draw normally
- **Add Anchor Point Tool**   Used to add anchor points to existing paths
- **Delete Anchor Point Tool**   Used to remove anchor points from existing paths
- **Convert Point Tool**   Used to convert between smooth (curved) points and corner points

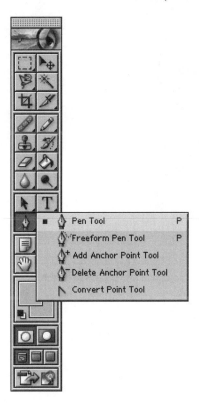

Clicking the Shape tool in the toolbox (as shown in the following illustration) reveals six variations on the tool:

- Rectangle Tool
- Rounded Rectangle Tool
- Ellipse Tool
- Polygon Tool
- Line Tool
- Custom Shape Tool

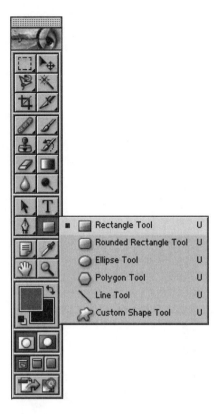

The Pen and Shape tools have several options that are displayed in the Options bar, but the options themselves vary according to which tool is selected. However, whether you've selected a Pen tool or a Shape tool, you can further clarify the type of vector selection you're creating by choosing between the following buttons in that Options bar. See Table 5-1 for a comparison of these three types of selections—Shapes, Paths, and Fills.

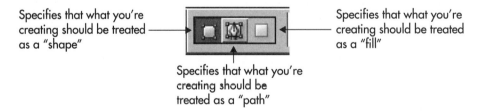

Specifies that what you're creating should be treated as a "shape"

Specifies that what you're creating should be treated as a "fill"

Specifies that what you're creating should be treated as a "path"

You can combine the Shape and Path tools to build complex paths. When doing so, you may need to select certain points within those paths. To do so, you use the Path Selection tool (found directly above the Pen tool in the toolbox). As shown in the following illustration, the Path Selection tool has two variations:

- **Path Selection Tool**   Used to select entire paths or path components

- **Direct Selection Tool**   Used to select path segments or points only

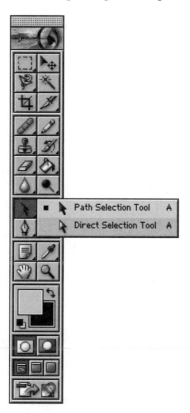

	Shape	Path	Fill
Automatically creates a new layer in the Layers palette	X		
Automatically creates a new working path in the Paths palette	X	X	
Fills the area within the selection with the color in the foreground swatch of the toolbox	X		X
Remains editable after deselected	X	X	
Alters the pixels within the selected area			X
Accessible from all Pen and Shape tools	X	X	X
Requires an editable layer to be highlighted in the Layers palette before use			X
Can be affected by an option from the Style menu	X		
Can be affected by an option from the Mode menu			X
Is deleted when Layer is deleted from Layers palette	X		X

Table 5-1   Comparison of the Three Options for Vector Selections: Shapes, Paths, and Fills

The Shape tools are discussed in more detail in Chapter 8.

All about Masks

While the basic selection tools included in Photoshop are perfectly suitable for most applications, Photoshop enables you to create intricate selections with a process called *masking*.

When you work with masks in Photoshop, you see neither those silly dancing ants nor the solid lines of paths. Instead, you can use brushes to *paint* your selections. In fact, when using masks, the term *selection* takes on a whole new meaning. Rather than being used as a synonym for "highlighted area," selection refers more to protected and unprotected areas of an image when masks are involved.

Masked areas of an image are protected from editing. For example, suppose I wanted to change the color of my daughter's bright-red sweatshirt in the following picture, because it is too dominant for the image. Selecting that sweatshirt with any of the normal selection tools—Magic Wand, Marquee, Lasso, and even the Pen tool—would be cumbersome and difficult.

▶ **NOTE**

To see how I ended up selecting only the color of this sweatshirt to edit, see the tip entitled "Use Quick Mask Mode for Quick Paint-by-Number Selections."

Painting a mask enables me to use a tool I'm really comfortable with—the paintbrush—in a way that is very forgiving. So when masking the sweatshirt in the previous illustration, if I start to get parts of the couch or my daughter's hair in the selection, I can easily fix that without having to fumble with those dancing ants again.

What Are Channels?

Channels contain color information about an image. For example, in RGB images, there are four channels—one that specifies where red is displayed in the image, one that specifies where green is displayed, one that specifies where blue is displayed, and one that shows a composite, or combined, color profile for the image.

When you save a selection or mask in Photoshop, it's placed in what's called an alpha channel, which can be accessed through the Channels palette. Unlike layer masks, which apply only to a certain layer or layers, masks saved in alpha channels typically apply to all layers in an image.

You create and edit masks in Photoshop with a variety of tools, but masks are typically grouped into three categories:

- **Quick masks** Temporary masks not saved anywhere in Photoshop
- **Channel masks** Permanent masks, saved in the Channels palette, that apply to the entire image
- **Layer masks** Permanent masks, saved in the Layers palette, that apply only to a certain layer or layers

▶ *NOTE*

The tips that follow in this chapter refer specifically to working with selections in Photoshop. In some instances, this involves the use of channels, layers, and masks. Additional tips related to these three items are also found in later chapters, particularly Chapter 6.

Use Quick Mask Mode for Quick Paint-by-Number Selections

Have you ever wished you could use the Paintbrush tool to make a quick selection? You can do so after first switching into Quick Mask mode in Photoshop.

▶ *NOTE*

Quick masks are different from real masks because they don't get saved. Like selections made with the Marquee tool, they are normally "forgotten" as soon as you deselect.

 To use Quick Mask mode for a quick paint-by-number type selection, first make sure the image you want to select part of is open in Photoshop. Then, double-click the Quick

Mask button in the toolbox, as shown here, or press Q on your keyboard to reveal the Quick Mask Options dialog box:

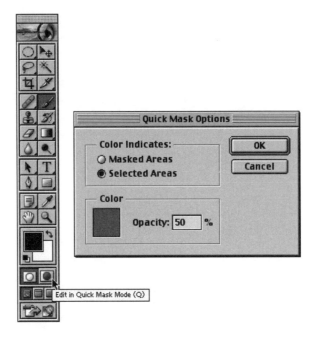

Within the Quick Mask Options dialog box, check Selected Areas. You can leave the quick mask color as red with a 50% Opacity setting, unless the bulk of your image is red—if it is, you'll probably want to change the quick mask color to something other than red.

Now that you're in Quick Mask mode, you can click the Paintbrush tool and select a brush from the Brushes palette to begin making your selection. Because of the options you just selected, the color you're painting with indicates which parts of the image you're adding to your selection.

As you're painting, you'll notice that the color in your foreground swatch is black. In this case, Photoshop uses black to indicate that you're adding to the selection, while white is used to subtract from a selection. When you're masking in Photoshop, black and white will be the only colors available.

▶ **QUICK TIP**

Made a mistake when painting your quick mask? No problem. Press X on your keyboard to switch the foreground and background colors, and then "erase" your mistake by painting with white.

Once you're finished "masking" your selection, click the button next to Quick Mask in the toolbox or press Q again on your keyboard to return to Standard mode.

Upon returning to Standard mode, your selection is now enclosed by the dancing ants, and can be edited, transformed, or manipulated as needed.

▶ **NOTE**

For tips on how to easily change the colors of things (like sweatshirts), check out Chapter 9.

Feather Selections for Soft Edges

By default, all of the selection tools in Photoshop have crisp edges. While this is suitable for most situations, it's sometimes useful to make selections that have soft, feathered edges, such as is shown in Figure 5-2.

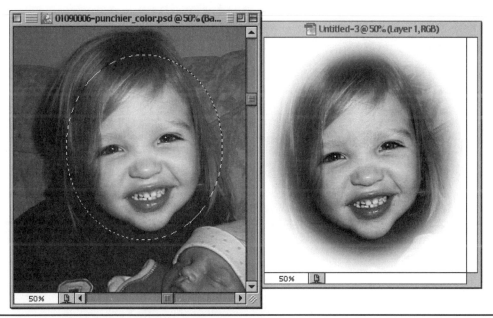

Figure 5-2   Feathering the edges of a selection enables you to create soft-edged images.

TRY IT To feather the edges of your selections, first make sure you have an image open in Photoshop. Then, click once on one of the Lasso or Marquee tools in the toolbox. The Options bar for those tools includes an option to Feather that is normally set to 0 px.

To create the soft edges like those shown in Figure 5-2, you need to increase this number. The number at which you ultimately set your Feather will determine two things:

- How wide you want your feathered edge to be
- How high the file's resolution is set

The wider you want your feathered edge to be, the higher you should set the Feather. Likewise, the higher the file resolution, the higher you need to set the Feather in order to see an effect, because the feather is measured in pixels.

Use the Inverse Command to Select the Opposite

Sometimes, the easiest way to make a selection might actually be to first select the opposite of what you want to select. For example, consider the Ducky.tif file found in the Samples folder of the Adobe Photoshop 7 folder. This file contains a single image of a yellow rubber duck on a white background. Because the background is a solid color—something easily selectable in Photoshop—you can use that background and the Inverse command to quickly select the duck.

TRY IT To use the Inverse command, first open the Ducky.tif file in Photoshop and use the Magic Wand tool to select only the white background within the image. Then, choose Select | Inverse to have Photoshop change your selection to be the opposite of the white background, which in this case is the rubber duck (see Figure 5-3).

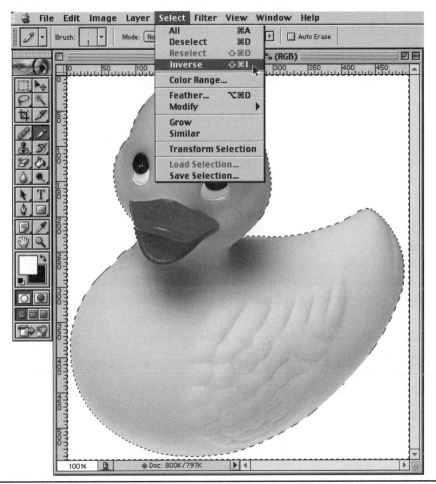

Figure 5-3   After selecting the white background in the Ducky.tif file, I choose Select | Inverse to have Photoshop select the exact opposite of the white background.

Some things to keep in mind when using this process are the following:

- You can use any selection tools to make the initial selection, and are not restricted to using the Magic Wand tool.

- When you do use the Magic Wand tool to make the initial selection, you may need to click the check box next to Contiguous in the options bar, if all the solid areas of color you want to select aren't touching.

- The Inverse command selects the exact opposite of what is currently selected, so make sure all the pixels you don't want to include in your final selection are selected before choosing Select | Inverse.

Use Keyboard Commands to Quickly Add to and Delete from Existing Selections

It is a common exercise in Photoshop to make a selection and then need to add to or delete from that selection instead of starting from scratch. While you can always use the Add and Delete buttons in the Options bar for selection tools, it's must quicker and easier to use the keyboard commands to do so.

TRY IT   To use a keyboard command to add to or delete from a selection, first click any of the bitmap selection tools—Marquee, Lasso, or Magic Wand—and make a selection in an open file in Photoshop. Then, follow these instructions:

1. To add to the existing selection, hold down the SHIFT key and use the selection tool again on your image. You'll notice that when holding down the SHIFT key in this instance, the cursor has a plus sign next to it.

2. To delete from the existing selection, hold down the ALT key (Windows) or OPTION key (Mac) and use the selection tool again on your image, somewhere inside the existing selection. You'll notice that when holding down the ALT key in this instance, the cursor has a minus sign next to it.

Use Multiple Tools Together for Quick Complex Selections

Sometimes, using a single selection tool is not sufficient for selecting everything you wish to within an image. At other times, a combination of selection tools can help in refining a selection. For example, suppose you want to quickly select the eagle's head in Figure 5-4 without the green background. One easy way to do this is to use a combination of the Marquee and Magic Wand tools.

▶ *NOTE*

The Marquee and Magic Wand tools can also be used in conjunction with the Lasso tools.

TRY IT   To select only the eagle's head without the background using multiple selection tools, first open Eagle.psd from the Samples folder within the Adobe Photoshop 7 folder on your computer. Then, use the Marquee tool to draw a rectangle around the eagle's head, as shown in Figure 5-4.

Then, click the Magic Wand tool from the toolbox and position it over the green background within your existing selection. Hold down the ALT key (Windows) or OPTION key (Mac) and click the green background to remove that background from the existing selection, as shown in Figure 5-5.

Figure 5-4   First, use the Marquee tool to draw a rectangular selection around the eagle's head.

Figure 5-5   Next, use the Magic Wand tool to remove the green background from the selection.

▶ *NOTE*

If you have trouble removing all of the green background at once, undo your operation (Edit | Undo) and make sure your Tolerance is set to 32 in the Options bar at the top of the screen for the Magic Wand tool. To make the edges of your selection smooth, place a check mark in the box next to Anti-aliased.

Use the Magic Eraser to Remove Areas of Color with a Single Click

Oftentimes, a designer needs to quickly remove an area of color from an image. Previously, this may have involved countless hours of erasing with the normal eraser, or drawing selections. An easier way to quickly remove an area of color is to use the Magic Eraser tool.

TRY IT   To quickly remove an area of color from an image, such as the green background from the Eagle.psd file in the Photoshop 7 Samples folder, click and hold on the Eraser tool in the toolbox to reveal two additional eraser tools. The tool at the bottom of the menu is the Magic Eraser, which is also accessible on your keyboard by pressing SHIFT-E. (You may have to press SHIFT-E several times until you cycle through the other eraser tools and reach the Magic Eraser.)

To use the Magic Eraser, click once anywhere within the green background or on whichever color range you wish to remove. Photoshop automatically removes the color from those pixels, leaving them transparent (as shown in Figure 5-6 by the gray blocks behind the eagle).

▶ *QUICK TIP*

Want to get rid of that green "fringe" around the edge of the eagle that's left over from the background? See the next tip, "Remove Fringe Areas to Clean up Selections."

You can edit the range of colors removed by increasing or decreasing the Tolerance in the Options bar; the higher the number, the wider the range of colors removed. For smooth edges, place a check mark in the box next to Anti-aliased. To restrict Photoshop to removing only pixels in the color range that are touching the one you click, place a check mark in the box labeled Contiguous. To reduce the opacity of the color range instead of removing it altogether, change the Opacity setting in the Options bar.

Remove Fringe Areas to Clean Up Selections

It is common that when you move or copy an irregularly shaped selection—particularly one with anti-aliased or soft edges—a few pixels tag along from outside the selection area. For example, when I used the Magic Eraser tool to quickly remove the green background from the Eagle.psd file found in the Photoshop 7 Samples folder in the previous tip, a few green pixels were stuck around the eagle's

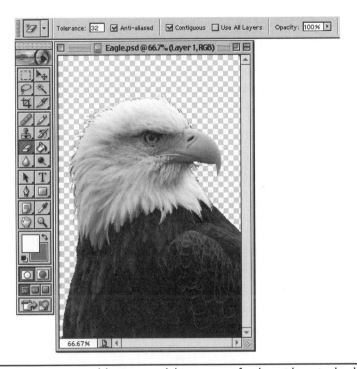

Figure 5-6 The Magic Eraser enables you to delete areas of color with a single click.

white head (refer to Figure 5-6). The Defringe command in Photoshop makes it easy to clean up selections like this one.

TRY IT To clean up selections that have leftover pixels of unwanted color—often called a halo—around the outside edge of a selection, first make sure the selection is on its own layer in Photoshop. For example, if you used the Magic Eraser to remove the green background from the Eagle.psd file in the previous tip, you are left with the eagle itself on Layer 1.

Then, choose Layer | Matting | Defringe and specify the amount of solid color pixels to remove from the edge of the layer. If you're unsure, it's best to try 1 pixel first, because you can always perform the action again to remove additional pixels of color.

Use the Single Row and Single Column Marquee Tools to Create Quick Borders

Two versions of the Marquee tool—the Single Row Marquee and Single Column Marquee—are rarely used by most designers. However, these two tools can be particularly useful to web designers who need to create quick single-pixel borders.

> *TRY IT* To create a quick single-pixel vertical border, first create a new layer in your destination file in Photoshop by clicking Layer | New | Layer or pressing SHIFT-CTRL-N (Windows) or SHIFT-CMD-N (Mac).

Then, click and drag the Marquee tool to reveal the Single Column Marquee tool. Click once within your image area, wherever you want the border to appear. Next, make sure the desired color of this border is in the foreground color swatch of the toolbox, and press ALT-BACKSPACE (Windows) or OPTION-DELETE (Mac) to fill the border with the foreground color.

To create a single-pixel horizontal border, repeat the preceding steps using the Single Row Marquee tool.

▶ | **QUICK TIP**

By default, the borders created with these tools span the entire width or height of the canvas. To restrict the width or height of your border, first make a selection with the normal Marquee tool to specify the boundaries of the border. Then, switch to the Single Row or Column Marquee tool and press ALT-SHIFT *(Windows) or* OPTION-SHIFT *(Mac) while clicking once at the desired location of your border.*

Stroke Selections to Create Quick Borders

When you need to outline an area of an image with a colored border, Photoshop's Stroke command is a good candidate for the job. This tool creates a hard-edged border around an existing selection, at whatever width you specify, using the color in the foreground swatch of the toolbox.

▶ **NOTE**

While this tip discusses using the Stroke command to stroke selections, you can also use the Stroke layer style to stroke the contents of an entire layer. This is discussed in more detail in Chapter 6.

▶ | **QUICK TIP**

I like to first create a new layer (choose Layer | New | Layer) on which to place my border so I can easily delete or edit it later if needed.

> *TRY IT* To stroke a selection and create a quick border, first make sure the color you want the border to be is visible in the foreground swatch of the toolbox. Then, make a selection in an open document in Photoshop with one of the selection tools.

After making a selection, choose Edit | Stroke to reveal an options window similar to this one:

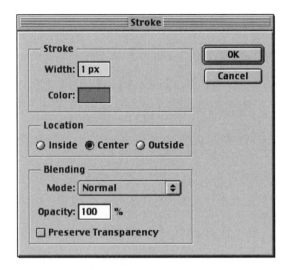

For Width, specify how wide you'd like your border to be, from 1 to 16 pixels. You can also change the color of the border by clicking within the colored box next to Color and specifying a new color.

For Location, specify where you'd like to place the border in reference to the existing selection—Inside, Center, or Outside. For Blending, specify how the color of the border should affect the color(s) beneath, as necessary.

Save Selections for Future Use

After you've made and lost several selections, you may find it necessary to save selections to avoid having to re-create them. Saved selections are stored in the Channels palette and can be easily reselected and edited as necessary.

 To save an existing selection, make sure the selection is active and choose Select | Save Selection to reveal an options window similar to the following:

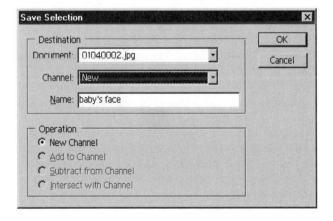

To save the selection in the current document, make sure the name of the current document is selected in the Document drop-down menu. The default of New in the Channel menu saves the selection as a new channel in the Channels palette, and is typically the only option you'll use.

In the Name text box, give the selection a name to help identify its contents. In the section labeled Operation, the default operation of New Channel is suitable in most cases. However, if you're trying to use the current selection to edit another saved selection, you'd need to choose one of the other options in that section.

▶ | **QUICK TIP**

Pressing ALT-H *(Windows) or* CMD-H *(Mac) can temporarily hide those dancing ants and make it easy to forget that a selection is active. An easy way to quickly determine if there are any active, yet hidden, selections in a document is to choose Select from the top menu and look at the option to Deselect. If that option is available, then a selection is active and perhaps hidden.*

TRY IT To load a selection at a later time, choose Select | Load Selection and specify the name of the selection to load from the Channel drop-down menu. When loading a selection, keep the following in mind:

1. You can load selections into the same layer from which they were selected or any other layer within the file.

2. You can load the opposite of any selection by clicking the check box next to Invert in the Load Selection dialog box.

3. If you have multiple files open that are the exact same size, you can load a selection from one file into another open file by specifying the source document in the Source drop-down menu.

▶ | **QUICK TIP**

To quickly load the contents of an existing layer as a "selection," hold down the ALT *(Windows) or* CMD *(Mac) key and click the layer in question.*

▼ Use the "Snap To" Feature to Assist in Drawing Selections

Sometimes, when drawing selections close to the edges of a canvas, such as with the Marquee tool, you might notice that the tool tries to "snap" to the edges of that canvas. This is caused by a default setting in Photoshop, where selections are set to Snap To Document Bounds.

▶ **NOTE**

The Snap To feature is also useful when performing actions such as cropping or drawing, if you want to snap to certain elements of an image.

While I like to turn off that feature when I need to make selections close to—but not touching—the edges of a canvas, it can be useful to leave it on in other cases. For example, the Snap To feature is available for snapping not only to a document's edges (or bounds), but also to its guides, grid, and slices. Photoshop 7 lets you turn each of these commands on and off independently, so you can effectively have your selections snap to the document guides, but not the grid.

▶ **QUICK TIP**

If you draw guides on your canvas, it can be particularly beneficial to let them help you draw selections—especially if you're a web designer planning to later use those same selections to slice your document into individual GIFs, JPEGs, and PNGs.

TRY IT ▶ To use the Snap To feature to assist in drawing selections, first decide what you'd like your selections to snap to. Then, select that option from the list by choosing View | Snap To.

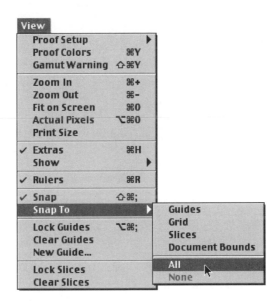

▶ **NOTE**

Some of these options will not be visible until they exist in your document. For example, until you draw guides, the Snap To | Guides option will be grayed out. To draw guides, first make sure your rulers are visible by pressing CTRL-R *(Windows) or* CMD-R *(Mac), and then click and drag away from a ruler into your image. To turn on the grid for your document, choose View | Show | Grid. To create slices, use the Slice tool in the toolbox.*

Copy Selections from One Image/Application to Another

When working with a file in Photoshop, you're not limited to using only elements within that file or, for that matter, within that application. Because most computers have a feature called the Clipboard, files from one application can be copied and pasted into another. This includes pieces or selections of files.

TRY IT To copy a selection between files, you have several options:

- Make a selection within the file from which you want to copy and choose Edit | Copy. Then, switch to the file you want to paste into and choose Edit | Paste. Note that Photoshop always pastes onto new layers.

- Make a selection within the file from which you want to copy. Switch to the Move tool and click and hold within the boundaries of the selection and drag it out of that file and into the file into which you want to paste it. Note that this really only works if both files are open and visible on the screen at the same time.

When you choose the Copy command in Photoshop, it only copies the contents of the currently active layer by default. To make a copy of the content within a selection from all layers in the file, choose File | Copy Merged instead of File | Copy.

▶ *CAUTION*

Photoshop automatically rasterizes vector-based selections when they are dragged into a file from outside of Photoshop. Table 5-2 lists some notes regarding copying selections from vector applications such as Adobe Illustrator to Photoshop.

▶ *QUICK TIP*

To copy a selection from one file and paste it inside of an existing selection in another file, use the Paste Into command (Edit | Paste Into).

Issue	Notes
Typography	When copying type from a vector-based file, you must first convert the type to outlines.
Paths	If you don't want your paths to become rasterized, hold down the CTRL (Windows) or CMD (Mac) key as you drag vector-based content into Photoshop.
Different file resolutions	When copying between two files with different file resolutions, the copied artwork always retains its original resolution.
Different color profiles	When copying between two files with different color profiles, you may be asked how to handle the color differences.

Table 5-2   Issues Involved in Copying Between Files

Export Paths to Illustrator

If you're working on a computer without enough memory to open Photoshop and Illustrator at the same time, you obviously can't use drag and drop to copy selections as discussed in the previous tip, "Copy Selections from One Image/Application to Another."

While you can always save bitmap images from Photoshop and open them in Illustrator, you can't save vector-based images out of Photoshop (even though you can open them in Photoshop). So what happens if you need to transfer vector paths created in Photoshop to a vector-based program? You can use the Export Paths command to do so.

TRY IT To export vector content to Adobe's vector-based program, Illustrator, choose File | Export | Paths To Illustrator when viewing a file containing paths. After choosing this command, specify the name of the path to export from the drop-down list of paths that exist in your document, and give the file a name.

▶ *NOTE*

Photoshop automatically gives the exported path an .ai file extension, which is readable as vector data in Illustrator.

Transform Selections with the Transform Command

In older versions of Photoshop, once you made a selection, you were stuck with its size and proportions. This meant if you made your selection just 1 pixel too short on one side, you'd have to deselect (Select | Deselect) and start over. Recent versions of Photoshop, however, have rectified this problem, and you can now easily edit selections without affecting their content.

The most efficient way to easily edit selections is to use the Transform command, because it enables you to scale, rotate, and move the selection all at once, without switching between multiple tools or commands.

TRY IT To use the Transform command to edit a selection, first make a selection within an open document in Photoshop. Then, choose Select | Transform Selection to cover the dancing ants around your selection to a box with "handles" or edit points at each of the corners, as well as in the center of each edge (see Figure 5-7).

> ▶ **QUICK TIP**
>
> *To force your transform to maintain the original proportions of the selection, hold down the SHIFT key while scaling or rotating the selection.*

If you move your cursor around the edges of the bounding box, you'll notice that the cursor changes slightly depending on which edge or handle you're near. For example, if the cursor is near a corner, the cursor changes to a curved line with arrows on both ends to indicate that by clicking now you can rotate the selection (see Figure 5-7).

Figure 5-7   By clicking and dragging from one of the corners in the selection, I can rotate this selection without editing the content within it.

▶ **NOTE**

Keep in mind that you're editing only the selection with this tool. That means you're not actually changing the content beneath it. To rotate, scale, or skew the content within a selection, choose Edit | Free Transform.

When you're satisfied with the edits to your selection, press the ENTER or RETURN key on your keyboard, or click the check mark button in the Options bar. To cancel the operation, press CTRL-. (Windows) or CMD-. (Mac), or click the button that looks like a zero with a line through it in the Options bar.

Use the Pen Tools to Make Detailed, Easily Changeable Selections

The Pen tools in Photoshop are excellent tools for making detailed and easily changeable selections, because instead of creating selections with dancing ants, they create vector-based paths that have anchor points along the way used to edit each piece of the "selection."

▶ *NOTE*

More information about the different types of paths and the tools used to create them is found in an earlier section of this chapter, "Making Vector Paths."

Paths created with the Pen tool are stored in the Paths palette. By default, they're stored as temporary or "working" paths until you save them (choose Save Path from the flyout menu in the Paths palette). In fact, these paths aren't really "selections"—that is, they won't allow you to select content within the file and edit it—until after you change them from vector-based paths to bitmap selections by choosing Make Selection from the Paths palette flyout menu.

Nonetheless, the Pen tool can be especially useful for drawing paths that you can edit before turning into bitmap selections.

TRY IT To use the Pen tools to make detailed, easily changeable selections in Photoshop, first open a file requiring such a selection. For practice, consider opening the Ducky.tif file found in the Samples folder within the Adobe Photoshop 7 folder.

Click the Pen tool in the toolbox to make it active. Then, move into the Ducky.tif file and begin clicking around the outside of the rubber duck. You can create two different types of lines with the Pen tool depending on how you click:

▶ *QUICK TIP*

Depending on the size of your monitor, it may be easier to zoom into the file to make really detailed paths. Press CTRL-+ *(Windows) or* CMD-+ *(Mac) to zoom in, or use* CTRL-- *(Windows) or* CMD-- *(Mac) to zoom out.*

1. To make straight segments, simply click and move to add anchor points along your path.
2. To make curved segments, click and drag before moving and clicking again. As you drag, the cursor pulls out a directional line that determines the angle and length of the curve on that part of the segment.

To close a path, position the cursor near the starting point until you notice a small circle appear next to the cursor. This indicates that when you click again, you'll close the path. To end a path without closing it, move the cursor away from the path and CTRL-click (Windows) or CMD-click (Mac).

TRY IT   To move an entire path, use the Path Selection tool, which is just above the Pen tool in the toolbox. To move or reshape segments of a path, click and hold on the Path Selection tool to reveal a flyout menu with an additional tool—the Direct Selection tool.

▶ QUICK TIP

If you created a straight segment but now want to change it to a curved segment (or vice versa), use the Convert Point tool, found at the bottom of the flyout menu for the Pen tool. Click and drag away from a straight anchor point to convert it into a curved anchor point. Click once on a curved anchor point to convert it to a straight anchor point.

The Direct Selection tool can be used to edit curved segments by first clicking the anchor point within the curved segment, which reveals small directional lines, as shown in Figure 5-8. To edit the slope and/or length of the curve, click and drag those directional lines.

▶ CAUTION

When drawing paths, use only as many anchor points as are necessary to create the intended path. Too many anchor points increase a file's size and can cause printing problems.

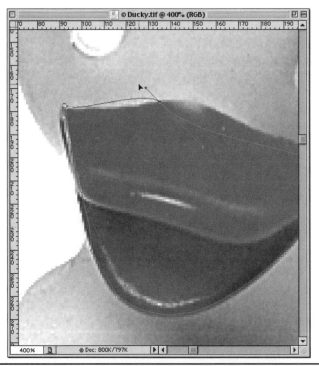

Figure 5-8   To edit curved anchor points, click and drag their directional lines.

TRY IT To add anchor points to an active path, use the Add Anchor Point tool, found in the flyout menu for the Pen tool. After selecting this tool, click anywhere on an active path to add a straight anchor point in that location. To add a curved anchor point, click and drag.

To delete anchor points from an active path, use the Delete Anchor Point tool, found in the flyout menu for the Pen tool. After selecting this tool, click any anchor point to delete it.

TRY IT To save a path for future use, highlight the path in the Paths palette and click the triangle in the upper-right corner to reveal a flyout menu. Choose Save Path from this menu and assign a name to the path. After you do so, the path will no longer be referenced as a "working path" in the Paths palette. Instead, it appears under its new name.

To delete any path from the Paths palette, highlight the path and click the Trash Can in the bottom of the Paths palette.

► | ## QUICK TIP

To "unselect" a path and hide its lines from view, choose Window | Paths to reveal the Paths palette. Then, click off of the active path to "turn it off." To "reselect" a path and make it active again, simply click the path name in the Paths palette.

Use the Magnetic Tools to Assist in Drawing Selections

If you need to make a selection around an object with clear distinction from its background, it's a good idea to turn your selection tool into a magnetic one. Two tools are capable of being made magnetic—the Lasso and the Freeform Pen tool.

TRY IT To make the Lasso tool magnetic, click and hold on the Lasso tool in the toolbox to reveal a flyout menu with additional options. At the bottom of that menu is the Magnetic Lasso tool.

After selecting this tool, click once in the location where you want your selection to begin. Then, move the cursor around the edge of the intended selection (see Figure 5-9 for an example). Click again once you get close to the beginning of the selection to close it. After closing the selection, you can switch to other selection tools to edit the selection, if necessary.

As you move your cursor around the edge of a selection, you'll notice that Photoshop adds anchor points along the way to anchor the selection against the border. The frequency of these points is controlled in the Options bar (see Figure 5-9). Other options you can control for the Magnetic Lasso are the following:

- **Width**   Used to specify how far away from the cursor Photoshop should look when detecting edges

- **Edge Contrast**   Used to specify how sensitive Photoshop should be to edges within an image; the higher the Edge Contrast, the more contrast that must be present before Photoshop will recognize it

Figure 5-9   Use the Magnetic Lasso tool to easily select objects that are against contrasting colors.

▶ *CAUTION*

Don't hold down the mouse button while you're moving the cursor around the selection—it works best if you click once to start the selection, and then release and move around the edge. However, if the Lasso doesn't snap to the edge as desired, you can click once to manually add an anchor point.

TRY IT   To make the Freeform Pen tool (found behind the Pen tool in the toolbox) magnetic, click the check box labeled Magnetic in the Options bar for the tool. Then, click once within the image to begin creating the path. After starting the path, move the cursor around the outside of the intended selection.

Avoid holding down the mouse button while moving around the path, for best results. Photoshop automatically adds anchor points where necessary, but you can manually add additional anchor points by clicking wherever you want the anchor points to appear.

To edit the options for the Magnetic Freeform Pen tool, click the inverted arrow next to the shape buttons in the Options bar, as shown in Figure 5-10, to reveal the following options:

• **Curve Fit**   Use a value between 0.5 and 10.0 pixels; the higher the value, the simpler the path with fewer anchor points.

- **Width**   Use a value between 1 and 256 to specify how far away from the cursor edges can be found.

- **Contrast**   Use a value between 1% and 100% to specify how sensitive Photoshop should be to edges within an image.

- **Frequency**   Use a value between 5 and 40 to specify how often Photoshop should add anchor points.

> ▶ **QUICK TIP**
>
> *Double-click to close the path.*

- **Pen Pressure**   Select this option if you have a pressure-sensitive pen and tablet and want to alter the Width option according to the pen pressure.

Save Selections as Clipping Paths to Define Transparent Sections of an Image

Suppose you want to use only the rubber duck from the Ducky.tif image (found in the Samples folder of the Adobe Photoshop 7 folder) in a page layout. In other words, you want to use the duck without

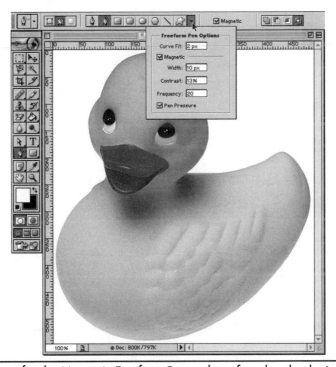

Figure 5-10   Options for the Magnetic Freeform Pen tool are found under the inverted arrow next to the shape buttons in the Options bar.

its white background. You can do so by first selecting the rubber duck and then saving that selection as a *clipping path.*

► **NOTE**

A clipping path defines the areas of an image that should display when the image is taken into a page-layout program and then printed.

TRY IT — To create a clipping path on an image, you must first save a selection. For practice, you can use the Ducky.tif image found in the Samples folder of the Adobe Photoshop 7 folder. After opening this file, select the rubber duck using any of the selection tools.

Then, convert the selection into a path by right-clicking (Windows) or CTRL-clicking (Mac) the selection and choosing Make Work Path. Using a value of 0.5 to 10.0 pixels, the tolerance level specifies how sensitive Photoshop should be to changes in the shape of the selection. The default of 2.0 pixels is usually sufficient; the higher the value, the fewer anchor points that are added and the smoother the resulting path. However, if you have problems printing the clipping path from your page-layout program, you might need to return to Photoshop and increase the tolerance here.

► **QUICK TIP**

This file has also been used in many of the other tips throughout this chapter. So if you're stuck on how to select only the rubber duck, see tips such as "Use the Inverse Command to Select the Opposite" or "Use the Magnetic Tools to Assist in Drawing Selections."

► **NOTE**

If you used the Pen tools to select the duck, you already have a work path and can skip the step of converting a selection to a path.

After converting your selection to a work path, you need to save it as a permanent path by highlighting the path in the Paths palette and choosing Save Path from the flyout menu, accessed by clicking the triangle in the upper-right corner of the palette.

Once you have saved the path you want to use as the clipping path, click the triangle in the upper-right corner of the Paths palette again and choose Clipping Path. The resulting menu asks you to choose which path to make the clipping path, and to identify a flatness level.

The flatness level refers to how the Postscript interpreter used in the printing process assigns the curved and straight-line segments. In most cases, you can leave this value blank and leave it up to the printer to determine. But if you have problems printing, you can use a value between 0.2 and 10.0, where 8 to 10 is usually good for high-resolution printing and 1 to 3 is usually better for low-resolution printing.

After clicking OK, your clipping path has been set. The only visible change in Photoshop to let you know this has occurred is in the Paths palette, where the path name itself changes from solid to outlined.

Use the Color Range Command to Select Precise Areas of Color

Using the Color Range command is similar to using the Magic Wand tool to select areas based on color. However, the Color Range command is a more precise way of selecting those areas because it lets you refine the selection without dealing with those sometimes pesky dancing ants.

TRY IT   To use the Color Range command to select precise areas of color, choose Select | Color Range. Use the Eyedropper tool—which is chosen by default upon opening the Color Range command—to select the primary areas of color you want to choose. When choosing colors, you can click anywhere within the actual image or within the preview pane shown in the Color Range window (see Figure 5-11).

▶ *NOTE*

Photoshop defaults to showing the boundaries of your selection in black and white, where the white areas are within the selection and the black areas are outside of the selection. When you first open the Color Range window, you may notice that some colors are highlighted already within the preview pane. This is because Photoshop automatically selects any colors within the image that match the current color in the foreground color swatch of the toolbox.

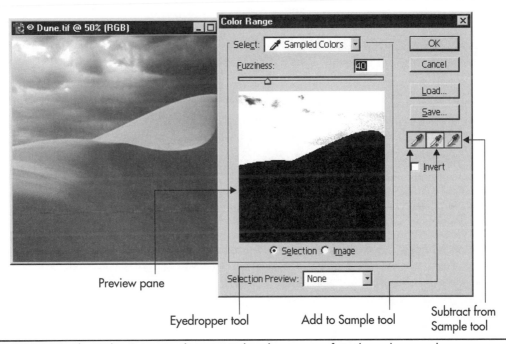

Preview pane

Eyedropper tool   Add to Sample tool   Subtract from Sample tool

Figure 5-11   Use the Color Range tool to precisely select areas of similar color or value.

To add to the selection of colors, hold down the SHIFT key while clicking, or click the Add To Sample button before selecting additional areas of color. To subtract from the selection of colors, hold down the ALT (Windows) or OPTION (Mac) key while clicking, or click the Subtract From Sample button before selecting additional areas of color.

When you're finished, you can click OK to return to your image, where the areas of color will be selected. Or you can click Save to save the selection for future use.

> ► **QUICK TIP**
>
> *Clicking Load allows you to load another selection in the Color Range tool, where you can then add to or subtract from the selection as needed.*

Use the Extract Command to Remove Objects from Complex Backgrounds

Photoshop's Extract command can be quite useful for removing objects from backgrounds, particularly objects that might otherwise be too complex to easily select with the selection tools. For example, suppose I wanted to extract my daughter from the background in the following image.

Although I might use the selection tools to painstakingly try to draw the selection, the Extract command can make the whole process a bit easier because you can work and rework the edges of the selection as much as necessary until you get it perfect.

 To use the Extract command to remove an object from a complex background, first make sure the file you want to edit is open in Photoshop. If you're working with a layered file, make sure the layer from which you want to extract an object is active in the Layers palette. Then follow these steps:

▶ **CAUTION**

Extracting an image in Photoshop causes the background to become lost. Therefore, if you want to keep a copy of that background, duplicate the layer before you proceed.

1. Choose Filter | Extract.

2. Use the Edge Highlighter tool (shaped like a marker in the Extract command's toolbox) to draw an outline around the object you wish to extract. Try to stay as close as possible to the edge of the object to avoid losing any piece of the object in the extraction. By default, the outline you draw appears in neon green in the preview.

▶ **QUICK TIP**

Put a checkmark next to the option Smart Highlighting under Tool Options to have Photoshop automatically snap to edges with a lot of contrast when drawing your outline. Or leave that box unchecked and just hold down the CMD key (Mac) or CTRL key (Windows) to temporarily use Smart Highlighting when drawing an outline.

3. Use the Eraser tool to fix any stray part of the outline you drew, but make sure the entire outline is complete. In other words, check to make sure there aren't any holes in your outline before proceeding to the next step, in which you fill the outline. To temporarily use the Eraser while drawing the outline with the Edge Highlighter tool, hold down the ALT (Windows) or OPTION (Mac) key.

4. Use the Fill tool (shaped like a paint bucket) to fill the outline and mark the area you want to retain and extract from the rest of the image, as I did in Figure 5-12.

5. Click Preview to see how the image will look when it's extracted to Photoshop.

In most cases, you'll want to adjust or edit the object before you actually extract it to Photoshop. You can do so—as I did to clean up the edges around my daughter's hair in Figure 5-13—with the Cleanup and Edge Touchup tools.

- Use the Cleanup tool to remove traces of the background around the object you're extracting. I find this tool to be especially useful for cleaning up edges, because it also softens the edges it cleans up. When working with the Cleanup tool, you can also hold down the ALT (Windows) or OPTION (Mac) key to temporarily add pixels from the background instead of remove them. (Press numbers 0 through 9 on your keyboard to adjust the pressure of your brush.)

- Use the Edge Touchup tool to smooth rough edges of the selection without softening them. When working with the Edge Touchup tool, hold down the CTRL (Windows) or CMD (Mac) key and drag from within the edge's borders outward to move the edge itself. (Press numbers 0 through 9 on your keyboard to adjust the pressure of your brush.)

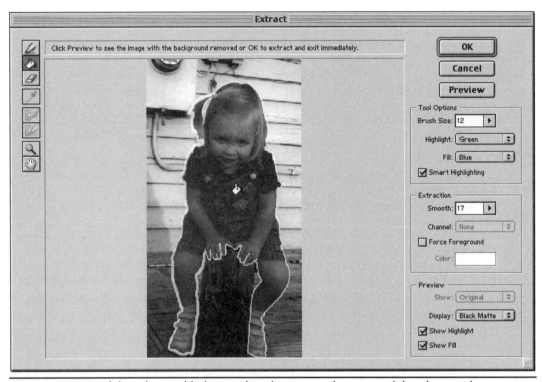

Figure 5-12 I used the Edge Highlighter tool to draw an outline around the object to be extracted, and then filled in the area I wanted to keep.

To return to viewing the original image, choose "Original" in the Show menu under Preview. Or you can choose one of the following backgrounds from the Display menu against which you can temporarily display the extracted object:

> **QUICK TIP**
>
> *Press* CTRL-+ *(Windows) or* CMD-+ *(Mac) to zoom in and get a closer view of the edges of your object. Then press* CTRL-- *(Windows) or* CMD-- *(Mac) to zoom out.*

- **None**   Displays the extracted image against the gray checkerboard used to symbolize transparency in Photoshop
- **Black Matte**   Displays the extracted image against solid black background
- **Gray Matte**   Displays the extracted image against a solid 50 percent gray background
- **White Matte**   Displays the extracted image against a solid white background
- **Other**   Displays the extracted image against the color of your choice
- **Mask**   Displays the extracted image as solid white against a black background

Figure 5-13   I used the Cleanup and Edge Touchup tools to smooth and soften the edges around my daughter's hair.

You can continue to clean up the edges as necessary, or you can even go back and redraw the edges, refill the center, and then re-extract the image. When you're satisfied with the object, click OK to formally extract the image to Photoshop, where the background pixels are erased and left transparent. You can then place the object against the background of your choice.

▶ **NOTE**

If you're working on the Background layer in a file, the layer is turned into a normal layer, and the "background" around the extracted image is erased to reveal the gray checkerboard pattern, as shown in Figure 5-14.

Figure 5-14   Because I was working with an image on a Background layer in Photoshop, the gray checkerboard pattern was made visible when the image was extracted.

CHAPTER 6

Using Layers

TIPS IN THIS CHAPTER

One of the key features of Photoshop is its use of layers. While they may seem small in comparison to other aspects of the program, it is only with the use of layers that most of the other features and commands are possible. If you're new to Photoshop, then such a large emphasis on layers begs the question, "What are layers?"

You might think of layers in Photoshop as being similar to clear sheets of acetate. Painters sometimes place these sheets of acetate over their paintings before making a potentially drastic change in the painting. By painting a quick sketch on the acetate instead of the canvas itself, a painter is giving herself the chance to say "forget it" and remove the change—before it was ever made permanent on the canvas.

Using layers in Photoshop is much the same. You can paint, draw, and make changes on a layer—your piece of acetate—without affecting the contents beneath the layer. In fact, in Photoshop, you can add multiple layers on top of each other as needed, and each layer is treated as a separate entity in Photoshop. This means you can edit the contents of each layer without changing the contents of other layers.

▶ **NOTE**

Whereas previous versions of Photoshop limited the number of layers you could create to 99, Photoshop 7 does not. You are now only limited in the number of layers you can add to an image by the memory on your computer.

At any time, you can change the stacking order of the layers, or assign styles to them. You can also group certain layers together—as if you were stapling them together—if you want those layers to take on similar characteristics.

When you save your file in a format other than Photoshop (PSD), the program asks you whether you want to "flatten layers," a process where all visible layers are merged together and hidden layers are thrown away. Most designers typically keep layered Photoshop files on hand for editing, and only save flattened versions, for example, for placement in page-layout programs, web-page layouts, or other final designs.

▶ **CAUTION**

Only Photoshop (.psd extension) and TIFF (.tif extension) files can be saved with layers. And while TIFF files can be saved with layers, most other programs will only display the flattened version—without layers.

The Layers Palette

When you create layers in Photoshop, they are stored in the Layers palette (choose Window | Layers to view). Layers appear differently in the Layers palette, depending on their type, as defined in Table 6-1 and shown in Figure 6-1. For example, layers within a layer set are indented beneath

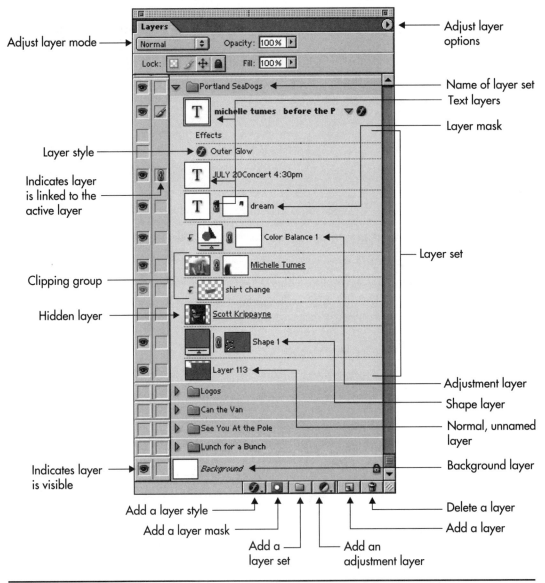

Figure 6-1 The Layers palette houses a variety of layer types, as defined in Table 6-1.

the name of the layer set. Layers associated with other layers—such as adjustment layers or layer styles—are further indented, and include arrows that point to the associated layer.

Type of Layer	Characteristics
Background layer	Recognized by its name—Background—shown in italics in the Layers palette Always exists at the bottom of the Layers palette because layers can't be placed under the background Only one Background layer can exist in a single image file Its opacity is set at 100% and can't be changed Can't be grouped with other layers Similar to the actual canvas of a physical painting Can be changed into a normal layer by double-clicking it
Layer (normal; also called an image layer)	Is transparent until content is added to it Has editable opacity and fill levels Can be grouped and/or linked with other layers Can be moved above or below other layers in the Layers palette Can be changed into a Background layer (if one doesn't already exist) by choosing Layer | New | Background From Layer Accepts layer styles and adjustment layers Can be renamed
Layer mask	Must be associated with a particular layer Can be linked to the associated layer Can be moved with the associated layer Has editable opacity and fill levels
Adjustment layer	Can be associated with another layer Can be grouped and/or linked with other layers Has editable opacity levels Can be moved above and below other layers in the Layers palette Affects all layers underneath it
Fill layer	Can be associated with another layer Can be grouped and/or linked with other layers Has editable opacity levels Can be moved above and below other layers in the Layers palette Does not affect the layers underneath it
Layer style	Must be associated with a particular layer Can be any of the following: Drop Shadow, Inner Shadow, Outer Glow, Inner Glow, Bevel and Emboss, Satin, Color Overlay, Gradient Overlay, Pattern Overlay, Stroke
Text layer	Accepts only vector-based text content Can be grouped and/or linked with other layers Has editable opacity and fill levels Can be moved above or below other layers in the Layers palette Accepts layer styles and adjustment layers Must be rasterized (changed from vector-based to bitmap) before accepting certain filters and effects

Table 6-1   Comparison of Different Types of Layers

Type of Layer	Characteristics
Shape layer	Contains a vector-based path Can be grouped and/or linked with other layers Has editable opacity and fill levels Can be moved above or below other layers in the Layers palette Accepts layer styles and adjustment layers
Clipping group	Contains several layers grouped together Contains a bottom layer (which is underlined in the Layers palette) that masks the contents of the grouped layers above it

Table 6-1   Comparison of Different Types of Layers *(continued)*

Layer Options

There are several ways to access options for the Layers palette and its individual layers. The most comprehensive of these is the Layer menu, which provides access to just about anything you want to do with or to a layer in Photoshop.

You can gain access to options more specific to the Layers palette by clicking the small triangle in the upper-right corner of the palette window.

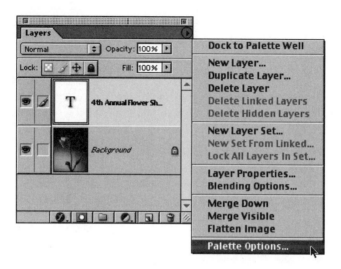

Finally, you can right-click (Windows) or CTRL-click (Mac) any particular layer in the Layers palette to see options specific to that layer, including Layer Properties, Blending Options, and the ability to duplicate or delete the layer.

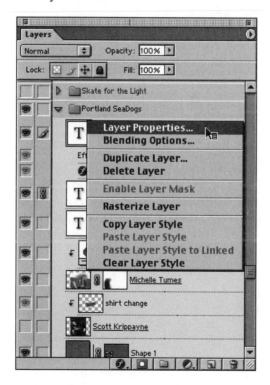

Blending Modes

In Photoshop, the effect layers have on one another is determined by three key things:

- **Stacking order**   Where a layer is in relation to other layers in the Layers palette
- **Opacity**   How transparent or opaque a layer is
- **Blending mode**   Specifies exactly how the pixels within a layer should affect those below it. In each of the various modes, Photoshop considers both the base color (the color of the pixels on the layer below the current one) and the blend color (the color of the pixels on the current layer).

▶ **QUICK TIP**

You can easily adjust the stacking order of layers simply by dragging and dropping them within the Layers palette. In addition, you can press CTRL-] *(CMD-] on the Mac) to bring a layer forward (or higher) in the stacking order, or* CTRL-[*(CMD-[on the Mac) to send it backward. Add the* SHIFT *key to those combinations to send the layer to the very top or bottom of the stacking order.*

There are six groups of different blending modes, as shown in the following illustration, and in the Blending Modes section of the color insert . Table 6-2 gives a brief description of each blending mode.

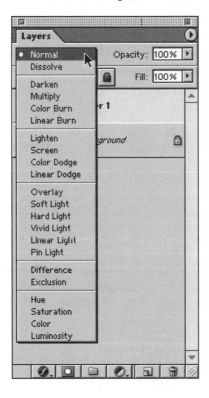

Blending Mode	Characteristics
Normal	Considered the same as "no blending mode" (default mode)
Dissolve	Scatters color throughout pixels Results appear "dithered" or "spotty"
Darken	Selects the darker color to display Replaces lighter pixels with darker ones Has no effect on darker pixels
Multiply	Multiplies base color with blend color Results always appear darker
Color Burn	Darkens base color to reflect blend color by increasing contrast Has no effect on white pixels
Linear Burn	Darkens base color to reflect blend color by decreasing brightness Has no effect on white pixels
Lighten	Selects the lighter color to display Replaces darker pixels with lighter ones Has no effect on lighter pixels
Screen	Multiplies the inverse of the blend and base colors Results always appear lighter
Color Dodge	Brightens base color to reflect blend color by decreasing contrast Has no effect on black pixels
Linear Dodge	Brightens base color to reflect blend color by increasing brightness Has no effect on black pixels
Overlay	Multiples or screens colors Effect depends on base color Preserves highlights and shadows Mostly affects midtones
Soft Light	Darkens or lightens colors Effect depends on blend color Similar to using a diffused spotlight
Hard Light	Multiplies or screens colors Effect depends on blend color Similar to using a harsh spotlight
Vivid Light	Burns or dodges colors by increasing or decreasing contrast Effect depends on blend color
Linear Light	Burns or dodges colors by decreasing or increasing brightness Effect depends on blend color

Table 6-2   Brief Description of Layer Blending Modes

Blending Mode	Characteristics
Pin Light	Darkens or lightens pixels Effect depends on blend color, which is considered the light source
Difference	Subtracts color with greatest brightness value Has no effect if blend color is black
Exclusion	Similar to Difference mode, but lower in contrast Has no effect if blend color is black
Hue	Uses luminance and saturation of base color and hue of blend color
Saturation	Uses luminance and hue of base color with saturation of blend color
Color	Uses luminance of base color with hue and saturation of blend color Preserves grays
Luminosity	Uses hue and saturation of base color with luminance of blend color Creates opposite effect of Color mode

Table 6-2   Brief Description of Layer Blending Modes *(continued)*

In addition to the blending modes listed in Table 6-2, two additional modes exist, but are only available when Lock Transparency is selected for a particular layer:

- **Behind**   Enables you to edit or paint only transparent parts of the layer
- **Clear**   Makes each edited pixel transparent on the layer

For a visual representation of each blending mode, see the "Layer Blending Modes" section of the color insert.

Managing Layers

Because you can have so many layers in a layered Photoshop document, it's important to properly manage those layers. If left unmanaged, the Layers palette can quickly become an overwhelming mess. For example, suppose you created a file with many layers, none of which had custom names, such as the one shown in Figure 6-2. While the thumbnail images on each layer can provide a bit of help, it's difficult to determine exactly what's on most layers. And what if you close the file and then need to edit it two weeks later? You'd need to click through each of the layers just to remind yourself of their contents.

To avoid situations like this, it's best to properly manage layers by doing the following:

- Give them descriptive names
- Group them into layer sets, wherever possible
- Link them to force movements and transformations to be applied uniformly
- Lock them to prevent unwanted changes

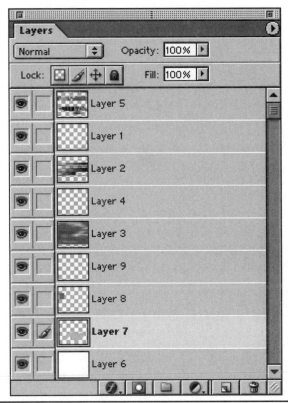

Figure 6-2   Files with unnamed layers, such as this one, are difficult to manage.

Tips in the following section explain how to perform each of these tasks, as well as other ways to use layers in Photoshop.

Turn On Thumbnail Views to Help Layer Recognition

The Layers palette includes the option to view a thumbnail of the contents of a particular layer, to the left of that layer's name. While thumbnails can cause the Layers palette to be longer, they can be quite helpful in determining the contents of a layer—particularly if the layer hasn't been named.

TRY IT   To turn on thumbnail views in the Layers palette, first choose Window I Layers to make sure the Layers palette is visible. Then, click the triangle in the upper-right corner of the palette to display a flyout menu of options. Choose Palette Options from the bottom of that menu to reveal the options shown next.

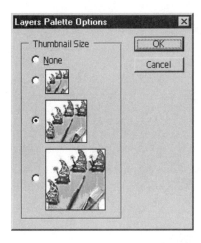

From this window, you can specify whether to display thumbnail views at all, and if so, the size at which they should be displayed.

Name Layers for Easy Recognition

When you look at the Layers palette for an image with unnamed layers, such as the one shown previously in Figure 6-2, it's often difficult to determine the contents of those layers. When the thumbnail icons are turned off, as they are in the following illustration, it's almost impossible to identify which layer you're looking for at any given time.

▶ *NOTE*

For information on how to turn on the thumbnail views in the Layers palette, see the previous tip, "Turn On Thumbnail Views to Help Layer Recognition."

One of the most efficient ways to speed up your use of the Layers palette is also the simplest of all management techniques—name your layers. You can name layers in Photoshop in two ways:

- As a layer is being created
- After a layer is created

While it may sound like more trouble than it's worth to go back and name all your layers after creating them, I can promise you it'll save lots of time in the long run, because you won't have to click through all the layers looking for a particular element.

▶ *NOTE*

Text layers are the only types of layers that are given names automatically by default. In this case, Photoshop names a text layer with the beginning of the text on that layer.

 To name a layer as it's being created, first make sure the Layers palette is open by choosing Windows | Layers and then perform any of the following tasks:

- Click the triangle in the upper-right corner of the palette and choose New Layer.
- Hold down the ALT (Windows) or OPTION key (Mac) while clicking the New Layer button at the bottom of the Layers palette.
- Choose Layer | New | Layer from the top menu.
- Press SHIFT-CTRL-N (Windows) or SHIFT-CMD-N (Mac).

In each of these four cases, you're presented with a dialog box similar to the one shown in Figure 6-3, in which you can give the layer a suitable name, as well as change its color, mode, and opacity.

▶ **QUICK TIP**

When you name a layer, you can also assign it a color. By assigning similar layers or groups of layers the same color, you can color-code your Layers palette and make it even easier to manage.

After naming a layer, the new name appears in the Layers palette. Whether or not the entire name is displayed in the Layers palette at once depends on the width of the Layers palette window and the length of the layer name. If you can't see the entire name of a particular layer, you can move your cursor over the layer name and leave it there for a few seconds. If there's enough room, Photoshop tries to show you the entire layer name in a tool tip.

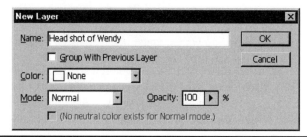

Figure 6-3   You can name a layer from within the New Layer dialog box.

  To name a layer after it's been created, first make sure the Layers palette is open by choosing Windows | Layers and then perform any of the following tasks:

- Double-click the layer name in the Layers palette and type the new layer name right within the Layers palette.
- Click once on the layer within the Layers palette and choose Layer Properties from the palette menu accessible from the upper-right corner of the palette.

Group Related Layers into Sets

The longer I work on a file in Photoshop, the more layers I add. After a certain amount of time, however, I always go back and group as many layers as possible into layer sets. Using layer sets in Photoshop is similar to using folders to organize the files on your hard drive. There are several additional benefits to using layer sets:

- Layer sets help to clean up the Layers palette by reducing clutter.
- You can easily move, hide, lock, delete, or duplicate all the layers within a layer set, in most cases with a single click.
- You can apply attributes such as adjustment layers and masks to an entire group of layers in a layer set.

When you create a new layer set, you can specify the blending mode of the set. By default, Photoshop sets the blending mode to Pass Through, to indicate that each layer within the set should use its own characteristics and blending mode. If you change the blending mode for the entire layer set, the layers within that set are treated as a single image—or composite—before being blended with the rest of the image according to that blending mode. For more information about blending modes, refer to "Blending Modes" earlier in the chapter.

▶ | **QUICK TIP**

When you group layers together in sets, you can also assign those sets a color. By assigning different layer sets different colors, you can further color-code your Layers palette and make it even easier to manage.

TRY IT   To group related layers into a layer set, first make sure the Layers palette is visible by choosing Windows I Layers. If you don't have another layered document with which you can test this tip, consider using the Banner.psd document—like I am—found in the Samples folder of the Adobe Photoshop 7 folder. It's a good file to practice with because it has many layers already defined, none of which are grouped into sets.

▶ **NOTE**

The layers in the Banner.psd file are actually parts of a web animation. To see it in action, choose File | Jump To | Adobe ImageReady 7.0. Then choose Window | Animation and click the Play button at the bottom of the Animation palette.

Once you've identified a few layers you want to group together, do one of the following things to create a new layer set:

- Choose Layer I New I Layer Set.
- Choose New Layer Set from the Layers palette menu accessible from the triangle in the upper-right corner of the palette.
- Click the New Layer Set button in the bottom of the Layers palette—it looks like a folder— and then double-click the layer set name in the Layers palette to name it.
- Hold down the ALT (Windows) or OPTION (Mac) key while clicking the New Layer Set button to name the set during creation.

After creating a new layer set, you can add layers to it by dragging them over the set's name in the Layers palette or above or below any existing layers within the set. When you add layers to a layer set in the former fashion, they are automatically added *below* any existing layers within the set. However, you can rearrange layers within a layer set as you would any normal layers by simply dragging and dropping them within the Layers palette window, as shown in the following illustration.

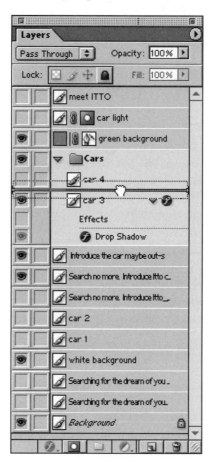

▶ | **QUICK TIP**

You can also quickly create a new layer set from an existing group of linked layers, by clicking one of the linked layers and choosing Layer | New | Layer Set From Linked.

TRY IT To hide all the lyers within a layer set, click the eye icon to the left of the layer set name, as in the following illustration. While turning off the eye icon makes *all* the layers of that layer set invisible on the canvas, turning it back on reveals only those individual layers that already have the eye icon visible. As shown here, when layers in a layer set are made invisible by the characteristics of the layer set, the eye icons for the individual layers are grayed out within the Layers palette.

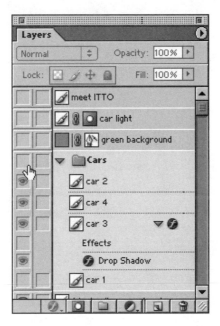

▶ **QUICK TIP**

You can also move all of the layers within a layer set together by first linking them. See the next tip for more information.

Link Layers to Transform Multiple Layers at Once

One of the great benefits of using layers in Photoshop is that you can move and transform elements from different layers independently but also together—as if they were on a single layer. To achieve this you must first link the layers together.

▶ **QUICK TIP**

Another benefit of linking layers together is the ability to quickly align and evenly distribute the contents of those layers. See the tip entitled "Align and Distribute Elements on Multiple Layers" later in the chapter.

TRY IT To link layers together, first make sure the Layers palette is visible by choosing Windows | Layers. Click once on the first layer you want to link to another. Then, click the box closest to the name of any other layer you want to link to the active one to place a small link icon in that box.

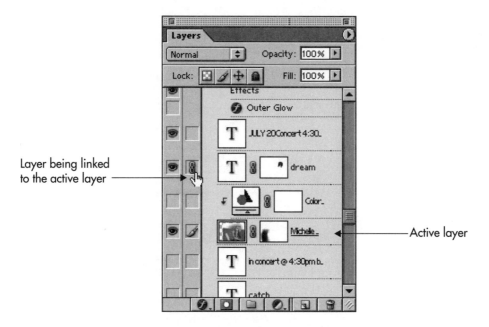

Layer being linked to the active layer

Active layer

Continue clicking to reveal link icons in each layer you want to link to the current layer.

▶ **NOTE**

To link all the layers within a layer set, first highlight the name of the layer set within the Layers palette. Then, click the box closest to the name of any layer within that set to reveal a link icon.

After linking layers, you can use the Move tool to move all of the elements at once. In addition, you can perform transformations, such as scaling or rotating, on all the elements on those layers at the same time simply by clicking any of the linked layers and performing the transformation as you normally would.

Merge Layers to Reduce File Size

Whenever you add another layer to a file in Photoshop, you also increase the file's size and amount of memory used. If you're working on a computer where memory and disk space is an issue, you'll want to keep track of how many layers you add to your files. More specifically, consider merged layers together whenever possible to reduce file size.

▶ *CAUTION*

While merging layers does reduce file size, avoid doing so until you're positive you won't need to edit the content of those layers independently.

TRY IT To merge layers together in Photoshop, first make sure the Layers palette is visible by choosing Window I Layers. Then, you need to rearrange the layers in your Layers palette so the layers you want to merge are stacked on top of one another. In other words, if you want to merge together two layers, named Headshot and New Hat, make sure those two layers are right next to each other in the Layers palette.

Click once on the top layer in the group you want to merge, and do one of the following to merge the currently selected layer with the one below it:

- Press CTRL-E (Windows) or CMD-E (Mac).

- Choose Layer I Merge Down.

- Click the triangle in the upper-right corner of the Layers palette and choose Merge Down from the flyout menu.

After merging layers, the merged layers take on the name and blending mode of the bottom layer in the group that was merged.

▶ *CAUTION*

Whenever you try to merge layers containing masks, Photoshop first applies that layer mask to the layer before merging. If that's not what you want, make sure to disable it (by right-clicking in Windows or OPTION-*clicking in Mac on the layer mask and choosing Disable Layer Mask) before merging.*

TRY IT If you need to merge several layers together, you can make the process go more quickly by first linking the layers together (click the box closest to the layer icon to reveal a link icon). Click one of the linked layers and choose Layer I Merge Linked or press CTRL-E (Windows) or CMD-E (Mac).

TRY IT To merge all the visible layers within a document, choose Layer I Merge Visible. After doing so, the only layers not merged will be those that are currently hidden. To merge all the layers in a document into a single layer is called *flattening* the document. This can be achieved by choosing Layer I Flatten Image, but it's wise to make sure you have saved a fully layered document before saving a flattened version.

▶ **QUICK TIP**

If you're planning to save an image in a format that doesn't support layers, it's a good idea to flatten the image before choosing File I Save or File I Save As. If you don't flatten your image before doing so, Photoshop requires you to save a flattened copy of the file instead of saving the file itself. So after saving the copy, you'll still be left with a layered Photoshop document to save or trash.

Align and Distribute Elements on Multiple Layers

Have you ever wished you could draw a guideline and quickly align the center of several text layers along that line, as I did in Figure 6-4? You can, if you first link the layers together, as discussed in the earlier tip, "Link Layers to Transform Multiple Layers at Once." And, in fact, you don't even have to draw the guideline.

Photoshop includes two commands used to align and distribute elements:

- **Align** Enables you to align several elements along a horizontal or vertical axis.
- **Distribute** Enables you to evenly distribute several elements either horizontally or vertically.

▶ *NOTE*

The Align and Distribute commands only work on layers containing pixels of at least 50 percent opacity.

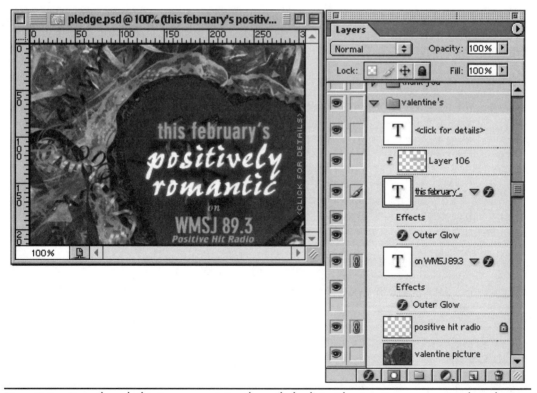

Figure 6-4 Even though this image contains three (linked) text layers, it was easy to align them along their horizontal centers by choosing Layer | Align Linked.

TRY IT To align elements on multiple layers, first make sure the layers are linked together by placing a link icon next to each layer name. Then, choose Layer | Align Linked and decide how you want to align the layers from the following flyout menu. Each option is described in Table 6-3.

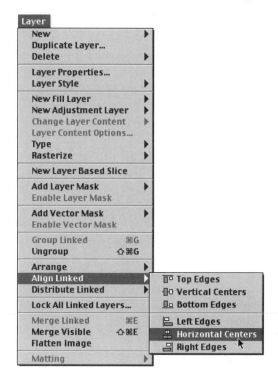

Align Option	Description
Top Edges	Aligns the top pixel of the active layer with the top pixel of the linked layer(s) or selection.
Vertical Centers	Aligns the pixel at the vertical center of the active layer with the pixel at the vertical center of the linked layer(s) or selection.
Bottom Edges	Aligns the bottom pixel of the active layer with the bottom pixel of the linked layer(s) or selection.
Left Edges	Aligns the leftmost pixel on the active layer with the leftmost pixel of the linked layer(s) or selection.
Horizontal Centers	Aligns the pixel at the horizontal center of the active layer with the pixel at the horizontal center of the linked layer(s) or selection.
Right Edges	Aligns the rightmost pixel on the active layer with the rightmost pixel of the linked layer(s) or selection.

Table 6-3   Options for the Align Command

▶ | **QUICK TIP**

You can also align a layer to a selection by first making a selection in the image and then selecting the layer in the Layers palette within which you want it to align. Then, choose Layer | Align To Selection and choose the appropriate option from the flyout menu.

TRY IT To evenly distribute elements on multiple layers, first make sure at least three layers are linked together by placing a link icon next to each layer name. Then, choose Layer | Distribute Linked and decide how you want to distribute the layers from the following flyout menu. Each option is described in Table 6-4.

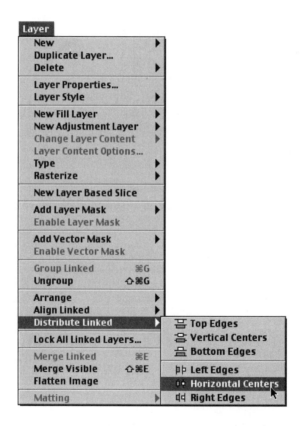

▶ **CAUTION**

To use the Distribute command, you must link at least three layers in the Layers palette.

Align Option	Description
Top Edges	Evenly spaces the linked layers, starting from the top pixel on each layer.
Vertical Centers	Evenly spaces the linked layers, starting from the vertical center pixel on each layer.
Bottom Edges	Evenly spaces the linked layers, starting from the bottom pixel on each layer.
Left Edges	Evenly spaces the linked layers, starting from the leftmost pixel on each layer.
Horizontal Centers	Evenly spaces the linked layers, starting from the horizontal center pixel on each layer.
Right Edges	Evenly spaces the linked layers, starting from the rightmost pixel on each layer.

Table 6-4   Options for the Distribute Command

Right-Click (CTRL-Click) to Jump to the Target Layer

Even after you name and group layers into sets to make things more manageable, it can still be cumbersome to have to scroll through long lists of layers to activate the one you need. To work around that issue, Photoshop is sensitive enough to how you click within the image window that you can click in a certain way to activate a list of each layer containing pixels under the spot in which you clicked.

 TRY IT   To quickly jump to a certain layer in the Layers palette, right-click (Windows) or CTRL-click (Mac) with the Move tool anywhere within the image window that contains pixels for the layer in question. For example, suppose you wanted to quickly activate the layer containing the text "July 20" in Figure 6-5 without scrolling through the 150+ layers (most of which are currently hidden) contained in the file.

By right-clicking (Windows) or CTRL-clicking (Mac) with the Move tool, I can access a menu of every layer—whether visible or not—with pixels beneath the cursor. To make the July 20 layer active, I simply select it from that list.

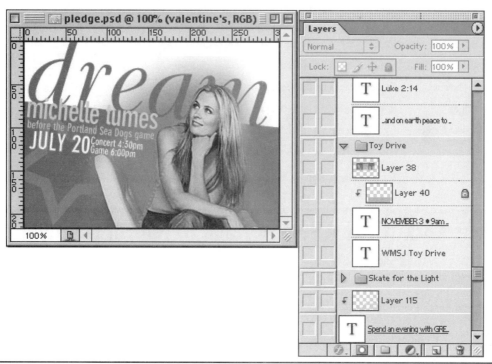

Figure 6-5   This file contains so many layers that it can take a long time scrolling to find the one I want in the Layers palette.

▶ | **QUICK TIP**

You can also choose Auto Select Layer from the Options bar for the Move tool, so the appropriate layer is automatically selected when you click on any part of it in the image window.

Lock Layers to Protect Their Contents

Photoshop allows you to lock layers entirely to prevent any edits or changes to their contents. Alternatively, you can lock certain characteristics of a layer to prevent changes only in the following areas:

- **Transparency**   Prevents editing any of the layer's transparent pixels; allows you to only edit the filled pixels on the layer.
- **Image**   Prevents editing the layer's pixels with the paint tools.
- **Position**   Prevents moving any of the layer's pixels.

You can recognize the difference between fully and partially locked layers by looking at the lock that appears next to the layer's name in the Layers palette—a solid lock indicates a fully locked layer, while an outlined lock indicates a partially locked layer.

TRY IT To lock a layer entirely to protect its contents from any modification, first make sure the Layers palette is visible by choosing Window | Layers. Click once on the layer in the Layers palette to make it active, and click the lock icon (the fourth button after Lock in the top of the Layers palette, as shown in Figure 6-6).

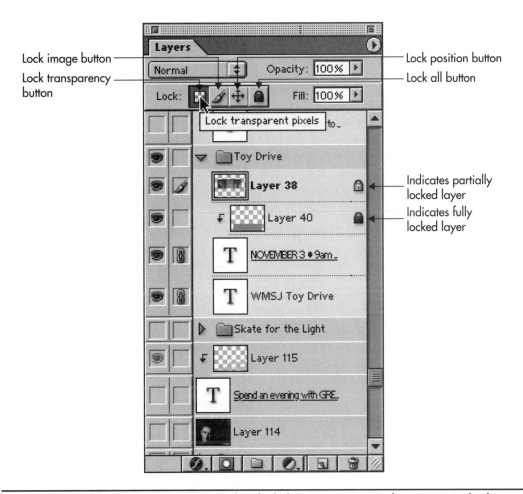

Figure 6-6 Click the first button next to Lock to lock the transparent pixels on a particular layer.

TRY IT   To lock a certain characteristic of a layer, click once on the layer in the Layers palette to make it active, and click the corresponding button from the three buttons immediately next to Lock in the Layers palette (as shown previously in Figure 6-6).

Adjust Opacity to Allow Layers Beneath to Show Through

Each layer—with the exception of the Background layer or a locked layer—has an adjustable opacity level that can be adjusted to allow the layers beneath to show through. The higher the opacity level, the less the layer below is able to be seen through the current layer.

In addition to a layer's opacity, you can adjust its fill opacity. The difference between the two is that a layer's opacity affects its blending mode, whereas the fill opacity affects only the transparency of the painted pixels on a layer and not any layer effects applied to it.

TRY IT   To change a layer's opacity (as in the example shown in Figure 6-7), do one of the following after clicking once on the layer in question in the Layers palette (choose Window | Layers to show the Layers palette):

- Type a new value into the Opacity text box or move the Opacity slider at the top of the Layers palette.
- Double-click the layer thumbnail in the Layers palette to reveal the Blending Options for that particular layer.
- Choose Layer | Layer Style | Blending Options.

TRY IT   To change a layer's fill opacity, do one of the following after clicking once on the layer in question in the Layers palette:

- Type a new value into the Fill text box (located below the Opacity text box) or move the Fill slider at the top of the Layers palette.
- Double-click the layer thumbnail in the Layers palette to reveal the Blending Options for that particular layer.
- Choose Layer | Layer Style | Blending Options.

Use Layer Styles to Customize Special Effects

Layer styles are special because they aren't stand-alone layers. Instead, they are special effects added to the contents of a particular layer. While older versions of Photoshop required you to go through

As the layer's opacity is reduced, the word "dream" fades away   Adjust the layer's opacity

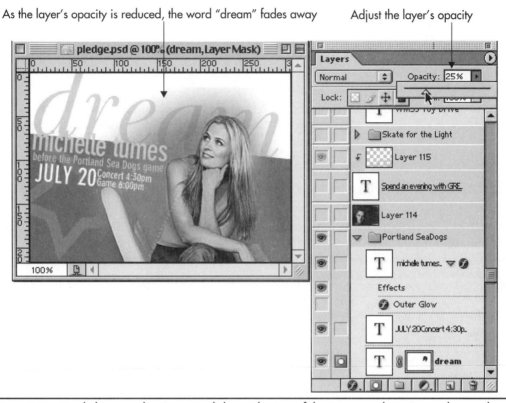

Figure 6-7   By clicking on the Opacity slider at the top of the Layers palette, I can change the opacity of the dream text layer.

sometimes painstaking processing to add effects like drop shadows to image elements, recent versions have included layer styles, which in effect do all the work for you.

Layer styles are available in the following categories, each of which can be added to layers with just a few clicks:

- Drop Shadow
- Inner Shadow
- Outer Glow
- Inner Glow
- Bevel and Emboss
- Satin

- Color Overlay
- Gradient Overlay
- Pattern Overlay
- Stroke

Once a style is added to and customized for one layer, it can be copied and pasted onto other layers with little hassle. Layer styles can also be disabled and reenabled independently of their parent layer.

▶ **QUICK TIP**

If you first link a group of layers together (by clicking in the second box on each layer), you can paste a layer style onto all the linked layers in just two steps—right-click (Windows) or CTRL-click (Mac) and choose Copy Layer Style, then Paste Layer Style To Linked.

TRY IT To add a layer style to a layer, first make sure the Layers palette is visible in Photoshop (choose Window | Layers) and that you have a layered file open. Then, choose a layer whose content doesn't bleed across all four canvas edges, so you will be able to actually see the effect of the layer style.

▶ **QUICK TIP**

Don't have a suitable layer in your file? Use the Type tool to create some random text, and you'll have a great layer for testing this tip.

Click once on the layer to which you want to add the layer style within the Layer palette; this makes that layer active. You can add a layer style either by choosing Layer | Layer Style from the top menu or clicking the Add Layer Style button at the bottom of the Layers palette. After doing so, choose which layer style to add from the menu and customize that effect in the Layer Style dialog box, as shown in Figure 6-8.

▶ **QUICK TIP**

If you customize a layer style, you can save it to use for other layers. To do so, click the New Style button in the Layer Style dialog box. Then, specify whether to include both the Layer Effects and Blending Options in the style and give your style a name. Saved styles are stored in the Styles palette, which can be found by choosing Window | Styles. For more tips on using the preset styles found in that palette, see Chapter 9.

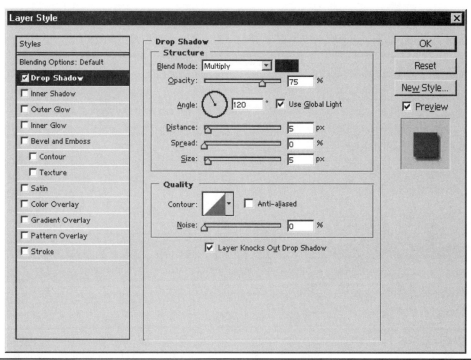

Figure 6-8 The Layer Style dialog box provides a way to customize each of the layer styles.

Add Adjustment and Fill Layers to Adjust Color on Single Layers Instead of Entire Images

When you want to experiment with the color of a specific layer or group of layers, as opposed to the entire image, you can use an adjustment or fill layer. The biggest benefit of using these special layers to make color changes is that adjustment and fill layers can easily be deleted or edited whenever you change your mind.

The key difference between adjustment and fill layers is that, by default, adjustment layers affect those beneath them, while fill layers do not. Also by default, both these types of layers have layer masks associated with them that specify which pixels the color changes affect.

There are three types of fill layers and 11 types of adjustment layers, as outlined in Tables 6-5 and 6-6.

▶ *CAUTION*

Adjustment and fill layers can't be edited in ImageReady, but they can be viewed in that program.

Fill Layer	Description
Solid Color	Fills the area with a solid color. The default color used is the one in the current foreground color swatch, but can be easily changed with the Color Picker.
Gradient	Fills the area with a color gradient. The default gradient used is the currently active one, but can be easily changed with the Gradient Editor.
Pattern	Fills the area with a saved pattern. The default pattern used is the currently active one, but can be easily changed in the pop-up window that is displayed.

Table 6-5   Types of Fill Layers in Photoshop

Adjustment Layer	Description
Levels	Changes the values of the highlights, shadows, and midtones using the Levels dialog box.
Curves	Changes the intensity values of pixels using a 0–255 scale, but keeps other values constant, using the Curves dialog box.
Color Balance	Changes the color balance between cyan and red, magenta and green, and yellow and blue within the shadows, midtones, and/or highlights using the Color Balance command.
Brightness/Contrast	Changes the values of the brightness and contrast using the Brightness/Contrast command.
Hue/Saturation	Changes the hue, saturation, and lightness of all colors, or reds, yellows, greens, cyans, blues, and magentas individually using the Hue/Saturation command.
Selective Color	Changes the characteristics of certain colors (reds, yellows, greens, cyans, blues, magentas, whites, neutrals, and blacks) individually with the Selective Color command.
Channel Mixer	Changes the characteristics of certain color channels (such as red, green, and blue in an RGB image) individually using the Channel Mixer dialog box.
Gradient Map	Changes the colors according to a saved gradient using the Gradient Map command.
Invert	Inverts the colors using the Invert command.
Threshold	Coverts the colors to high-contrast, black-and-white images using the Threshold command.
Posterize	Converts the colors into large, flat areas of color based on the number of tonal levels specified in the Posterize command. Note that the number of levels specified is applied to each channel in an image (i.e., four levels in an RGB image creates 12 colors: four for red, four for green, and four for blue.)

Table 6-6   Types of Adjustment Layers in Photoshop

To add an adjustment or fill layer to a file in Photoshop, first make sure the Layers palette is visible (choose Window I Layers) and do one of the following:

- Click the New Adjustment Layer button at the bottom of the Layers palette (as shown in the following illustration) and specify which type of layer to add (as described in Tables 6-5 and 6-6).
- Choose Layer I New Fill Layer or Layer I New Adjustment Layer and specify which type of layer to add (as described in Tables 6-5 and 6-6).

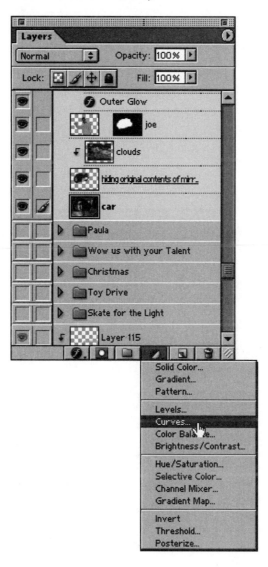

> ### QUICK TIP
>
> *By default, adjustment layers affect all layers below them in the Layers palette. If you need to restrict an adjustment layer to affect a certain group of layers, consider placing those layers in a layer set, as discussed in the earlier tip, "Group Related Layers into Sets." Another option is to use a clipping group, as discussed in the following tip, "Use Clipping Groups to Mask One Layer with the Contents of Another."*

After the new layer is added to the Layers palette, you'll notice that it has two thumbnails instead of one. The second thumbnail displays the contents of the layer mask. So to edit the adjustment or fill layer itself, double-click the first thumbnail. To edit which pixels on the layer are affected by the adjustment or fill layer, double-click the second thumbnail.

Figure 6-9 shows an example of a Curves adjustment layer that affects the layer below it called car. Because the adjustment layer is contained in a layer set, it only affects those layers that are below it in the set—in this case, it's just the layer called car.

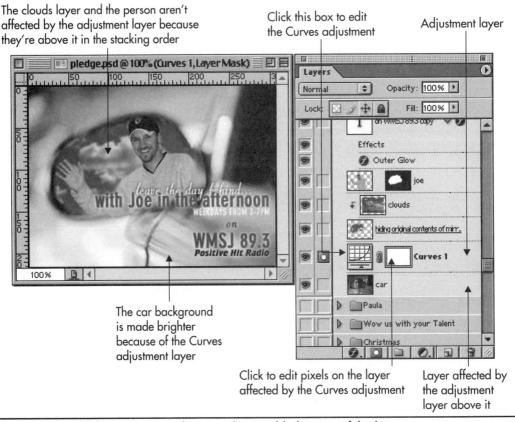

The clouds layer and the person aren't affected by the adjustment layer because they're above it in the stacking order

Click this box to edit the Curves adjustment

Adjustment layer

The car background is made brighter because of the Curves adjustment layer

Click to edit pixels on the layer affected by the Curves adjustment

Layer affected by the adjustment layer above it

Figure 6-9   This file has a Curves adjustment layer added to one of the layer sets.

Use Clipping Groups to Mask One Layer with the Contents of Another

After spending any amount of time working in Photoshop, you eventually wonder how to cover only a part of one image with another. The answer to that question brings me to one of my favorite aspects of Photoshop—clipping groups. Although the somewhat difficult-sounding name may turn some beginning users off, clipping groups are quite easy to create and use.

In a clipping group, the bottom layer is used as a mask for any layers above it in the group. Consider Figures 6-10 through 6-12. Figure 6-10 shows the background I used in a banner for a DJ at a local radio station. Because the DJ is on air during the afternoon "drive time," I wanted to show him in the side-view mirror of a car. I picked the image shown in Figure 6-10 as a starting point.

> **QUICK TIP**
>
> *You can recognize clipping groups in the Layers palette because the bottom layer's name is underlined, and the thumbnails of the other layers in the group are indented next to a small arrow pointing down.*

To conceal the existing image in the mirror, I added a new layer and painted with gray just over the part of the mirror I wanted to replace, as shown in Figure 6-11. Then, I brought in a picture of clouds and one of the DJ. To get those two images to display only in the area of the mirror— specifically in the area where I painted with gray— I used them in a clipping group with that painted gray layer. Figure 6-12 shows the final result.

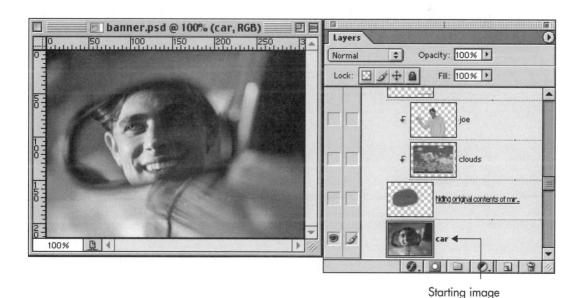

Starting image

Figure 6-10   To create a fun banner for the afternoon DJ at a local radio station, I start with this image of a car and side-view mirror.

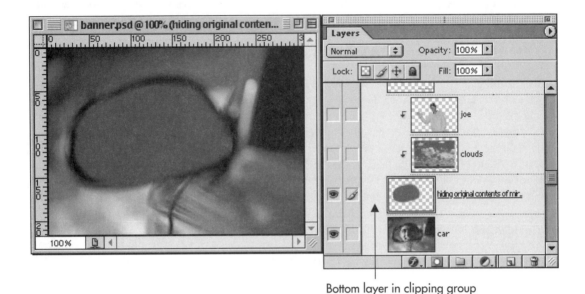

Bottom layer in clipping group

Figure 6-11   I add a new layer and cover the existing image in the mirror to prepare for adding in the DJ.

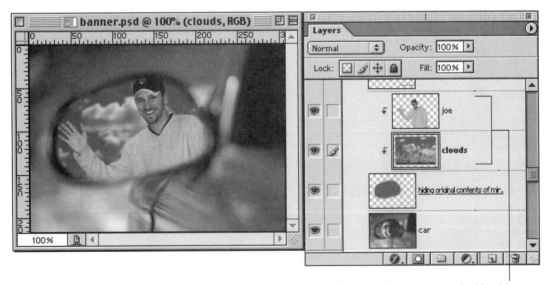

These two layers are masked by the bottom layer in this clipping group

Figure 6-12   After I use the DJ and clouds in a clipping group with the layer covering the previous image in the side-view mirror, the result is just what I was looking for.

TRY IT To create a clipping group, first make sure the Layers palette is visible by choosing Window I Layers. Then, position all the layers you want in your clipping group next to each other in the Layers palette; the layer that will mask all the other layers of the clipping group should be at the bottom of that group.

After the layers are in position, hold down the ALT (Windows) or OPTION (Mac) key and move the cursor over the line separating two of the layers in the Layers palette. When you see the cursor change to display two overlapping circles (as shown in the following illustration), click. Repeat this process until you've added all the necessary layers to your clipping group.

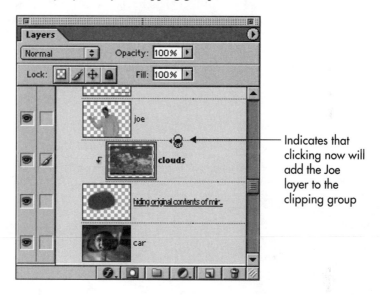

Indicates that clicking now will add the Joe layer to the clipping group

Alternatively, you can also create a clipping group by first linking the layers in question and then choosing Layer I Group Linked.

▶ | **QUICK TIP**

To remove a layer from a clipping group, ALT-*click or* OPTION-*click again in between the two layers. To remove all layers from a clipping group, choose Layer I Ungroup.*

Use Masks to Temporarily Hide Parts of Layers

Sometimes it's better to hide parts of layers instead of delete them. When this is the case, a layer mask is the perfect tool for the job because of the amount of flexibility it offers. For example, suppose you wanted to see what a photo of my Aunt Ginny looked like without Uncle Bernie standing next to her. You could add a layer mask to the layer and temporarily hide the part of the image containing Uncle Bernie.

When you use a layer mask to hide part of an image, you can use the painting tools to "paint away" the part you don't want. At any time, however, you can "erase" what you've painted, in which case the parts that were hidden reappear. Consider Figures 6-13 through 6-15. In this example, I wanted to put a photo of the evening DJ at a local radio station into a picture of the moon for a banner advertising his show. However, I wasn't sure exactly how much of his face I wanted in the moon, so instead of deleting the rest of him, I painted it away using a layer mask.

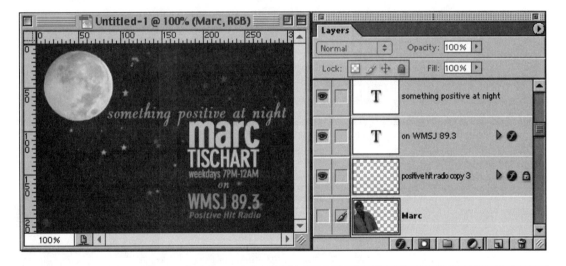

Figure 6-13   This is the banner before I added a photo of the evening DJ to the moon.

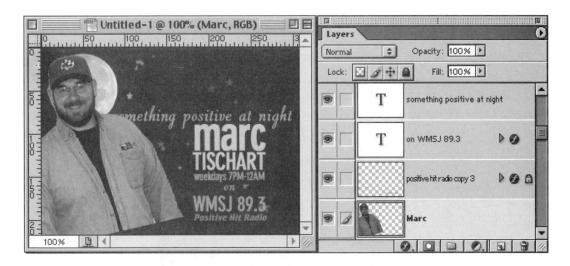

Figure 6-14   After bringing in the photo of the evening DJ, I sized and rotated it according to how I wanted it displayed in the moon.

The black of the layer mask indicates hidden parts, while the white shows which parts of the layer are displayed

Figure 6-15   To block out everything except a portion of the DJ's face, I added a layer mask and painted away the rest of his body to produce this final result.

TRY IT — To add a layer mask to hide part of a layer, first make sure the Layers palette is visible by choosing Window | Layers, and then click once on the layer to which you want to add a mask. Then, create the layer mask by doing one of the following:

- Click the Add Layer Mask button at the bottom of the Layers palette, and use the paint tools to hide aspects of the layer.

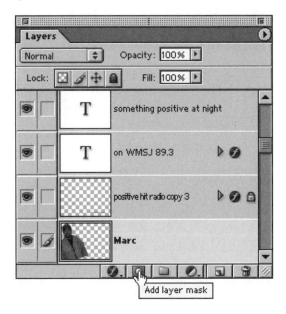

- Select the area you want to be visible (not hidden) and click the Add Layer Mask button at the bottom of the Layers palette to automatically create a mask that hides all of the areas outside of the current selection.

A layer mask is displayed as a second thumbnail on the layer in the Layers palette. To edit the actual pixels on the layer, click once inside the regular layer thumbnail. To edit the layer mask, click once inside the layer mask thumbnail. You can tell when the actual pixels on the layer are currently active because there is an outline around the regular layer thumbnail. Likewise, when the layer mask is active, its thumbnail is outlined.

Regardless of which way you go about creating the layer mask, you can always go back and edit it as necessary. When using the paint tools to edit a layer mask, understand that painting with white reveals areas of the layer, while painting with black hides them. In fact, notice that when the layer mask thumbnail is outlined—indicating it's currently active and editable—the only colors available to you are black and white.

▶ **QUICK TIP**

Right-click (Windows) or OPTION-*click (Mac) on a layer mask thumbnail to reveal additional options, such as the ability to discard or disable it.*

COLOR SWATCHES

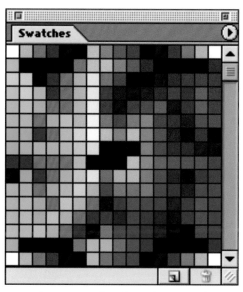

Visibone 2 Web-safe Color Swatches
(free download from www.visibone.com)

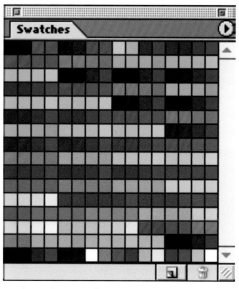

Photoshop Web Hues Color Swatches

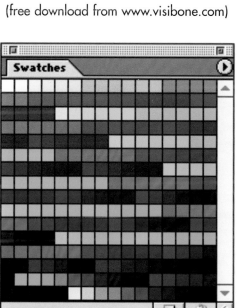

Photoshop Windows Color Swatches

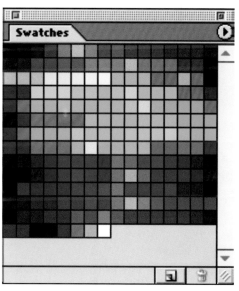

Photoshop Mac OS Color Swatches

LAYER BLENDING MODES

Background

Layer 1

Dissolve, 50% opacity

Darken

Multiply

Color Burn

Linear Burn

Lighten

Screen

Color Dodge

Linear Dodge

Overlay

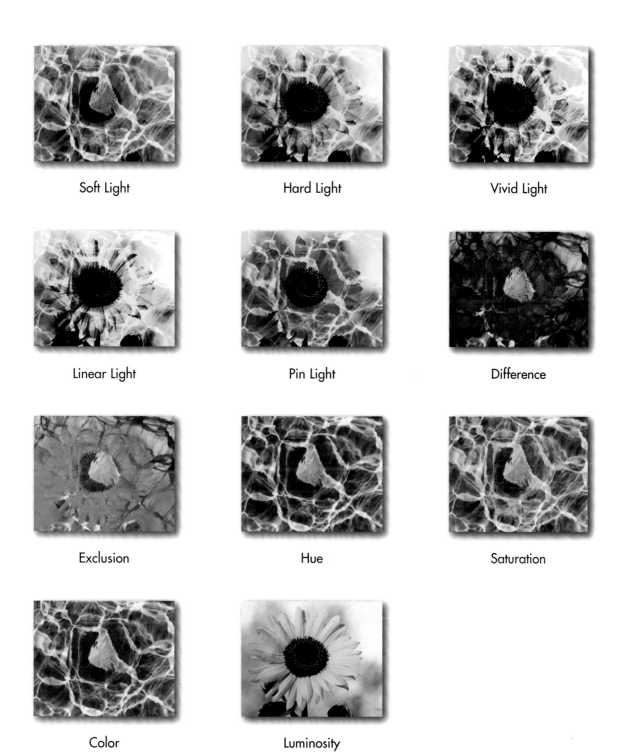

Soft Light

Hard Light

Vivid Light

Linear Light

Pin Light

Difference

Exclusion

Hue

Saturation

Color

Luminosity

TOOL BLENDING MODES

Normal, 100% opacity

Normal, 50% opacity

Dissolve

Behind

Clear (to white background)

Darken

Multiply

Color Burn

Linear Burn

Lighten

Screen

Color Dodge

Linear Dodge

Overlay

Soft Light

Hard Light

Vivid Light

Linear Light

Pin Light

Difference

Exclusion

Hue/Color

Saturation

Luminosity

LAYER STYLES

Paw print layer on solid background with no layer style attached

Paw print layer with Drop Shadow layer style attached (Distance: 12px; Size: 12px; all other settings at default values)

Paw print layer with Inner Shadow layer style attached (Distance: 12px; Size: 12px; all other settings at default values)

Paw print layer with Outer Glow layer style attached (Mode: Normal; Color: C-6% M-0% Y-96% K-0%; Size: 30px; all other settings at default values)

Paw print layer with Bevel and Emboss layer style attached (Style: Inner Bevel; Technique: Smooth; Direction: Up; Size: 25px; all other settings at default values)

Paw print layer with Bevel and Emboss layer style attached (Style: Pillow Emboss; Technique: Smooth; Direction: Up; Size: 25px; all other settings at default values)

Paw print layer with Satin layer style attached (Distance: 150px; Size: 100px; Contour: Ring-Double; all other settings at default values)

Paw print layer with Color Overlay layer style attached (all settings at default values)

Paw print layer with Inner Glow layer style (Size: 20px; all other settings at default values) and Drop Shadow layer style attached (Distance: 12px; Size: 12px; all other settings at default values)

Paw print layer with Gradient Overlay layer style attached (Gradient: Blue, Red, Yellow; all other settings at default values)

Paw print layer with Pattern Overlay layer style attached (Pattern: Ivy Leaves; all other settings at default values)

Paw print layer with Stroke layer style attached (Size: 10px; Color: dark blue; all other settings at default values)

CREATIVE EFFECTS

The original photo (left) showed a white house. A technique outlined in Chapter 9 was used to paint the house blue (well, at least in the photo). See "Change the Color of Someone's Shirt, Shoes, Bag, or Any Other Object in a Photo."

In the original photo (left) the faces appeared a bit ashen. A technique discussed in Chapter 9 was used to change that (right). See "Make the Color of Human Faces More Vivid."

The original black and white image (top) was painted with color to give the appearance that the people were "infused with color" upon stepping into the water (bottom). See "Add Color to Black and White Images" in Chapter 9.

The image above is a true duotone, created in Photoshop with two specified Pantone colors, to be used in a print spread with limited color output. By contrast, the image below is a fake duotone, using a technique discussed in Chapter 9, created purely for the sake of creativity. See "Create a Fake Duotone."

A normal grayscale image (a portion of which is shown above, left) can by turned into a bitmap image (above, right) using the technique discussed in Chapter 9. The image can then be colorized (below) and manipulated to produce some very creative effects. See "Use Bitmap Mode to Create Interesting Effects."

WEB COMPRESSIONS

The Color Table palette in ImageReady and the Color Table in the Save For Web dialog box in Photoshop display the colors in the palette of GIF and PNG-8 files. A dot inside a color indicates it is web-safe. A small white square in the bottom-right corner of a color swatch indicates it is locked and can't be removed from the palette. These three images show how different color tables are tied to the images they represent.

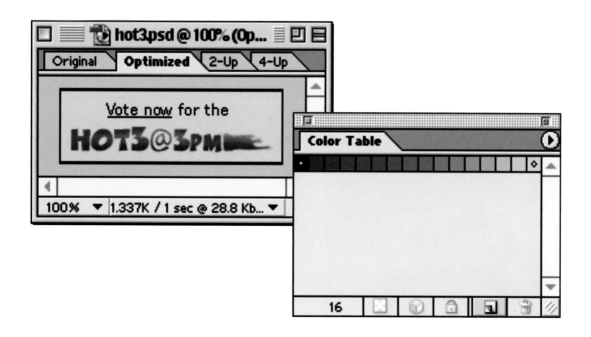
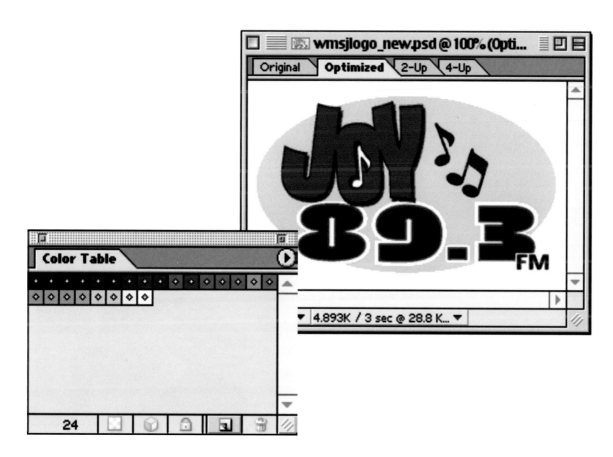

Photographic content containing text can sometimes be difficult to compress, because the text typically looks best when saved as a GIF and photographs always look best as JPEGs. The left image above shows the original file. To the right, I tried using the saved setting called GIF 32 Dithered, which compresses the file as a GIF with 32 colors and uses dithering. Below, I tried JPEG compression, first (left) using the Low setting (10% quality) and second (right) using the Medium setting (30% quality).

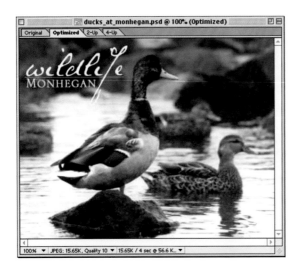 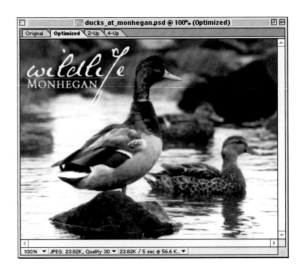

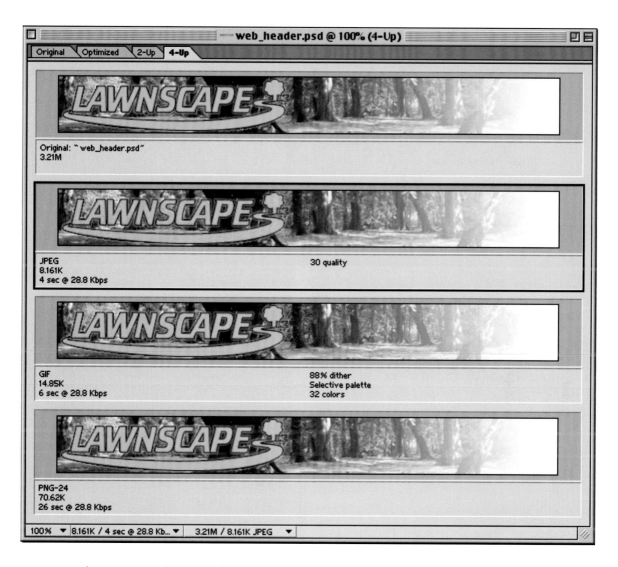

When trying to determine the best file format for the job, use the 4-Up tab in Photoshop's Save For Web dialog box and ImageReady's image window to compare up to four different compression settings. In this example, I was able to quickly determine that a low-quality JPEG (30% quality) was the best file format for this job.

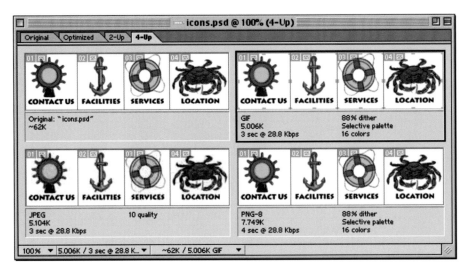

As done with the image on the previous page, I use the 4-Up tab in ImageReady's image window to compare three different compression settings next to the original image. In this example, I was able to quickly determine that the GIF format was best for these small navigational icons. Not only do the images look better as GIFs than as JPEGs, but the GIFs are also the smallest file size.

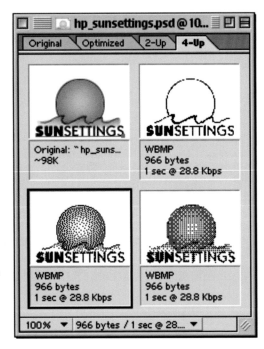

Devices like handheld computers aren't able to display the normal JPEG and GIF graphics of most web sites. Instead, to enable users of handheld devices to see your images, you use the two-color WBMP file format (example right). Clockwise from top left: Original; WBMP with No Dither; WBMP with Pattern Dither; WBMP with Diffusion Dither set to 88%.

CHAPTER 7

Using Text

TIPS IN THIS CHAPTER

Type in Photoshop has come a long way. While older versions of the application greatly restricted your use of typography in Photoshop, recent updates have changed it so that Photoshop can create crisp, resolution-independent type with relative ease. This chapter opens with a discussion of how to use the Type tools and their associated palettes for web and print design, followed by a wide variety of tips and techniques on the topic.

All about the Type Tools

One tool in particular—the Type tool—from the toolbox is used to access all the type aspects of Photoshop. Clicking and holding on the Type tool in the toolbox, as shown in the following illustration, reveals four variations:

- **Horizontal Type Tool**   Creates text along a horizontal axis
- **Vertical Type Tool**   Creates text along a vertical axis
- **Horizontal Type Mask Tool**   Creates a selection along a horizontal axis based on the outline of the text typed
- **Vertical Type Mask Tool**   Creates a selection along a vertical axis based on the outline of the text typed

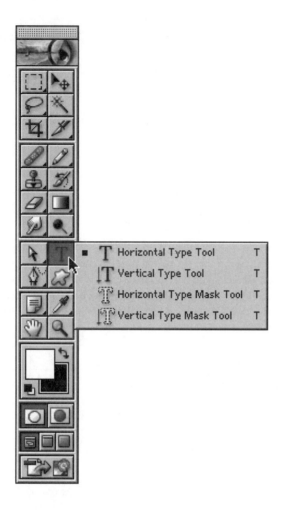

▶ *CAUTION*

When the Type tool is selected in the toolbox, many of the options in the top menus are unavailable. So if you need to create a new file, for example, you must first click off the Type tool by selecting a tool such as Move before choosing File | New.

The key difference between the two Type tools and the two Type Mask tools is this: the normal Type tools create new layers to house the text they create, while the Type Mask tools simply create selections (remember those dancing ants?) without creating layers. (The following illustration helps point out the difference visually.) Once you make a selection with a Type Mask tool, you can create a new layer, if needed, on which you can fill the selection.

Selection created with Horizontal Type Mask tool

Type created with Vertical Type tool

► **NOTE**

While you're using a Type Mask tool to make a text-based selection, the letters appear filled with a solid color. This is only to help you visualize the text; after you're finished, the letters switch from being filled in to being outlined by the dancing ants.

Clicking any of these tools in the toolbox reveals several items in the Options bar, where you can specify the direction of the text and its font family, face and size, alignment, and color. You can also add anti-aliasing to create soft edges, or warp the text along a curve. These options are pointed out in Figure 7-1.

In addition to these options, there are two palettes that provide access to important information about your text:

- Character palette
- Paragraph palette

QUICK TIP

Using Photoshop to create text that will be printed? Keep your text in vector format whenever possible and save the file as an EPS file, which will retain the vector data. If you rasterize it (or save it in a file format that rasterizes it), make sure your file resolution is at least 200 dpi, and use large point sizes (such as 48 pt and above).

The Character Palette

The Character palette (choose Window I Character) provides access to information specific to each individual letter or word. As you can see in the following illustration, some of this information duplicates that found in the Options bar for the Type tool (as shown previously in Figure 7-1). For example, you can change the font family, style, and size in both the Character palette and the Options bar for the Type tool.

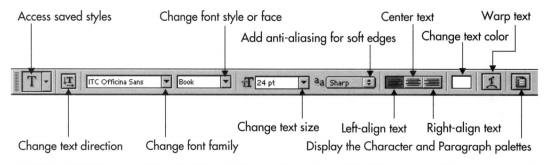

Figure 7-1   Options for the Type tools include font family, style, size, color, alignment, and direction.

Change font family —

Change kerning (space between two characters) —

Scale the text vertically —

Set a baseline shift for superscript or subscript text —

Set the language of the text (used for spelling and hyphenation) —

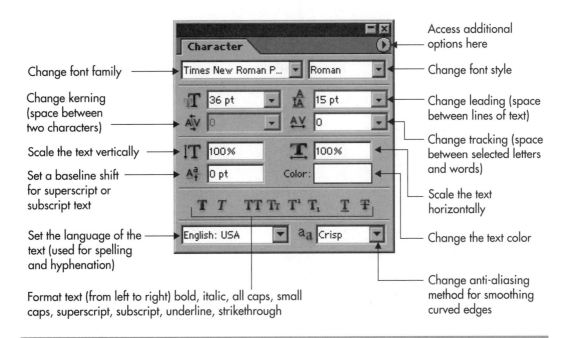

— Access additional options here

— Change font style

— Change leading (space between lines of text)

— Change tracking (space between selected letters and words)

— Scale the text horizontally

— Change the text color

— Change anti-aliasing method for smoothing curved edges

Format text (from left to right) bold, italic, all caps, small caps, superscript, subscript, underline, strikethrough

---

► ### QUICK TIP

You can also use key commands to adjust the tracking, kerning, and leading between a group of letter or words. See Table 7-1 for details.

The Paragraph Palette

The Paragraph palette provides access to formatting options specific to whole paragraphs of text. For example, you can use this palette to align paragraphs to the left, right, or center. You can also access justification and hyphenation options using the triangle in the upper-right corner of the palette.

Align right —
Align center —
Align left —

Indent entire left margin —
Indent first line only —

Add space above paragraph —

Automatically hyphenate words across lines —

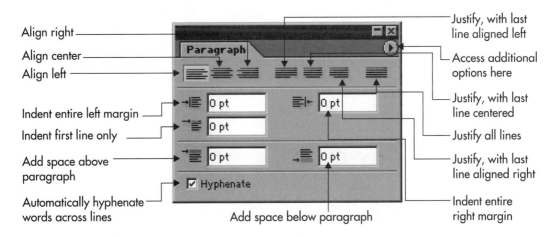

— Justify, with last line aligned left

— Access additional options here

— Justify, with last line centered

— Justify all lines

— Justify, with last line aligned right

— Indent entire right margin

Add space below paragraph

Text Adjustment		Keyboard Shortcuts	
Name	Description	To Increase	To Decrease
Kerning	Space between two individual letters	Put the cursor between the two letters to affect and press ALT-RIGHT ARROW (Windows) or OPTION-RIGHT ARROW (Mac).	Put the cursor between the two letters to affect and press ALT-LEFT ARROW (Windows) or OPTION-LEFT ARROW (Mac).
Tracking	Space between a group of letters or words	Highlight the text and press ALT-LEFT ARROW (Windows) or OPTION-LEFT ARROW (Mac).	Highlight the text and press ALT-RIGHT ARROW (Windows) or OPTION-RIGHT ARROW (Mac).
Leading	Space between lines of text	Select specific lines to affect and press ALT-DOWN ARROW (Windows) or OPTION-DOWN ARROW (Mac).	Select specific lines to affect and press ALT-UP ARROW (Windows) or OPTION-UP ARROW (Mac).
Baseline Shift	Shifts bottom of character(s) higher or lower than rest of text, such as Product™ or H_2O	Highlight the text and press SHIFT-ALT-UP ARROW (Windows) or OPTION-ALT-UP ARROW (Mac).	Highlight the text and press SHIFT-ALT-DOWN ARROW (Windows) or OPTION-ALT-DOWN ARROW (Mac).

Table 7-1 Keyboard Shortcuts for Common Typographic Tasks

Create a Single Line of Text along a Horizontal Axis

The most basic Type tool is the most commonly used. The Horizontal Type tool creates single lines of text along a horizontal axis. Each time you click inside your canvas with the Type tool, a new layer is created in the Layers palette to house the text you're about to create. The one exception to this is when you click on a location that already contains text. In this case, Photoshop activates the layer containing that text to enable you to edit it.

TRY IT To create a layer of text along a horizontal axis, click the Type tool in the toolbox to activate it. Then, click inside the boundaries of your canvas wherever you want to create text, and begin typing. You can customize the font details either in the Options bar or the Character palette (choose Window | Character).

QUICK TIP

By default, text is aligned along the left edge of wherever you clicked. So if you clicked in the center of the canvas because you wanted to create centered text, click the Center Text button in the Options bar. Likewise, click the Align Right button to align the text along the right edge of wherever you clicked.

When you are satisfied with your text, click the check mark at the right end of the Options bar to commit the text to its layer. Alternatively, you can click any other tool in the toolbox or on a layer in the Layers palette to commit the text to its layer. To cancel the text layer, click the X button at the right end of the Options bar or press CTRL-. (Windows) or CMD-. (Mac).

▶ *NOTE*

Text created like this is also called point type because it's treated as a single line of text only. To create multiple lines of text that can be edited as a whole, see the tip "Create and Modify Multiple Lines of Text" later in the chapter.

Create a Single Line of Text along a Vertical Axis

Text along a vertical axis can be displayed in two different ways.

By default, Photoshop creates vertical text with one letter on top of the next, as shown along the left edge of the previous illustration. Like the text created with the Horizontal Text tool, text created with the Vertical Text tool is automatically placed on its own layer in the Layers palette.

To create a layer of text along a vertical axis, click and hold on the Type tool in the toolbox to reveal a pop-up menu of additional tools. Select the second tool—the Vertical Type tool.

▶ | **QUICK TIP**

You can also rotate between the different Type tools by typing SHIFT-T *multiple times until the tool you wish to use is displayed in the Type tool spot in the toolbox.*

Then, click inside the boundaries of your canvas wherever you want to create text, and begin typing. You can customize the font details, including how the text is aligned on the canvas, either in the Options bar or the Character palette (choose Window | Character).

When you are satisfied with your text, click the check mark at the right end of the Options bar to commit the text to its layer. Alternatively, you can click any other tool in the toolbox or on a layer in the Layers palette to commit the text to its layer. To cancel the text layer, click the X button at the right end of the Options bar or press CTRL-. (Windows) or CMD-. (Mac).

▶ **NOTE**

Text created like this is also called point type because it's treated as a single line of text only. To create multiple lines of text that can be edited as a whole, see the tip "Create and Modify Multiple Lines Text" later in the chapter.

TRY IT To switch the display of the letter from being one on top of another to side by side, click the small triangle in the upper-right corner of the Character palette to reveal the palette menu. Uncheck the option Rotate Character to cause your text to display side by side.

Use the Type Mask Tool to Create Selections of Text

Suppose you want to remove a portion of a textured leaf background in the shape of the word "autumn," as shown in Figure 7-2. One way to accomplish this might be to first make a selection in the shape of "autumn" using the Type Mask tool.

Contrary to how the normal Type tool automatically creates a new layer on which to house its text, the Type Mask tool simply creates a selection—with dancing ants—around the outside of the text created. Like other selections made with the Marquee or Lasso tools, this selection is not saved in any palette until you choose Select | Save Selection to save it to the Channels palette.

While the text is being typed, Photoshop temporarily slips into Quick Mask mode. (Depending on your settings, you may notice your screen turn a bit pink or red because of this.) After you've completed the text, the program returns to Normal mode and displays the text with dotted outlines instead.

▶ **NOTE**

For more information on selections and Quick Mask mode, refer to Chapter 5.

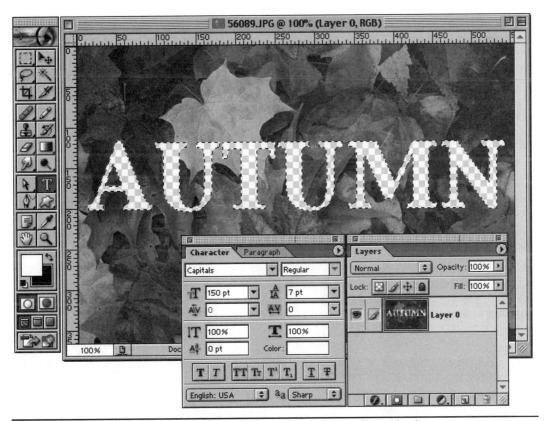

Figure 7-2   The Type Mask tool is useful for creating selections of text like this one.

TRY IT To create a selection of text, click and hold on the Type tool in the toolbox to reveal a pop-up menu of additional tools. Select the third or fourth tool—the Horizontal Type Mask tool or the Vertical Type Mask tool—depending on whether you want to create horizontal or vertical text selections.

> **QUICK TIP**
>
> *You can also rotate between the different type tools by pressing SHIFT-T multiple times until the tool you wish to use is displayed in the Type tool spot in the toolbox.*

Then, click inside the boundaries of your canvas wherever you want to create text and begin typing. You can customize the font details, including how the text is aligned on the canvas, either in the Options bar or the Character palette (choose Window | Character).

When you are satisfied with your text, click the check mark at the right end of the Options bar to turn it into a selection. Alternatively, you can click any other tool in the toolbox or on a layer in the Layers palette to turn it into a selection. To cancel the text layer, click the X button at the right end of the Options bar or press CTRL-. (Windows) or CMD-. (Mac).

► NOTE

Text created like this is also called point type because it's treated as a single line of text only. To create multiple lines of text that can be edited as a whole and turned into a selection, see the following tip, "Create and Modify Multiple Lines of Text."

TRY IT After your text has been turned into a selection—complete with dancing ants and all— you need to use the selection tools to edit or move it. To move the selection without affecting the image beneath it, use the Marquee tool. To move the contents of the layer within the selection, use the Move tool. For more tips on using the selection tools, refer to Chapter 5.

Create and Modify Multiple Lines of Text

Whenever you want to create multiple lines of text, such as paragraphs, that are modified together and restricted within a specific bounding box, you need to use the Type tools a bit differently than normal. For example, to create a single line of text in Photoshop, you click once with the Type tool anywhere within your canvas. But to create multiple lines of text, you must click and drag with the Text tool to define the boundaries of your text lines.

TRY IT To create multiple lines of text, click the Type tool in the toolbox. Then click and drag with the Text tool inside of your canvas to define the boundaries of your text lines. Alternatively, you can press the ALT (Windows) or OPTION (Mac) key while clicking inside the canvas window to display the Text Box Size dialog box. From this window, you can specify numeric pixel sizes for the height and width of your paragraph.

► **NOTE**

You can use any of the four variations of the tool to create paragraphs of text in this fashion. Refer to the previous three tips for descriptions of how to use these tools to create single lines of text.

After you release the mouse or enter height and width values into the Text Box Size dialog box, you'll notice a bounding box is visible around the outside edge, as shown in Figure 7-3. This box is similar to the bounding box that appears around selections after you choose Edit | Free Transform, because it also contains anchor points that can be dragged to transform the size and shape of the paragraph. Click and drag any of these anchor points to transform the box.

It was amazing... like fireworks going off in my head at the same moment our worlds collided. How was I supposed to respond? Only

A plus sign like this within the bottom right anchor indicates that there is more text that can't fit inside the bounding box

Figure 7-3   The shape of this bounding box can easily be edited to change the display of the text on the canvas.

TRY IT You can use the many options available to the Type tool to edit paragraphs of type. For example, to specify the alignment or justification options for the paragraph, or to add space above or below the paragraph, choose Window | Paragraph to display the Paragraph palette. To increase or decrease the space between the lines of text within the paragraph, choose Window | Character to display the Character palette, and then adjust the leading.

QUICK TIP

Already created several lines of text the hard way—by pressing the RETURN or ENTER key on your keyboard after each line? No problem. You can go back and convert point type into paragraph type by first activating the type layer in question, and then choosing Layer | Type | Convert To Paragraph Type. The next time you click within the text to edit it, you'll notice a bounding box appear around its edges that can be easily moved or transformed.

Add Anti-Aliasing to Smooth Edges

Anti-aliasing allows you to create smoothed edges, specifically on curved type, by adding partially colored pixels that appear to fade into the background. Photoshop includes five options for anti-aliasing:

- **None**   No anti-aliasing
- **Sharp**   Causes text edges to seem quite sharp
- **Crisp**   Causes text edges to seem moderately sharp
- **Strong**   Causes text to seem heavier or bolder, as opposed to sharper
- **Smooth**   Causes text edges to seem smoother, as opposed to sharper

In many cases, the differences between each of the last four types of anti-aliasing are almost unnoticeable when viewed at 100 percent. For examples of each, see Figure 7-4.

CAUTION

Anti-aliasing adds colors to your image, so if you're concerned about file size, consider choosing None to reduce the number of colors in your image. The trade-off is that any curved edges in your text will appear jagged and rough.

TRY IT To change the anti-aliasing method for text before it's created, click first on any Type tool in the toolbox. Then, click the Anti-aliasing drop-down menu in the Options bar or the Paragraph palette and select the desired method.

To change the anti-aliasing method for text that's already been created, use the Type tool to highlight the text before changing the method in the Options bar or the Paragraph palette.

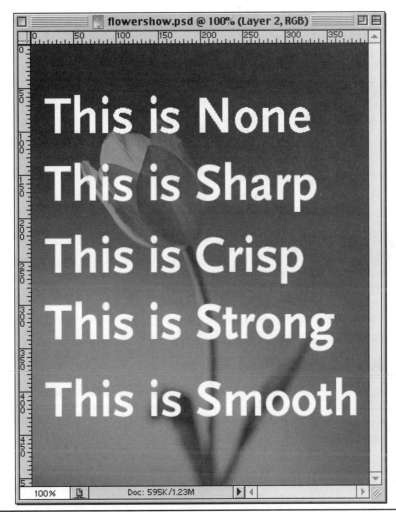

Figure 7-4 There are five variations of anti-aliasing, but only one—None—is truly different than the rest.

Change Text Color

What good is editable text if you can't change its color? With Photoshop, you don't even have to ask that question, because there are many ways to edit the color of text both before and after it's been created.

TRY IT To specify the color of text before creating it, click once on the foreground color swatch in the toolbox and select the color in which you want your text to be displayed. By default, Photoshop always creates text using the color in the foreground color swatch.

To change the color of selected text after it's been created, highlight the text in question with the Type tool and do one of the following:

- Click the color box in the Options bar to bring up the Color Picker, from which you can select a different color for your text.

- Choose Window | Character to make the character palette visible. Click the color box in the Character palette to bring up the Color Picker, from which you can select a different color for your text.

- Choose Layer | Layer Style | Color Overlay to add an overlay of color to the layer. You can further refine the color by specifying a blend mode and opacity level from within the Color Overlay options.

▶ **QUICK TIP**

Press ALT-BACKSPACE *(Windows) or* OPTION-DELETE *(Mac) to quickly fill an entire text layer with the color currently shown in the foreground color swatch. Use* CTRL-BACKSPACE *(Windows) or* CMD-DELETE *(Mac) to fill with the background color swatch instead.*

Spell-Check Photoshop Text

Long awaited by Photoshop fans is the ability to spell-check text right within Photoshop. You can use the Check Spelling command to have Photoshop compare the words used in your document to those in its internal dictionary. When a word in your document is not found in Photoshop's dictionary, the program prompts you to change or ignore the misspelling, or add it to the dictionary, as shown in Figure 7-5.

 Before you can spell-check your document, you need to make sure the correct language is specified in the Character palette, so Photoshop knows which dictionary to use. Choose Window | Character to display the Character palette, and select the appropriate language from the menu at the bottom. The default is English: USA.

To spell-check all the text in a document, choose Edit | Check Spelling. (To spell-check specific text, highlight the text with the Type tool before choosing Edit | Check Spelling.)

▶ **NOTE**

If there isn't any text selected, Photoshop automatically begins checking the text on all layers in your document when you choose Edit | Check Spelling. To force it to check only text on a single layer, you need to remove the check mark next to Check All Layers in the dialog box that appears when Photoshop finds a misspelling, as shown in Figure 7-5.

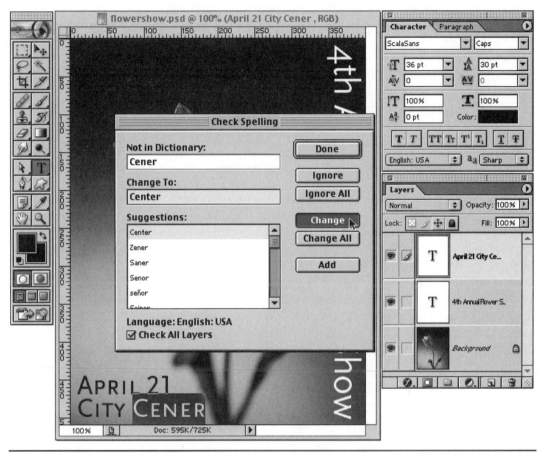

Figure 7-5   Photoshop's Check Spelling command identifies words that aren't found in its internal dictionary and prompts you to ignore, change, or add them.

When Photoshop finds a misspelled word, choose Ignore to leave the word unchanged. If the word appears more than once in your document and you want to leave it unchanged every time it appears, click Ignore All. To change a misspelled word, select the correct spelling from the list of options on the left or type a new spelling and click Change. If the word appears more than once in your document and you want to change every instance in which it is misspelled, click Change All.

> ▶ **QUICK TIP**
>
> *To prevent Photoshop from identifying a specific word as a misspelling in the future, you can choose Add to add it to Photoshop's dictionary.*

Control How Words Wrap Across Lines in Paragraphs

When you create paragraphs of text, the default is that the right edge of each paragraph is ragged, or not aligned, because one line of the paragraph may have more than another. However, if you choose to justify the lines of a paragraph, the program attempts to force those lines to align on both the left and right sides. To do this, some letters, words, or individual character glyphs may need to be expanded or compressed.

TRY IT   To specify which type of justification (if any) should be used for a paragraph, click once on the type layer within the Layers palette to make it active (choose Window | Layers to display this palette). Then, choose Window | Paragraph to display the Paragraph palette.

The last four of the seven button icons across the top of the palette deal with justification, and provide visual clues as to what each button does. For example, click the Justify Last Left button to force all the lines of the paragraph except the last one to align on both the left and right edges. With this setting, the last line is aligned left, but left ragged on the right side. Click one of these buttons to first specify how your paragraph should be justified.

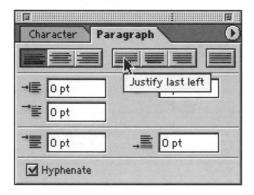

▶ *NOTE*

Sometimes, when Photoshop justifies text, it needs to hyphenate words to make them fit. To customize the hyphenation settings in Photoshop, see the next tip, "Control How Words Break Across Lines in Paragraphs."

Option	Range of Values	Value at Which No Change Occurs
Word Spacing (space between words)	0% to 1000%	100%
Letter Spacing (space between letters)	–100% to 500%	0%
Glyph Spacing (width of characters)	50% to 200%	100%

Table 7-2 Additional Justification Options

TRY IT To further customize exactly how Photoshop justifies your text, such as how much it can compress or expand words and letters, click the arrow in the upper-right corner of the Paragraph palette to reveal the palette menu. Then select Justification from the menu to adjust the options shown here, with the values listed in Table 7-2.

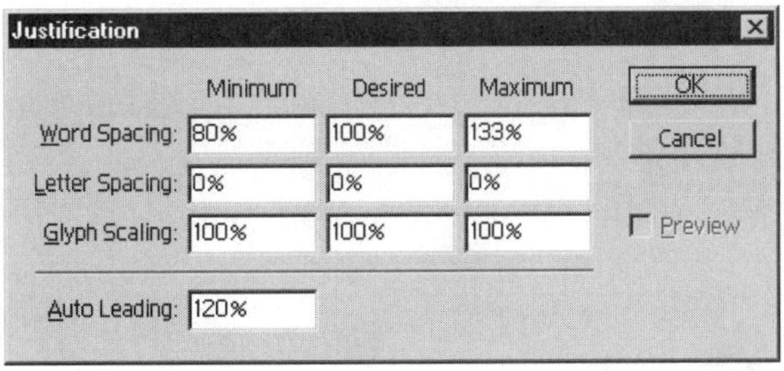

Control How Words Break Across Lines in Paragraphs

When justification is selected, Photoshop attempts to force the lines of the paragraph to align on both the left and right sides. During justification, the program might try to hyphenate words across those lines because, when hyphenation is allowed, words can be broken into parts that more easily fit onto each line.

You can specify whether or not to allow hyphenation as well as specific instances when hyphenation should or should not occur.

▶ NOTE

For proper handling of breaks within words, make sure the correct dictionary is selected in the Character palette (choose Window | Character).

TRY IT To turn hyphenation on or off for justified paragraphs in Photoshop, choose Window | Paragraph to display the Paragraph palette. Photoshop defaults to allowing hyphenation, as you can tell by the check mark in the box next to Hyphenate at the bottom of the Paragraph palette. To turn off the hyphenation feature, uncheck that box.

TRY IT To further customize specific instances when words should or shouldn't be hyphenated, click the triangle in the upper-right corner of the Paragraph palette to reveal the palette menu. Select Hyphenation to display a set of options similar to those shown in the following illustration.

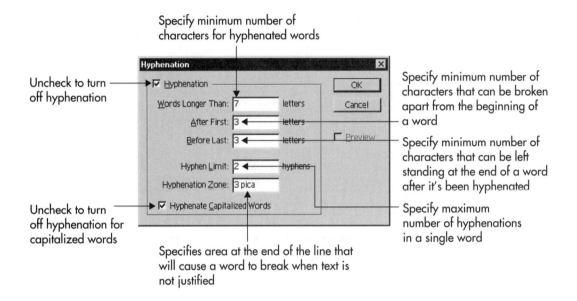

Specify minimum number of characters for hyphenated words

Uncheck to turn off hyphenation

Specify minimum number of characters that can be broken apart from the beginning of a word

Specify minimum number of characters that can be left standing at the end of a word after it's been hyphenated

Uncheck to turn off hyphenation for capitalized words

Specify maximum number of hyphenations in a single word

Specifies area at the end of the line that will cause a word to break when text is not justified

---

▶ **QUICK TIP**

Have a name or other word you don't want to be hyphenated? Highlight the text you don't want to break, click the triangle in the upper-right corner of the Paragraph palette, and choose No Break.

Use the Appropriate Composition Method for Paragraphs of Text

When you justify a paragraph of text as discussed in the previous two tips, you're telling Photoshop to force the majority of the lines within that paragraph to line up along both the left and right sides. Sometimes this means words must be broken apart and hyphenated, or extra space must be added between words to make all the lines "fit."

Ever wonder how Photoshop determines where to hyphenate or add space? When you make selections in the options for word spacing, letter spacing, glyph spacing, and hyphenation in Photoshop, the program takes that information and evaluates it to determine the best possible line breaks. This is called the *composition method,* and there are two possible composition methods in Photoshop:

- **The Every-line Composer**   Considers multiple lines at once and gives highest importance to keeping an evenness of letter and word spacing, and avoids hyphenation whenever possible
- **The Single-line Composer**   Considers one line at a time and compresses or expands word spacing before hyphenating, but does hyphenate to avoid altering letter spacing whenever possible

If you have a paragraph of text that isn't breaking as you'd like it to, try adjusting the composition method by switching between these two composers to find the best match for your situation.

TRY IT   To adjust the composition method for a section of text, first use the Type tool to highlight the text in question. Then choose Window | Paragraph to make sure the Paragraph palette is visible.

Click the triangle in the upper-right corner of the palette window to access the palette menu. Select Adobe Every-line Composer or Adobe Single-line Composer as needed. The currently selected option is identified with a check mark.

Find and Replace Words or Characters in Photoshop

Now that more people are using Photoshop to produce larger quantities of text, it's possible to encounter a situation where you need to replace a word that appears multiple times within a single file. Suppose, for example, you created an animation in Photoshop that contained 30 type layers. Each layer contained essentially the same text, but moved the text to a different location on the screen, so when the animation was played back, it appeared to jump all over the page. What if you needed to change one of the words that happened to be located on all 30 layers? Photoshop's Find And Replace Text command makes this task quick and painless.

TRY IT   To find and replace words or characters on a single layer in Photoshop, select the layer
that contains the text in question from within the Layers palette (choose Window | Layers).
Then choose Edit | Find And Replace Text. (If you're hoping to find and replace text across multiple
layers, simply choose Edit | Find And Replace Text.) In either case, you're presented with a dialog
box such as the following, where you can specify the text to find and, if necessary, the text with which
to replace it.

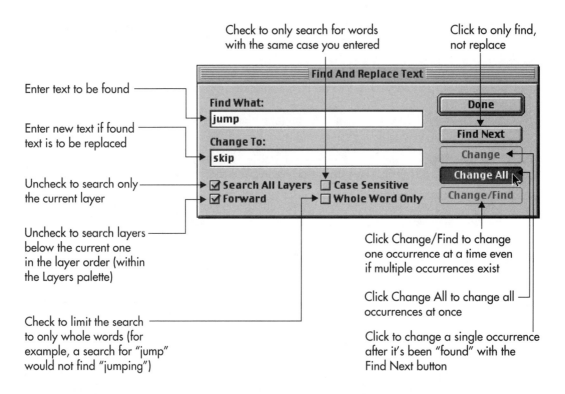

Check to only search for words
with the same case you entered

Click to only find,
not replace

Enter text to be found

Enter new text if found
text is to be replaced

Uncheck to search only
the current layer

Uncheck to search layers
below the current one
in the layer order (within
the Layers palette)

Check to limit the search
to only whole words (for
example, a search for "jump"
would not find "jumping")

Click Change/Find to change
one occurrence at a time even
if multiple occurrences exist

Click Change All to change all
occurrences at once

Click to change a single occurrence
after it's been "found" with the
Find Next button

Align Text on Multiple Layers

Suppose you're working on a design for which you created several layers of text, each with a single
word on it, that you needed to align down the center of the canvas, as shown in Figure 7-6. If you link
those layers together in Photoshop, you can easily align them with just a few clicks of the mouse.

TRY IT   To align two or more layers, first choose Window | Layers to make sure the Layers
palette is visible. Then click once on one of the layers to activate it in the Layers palette.
Click in the empty box next to each of the other layer names that you want to link to the active layer.
(When layers are linked to the currently active layer, a small chain icon appears in the previously
empty box next to the layer's name.)

Figure 7-6 After drawing a guide in the center of my canvas and specifying the appropriate alignment and snap options, I can easily align my text in the center of the image.

After your layers are linked, decide how to align them and choose Layer | Align Linked and the appropriate option. For details on how each particular alignment option works, see the tip titled "Align and Distribute Elements on Multiple Layers" in Chapter 6.

TRY IT If you want to align the layers with a specific spot or axis in the image canvas, draw a guide in that location. (To draw a guide, first press CTRL-R on Windows or CMD-R on Mac to display the rulers. Then, click and drag into the canvas from one of those rulers to create a guide.)

Choose View | Snap To | Guides and, with the Move tool, move the text from one of the layers toward the guide to which you want it aligned. Because the other layers are linked to the one you're moving, those will also move and align with the guide.

> ## QUICK TIP
>
> *Need to create a guide in the exact vertical or horizontal center of the canvas? Choose View | Snap To | Document Bounds. Then, click once on the Background layer in the Layers palette to activate it before drawing your guide, and you'll notice it "snaps" to the center of the canvas quite easily. This is because when drawing guides with Snap To Document Bounds selected, Photoshop also snaps to the center of the layer's contents.*

Use the Free Transform Command to Scale, Skew, Rotate, Distort, or Change the Perspective of Text

A great benefit of text in Photoshop now is that you can scale, skew, rotate, distort, or change the perspective of text without compromising your ability to edit it as necessary. This means you can rotate a phrase to display diagonally across the screen—as I did with the text "To my love" in Figure 7-7—

Figure 7-7   I used the Free Transform command to rotate this text along the edge of the box of candy.

and two weeks later come back and change a word in the phrase without having to retype the text or reapply the rotation.

The easiest way to apply all five of these types of transformations on text in Photoshop is to use the Free Transform command. However, you can also perform each of these transformations independently—as well as several others—from the Transform command menu (Edit | Transform).

▶ | ## QUICK TIP

To constrain the proportions of the original text, hold down the SHIFT *key while making any transformations.*

TRY IT   To scale, skew, and/or rotate text from a single command, choose Window | Layers to make sure the Layers palette is visible on the screen. Click once on the type layer you want to transform and press CTRL-T (Windows) or CMD-T (Mac) to quickly access the Free Transform command (which is also accessible by choosing Edit | Free Transform).

Click and drag the anchor points on the bounding box that appears around your text to transform it. In some cases, you need to hold down keys on the keyboard while dragging to perform different types of transformations:

- To rotate the text, move the cursor just outside one of the corners of the box until you see the cursor change to a curved, two-sided arrow, then click and drag.

- To shrink or expand the text, click and drag an anchor point halfway down a side of the bounding box.

- To skew the text, press CTRL-SHIFT (Windows) or CMD-SHIFT (Mac) while dragging a side anchor point.

- To distort the text freely, press CTRL (Windows) or CMD (Mac) while dragging an anchor point; to distort in relation to the center point on an edge of the bounding box, press ALT (Windows) or OPTION (Mac) instead.

- To adjust the perspective of the text, press CTRL-ALT-SHIFT (Windows) or CMD-OPTION-SHIFT (Mac) while dragging a corner anchor point.

At any point, you can type CTRL-Z (Windows) or CMD-Z (Mac) to undo the last transformation performed. When you're satisfied with your transformation, press RETURN or ENTER on the keyboard to commit the changes. Press CTRL-. (Windows) or CMD-. (Mac) to cancel the operation.

▶ | ## QUICK TIP

Right-click (Windows) or CTRL-CLICK *(Mac) within the bounding box to specify the exact type of transformation you want to use.*

Use the Warp Text Command for Curved Lines of Text

When simple rotations or distortions aren't enough, the Warp Text command can be used to distort type into shapes such as arcs—like the one in Figure 7-8 along the edge of the watermelon rind. In fact, the Warp Text command includes 15 shapes for warping text, as shown in the following illustration.

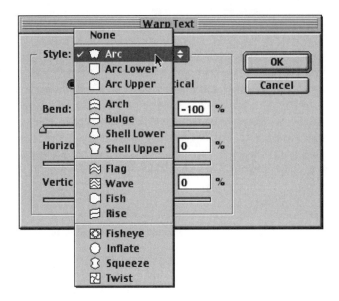

As with transformations performed by the Free Transform command (as discussed in the previous tip), warped type remains editable in Photoshop. Furthermore, you can change the shape of the warp itself at any time.

TRY IT   To warp text in Photoshop, first use the Type tool to create a new type layer containing the text you want to warp. Make sure the Layers palette is visible by choosing Windows | Layers, and click once on the type layer in question to activate it. Then click the Warp Text button in the Options bar.

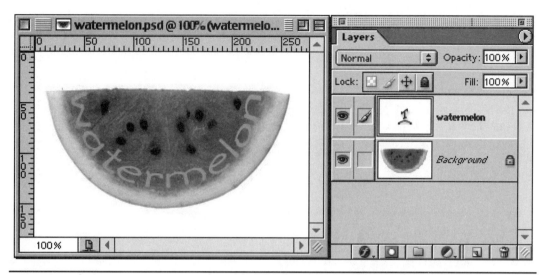

Figure 7-8   The Warp Text command enabled me to easily arc this text along the upper edge of the watermelon rind.

or choose Layer | Type | Warp Text to display the Warp Text dialog box.

Select the warp style

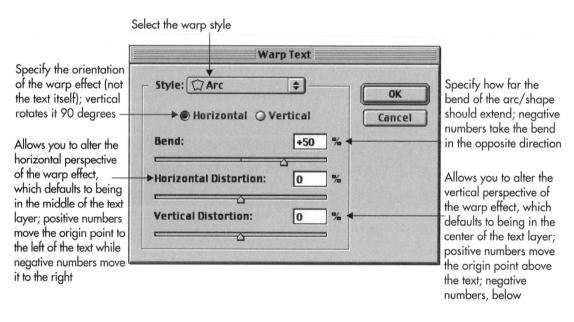

Specify the orientation of the warp effect (not the text itself); vertical rotates it 90 degrees

Allows you to alter the horizontal perspective of the warp effect, which defaults to being in the middle of the text layer; positive numbers move the origin point to the left of the text while negative numbers move it to the right

Specify how far the bend of the arc/shape should extend; negative numbers take the bend in the opposite direction

Allows you to alter the vertical perspective of the warp effect, which defaults to being in the center of the text layer; positive numbers move the origin point above the text; negative numbers, below

▶ *NOTE*

You can't apply the Warp Type command to text with Faux Bold formatting. In addition, you can't warp any bitmap type that doesn't contain outlines.

The best effects are often those that result from trying several of these numbers and options before clicking the OK button. Because Photoshop shows you the results of the warp as you're setting the options, it can be quite fun to get in there and really play around with the Warp Text command. In addition, don't forget you can always use the Free Transform command (as discussed in the preceding tip) to apply additional transformations to the text after warping it.

Apply Gradients to Text

If you try to use the Gradient tool on a type layer in Photoshop, you'll receive an alert that warns, "Could not use the gradient tool because the pixels in a type layer cannot be edited without first rasterizing the layer." While you could rasterize your type layer to use the Gradient tool and apply a gradient to it, that would cause your type to no longer be editable.

Instead, you can apply the Gradient Overlay layer style on your type layer. Figure 7-9 shows an example, and the following tip provides the details.

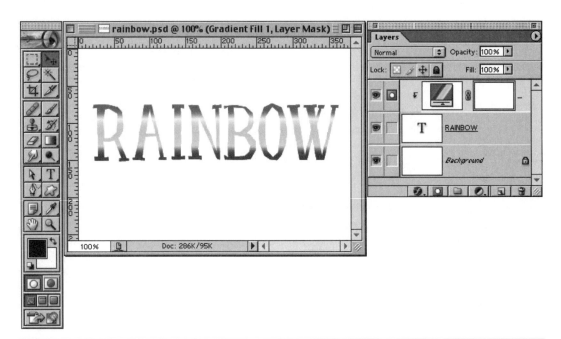

Figure 7-9   To easily fill the word "rainbow" with a rainbow gradient, I used the Gradient Overlay layer style.

TRY IT　To apply a gradient to text, first use the Type tool to create a new text layer in Photoshop. Choose Window | Layers to make sure the Layers palette is visible, and click once on the text layer in question to make it active. Then click the first button at the bottom of the Layers palette and select Gradient Overlay, or choose Layer | Layer Style | Gradient Overlay to reveal the following options.

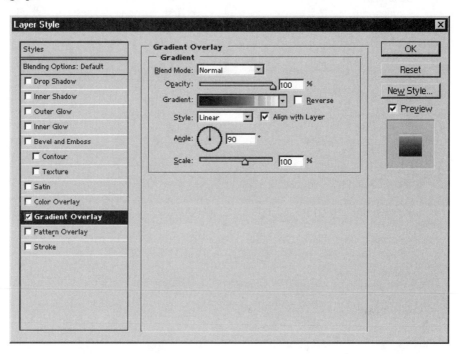

Use this window to select the type of gradient you want to apply, as well as its style (linear, radial, and so forth), angle, blend mode, opacity, and scale. When finished, click the OK button.

To edit the style after it's been applied to the layer, double-click the *f* button.

► ### QUICK TIP

Not satisfied with the list of predefined gradients in the Gradient menu? Click the triangle in the upper-right corner of that pop-up menu and choose New Gradient to design your own, or load additional sets of gradients from the list at the bottom of the menu.

Fill Text with Patterns

Normally, you can fill layers in Photoshop with patterns or textures by choosing Edit | Fill and selecting Pattern from the Use menu. However, if you try to choose Edit | Fill when a type layer is currently active in the Layers palette, you'll notice that option is grayed out and not available.

Instead, you can apply the Pattern Overlay layer style on your type layer. Figure 7-10 shows an example, and the following tip provides the details.

TRY IT   To apply a pattern to text, first use the Type tool to create a new text layer in Photoshop. Choose Window | Layers to make sure the Layers palette is visible, and click once on the text layer in question to make it active. Then, click the first button at the bottom of the Layers palette and select Pattern Overlay, or choose Layer | Layer Style | Pattern Overlay to reveal the following options.

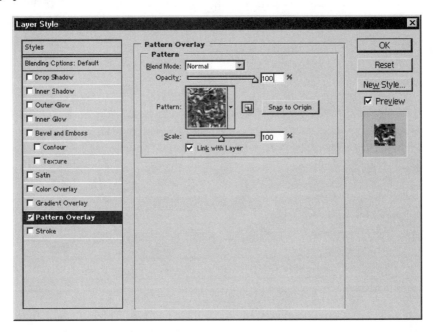

Use this window to select the type of pattern you want to apply, as well as its blend mode, opacity, and scale. When finished, click the OK button.

To edit the style after it's been applied to the layer, double-click the *f* button.

► **QUICK TIP**

Not satisfied with the list of predefined patterns in the Pattern menu? Click the triangle in the upper-right corner of that pop-up menu and choose New Pattern to design your own, or load additional sets of patterns from the list at the bottom of the menu. (See the tip entitled "Create Custom Patterns" in Chapter 8 for details on how to create your own.)

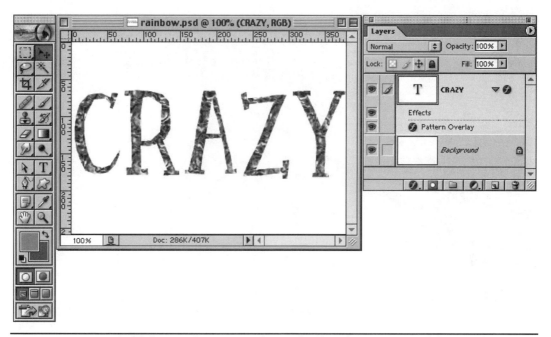

Figure 7-10   To easily fill the word "crazy" with a multicolored pattern, I used the Pattern Overlay layer style.

Fill Text with Photos or Other Images

A great way to enhance otherwise flat and boring typography is to fill it with photos or other continuous tone imagery. This can easily be accomplished in Photoshop using clipping groups—a process in which one layer masks the contents of another. In this case, the type layer acts as a mask to only allow the contents of a photograph to show through within the boundaries of the text.

▶ **NOTE**

Clipping groups are discussed in more detail in Chapter 6.

TRY IT ▶   To fill a type layer with a photo, first choose Window I Layers to make sure the Layers palette is visible, and that it includes both a layer with text on it and another layer with a photograph.

Then, position the layer with the photo directly above the type layer in the Layers palette. Hold down the ALT (Windows) or OPTION (Mac) key and click the line in between the two layers in the Layers palette to combine them into a clipping group. After doing so, the type layer becomes underlined in the Layers palette and filled with the contents of the layer above (see Figure 7-11 for an example).

Figure 7-11   To add a bit of texture to the words "Fall Frolic" in this image, I filled them with
a photo of leaves.

Add Layer Styles to Create Easy Drop Shadows and Other Special Effects

Layer styles are special because they aren't stand-alone layers. Instead, they are special effects added
to the contents of a particular layer. While older versions of Photoshop required you to go through
sometimes painstaking processing to add effects like drop shadows to text, recent versions have
included layer styles, which in effect do all the work for you.

> ### QUICK TIP
>
> *For full color examples of these layer styles, see the Layer Styles section of the color insert.*

Of course, multiple styles can be used together to further enhance the text. For example, adding a drop shadow to a text layer that already has a bevel and emboss effect gives you a three-dimensional look.

Once a style is added to and customized for one type layer, it can be copied and pasted onto other type layers with little hassle. Layer styles can also be disabled and re-enabled independently of their parent layer.

TRY IT To add a layer style to a layer of text, first use the Type tool to create some text. Make sure the Layers palette is visible in Photoshop (choose Window | Layers) and that you have your type layer selected in that palette.

You can add a layer style by either choosing Layer | Layer Style from the top menu or clicking the Add Layer Style button at the bottom of the Layers palette. After doing so, choose which layer style to add from the menu, and customize that effect in the Layer Style window, as discussed in Table 7-3. (The Color Overlay, Gradient Overlay, and Pattern Overlay layer styles were discussed previously and aren't included in Table 7-3.)

▶ **QUICK TIP**

If you first link a group of layers together (by clicking in the second box on each layer), you can paste a layer style onto all the linked layers in just two steps—right-click (Windows) or CTRL-*click (Mac) and choose Copy Layer Style | Paste Layer Style To Linked.*

Layer Style/Text Effect	Notes
Drop Shadow: Text appears to float on the page Inner Shadow: Text appears recessed into the page	-Adjust Blend Mode to change how the shadow reacts to pixels below it -Adjust Opacity of the shadow -Select Use Global Light to keep the direction of the light source constant throughout the entire image -Adjust Angle to change the direction of the light source -Adjust Distance to change how recessed the text appears -Adjust Choke (Inner Shadow) and Spread (Drop Shadow) to shrink the edges of the inner shadow or enlarge a drop shadow -Adjust Size to change the width of the shadow -Adjust Contour to alter the way the shadow fades -Select Anti-aliased to soften rounded edges -Adjust Noise to dither the shadow

Table 7-3   Layer Styles and Associated Options when Added to Type Layers

Layer Style/Text Effect	Notes
Outer Glow: Text appears backlit or glowing Inner Glow: Text appears to glow from inside its borders	-Adjust Blend Mode to change how the glow reacts to pixels below it -Adjust Opacity of the shadow -Adjust Noise to dither the glow -Adjust Color of glow -Adjust Gradient to add additional colors to the glow -Select Technique for softer, slightly blurred glows, or precise, tighter glows -Select Source (Inner Glow): Where the glow emanates from -Adjust Choke (Inner Glow) and Spread (Outer Glow) to shrink the edges of the inner glow or enlarge the edges of an outer glow -Adjust Size to change the width of the glow -Adjust Contour to alter the way the glow fades -Select Anti-aliased to soften rounded edges -Adjust Range to affect how the contour sits on the overall scheme of the glow; lower it to expand, raise it to shrink -Adjust Jitter to add random colored pixels to glows that already have multiple colors
Bevel and Emboss: Text can appear embossed into or above the page, depending on how the highlights and shadows are combined	-Specify the Style: Outer Bevel (affects only the areas *around* the text), Inner Bevel (affects only the areas *within* the text), Emboss (adds both an Outer and Inner Bevel), Pillow Emboss (adds an Inner Bevel but switches the colors in the Outer Bevel), Stroke Emboss (adds a bevel inside an outline created with the Stroke effect) -Specify the Technique: Smooth creates a blurred bevel, Chisel Hard creates a hard-edged bevel, and Chisel Soft is somewhere in between those two -Adjust Depth to increase the contrast -Specify Direction (up or down) to determine whether text looks recessed or truly embossed -Adjust Size of the bevel -Adjust softness of any blur in the beveled edges -Select Use Global Light to keep the direction of the light source constant throughout the entire image -Adjust Angle to change the direction of the light source -Adjust Altitude of light along a semicircle in the sky; 90 degrees is directly overhead -Select Contour to add texture in the beveled edge -Select to add texture to the text itself -Specify the Blend Modes, Color, and Opacity of the highlight and shadow

Table 7-3 Layer Styles and Associated Options when Added to Type Layers *(continued)*

Layer Style/Text Effect	Notes
Satin: Text appears shiny through the use of subtle contoured color variations	-Adjust Blend Mode to change how the overlay reacts to pixels below it -Adjust Opacity of the overlay -Adjust Angle of the contoured fill -Adjust Distance between the intersection of two contours -Adjust Size of total effect -Select Anti-aliased to soften rounded edges -Select Invert to achieve the opposite effect as normal
Stroke: Text is outlined	-Adjust Size of stroke to change its width -Adjust Location of stroke to move it in relationship to the text itself -Adjust Blend Mode to change how the stroke reacts to pixels below it -Adjust Opacity of the stroke -Specify and assign the Fill Type: Color, gradient, or pattern

Table 7-3   Layer Styles and Associated Options when Added to Type Layers *(continued)*

► | **QUICK TIP**

If you customize a layer style, you can save it to use for other layers. To do so, click the New Style button in the Layer Style dialog box. Then, specify whether to include both the Layer Effects and Blending Options in the style, and give your style a name. Saved styles are stored in the Styles palette (Window | Styles). For more tips on using the preset styles found in that palette, see Chapter 9.

Simulate HTML Text in Web Mockups

Perhaps the most common use of Photoshop text currently is in web development, because for web designers, Photoshop is often both the design and page layout program.

Text created in web design mockups typically falls into one of two categories—text to be made into a web graphic or text that will ultimately be rendered by the browser as HTML text. It is the latter category that this tip applies to, because the former (text to be made into a web graphic) isn't affected by HTML.

In particular, many web designers create detailed design mockups that are presented to the client for sign-off before the code development process begins. Because of the nature of HTML text and how it is rendered differently by various browsers and operating systems, there are certain things you can do in Photoshop to more accurately simulate it. The more accurate your mockup is, the happier the client will be when the final product looks just as they expected it to.

TRY IT To accurately simulate HTML text in Photoshop, open a web design mockup and activate one of the type layers containing text that will ultimately be rendered by the browser. Then, check to make sure you have addressed each of the following issues:

- Turn off anti-aliasing, because text rendered by the browser is never anti-aliased (in other words, it always has hard edges). Select the type in question with the Type tool and choose None from the Anti-Aliasing Method drop-down menu in the Options bar or the Character palette.

- Mac designers: Set the font size between 1 and 2 pts larger, because Windows text typically displays larger than that on a Mac. In other words, if you plan to use 10 pt text in HTML, set the font size to 12 pt in your mockup to accurately show how the text will likely display on a Windows machine.

- Windows designers: Avoid font sizes below 9 pt, because text on a Mac typically displays smaller than that on a PC and can become unreadable.

- Use the appropriate text, link, and visited link colors.

- Use single-spaced text, because paragraphs displayed in HTML are single-spaced by default. In other words, if your font size is 12 pt, use the default leading of 14 pt. Likewise, if your font size is 10 pt, set the leading to 12 pt.

- Avoid using Photoshop's built-in underline feature when simulating HTML text links under 10 pts in size. It creates an underline that touches the bottom of the text, even though HTML link underlines never touch the bottom of the text. If you need to add an accurate underline to small text, you can use the Pencil tool with a single-pixel brush to draw one in on a new layer. (Sorry!) Or, you can use the inaccurate underline and alert the client that it will display accurately when the text is ultimately rendered by the browser.

- Avoid using special formatting techniques, such as adjusting the leading, kerning, or tracking in the Character palette, when simulating HTML text because these aren't available in traditional HTML. If you do choose to use these formatting techniques by employing Cascading Style Sheets on your site, be sure to let your client know they won't be visible to viewers of older browsers.

▶ | **QUICK TIP**

If you don't have a web design mockup with which to test this technique, open a new file and create a type layer with several sentences of text that might be found on a web page. Highlight a word that might be linked to another page and click the Underline button in the Character palette to underline it.

Rasterize Type Layers to Apply Photoshop Filters

Photoshop has a large assortment of special-effects filters that can add a great amount of pizzazz to text layers, as well as any other layers in your image. However, due to the nature of most filters, they can't be applied to layers with vector-based data, including type layers. Therefore, before you can apply a filter to text in Photoshop, you must change it from vector-based to bitmap-based—a process called *rasterization*.

▶ *CAUTION*

The drawback of rasterizing your type layer is that once you do it, the text on that layer is no longer editable. This means if you later determine that the text should be spelled differently, you'll have to re-create it and reapply the filter.

 There are several ways to rasterize type layers in Photoshop:

- Right-click (Windows) or CTRL-click (Mac) the type layer and choose Rasterize Layer.
- Click once on the type layer in the Layers palette and choose Layer | Rasterize | Type.
- Click once on the type layer in the Layers palette and choose a filter from the Filter menu. Doing so prompts Photoshop to alert you that the type must be rasterized before the filter can be applied. Click OK to rasterize.

Save Type Settings for Customized "Style Sheets"

Suppose you were working on a series of mockups depicting several pages within a web site, or a series of ads for a single campaign. In either case, you likely have certain styles that will be applied to a variety of text across several files. For example, all the buttons on one client's web site might have the following characteristics:

- **Font**   Tahoma bold
- **Size**   14 pt
- **Color**   Red (#FF0000)
- **Anti-Aliasing**   Strong
- **Layer style**   Drop Shadow

After saving these characteristics as part of a preset type style, you can create new text layers or selections with those same characteristics quickly and easily.

TRY IT —— Before you can save a customized "style sheet," click the Type tool in the toolbox and
adjust all the type options according to the style you have in mind. Then, click the first
button in the Type option bar to reveal the Tool Preset picker. Once the picker is displayed, do one
of the following to save the current type settings:

- Click the Create New Tool Preset button along the right edge of the picker, as shown in
  Figure 7-12.
- Choose New Tool Preset from the picker menu, accessible by clicking the triangle in the
  upper-right corner of the picker.

In either case, you are prompted to give the preset (style sheet) a name and click OK. After doing
so, you'll notice the name is listed in the picker.

TRY IT —— To access the style sheet at a later time, simply click the Tool Preset picker button in the
Options bar again and select the name of the style sheet from the available list. Then create
your new text, which will take on the characteristics of the previously saved style sheet.

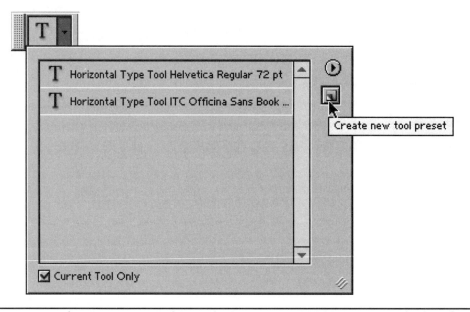

Figure 7-12   Use the Create New Tool Preset button to save type settings as a style sheet for
future use.

Create Text along a Path

Often, text that follows an irregularly shaped path can be a great attention-getter in all types of designs. However, it is not easily achieved in Photoshop, because the program doesn't ship with a command or tool making it possible to create text along a path. So why am I including a tip titled "Create Text along a Path" in a Photoshop book if it's not possible? The answer is that it is possible—see the following illustration—if you're willing to do a little extra work and perhaps shell out some extra cash, if you need to buy a program like Adobe Illustrator.

There are two common techniques used to create text along a path in Photoshop:

- Create the text along a path in a vector-based program such as Adobe Illustrator, save it as either an AI or EPS file, and bring it into Photoshop.
- Use a plug-in tool called PhotoGraphics, which is made available by Extensis.

There are pros and cons to each technique, but the quickest and easiest way to add text along a path is to use the PhotoGraphics plug-in, because it works right within Photoshop and there's no need to launch an additional program like Adobe Illustrator.

▶ *NOTE*

Extensis has unfortunately discontinued PhotoGraphics,. However, you can still download it from www.download.com. (Search for PhotoGraphics to appropriate plug-in for your operating system.)

TRY IT   To create text along a path using Extensis PhotoGraphics, first make sure the tool is loaded and available from within Photoshop. Before launching PhotoGraphics, choose Window | Layers and click on the layer you want to see when working in PhotoGraphics. Then, launch the tool by choosing Filter | Extensis | PhotoGraphics from the top menu in Photoshop to reveal a set of windows similar to those shown in Figure 7-13.

Use the Pen tool to draw a path however you want it to appear. Because the tool is similar to the Pen tool in Photoshop, you use it in basically the same way. Click the Options tab in the floating palette to reveal options for the Pen tool.

After you're finished drawing the path along which you want the type to run, click the Type tool, click the path wherever you want the type to begin, and start typing. Use the Text palette and other aspects of PhotoGraphics to adjust the text as needed.

▶ **QUICK TIP**

To adjust where the type begins on the path, after it's been created, use the Move tool and click just under the first letter. Drag it to wherever you want it to begin on the path.

When you're satisfied with the way the text along a path looks, click the Apply button to apply the text on the currently active layer in Photoshop, or click the Apply To New Layer button to save it to a new layer in Photoshop.

▶ *NOTE*

While the text itself will not be editable in Photoshop, you can return to PhotoGraphics and re-edit the text or curve as needed.

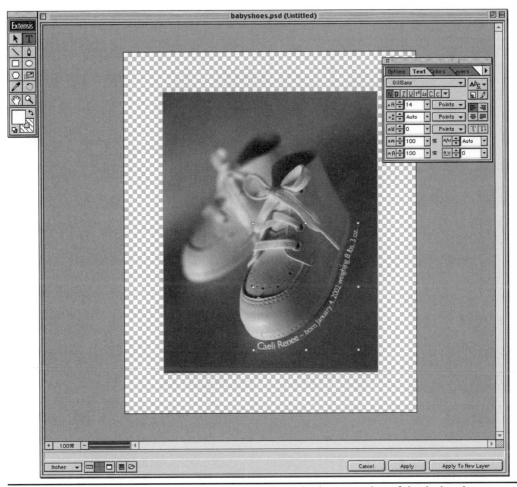

Figure 7-13   I used PhotoGraphics to add type along the bottom edge of this baby shoe
in Photoshop.

CHAPTER 8

Drawing and Painting

TIPS IN THIS CHAPTER

Drawing and painting in Photoshop not only are fun, but also are quite easy to do with Photoshop's wide variety of tools. The first part of this chapter identifies each of the painting and image editing tools in Photoshop, as well as the tools used to draw shapes. From there, the discussion moves on to the palettes involved, specifically the new Brushes and Tool Presets palettes, before listing many techniques and tips for using these tools and palettes.

▶ **NOTE**

As I sought to show you as many tips as possible related to Photoshop's vast abilities related to drawing and painting, this chapter grew and grew. Therefore, when reading this chapter, be aware that its contents are a lot to digest in one sitting! That's the bad part. The good part is that the chapter's length and depth will help you get the most out of Photoshop's excellent toolbox of options for drawing and painting.

All about the Tools

Photoshop enables you to draw and paint pixels and vectors with paintbrushes, airbrushes, pencils, rubber stamps, sponges, and much more. In general, these can be grouped into three categories—paint tools, image editing tools, and shape tools.

▶ **QUICK TIP**

Most of these tools give you the option to specify a blend mode—telling Photoshop how to handle the interaction between the edited pixels and those beneath them. See the Blending Modes section in the color insert for color representations of each blend mode.

Paint Tools

The paint tools in Photoshop typically encompass the following tools—grouped into sets according to their location in the toolbox:

- Brush and Pencil
- History Brush and Art History Brush
- Gradient and Paint Bucket
- Eraser, Background Eraser, and Magic Eraser

Brush and Pencil

While both tools are used to paint with the current foreground color located in the toolbox, the Brush and Pencil tools in Photoshop also have distinct and easily identifiable differences. First and foremost, the Brush tool is capable of producing soft, anti-aliased edges, while the Pencil tool creates hard-edge, aliased lines. The other differences lie in the options for each tool, as discussed in Table 8-1.

Figure 8-1 shows where the Brush and Pencil tools are located in the toolbox, and the following illustration gives a quick look at some strokes applied with each tool.

▶ **QUICK TIP**

Press SHIFT-B *on your keyboard to switch between the Brush and Pencil tools. Hold down the* SHIFT *key while dragging to draw a straight line with either tool.*

History Brush and Art History Brush

The history brushes are different from the Pencil and normal Brush because they paint from the History palette instead of from the color in the foreground swatch of the toolbox. In fact, the History Brush and the Art History Brush don't really paint with specific colors at all. Instead, these two tools paint from specific states within the history of the image.

For example, suppose you wanted to restore a certain piece of an image to how it looked when you first opened the file. You can do so by painting back the area with the History Brush. (See the tip "Restore Part of an Image to the Previously Saved Version," later in this chapter.) Or suppose you applied a motion blur (Filter | Blur | Motion Blur) to an image of a woman riding a bicycle, but choose Edit | Undo because you didn't like how the blur looked on the entire image. You could use the Art History Brush to selectively paint back the motion blur only in the areas where it seemed appropriate.

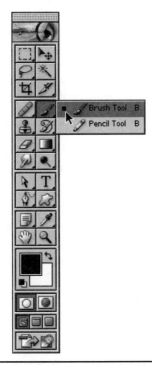

Figure 8-1   The Pencil tool is grouped with the Brush tool in the toolbox.

Brush Tool	Pencil Tool
Creates soft strokes	Creates hard-edged lines
Has an option for flow rate, which tells how quickly paint is applied by the brush	Has an option to auto-erase, where foreground color is "erased" to background color when foreground color is under the cursor as it's clicked
Has an option for opacity, which indicates the maximum amount of paint that can be applied at once	Has an option for opacity, which indicates the maximum amount of paint that can be applied at once
Has an option for blending mode, which controls how pixels are affected by the colors applied with the tool	Has an option for blending mode, which controls how pixels are affected by the colors applied with the tool
Can be used with a variety of brushes found in the Brushes palette	Can be used with a variety of brushes found in the Brushes palette
Can be used as an airbrush to spray jets of color applied in gradual tones	

Table 8-1   Comparison of the Brush and Pencil Tools

The key difference between these two types of history brushes is that, while they both paint from states within the History palette, only the Art History Brush allows you to edit the style, area, and tolerance of the brush strokes. The result is that strokes applied with the Art History Brush tend to be more "artistic" in nature than those applied with the History Brush. (See the tips "Restore Part of an Image to the Previously Saved Version" and "Use the Art History Brush to Combine Creative Effects.")

Figure 8-2 shows where the History Brush and Art History Brush tools are located in the toolbox.

QUICK TIP

Press SHIFT-Y *to switch between the History Brush and Art History Brush tools.*

Gradient and Paint Bucket

When you want to quickly fill large areas with a single color, the Paint Bucket tool is the likely candidate. As shown in Figure 8-3, the Paint Bucket tool is grouped with the Gradient tool in the toolbox. The Gradient tool also allows you to fill large areas with color, only it fills with gradations of one or more colors, as defined in the Gradient Editor.

Both the Gradient and Paint Bucket tools can be applied to entire images or selected areas within an image. Additional characteristics and options for each tool are shown in Figures 8-4 and 8-5.

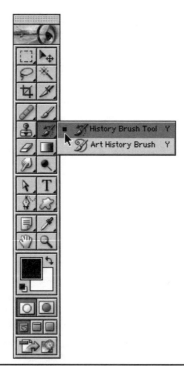

Figure 8-2   The Art History Brush is grouped with the History Brush in the toolbox.

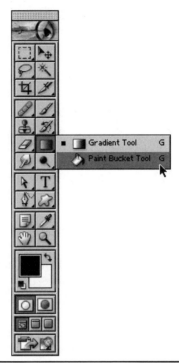

Figure 8-3   The Paint Bucket tool is grouped with the Gradient tool in the toolbox.

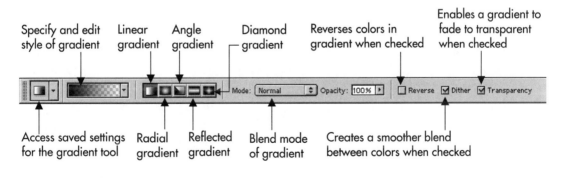

Figure 8-4   Options for the Gradient tool

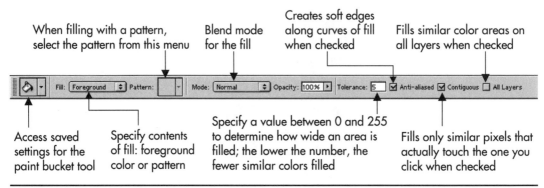

When filling with a pattern, select the pattern from this menu

Blend mode for the fill

Creates soft edges along curves of fill when checked

Fills similar color areas on all layers when checked

Access saved settings for the paint bucket tool

Specify contents of fill: foreground color or pattern

Specify a value between 0 and 255 to determine how wide an area is filled; the lower the number, the fewer similar colors filled

Fills only similar pixels that actually touch the one you click when checked

Figure 8-5   Options for the Paint Bucket tool

Eraser, Background Eraser, and Magic Eraser

The eraser tools (shown in Figure 8-6) are so named because, by default, they remove pixels of color from an image. However, depending on the options you assign to the tools, they can also be used to add pixels of color in an image.

When working with the Eraser tool, what appears after you "erase" depends on several things:

- If you're working on the Background layer or a layer whose transparency is locked, the Eraser erases to reveal the color currently located in the background color swatch.

- If you're working on any other layer, the Eraser erases to transparency (shown by the checkerboard pattern in Photoshop).

- If Erase To History is selected as an option of the Eraser tool, the Eraser erases to the selected state in the image's history. (See the tip "Restore Part of an Image to the Previously Saved Version" later in this chapter for details.)

Both the normal Eraser and the Background Eraser give you the option of selecting a brush style and size. In addition, the normal Eraser also allows you to select a mode—Pencil, Brush, or Block. This means you can erase with the hard edges of the

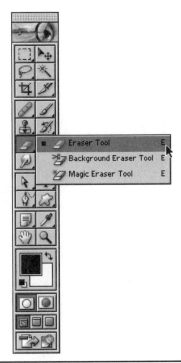

Figure 8-6 The Background Eraser and Magic Eraser are grouped with the normal Eraser in the toolbox.

Pencil tool, the soft edges of the Brush tool, or a flat, rectangular block similar to those chalkboard erasers from school.

▶ **NOTE**

See the tips "Use the Magic Eraser to Remove Areas of Color with a Single Click" and "Use the Background Eraser to Remove Solid Color Backgrounds" in Chapter 5 for details on using the Magic Eraser.

Image Editing Tools

Photoshop's image editing tools are a top-notch set of tools that enable you to edit photographs in much the same way as photographers have done in the darkroom for years. In fact, where the capabilities of darkroom editing stop, they only just begin in Photoshop. Each of the following tools—grouped into sets according to their location in the toolbox—perform distinct functions in Photoshop:

- Blur, Sharpen, and Smudge
- Dodge, Burn, and Sponge
- Clone Stamp and Pattern Stamp
- Healing Brush and Patch

Blur, Sharpen, and Smudge

For the most part, these tools do exactly what their names say—the Blur tool blurs or softens edges, the Sharpen tool increases focus to sharpen areas, and the Smudge tool works a bit like finger painting to smudge areas. All three of these tools (shown in Figure 8-7) give you the option of choosing a brush size and style.

See the tips "Use the Blur and Sharpen Tools to Adjust the Focus Within Small Areas of an Image" and "Use the Smudge Tool to Enlarge an Image's Canvas Size" in this chapter for details on using these tools.

> ### QUICK TIP
>
> *Press* SHIFT-R *to switch between the Blur, Sharpen, and Smudge tools.*

Dodge, Burn, and Sponge

The Dodge, Burn, and Sponge tools (shown in Figure 8-8) most closely simulate effects produced in the photographic darkroom. For example, photographers in a darkroom commonly hold their hands or other objects over a photograph to block the light from reaching it, in a technique called *dodging*. Dodging in Photoshop produces the same result—the dodged area is lightened. Likewise, photographers can increase a photograph's exposure to the light to darken it, in a process called *burning*. For details on using these two tools, see the tip "Use the Dodge and Burn Tools to Adjust the Exposure of an Image."

Figure 8-7   The Sharpen and Smudge tools are grouped with the Blur tool in the toolbox.

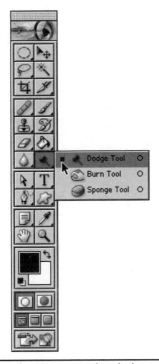

Figure 8-8   The Burn and Sponge tools are grouped with the Dodge tool in the toolbox.

> **QUICK TIP**
>
> Press SHIFT-O *to switch between the Dodge, Burn, and Sponge tools.*

The third tool in this group, the Sponge tool, is used in a similar fashion, but instead of affecting the darkness or lightness of an image, it affects the saturation. When using the Sponge tool, you must first specify whether to desaturate (reduce the intensity of) or saturate (increase the intensity of) the area. You must also choose a brush and specify the flow, which refers to how quickly the area is affected by the Sponge tool.

> **QUICK TIP**
>
> Press SHIFT-S *to switch between the Clone Stamp and Pattern Stamp tools.*

Clone Stamp and Pattern Stamp

The two rubberstamp tools (shown in Figure 8-9) can be applied to an image using any brush of your choosing, but the way in which each tool edits the image is distinctly different. The Clone Stamp paints by copying an area of the image and pasting it into another area, just as cloning an object duplicates it. By contrast, the Pattern Stamp tool simply paints with a pattern.

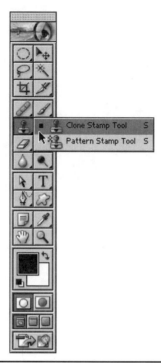

Figure 8-9 The Pattern Stamp tool is grouped with the Clone Stamp tool in the toolbox.

See the tip "Duplicate Part of an Image with the Clone Stamp" for details on using the Clone Stamp tool.

Healing Brush and Patch

The Healing Brush and Patch tools (both of which are wonderful new additions to Photoshop in version 7) might be considered by some people to be advanced Clone Stamp tools, because both of these tools work similarly to the Clone Stamp tool—all three tools enable you to copy from one area of an image and paste into another area using a paintbrush. (For a comparison of these three tools, see Table 8-2.)

However, the huge benefit of the Healing Brush and Patch tools is that both of these tools make color and tonal corrections to the "pasted" area after you're finished painting. These corrections cause the pasted area to blend better and evenly match the pixels surrounding it.

The difference between the Healing Brush and Patch tools is that the Healing Brush enables you to paint the pasted area into the image with a brush, whereas the Patch tool gives you the option of using the selection tools to copy and paste with color and tonal correction. Figure 8-10 shows the location of these two tools in the toolbox. For details on using these two tools, see the tip "Remove Blemishes with the Patch and Healing Brush Tools" later in the chapter.

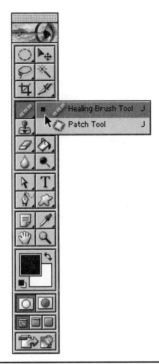

Figure 8-10   The Patch tool is grouped with the Healing Brush tool in the toolbox.

▶ | **QUICK TIP**

Press SHIFT-J *to switch between the Healing Brush and Patch tools.*

▶ **NOTE**

This first incarnation of the Healing Brush tool is really quite simple and can only be used with a normal, round brush. This means you don't have access to the entire Brushes palette when using the Healing Brush. Instead, click the brush in the Options bar to edit its size, diameter, angle, hardness, spacing, and roundness.

Shape Tools

Unlike strokes painted with the Brush or Pencil tool, shapes are easy to select, edit, and move independently of each other, because shapes—like paths drawn with the Pen tool—are object-oriented and vector-based. This also means shapes are resolution-independent and can be printed with crisp edges at any size or resolution.

Feature	Clone Stamp Tool	Healing Brush Tool	Patch Tool
Allows you to copy and paste areas of images by painting with brushes	Yes	Yes	No
Allows you to copy and paste areas of images by selecting with a lasso	No	No	Yes
Allows you to copy from one layer and paste into another	Yes	No	No
Can be used on transparent layers	Yes	No	No
Performs color and tonal corrections to the pasted area	No	Yes	Yes
Performs the copy and paste on the fly, as you're painting/selecting	Yes	No	No
Painting can be done with any of the brushes available in Photoshop	Yes	No	No
Allows "copy" and "paste" strokes to be aligned with each other	Yes	Yes	No
Blending mode can be adjusted	Yes	Partial list only	No
Pasted area can be filled with pattern	Yes	Yes	Yes

Table 8-2   Comparison of the Clone Stamp, Healing Brush, and Patch Tools

▶ **NOTE**

The shape tools were introduced in Chapter 5, because they are edited with the pen tools, which are commonly used to make selections. For a comparison of how the shape and pen tools work with paths, refer to Chapter 5.

There are five permanent shape tools—Rectangle, Rounded Rectangle, Ellipse, Polygon, and Line—and one Custom Shape tool, which can be used to access any of the vast number of other shapes that ship with the program. Figure 8-11 shows where each of the shape tools are located in the toolbox.

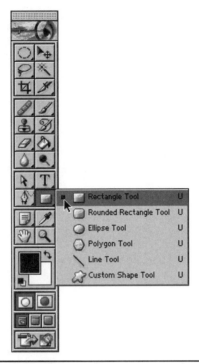

Figure 8-11   The Rounded Rectangle, Ellipse, Polygon, Line, and Custom Shape tools are grouped with the Rectangle tool in the toolbox.

When a shape tool is selected from the toolbox, the options bar at the top of the screen is displayed, similar to the one shown in the following illustration.

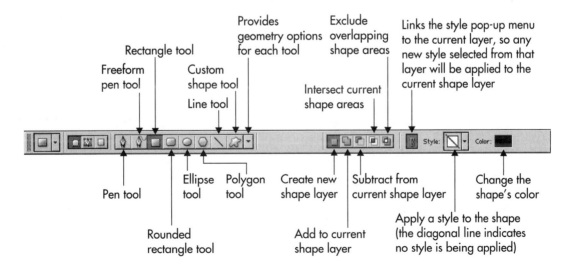

The various settings for each of the shape tools are accessed by clicking the inverted triangle to the right of the shape buttons in the Options bar, and are discussed in Table 8-3 and throughout this chapter.

> ▶ **QUICK TIP**
>
> *Press* SHIFT-U *to switch between the shape tools.*

Option	Action (When Selected)	Rectangle	Rounded Rectangle	Ellipse	Polygon	Line	Custom Shape
Unconstrained	Doesn't limit the size or proportions of the shape	X	X	X			X
Square	Restricts the proportions of the rectangle to a square	X	X				
Fixed Size	Creates a shape in the exact size entered, using the Width (W) and Height (H) fields	X	X	X			X
Proportional	Restricts the proportions of the shape, based on the values entered in the Width (W) and Height (H) fields	X	X	X			X
From Center	Draws the shape from its center point instead of a corner point	X	X	X			X
Snap to Pixels	Causes the edges of the shape to align with the edges of pixels; in other words, the shape can't begin at 200.5 pixels across the screen—it must start at either 200 or 201 pixels	X	X				
Radius	Defines the corner radius of rounded rectangles, and the distance from the center to the outer points of polygons		X		X		
Circle	Restricts the proportions of the ellipse to a circle			X			
Sides	Defines the number of sides in the shape				X		

Table 8-3   Shape Options For Each Tool Are Designated by an X

Option	Action (When Selected)	Rectangle	Rounded Rectangle	Ellipse	Polygon	Line	Custom Shape
Smooth Corners Smooth Indents	Causes any sharp corners to be rounded and smooth				X		
Star Indent Sides By	Creates a star polygon; the percentage entered indicates the portion of the star's radius used by the points				X		
Arrowheads (Start and End)	Adds an arrowhead to the end(s) of the line (additional options appear when selected, where you define the shape of the arrowheads)					X	
Width Height	Defines proportions of arrowheads using values of 10 – 1000% for width and 10 – 5000% for height (only used when arrowheads are added to the line)				X		
Concavity	Defines the amount of curve in the fullest part of the arrowhead, using a value of –50% to +50% where 0% contains no curve (only used when arrowheads are added to the line)					X	
Weight	Defines the thickness of a line in pixels					X	
Shape (select menu in Options bar)	Identifies the custom shape being drawn						X
Defined Proportions	Creates a custom shape with the exact proportions in which the shape was created						X
Defined Size	Creates a custom shape with the exact size in which the shape was created						X

Table 8-3   Shape Options For Each Tool Are Designated by an X *(continued)*

> ▶ **QUICK TIP**
>
> *If you have multiple shapes on different layers in a file, you can quickly align and/or distribute them. Select one of the layers and place link icons in the empty boxes next to the other shape layers to link them all together. Then, choose Layer | Align Linked or Layer | Distribute Linked.*

All about Brushes

Almost all of the tools discussed so far in this chapter have one thing in common—brushes. This means the tools require you to select a brush size and style. The Brushes palette (shown in the following illustration and accessible by choosing Window | Brushes) is your newly improved, one-stop shopping for all things related to brushes in Photoshop. In fact, there are so many options in this one palette that it's easy to get lost just "playing" (well, for me at least).

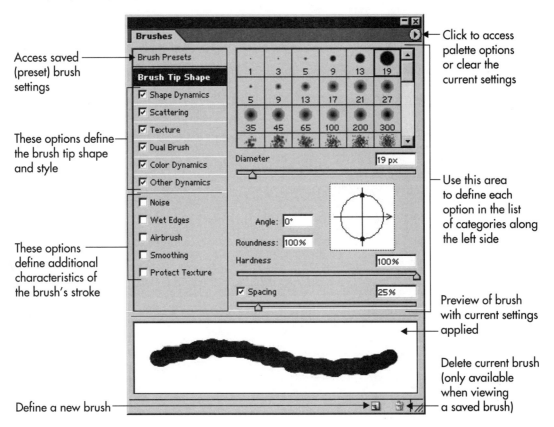

This palette is accessible any time you use a tool in the toolbox that needs a "tip size." That includes each of the following:

- Brush
- Pencil
- History Brush
- Art History Brush
- Eraser
- Clone Stamp
- Pattern Stamp
- Dodge
- Burn
- Sponge
- Blur
- Sharpen
- Smudge

After opening the Brushes palette, you can turn on or off each of the various options independently of one another.

▶ **NOTE**

The Brushes palette is not available for the Healing Brush, but you can set some brush options in the mini-brushes palette (called the Brush pop-up palette), accessible by clicking the brush sample display in the Options bar.

The vast majority of the tips in this chapter have you accessing the Brushes palette in some way, shape, or form, but pay special attention to those titled "Use Brush Presets" and "Create and Save Custom Brushes" because those are sure to increase your productivity with the tool.

Use Brush Presets

Photoshop ships with its Brushes palette already loaded with a set of brushes. These brushes have certain settings attached to them and are called *brush presets*. Whether you're looking for a predefined brush to use for quick touch-ups or one in an interesting shape, the brush presets are a great place to start.

▶ *NOTE*

Don't let the name "preset" throw you—brush presets are just brushes saved with certain settings in Photoshop.

 To access the brush presets, click a tool requiring a brush (such as the Brush or Pencil tool) and perform one of the following:

- Choose Window | Brushes and click the first option on the left side, labeled Brush Presets, to reveal a display similar to the one shown in Figure 8-12.
- Click the brush sample display in the Options bar to reveal the Brush pop-up palette, which is shown in Figure 8-13.

After performing either task, you'll be presented with a list of brushes, which by default begins with a single-pixel, hard-edged round brush. Scroll down the list to see and access additional brushes. Click once on any brush to activate it. You can edit the settings of a preset brush by choosing from the various options along the left side of the Brushes palette.

▶ **QUICK TIP**

When viewing brush presets in the Brushes palette, simply hold your cursor over the brush's name for a few seconds to reveal how it will display in the preview window.

TRY IT You're not stuck with only round brushes in Photoshop! In fact, Photoshop 7 ships with more brushes than ever before. To load some of these additional brush sets, click the small triangle in the upper-right corner of the Brushes palette or the Brush pop-up palette and choose one of the following:

- **Reset Brushes** Select to replace or append the current brushes with the default round brushes
- **Load Brushes** Select to load additional brushes that will appear after the existing brushes in the Brush Presets
- **Save Brushes** Select to save the current set of brushes
- **Replace Brushes** Select to load additional brushes that will replace the existing brushes in the Brush Presets

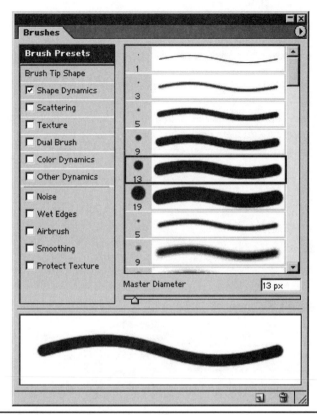

Figure 8-12   Click Brush Presets in the Brushes palette to access the saved brushes in Photoshop.

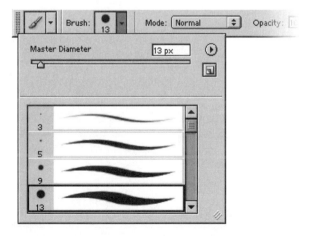

Figure 8-13   Click the brush sample in the Options bar to reveal the Brush pop-up palette, which also displays brush presets.

Or choose from one of the additional brush libraries listed at the bottom of the menu (as shown in the following illustration) and Photoshop will prompt you whether to *append* or *replace* the existing brushes in the Brush Presets window.

▶ **NOTE**

Choosing to append adds the brushes to the current list, while choosing to replace removes the existing brushes before adding the new ones.

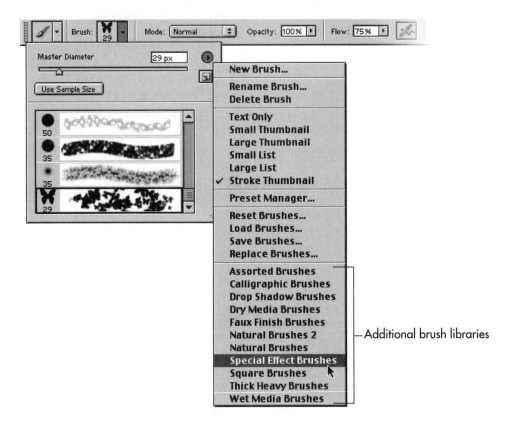

—Additional brush libraries

> ▶ **QUICK TIP**
>
> *You can customize the look of the Brush Presets by clicking the small triangle in the upper-right corner of the Brushes palette or the Brush pop-up palette and choosing from one of the views in the third section—Text Only, Small Thumbnail, Large Thumbnail, Small List, Large List, or Stroke Thumbnail. (Note that depending on how large your screen is, that small triangle may not appear in the upper-right corner of the Brushes palette. Instead, it may appear directly to the right of the palette title.)*

Load Additional Shapes

In addition to the custom shapes that are loaded into Photoshop by default, you can load a number of other libraries of custom shapes, including animals, ornaments, and talk bubbles.

> ▶ **QUICK TIP**
>
> *You can also use the Preset Manager to load shape libraries. See the tip "Use the Preset Manager to Manage Saved Tool Settings" later in the chapter.*

TRY IT   To load additional shapes, select the Custom Shape tool from the toolbox or the Options bar. Then, click the shape preview to open the Custom Shape Picker and select one of the following options:

- **Reset Shapes**   Select to replace or append the current shapes with the default custom shapes
- **Load Shapes**   Select to load additional shapes that will appear after the existing shapes in the Custom Shape Picker
- **Save Shapes**   Select to save the current set of shapes
- **Replace Shapes**   Select to load additional shapes that will replace the existing shapes in the Custom Shape Picker

Or choose from one of the additional shape libraries listed at the bottom of the menu (as shown in the following illustration) and Photoshop will prompt you whether to *append* or *replace* the existing shapes in the Custom Shape Picker.

▶ *NOTE*

Choosing to append adds the shapes to the current list, while choosing to replace removes the existing shapes before adding the new ones.

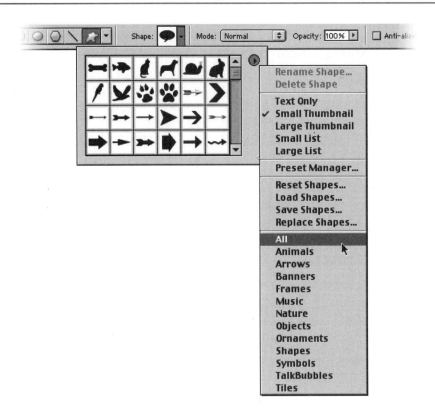

Load Additional Patterns

In addition to the patterns that are loaded into Photoshop by default, you can load a number of other libraries of patterns, including animals, ornaments, and talk bubbles.

 To load additional patterns, perform one of the following tasks to access the pattern picker:

- Select an area to fill with a pattern, and choose Edit | Fill. For Use, select Pattern and click the pattern sample.
- Select a tool capable of filling with a pattern, such as the Pattern Stamp, Healing Brush, or Patch tool. Click the pattern sample in the Options bar.

▶ | **QUICK TIP**

You can also use the Preset Manager to load pattern libraries. See the tip "Use the Preset Manager to Manage Saved Tool Settings" later in the chapter.

Then, select one of the following options after clicking the small arrow in the upper-right corner:

- **Reset Patterns**   Select to replace or append the current patterns with the default patterns
- **Load Patterns**   Select to load additional patterns that will appear after the existing patterns in the pattern picker
- **Save Patterns**   Select to save the current set of patterns
- **Replace Patterns**   Select to load additional patterns that will replace the existing patterns in the pattern picker

Or choose from one of the additional pattern libraries listed at the bottom of the menu (as shown in the following illustration) and Photoshop will prompt you whether to *append* or *replace* the existing patterns in the pattern picker.

▶ **NOTE**

Choosing to append adds the patterns to the current list, while choosing to replace removes the existing patterns before adding the new ones.

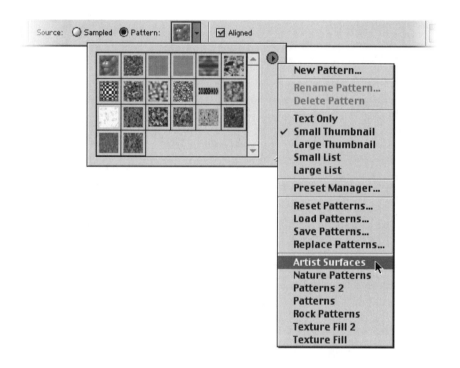

Create and Save Custom Brush Tips, Shapes, and Patterns

In addition to loading the brush tips, shapes, and patterns that ship with Photoshop, you can create your own quite easily. One of my favorite applications of this tip is in creating a custom signature stamp. For example, suppose you were a painter who commonly created work in Photoshop. You could "sign" a blank Photoshop file, save it as a brush tip, and then simply paint your signature on any finished piece of art.

▶ **NOTE**

This tip is specifically for creating a custom brush tip, and not a custom brush. The difference is that brush tips are used by a variety of different brush styles and techniques. See the following tip, "Create and Save Custom Brushes," for more details.

TRY IT   To create and save your own custom brush tips, shapes, and patterns, open a new file in Photoshop and draw whatever you'd like to use as the brush, shape, or pattern on a new layer. When doing so, refer to Table 8-4 for a few important restrictions. Then, use the Rectangle Marquee and make sure the Feather option is set to 0 pixels. Select the area of the image you wish to use as the custom brush tip, shape, or pattern and choose one of the following commands, depending on what you're creating:

- Edit | Define Brush
- Edit | Define Pattern
- Edit | Define Custom Shape

Give the brush tip, pattern, or shape a name and click OK to continue, as shown in the following illustration.

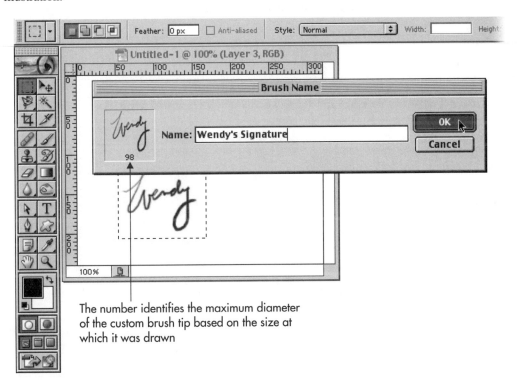

The number identifies the maximum diameter
of the custom brush tip based on the size at
which it was drawn

Item	Maximum Size	Color Mode	Other Notes
Custom brush tip	2500 pixels by 2500 pixels	Black and white (for hard-edged brushes) or grayscale (for soft brushes)—if you define a brush that contains color, the color is converted to grayscale when the brush is saved	Works best when the brush tip is drawn against a solid white background. Create the brush as large as you ever intend to use it, because although you can shrink a custom brush's diameter, you can't increase it beyond the original size.
Custom pattern	n/a	Color mode of current document	Smaller patterns typically work better than larger ones. Consider how the pattern will tile when repeated in Photoshop or a web browser (see Chapter 4 for more details on creating seamless web page backgrounds).
Custom shape	n/a	No color mode, saved as vector art only	Must be drawn with the pen or shape tools as a path or vector mask.

Table 8-4   Tips for Creating Custom Brush Tips, Patterns, and Shapes

---

QUICK TIP

The spacing for a custom brush tip is 25% by default, and although you can adjust it each time you use it, you can't adjust the spacing or other settings of a brush before defining it. To save the settings for a brush using a custom brush tip, click the Brush Preset tab on the left side of the Brushes palette. Then, click the triangle in the upper-right corner of the palette (or next to the palette name) and choose New Brush. The new brush will be defined and saved in the Brush Preset window, as discussed in the following tip, "Create and Save Custom Brushes."

 To use a custom brush, shape, or pattern, access the appropriate palette—Brushes, Custom Shape Picker, or pattern picker—and select your new item from the list.

Create and Save Custom Brushes

The previous tip discussed creating custom brush tips. This tip expands on that tip to show you how to create custom brushes. To understand the difference, consider the following analogy. When you decorate cakes, you can use a flower-shaped decorator's tip to create all sorts of flowers. But to create daisies, you have to use the flower-shaped tip, white icing, and a dot of orange in the center. Creating flowers can be done with the tip, while creating a specific type of flower—in this case a daisy—requires the use of the flower tip as well as several additional techniques.

In Photoshop, you can use a flower-shaped brush tip to create a variety of flowers, but to create a string of daisies that scatter in a variety of sizes and opacities, you use a flower-shaped brush tip, plus a variety of other settings. After making those settings in the Brushes palette, you can save the whole package—the tip you used and any settings you made—as a *brush preset*.

TRY IT   To create a custom brush, select a painting tool that uses the Brushes palette, such as the Brush or Pencil. Then, choose Window | Brushes or click the Brushes palette button to the right of the Options bar. Select the brush tip you want to use and make any additional changes to the settings for that brush, such as the spacing and diameter.

Check and uncheck each of the other setting options along the left side of the Brushes palette, depending on which options you want saved with this brush. For example, if you have a pressure-sensitive drawing tablet and you want to make the opacity vary according to the pressure of the pen on the tablet, place a check in the box labeled Other Dynamics and choose Pen Pressure for the control of the Opacity Jitter. The result of your settings is displayed in the preview pane at the bottom of the Brushes palette.

After you're finished adjusting the settings for your brush, click the triangle in the upper-right corner of the palette and choose New Brush. Give the brush a name to help identify its settings, and click OK.

To access a saved brush, click the Brush Presets option in the upper-left corner of the Brushes palette and choose your brush from the list.

QUICK TIP

To save this brush—along with any others currently loaded into the brush presets—for use on another computer, click the triangle in the upper-right corner of the Brushes palette (or next to the palette title) and choose Save Brushes. Give the brush library a name, using the extension .abr, and identify where to save it. By default, brush libraries are stored in the Brushes folder within the Presets folder for Adobe Photoshop 7.

Create and Save Custom Tool Settings

The previous two tips discussed, in order, creating a custom brush tip and creating a custom brush. This tip takes that process one step further by showing you how to create a custom tool. While a custom brush can contain tip and other settings within the Brushes palette, it can't contain options set outside of the Brushes palette.

For example, suppose you wanted to create a string of daisies that scatter in a variety of sizes and opacities, as well as in specific colors and using the Multiple blending mode. Because the colors and blending mode of the Brush tool are set outside of the Brushes palette, those options won't be captured if you choose New Brush from the Brushes palette flyout menu. Instead, to capture settings made outside the Brushes palette—such as colors or blending modes—you save them as a tool preset.

This is just the tip of the iceberg, really. Consider creating a setting that automatically selects all the options needed to crop an image to 4×5 inches and 300 dpi with one click. Or, try using a tool preset to give one-click access to all of your favorite typographic settings—font family, style, weight, color, size, alignment, and so on. The possibilities really are limitless.

TRY IT   To create a custom tool setting—in this case for the Brush tool—select the Brush tool from the toolbox. Choose Window | Brushes or click the Brushes palette button to the right of the Options bar. Select the brush tip you want to use and make any additional changes to the settings for that brush, such as the spacing and diameter.

Check and uncheck each of the other setting options along the left side of the Brushes palette, depending on which options you want saved with this brush. Make additional selections within the Options bar as needed. Finally, make sure any colors you want saved with these settings are currently located in the foreground and background color swatches.

▶ **NOTE**
_____

You can save settings for all tools in the Photoshop toolbox using these same basic steps.
_____

TRY IT   To save the current settings for the Brush tool as a tool preset, first choose Window | Tool Presets to open the Tool Presets palette. Click the triangle in the upper-right corner of the palette and choose New Tool Preset (as shown in Figure 8-14) or click the New Tool Preset button at the bottom of the palette (next to the trash can icon). Give the tool a name to help identify its settings and click OK. To access and manage tool presets, see the following tip.

▶ **NOTE**
_____

Some tools, such as the Brush tool, have additional options within the New Tool Preset dialog box. For example, when saving a tool preset for the Brush tool, you can choose whether to include the current colors in the saved settings. Or, when saving a tool preset for the Gradient tool, you can choose whether to include the currently selected gradient in the saved settings.
_____

Use the Preset Manager to Manage Saved Tool Settings

Tool presets can significantly increase your productivity and efficiency in Photoshop because they enable you to save settings you might otherwise have to remake over and over again. For example, I use a pressure-sensitive drawing tablet for all my Photoshop work. I like to customize a variety of

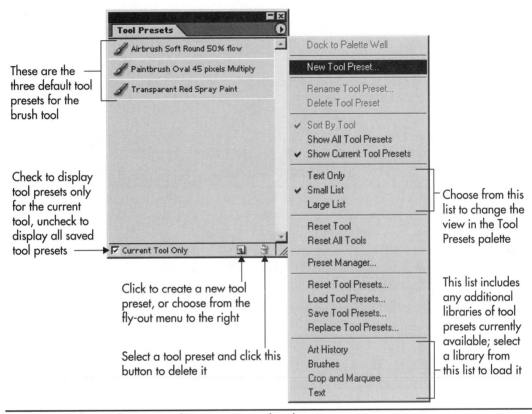

These are the three default tool presets for the brush tool

Check to display tool presets only for the current tool, uncheck to display all saved tool presets

Click to create a new tool preset, or choose from the fly-out menu to the right

Select a tool preset and click this button to delete it

Choose from this list to change the view in the Tool Presets palette

This list includes any additional libraries of tool presets currently available; select a library from this list to load it

Figure 8-14   The Tool Presets palette stores saved tool settings.

tools so settings like opacity and size are dictated by the amount of pressure I place with the pen on the tablet. To avoid re-creating these settings every time I want to use them, I can save them as tool presets and use the Preset Manager to access and organize them.

▶ **NOTE**

For information on how to save a tool preset, see the previous tip, "Create and Save Custom Tool Settings."

TRY IT To use the Preset Manager, choose Window | Tool Presets to open the Tool Presets palette. Then, click the triangle in the upper-right corner and choose Preset Manager from the flyout menu to reveal the following window:

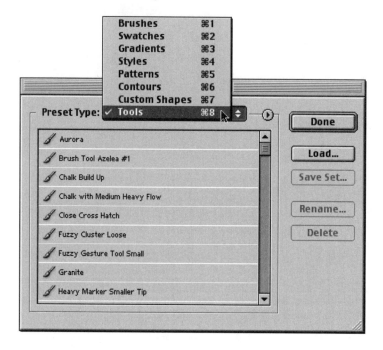

From this window, you can manage not only all tool presets but also the following other saved settings by choosing them from the pop-up menu or pressing the associated key commands:

- Brushes
- Swatches
- Gradients
- Styles
- Patterns
- Contours
- Custom Shapes

> **QUICK TIP**
>
> *To rename a preset, simply double-click it in the Preset Manager and begin typing.*

TRY IT To reorganize the order in which the tool presets display, you can click individual presets and drag and drop them in the same way you move layers within the Layers palette. (Note that you can reorder presets only within the Preset Manager, and not within the actual Tool Presets palette.)

To move more than one preset at the same time, select the first one and hold down the SHIFT key before selecting the additional presets you want to move.

TRY IT To save a group of presets as a library, which can then be loaded into Photoshop on another computer as needed, click the Save Set button on the right side of the Preset Manager. To save select presets, and not all of those currently visible in the Preset Manager, SHIFT-click the presets to highlight them before choosing Save Set. Give the set a name, using the .tpl extension, and designate where to save the file on your hard drive before clicking OK.

To load saved presets, click the Load button on the right side of the Preset Manager and identify the preset library you want to load.

> **QUICK TIP**
>
> *Photoshop ships with some additional preset libraries in its Presets folder. Have fun experimenting with the different tool settings in these libraries by choosing the library's name from the button of the flyout menu in the Preset Manager.*

Use Photoshop's Pattern Maker

Photoshop 7's Pattern Maker command makes it easy to create patterns out of any part of an image. For example, I recently wanted to fill part of a design with an abstract pattern based on the American flag. While I certainly could have tried creating this pattern by hand, Pattern Maker was able to give me a wide variety of patterns to choose from based on this theme in no time at all.

TRY IT To use Pattern Maker, you first need to open an image in Photoshop on which to base your pattern. So when I wanted to create a pattern based on the American flag, I opened the following image from Photodisc (www.gettyimages.com/photodisc):

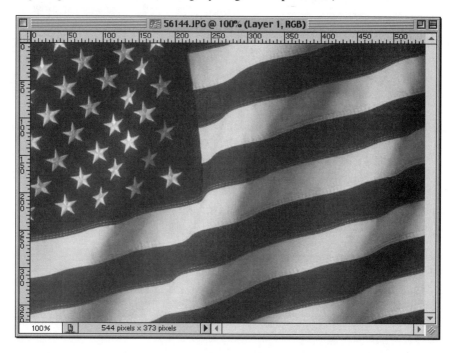

After opening the file, move to the layer containing the image and decide whether to base your pattern on the entire image or a select part. If you're basing it on a select part, use the Marquee tool to select that part before continuing. Once you're ready to create the tile, choose Filter | Pattern Maker to reveal a window similar to the one shown in Figure 8-15, where you can preview and customize your patterns.

Click Generate to ask Photoshop to create a pattern based on the current selection in the window. The default size for patterns created by Pattern Maker is 128 by 128 pixels. You can change the size by entering different numbers in the Width and Height boxes in the Tile Generation section. Or, to create one pattern the entire width and height of the current file, click the Use Image Size button.

Photoshop generates a single pattern the size specified and tiles it across and down the available window space in an evenly spaced grid. To vary that grid somewhat, choose Vertical or Horizontal from the Offset menu and specify the offset amount below that.

▶ **NOTE**

If your image size is 128×128 pixels—and your pattern size is the same—you'll only see one instance of the pattern in the window and won't get to see how it looks tiled. To properly preview your pattern in Pattern Maker, make sure the file you're working with is larger than the pattern you're creating.

With the Marquee tool, you can change the selected area on which the pattern is based

Check to see the edges of the pattern's tiles in the preview window

Increase the smoothness to lower the contrast between the pattern's edges

Increase the detail to attempt to keep aspects of the pattern "whole" and not broken into as many little pieces

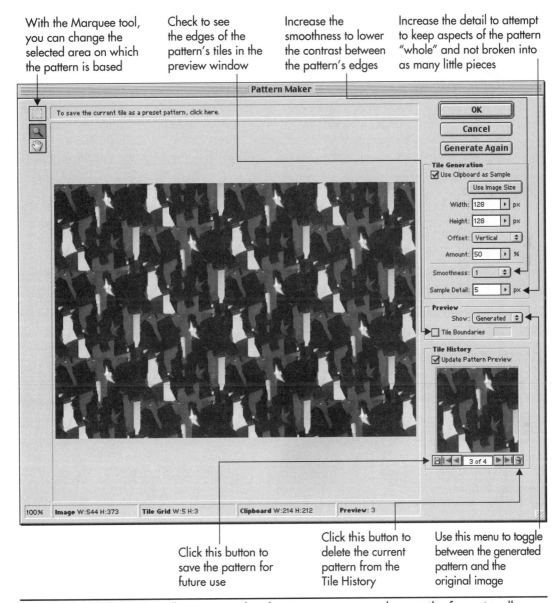

Click this button to save the pattern for future use

Click this button to delete the current pattern from the Tile History

Use this menu to toggle between the generated pattern and the original image

Figure 8-15   The Pattern Maker command makes it easy to create abstract tiles from virtually any image.

You can change the settings and have Photoshop generate a new pattern as many times as you'd like. Luckily, Photoshop saves each pattern in the Tile History section of the screen so you can return to previous patterns later if you decide those first ones were really the best of the bunch.

When you're satisfied with the pattern(s) created, you have two options:

- Make sure the pattern you like best is currently visible and click OK. This causes Photoshop to fill the current layer with the pattern you selected.

- Make sure the pattern you like best is currently visible in the Tile History section of the window, and click the small disk icon below the preview to save the pattern as a preset. This allows you to use it later to paint or fill areas of your image, as discussed in the next tip, "Paint with Patterns." Then, if you want Photoshop to also fill the current layer with the selected pattern, click OK. Otherwise, click Cancel to return to the normal view without filling the image with the pattern.

▶ | **QUICK TIP**

If you want the pattern to fill a new, empty layer in Photoshop instead of the one containing your image, perform the following steps before starting Pattern Maker. Select the area on which you want to base your pattern and choose Edit | Copy. Then, create a new layer and make the new layer active by clicking it once within the Layers palette. Launch Pattern Maker (Filter | Pattern Maker) and click the box next to Use Clipboard As Sample before clicking the Generate button.

Paint with Patterns

A great way to add dimension to shapes that otherwise might appear flat and dull is to fill them with patterns in Photoshop. One way to accomplish this is by painting directly with a saved (preset) pattern.

▶ **NOTE**

Another way to fill an area with a pattern or other image is to use a clipping group. For details on using this technique, see the tip "Use Clipping Groups to Mask One Layer with the Contents of Another" in Chapter 6.

TRY IT — To paint with a saved pattern in Photoshop, make sure the file in which you want to work is open and the layer on which you want to paint is currently selected before you perform the following tasks.

1. Choose the Pattern Stamp tool (hidden behind the Clone Stamp tool) from the toolbox.
2. Select the pattern with which you want to paint from the pattern picker in the Options bar.

▶ **NOTE**

Not happy with the existing patterns in the pattern picker? You can click the small triangle to the right in the pattern picker and choose from additional libraries of patterns at the bottom of the list, or create your own. See the previous tip, "Create and Save Custom Brush Tips, Shapes, and Patterns," for details.

3. Select an appropriately sized brush tip by clicking the brush sample in the Options bar or using the Brushes palette.

4. Select in the Options bar the appropriate blending mode in which to paint.

5. Specify in the Options bar the opacity at which to paint.

6. Specify in the Options bar the flow rate (how much paint is applied at once) for each stroke.

7. Click the button in the Options bar to enable the airbrush, as needed.

8. Click the check box next to Aligned to cause the painting you perform to match with the pattern. In other words, each time you click the image to paint, Photoshop matches your location in reference to where you started painting with the pattern. When the Aligned box is left unchecked, Photoshop begins painting with the pattern from the same point in the pattern each time you click in the image.

9. Click the check box next to Impressionist to cause Photoshop to apply the pattern in a softer and lighter way than it normally would. (Note that if the details of your pattern are small, using this option may result in very little of the pattern actually showing up.)

10. Begin to paint within your image wherever you want the pattern to appear.

Figure 8-16 shows an example of how I painted with the Light Marble pattern that ships with Photoshop (click the triangle in the upper-right corner of the pattern picker and choose Rock Patterns to load it) to give an egg a crackled look. To retain the darks and lights of the egg, I painted my pattern on a new layer whose blending mode was set to Linear Burn.

QUICK TIP

If you want to restrict the pattern to appear only in a certain area, consider first selecting the area in which you want to paint with one of the selection tools. Then, if it's difficult to see where to paint because of the "dancing ants," press CTRL-H *(Windows) or* CMD-H *(Mac) to temporarily hide the selection outline.*

Paint with Texture

When you want to give an image a bit of texture, the best way to do so is to actually paint the texture right onto the image, as if applying textured paint onto the canvas. Whereas the previous tip, "Paint with Patterns," might be considered painting with textured paint, another way to go about this process is to give the brush itself the texture. The new Brushes palette gives you the option to do just that.

Figure 8-17 shows how I painted with texture applied to my brush tip to add texture to another Easter egg.

A marbled texture was
painted on this egg

Figure 8-16 I used the Pattern Stamp tool to add a marble pattern to the green egg in the front
of this image.

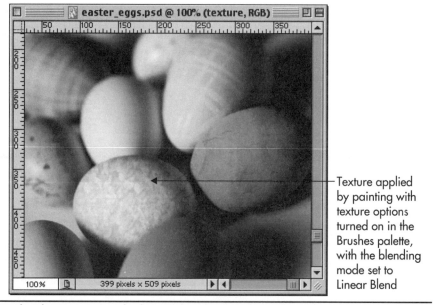

Texture applied
by painting with
texture options
turned on in the
Brushes palette,
with the blending
mode set to
Linear Blend

Figure 8-17 I painted with a texture applied to my brush to texturize this colored egg.

TRY IT To paint with texture in Photoshop, first make sure the file in which you want to work is open and the layer on which you want to paint is currently selected before performing the following tasks:

1. Select the Brush or Pencil tool from the toolbox.
2. Choose Window | Brushes or click the button in the Options bar to access the Brushes palette.
3. Select the brush tip you wish to use and any other desired settings.
4. Select Texture from the list of options on the left side of the Brushes palette to reveal the Texture choices. (Click the name Texture to access the choices; click the check box next to it to turn Texture on for the current brush tip.)
5. Select the actual texture to be applied to the brush from the texture picker by clicking once on the inverted triangle and choosing from the available options.

QUICK TIP

To load additional textures into the texture picker, click the small triangle in the texture picker and choose from any of the texture libraries at the bottom of the pop-up menu.

---

6. Choose from the remaining options to customize the texture, as shown in the following illustration, and begin painting.

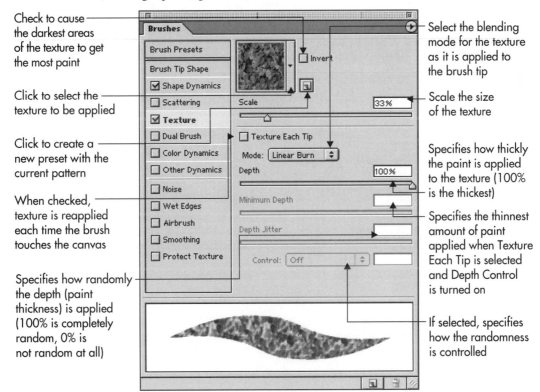

Check to cause the darkest areas of the texture to get the most paint

Click to select the texture to be applied

Click to create a new preset with the current pattern

When checked, texture is reapplied each time the brush touches the canvas

Specifies how randomly the depth (paint thickness) is applied (100% is completely random, 0% is not random at all)

Select the blending mode for the texture as it is applied to the brush tip

Scale the size of the texture

Specifies how thickly the paint is applied to the texture (100% is the thickest)

Specifies the thinnest amount of paint applied when Texture Each Tip is selected and Depth Control is turned on

If selected, specifies how the randomness is controlled

Paint with Two Brushes at Once

One of the exciting things about the new Brushes palette in Photoshop 7 is the way in which you can combine two brush tips to create a third, truly unique one. For example, you might start with a hard-edged, round brush tip about 30 pixels in diameter, and then add a brush tip shaped like a maple leaf. Then, scatter the leaves within the stroke, and the result might look something like this:

TRY IT To paint with two brushes at once, first make sure the file in which you want to work is open and the layer on which you want to paint is currently selected before performing the following tasks:

1. Select the Brush or Pencil tool from the toolbox.

2. Choose Window | Brushes or click the button in the Options bar to access the Brushes palette.

3. Select the initial brush tip you wish to use and any other desired settings.

4. Select Dual Brush from the list of options on the left side of the Brushes palette to reveal the Dual Brush choices. (Click the name Dual Brush to access the choices; click the check box next to it to turn Dual Brush on for the current brush tip.)

5. Select the second brush tip to be applied from the brush picker.

► | **QUICK TIP**

To load additional brush tips, click Brush Presets from the left menu and then click the small triangle in the upper-right corner of the Brushes palette. Choose from any of the additional libraries at the bottom of the pop-up menu.

6. Choose from the remaining options to customize the dual brush, as shown in the following illustration, and begin painting.

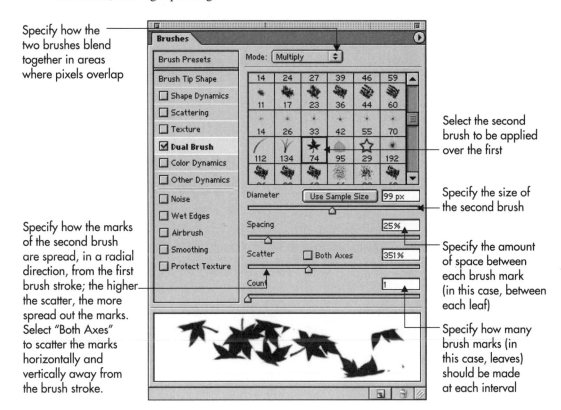

Specify how the two brushes blend together in areas where pixels overlap

Select the second brush to be applied over the first

Specify the size of the second brush

Specify how the marks of the second brush are spread, in a radial direction, from the first brush stroke; the higher the scatter, the more spread out the marks. Select "Both Axes" to scatter the marks horizontally and vertically away from the brush stroke.

Specify the amount of space between each brush mark (in this case, between each leaf)

Specify how many brush marks (in this case, leaves) should be made at each interval

Scatter Brush Strokes to Achieve Unique Paint Textures

Another great feature of the new Brushes palette is the ability to scatter brush strokes. If you've ever wanted to apply a stroke of paint in a somewhat random pattern across the screen, instead of in a perfect row, this is the technique for you. You can specify both how the brush marks are scattered across the stroke and how many marks are applied throughout the stroke. For example, here's what a stroke looks like without scattering:

And here's the same stroke applied with the Scatter option set to 500%:

TRY IT   To scatter brush strokes in Photoshop, first make sure the file in which you want to work is open and the layer on which you want to paint is currently selected before performing the following tasks:

1. Select the Brush or Pencil tool from the toolbox.
2. Choose Window | Brushes or click the button in the Options bar to access the Brushes palette.
3. Select the initial brush tip you wish to use and any other desired settings.
4. Select Scattering from the list of options on the left side of the Brushes palette to reveal the Scattering choices. (Click the name Scattering to access the choices; click the check box next to it to turn Scattering on for the current brush tip.)
5. Specify the amount of scattering you'd like to use with the brush.

▶ **QUICK TIP**

To preview the effects that increasing or decreasing the scattering has on your brush stroke, use the slider to enter a value and watch the preview window below as you slide.

6. Choose from the remaining options to customize the brush scattering, as shown in the following illustration, and begin painting.

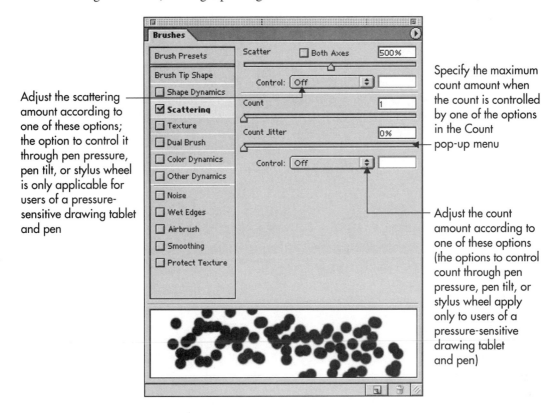

Adjust the scattering amount according to one of these options; the option to control it through pen pressure, pen tilt, or stylus wheel is only applicable for users of a pressure-sensitive drawing tablet and pen

Specify the maximum count amount when the count is controlled by one of the options in the Count pop-up menu

Adjust the count amount according to one of these options (the options to control count through pen pressure, pen tilt, or stylus wheel apply only to users of a pressure-sensitive drawing tablet and pen)

Vary Paint Settings According to Pen Pressure

Many of the preceding tips in this chapter discussed a technique new to Photoshop 7: jittering. Jittering allows you to vary certain brush settings according to one of the following:

- **Fade**   Fades an effect in the specified number of steps
- **Pen Pressure**   Adjusts the effect based on the amount of pressure applied with a pressure-sensitive drawing pen

- **Pen Tilt**   Adjusts the effect based on the angle of the pressure-sensitive drawing pen in relation to the drawing tablet
- **Stylus Wheel**   Adjusts the effect based on the position of the pressure-sensitive pen's thumbwheel

The last three options—Pen Pressure, Pen Tilt, and Stylus Wheel—are only available to users of pressure-sensitive drawing tablets, such as those made by Wacom (www.wacom.com).

If you do have a drawing tablet, be sure to take advantage of these settings to achieve more realistic drawing and painting strokes. You can apply a jitter to the following brush controls:

- Tip size
- Tip angle
- Tip roundness
- Scattering
- Texture depth
- Color
- Opacity
- Flow

When applying a jitter, you specify it using a percentage: 0% causes there to be no change in the effect from the fade or pen options, while 100% uses the maximum amount of change.

▶ | **QUICK TIP**
_____

If you've never used a drawing tablet, I highly recommend trying one out. I use mine not only for all my Photoshop work, but also for all other pointing and clicking! My mouse is rarely used, if ever. Once you get used to it, a pressure-sensitive pen not only is easier to draw with—it's just like using a regular pen or pencil—but also is better for your hands. See www.wacom.com for more information.

TRY IT   To vary paint settings, such as the opacity, according to the pen pressure, be sure your pressure-sensitive drawing tablet is installed and properly connected to your computer. Select one of the brush tools in the toolbox and choose Window | Brushes or click the button in the Options bar to access the Brushes palette.

▶ *CAUTION*

If a tablet is not installed and/or properly connected, a warning icon appears when you select one of the pen controls in the Brushes palette.

Choose the appropriate menu in the Brushes palette, depending on which option you want to vary, and adjust the settings as desired:

- **Tip size**   Listed under Shape Dynamics
- **Tip angle**   Listed under Shape Dynamics
- **Tip roundness**   Listed under Shape Dynamics
- **Scattering**   Listed under Scattering
- **Texture depth**   Listed under Texture
- **Color**   Listed under Color Dynamics
- **Opacity**   Listed under Other Dynamics
- **Flow**   Listed under Other Dynamics

▶ *QUICK TIP*

If you want to vary a setting like Opacity according to your pen pressure more times than not, save your options as a brush preset. See the earlier tip "Create and Save Custom Tool Settings."

Change the Brush Size with One Click

One of the biggest timesavers I use on a daily basis in Photoshop is this: using the shortcuts and key commands to quickly change the dynamics of my brush without accessing the Brushes palette.

TRY IT   To quickly change the size of your brush tip while painting in Photoshop, make sure you have a paint tool selected in the toolbox and an available layer active in the Layers palette. Then, right-click (Windows) or CTRL-click (Mac) anywhere within your image to access a pop-up menu with simple brush options like the one shown in the following illustration. Use the slider in this menu to adjust the size of your current brush tip.

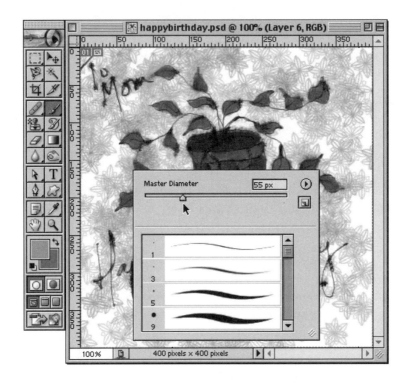

Use the Blur and Sharpen Tools to Adjust the Focus Within Small Areas of an Image

When you want to draw attention to certain areas within an image by adjusting the focus, the Sharpen tool is well suited for the job. Likewise, when you need to take attention away from areas within an image by reducing the contrast between the details, the Blur tool is a likely candidate. Both of these tools enable you to use brushes and all the settings in the Brushes palette to "paint" the adjustments into the image as needed.

TRY IT To use the Blur and Sharpen tools to adjust focus within small areas of an image, first make sure you have the file you want to edit open in Photoshop. Open the Layers palette (choose Window I Layers) and select the layer containing the part you want to blur or sharpen. Then, select the appropriate tool (Blur or Sharpen) from the toolbox.

Click the button to the far right of the Options bar or choose Window | Brushes to access the Brushes palette, and select a good brush for the job. If you need to blur or focus a very small, specific area, then the harder-edge brushes are fine. However, if you want to blur or focus a bit larger area, and keep the edges feathered, I find the softer brushes work better.

▶ *CAUTION*

Avoid being heavy-handed with the Sharpen tool, as it is meant to be used in moderation. If you click and hold for too long in one spot with the Sharpen tool, you will likely find your images changing to resemble tiny pieces of fluorescent confetti.

In the Options bar, select the blending mode to specify how your brush affects the pixels it touches by choosing one of the following:

- Normal
- Darken
- Lighten
- Hue
- Saturation
- Color
- Luminosity

Then specify the strength of each stroke.

Finally, check the box next to Use All Layers to instruct Photoshop to blur or sharpen on all layers at once, instead of just the active one.

▶ *QUICK TIP*

To blur or sharpen an entire layer or image—as opposed to small sections of the image—use filters instead. Try experimenting with one of the blur filters by choosing Filter | Blur and picking one in the menu. Or try the sharpen filters, which can be found by choosing Filter | Sharpen.

Use the Smudge Tool to Enlarge an Image's Canvas Size

I create a lot of collages that become banners for web pages. For example, one of my clients—a radio station—has a banner on its home page that rotates every 10–15 seconds. I create new banners for the radio station all the time, but each must be the exact same size. Sometimes the backgrounds of the photos I use don't fill the designated space, so I have to force them to do so. My favorite way to do this is using the Smudge tool.

Figure 8-18   The image I found to use for this banner needed more added to the background.

Figure 8-18 shows an example where I needed to create a banner to advertise the morning DJ, who goes on the air at 5 A.M. I found a great photo of an alarm clock that is already set to 5 A.M., but its background isn't wide enough to fill the entire size of the banner. I can't resize the photo because then the clock wouldn't fit in the banner, so the Smudge tool is my preferred method of adding to the background. Figure 8-19 shows the final result after smudging the background to make the image large enough to fit the banner's dimensions.

TRY IT   To use the Smudge tool to enlarge an image's canvas size, first make sure the image is open in Photoshop and the layer in question is selected in the Layers palette. Select the Smudge tool from the toolbox by clicking and holding on the Blur tool or pressing SHIFT-R several

Figure 8-19   The Smudge tool worked quite well to provide the needed addition to the background.

times until the Smudge tool is displayed. Then, choose a large, soft, round brush if you need to smudge a large area like I did in Figure 8-19.

> ### ▶ QUICK TIP
>
> *If you have a pressure-sensitive drawing tablet and pen, set your options to adjust the strength of the smudge according to your pen's pressure for more control over the smudged area.*

Click just within the edges of the image and drag the cursor away from the edge toward the area you need to fill. Repeat this process as many times as needed to create the desired effect. The following illustration shows how I started working at the bottom of the image, where I was most concerned about keeping the reflections from the alarm clock.

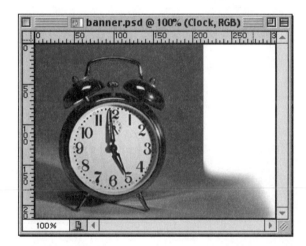

Because the top portion of the image doesn't really contain any textures I need reproduced in the added background, I can speed up the process by doing something we all loved as a kid—finger painting. Click the box in the Options bar to activate Finger Painting for the Smudge tool.

Then, use the Eyedropper tool to pick up a color from the image and place it in your foreground color swatch. To help understand why this is important, consider this analogy—Finger Painting with the Smudge tool is like putting a dab of the color paint in the foreground color swatch onto your finger and then using it to smear part of a canvas already wet with oil paints. By contrast, normal use of the Smudge tool smudges the wet colors already on the canvas with a clean finger.

Use the Dodge and Burn Tools to Adjust the Exposure of an Image

If you've ever taken an over- or underexposed photograph and wished you could "fix" it, this technique is for you. Likewise, if you've ever simply wanted to adjust the exposure of an image in order to shift the viewer's attention, this technique is for you. Photoshop contains two tools—Dodge and Burn—that are replicas of tools photographers use in the darkroom to adjust the exposure of an image.

Compare Figures 8-20 and 8-21 to see how adjusting the exposure of an image can refine the viewer's focus to a specific area. In this case, I burned (darkened) the background and outer edges of my daughter's face to make it recede further into the background, while dodging (lightening) the highlights on her face to make them stand out in a more three-dimensional way.

TRY IT   To use the Dodge and Burn tools to adjust the exposure within an image, first make sure you have the file you want to edit open in Photoshop. Open the Layers palette (choose Window | Layers) and select the layer containing the part you want to blur or sharpen. Then, select the appropriate tool (Dodge or Burn) from the toolbox.

> ### QUICK TIP
>
> *Select the Dodge tool to lighten areas. Select the Burn tool to darken areas.*

Click the button to the far right of the Options bar or choose Window | Brushes to access the Brushes palette, and select a good brush for the job. If you need to dodge or burn a very small, specific area, then the harder-edge brushes are fine. However, if you want to dodge or burn a bit larger area and keep the edges feathered, I find the softer brushes work better.

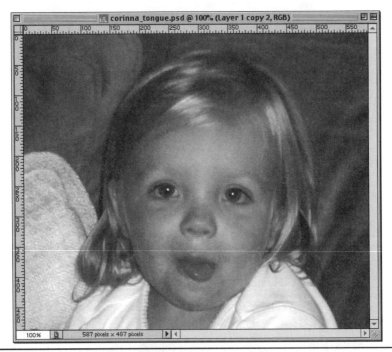

Figure 8-20   Untouched photo of my daughter

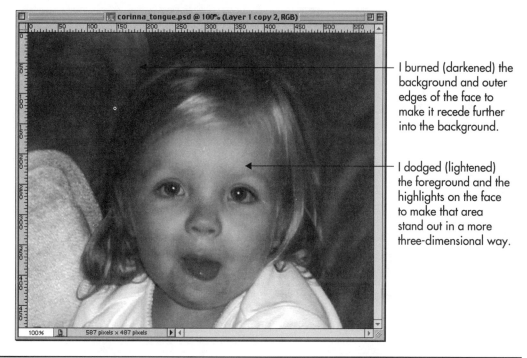

I burned (darkened) the background and outer edges of the face to make it recede further into the background.

I dodged (lightened) the foreground and the highlights on the face to make that area stand out in a more three-dimensional way.

Figure 8-21   Retouched photo of my daughter, in which the Dodge and Burn tools were used to adjust the exposure of the image

In the Options bar, select the range to specify which areas of the image the exposure affects:

- Shadows
- Midtones
- Highlights

Then specify the exposure level of each stroke.

▶ **QUICK TIP**

To dodge or burn only a specific area of an image, use a selection tool to select the area before painting in it.

Change the Blending Mode to Paint Highlights and Shadows

I often use Photoshop to create my own web icons and drawings, such as the one shown in the following illustration. In cases like this one, I can add a lot to otherwise flat-color drawings by painting in highlights and shadows. To see what I mean, compare the before and after view of a portal illustration for a marina, shown here on the left and right, respectively. The shadows and highlights around the rim of the hand-drawn portal were added by painting with black and white.

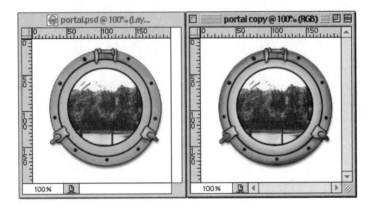

However, if I had just painted with black and white using the normal blending mode, the "highlights" and "shadows" would have been too harsh. Instead, to allow the highlights and shadows to properly blend with the image, I painted the highlights using the Screen blending mode and the shadows using the Multiply blending mode.

TRY IT To paint realistic highlights and shadows into an image, make sure the image is open and the layer on which you want to paint is currently selected. Select the Brush tool from the toolbox and pick an appropriately sized brush with which to paint.

> ### QUICK TIP
>
> *I like to paint on a new layer, so I can easily turn the layer off to compare how the image looked with and without the new additions.*

Before you begin painting your highlight, switch the blending mode in the Options bar to Screen for highlights or Multiple for shadows. Then, paint your highlights and shadows as needed.

Duplicate Part of an Image with the Clone Stamp

The Clone Stamp is one of my favorite tools in Photoshop, simply because of how fun it is to work with. I've enjoyed using it to perform such tasks as removing ex-family members from photos and adding extra eyes/ears/nose/toes to annoying family members' faces. (In fact, to test this tip while also having a bit of fun, I recommend you try it on a photo of an old boyfriend or girlfriend.)

TRY IT   But seriously, to duplicate part of an image with the Clone Stamp, you first need to make sure the image you want to edit is open in Photoshop and the active layer contains the part of the image you wish to copy. Click the Clone Stamp tool in the toolbox and select an appropriately sized brush for the job.

QUICK TIP

If you need to copy a small, specific area, try a small, hard-edged brush. If you need to copy a larger area, or one without clear edges, try a larger, softer brush.

From the Options bar, specify the following:

- Select the blending mode to specify how the new pixels you apply should interact with those already existing in the image.

- Specify the opacity of your brush strokes to define how much of the image below shows through the pasted area.

- Define the flow rate to identify how much "paint" is applied at once, and click the airbrush button to "spray" the effect rather than "brush" it.

- Choose Aligned to cause Photoshop to keep track of your brush strokes so each new stroke picks up where the previous one left off performing the copy and paste. Leaving the Aligned option unchecked causes Photoshop to start from the beginning each time you click the image to paint.

- Choose Use All Layers to copy from a layer other than the active one. If this option is left unchecked, you can only copy and paste within the currently active layer.

To specify from which part of the image you'd like to copy, ALT-click (Windows) or OPTION-click (Mac). Then, move to the location in which you want to paste it, and begin dragging in the window with the Clone tool.

For example, when I wanted to add more blocks to the image shown in Figure 8-22, I first OPTION-clicked (on my Mac) in the center of the Y block on the right to copy it. Then, I moved to the left a little bit and began dragging (painting) to paste the block in that location. I prefer to work on a new layer when pasting, so I have the option of removing the pasted element or editing it as needed.

Then I began dragging here
to paste the copied image

First I clicked here to "sample"
the spot I wanted to copy

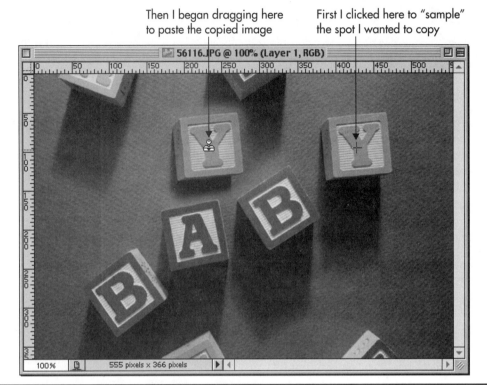

Figure 8-22   I used the Clone tool to duplicate a block in this image.

> ▶ | **QUICK TIP**
>
> *You can also use the Clone tool to copy and paste between multiple files open in Photoshop.*
> ALT-*click (Windows)/*OPTION-*click (Mac) to sample the area from which to copy in one image,*
> *and then drag in the other image to paste the sampled area.*

Remove Blemishes with the Patch and Healing Brush Tools

A common task for designers working in Photoshop is to remove blemishes or other unneeded items from images. In the past, the Clone tool was the best tool for the job, and although that tool is still a good candidate in many cases, the Healing Brush and Patch tools are coming on strong. Both tools not only copy and paste between areas of an image, but also add color and tonal correction to cause the pasted area to more closely fit with the pixels around it.

Suppose, for example, I wanted to remove the top leaf from the clover shown in Figure 8-23. Using the Clone tool, I could tediously try to paint out the clover and replace it with a sample from the adjacent background gradient. However, matching the gradient would not be easy. Believe it or not, I can remove the top leaf with the Patch tool in a matter of ten seconds and then touch up with the Healing Brush tool, and you'd never know it was there. Compare Figures 8-23, 8-24, and 8-25 to see what I mean.

▶ *CAUTION*

The code behind the Healing Brush tool uses Photoshop's Image Cache to perform the behind-the-scenes computation necessary for these tools. Choose Edit | Preferences | Image Cache to check your settings. To avoid problems, leave it at the default setting of 4.

TRY IT   To use the Patch and Healing Brush tools to remove blemishes or other areas from an image, first make sure the image you want to edit is open in Photoshop and the layer containing the area you want to edit is active in the Layers palette. Then, select either the Healing Brush or the Patch tool, depending on how you want to remove the area.

▶ *QUICK TIP*

To remove an area with selection tools, choose the Patch tool. To remove an area by painting it out with a brush, choose the Healing Brush.

Figure 8-23   Untouched photo

Figure 8-24 Photo after the Patch tool was used to remove the top leaf

Figure 8-25 Photo after the Healing Brush tool was used to touch up the base of the top leaf and a few other areas

When using the Patch tool, draw around the area you want to remove. The tool works just like the Lasso tool, so you can hold down the SHIFT key and drag to add to your selection, or press ALT (Windows)/OPTION (Mac) while dragging to subtract from your selection. When you're finished selecting the area to remove, click inside the selected area and drag the selection outline over to the area with which you want to replace it. In Figure 8-23, I selected the top leaf and then dragged the selection outline to the left to cover the leaf with the gradient from the background in that area.

When using the Healing Brush tool, select the brush size, hardness, spacing, angle, and roundness by clicking the brush sample in the Options bar to reveal the Brushes pop-up palette. A relatively small, hard brush typically works best. Specify the blending mode of the area being "healed."

> **QUICK TIP**
>
> *When using the Healing Brush to fix images containing sand, hair, or other noisiness, try working with the blending mode set to Replace and using a smooth brush for best results.*

Click the box next to Aligned to cause Photoshop to keep track of your brush strokes so each new stroke picks up where the previous one left off performing the copy and paste. Leaving the Aligned option unchecked causes Photoshop to start from the beginning each time you click the image to paint.

Work as you would with the Clone tool, by ALT-clicking (Windows) or OPTION-clicking (Mac) first on the area you want to copy, and then dragging in the area you want to paste to. Wait a few seconds after making a stroke to see the color and tonal corrections be applied to the area you edited. If you need to make corrections to a precise area without affecting the surrounding pixels, make a selection with the selection tools before painting with the Healing Brush.

> **QUICK TIP**
>
> *Use the Fade command (Edit | Fade) to reduce the opacity of the effects of the Healing Brush or Patch tool. However, you can only apply the Fade command immediately after using the Healing Brush or Patch tool. If you perform another action first, the Fade command becomes inaccessible and can only be reached by stepping back a step in your History palette (choose Window | History).*

Restore Part of an Image to the Previously Saved Version

While the File | Revert command is great for reverting an entire image to its previously saved version, there are times when you only need to revert a portion of an image. In a case like this, you can use brushes to actually paint back the previously saved version on a part of an image.

TRY IT Before restoring part of an image, you need to open the History palette (choose Window | History) and click once in the first box next to the state or snapshot from which you wish to restore. For example, if you want to restore part of an image all the way back to the way it looked when you first opened it, select the first snapshot at the top of the History palette with the name of your file. If you instead want to restore to how the file looked about ten minutes ago, look for the action you performed at that time in your History palette and select that state.

▶ **QUICK TIP**

If you're not sure what the image looked like at a given state or snapshot in your History palette, click once on the state or snapshot's name, and Photoshop will show you how things looked at that time. Be careful not to perform any edits or actions on your image while you're reviewing how things looked, or you'll cause the rest of the states after that one to disappear. When you're ready, click once on the last state in the History palette to return to the current state.

After you select the state from which you want to restore part of your image, begin restoring using either of the following techniques:

- Use the History Brush tool to paint from a selected point in the History palette
- Use the Eraser tool with the Erase To History option selected, to erase to a selected point in the History palette

▶ **NOTE**

Another way to restore part of an image to a previously saved version is to select the area you want to restore and choose Edit | Fill. Then, specify History as the Use. As with painting to restore a part of an image, this technique also requires you to first select the state to which you want to restore, from within the History palette.

▶ **QUICK TIP**

When using the Eraser tool with the Erase To History option selected, you can quickly shift to using the regular Eraser tool by holding down the ALT *(Windows) or* OPTION *(Mac) key while erasing.*

Use the History Brushes to Combine Creative Effects

Sometimes when I'm working in Photoshop, I like the way an applied effect looks on one part of the image but not on the rest. When this happens, it can be difficult to retain the effect in only one area without compromising the rest of the image. However, it doesn't have to be difficult if you use the history brushes.

Consider the image shown in Figures 8-26 and 8-27. Figure 8-26 shows an untouched photo I wanted to use as a background for advertising a theme dinner. To give the photo a more painterly

Figure 8-26   Untouched photo

Figure 8-27   Photo after Paint Daubs filter was applied

look, I applied the Paint Daubs filter (Filter | Artistic | Paint Daubs), as shown in Figure 8-27. However, I wasn't happy with just how painterly the elements in the foreground had become, and wanted to regain some of the clarity in those areas from the original image.

So, I created a snapshot of the image with the Paint Daubs filter applied, and then moved back in the History palette to return to the image before I applied the filter. I used the Art History Brush—which paints from the history but with stylized strokes—to paint from the new snapshot in the areas where I wanted to add the Paint Daubs effect. Then, to retain clarity in areas where I lost it, I used the normal History Brush and painted from the original snapshot. Figure 8-28 shows my final image.

TRY IT   To use the history brushes to combine creative effects in Photoshop, first make sure you have the image you want to work with open in Photoshop. Then, make a change to the entire image, such as by applying one of the filters located in the Filter | Artistic menu. (For example, in Figure 8-27, I applied the Paint Daubs filter to my image.)

Choose Window | History to reveal the History palette. Click the button at the bottom of the palette to create a new snapshot based on how the image looks now that the filter has been applied.

Figure 8-28   Final piece

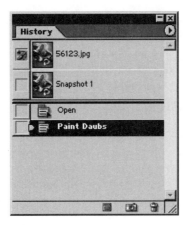

Now click once on the original snapshot in the History palette to return the image to its original state. Another way to go back in the history of the image is to click on preview steps within the History palette until the image looks as it did before you applied the filter.

To reveal some of the effect of the Paint Daubs filter, you can paint from the history using one of the history brushes. Select the appropriate history brush from the toolbox and adjust its size and shape by clicking on the brush sample in the Options bar.

► **QUICK TIP**

If you want to paint with normal brushes, use the History Brush. Or, to paint with stylized brushes, use the Art History Brush.

When using the Art History Brush, you also need to specify which type of stylized brush you want to use from the following list, as well as the area around the brush affected by it and the tolerance level. Note, the higher the tolerance level, the more Photoshop limits your strokes to only affect areas distinctly different from those in the history state from which you're painting.

- Tight Short
- Tight Medium
- Tight Long
- Loose Medium
- Loose Long
- Dab
- Tight Curl
- Tight Curl Long
- Loose Curl
- Loose Curl Long

When you've made all the appropriate changes to the settings, you just need to return to the History palette to specify from which layer you want to paint. To do that, click once in the empty box next to the snapshot or history state name you want to reveal with your brush strokes. For testing this technique, click next to Snapshot 1 to add some of those Paint Daubs back into the image. Now you're ready to click and drag in the image to paint.

▶ | **QUICK TIP**

Don't be afraid to experiment! Try performing other filters on the image and creating new snapshots from each one, which you can then use to paint from with one of the history brushes. Likewise, try experimenting with the different stylized artistic brushes using the Art History Brush, for some really creative effects.

Add Layer Styles to Shapes for Quick and Easy Buttons

Creating buttons and navigational systems for web pages is a very common task for web designers. Using the shape tools to create those buttons offers added flexibility over drawing them with the Pencil or Brush tool because shape tools draw resolution-independent artwork that can be easily resized at will. In addition, you can quickly add a drop shadow or emboss effect (or both, as shown in the following illustration) to a button just by adding the appropriate layer style or styles.

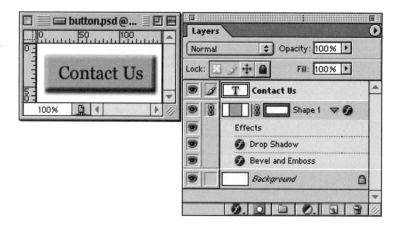

TRY IT To create quick and easy Web buttons using shapes and layer styles, first make sure the file you want to work with is open in Photoshop. Select the appropriate shape tool from the toolbox, depending on which type of shape you want to draw—rectangle, rounded rectangle, ellipse, polygon, line, or custom shape.

For example, Figure 8-29 shows how I drew three leaves with the Custom Shape tool in the form of a maple leaf and added text inside each leaf to define the links. (Click the triangle in the upper-right

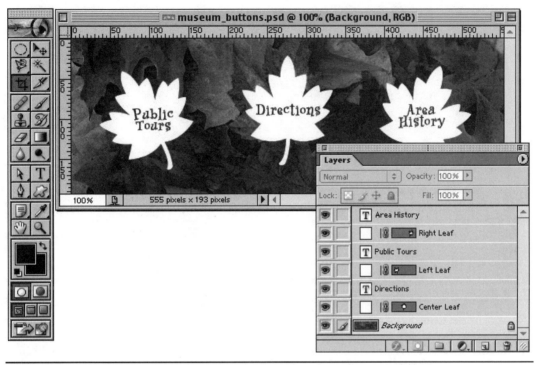

Figure 8-29   I used the maple leaf Custom Shape tool to draw three maple leaves.

corner of the Custom Shape selector and choose All to load all custom shapes, including this one.) For two of the shapes, I choose Edit | Free Transform and dragged just outside one of the corners to slightly skew them.

After drawing the shapes you want to use for buttons, click once on one of the shape layers in the Layers palette to make it active. Click the Layer Styles button (ƒ) and select a style to add. Figure 8-30 shows how I added two styles to the first maple leaf—Outer Glow, and Bevel and Emboss.

► **QUICK TIP**

Wondering how I got the leaf to look "cut out" of the leaf background in Figure 8-30? Choose Bevel and Emboss from the Layer Styles menu and select Inner Bevel for the Style, Smooth for the Technique, and Down for the Direction. The other options can be left at their defaults.

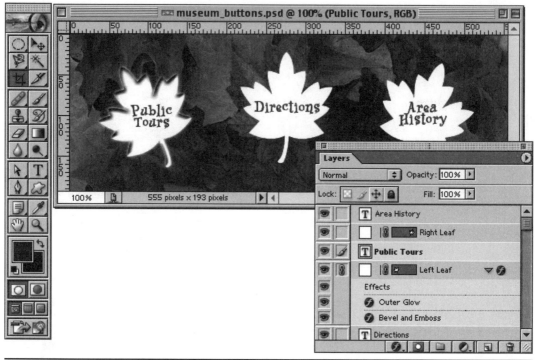

Figure 8-30 After drawing and rotating the first shape, I added two layer styles to give it a "cut out" effect.

Use Font Dingbats for Easy Icons

Photoshop 7 ships with a wide variety of custom shapes, just a portion of which are shown in Figure 8-31. These custom shapes are perfect for creating icons, such as those commonly used in web and interface design. You can further add to this library by converting font dingbats to shapes.

Dingbats are font families in which each letter is replaced by a shape, drawing, or icon. You probably have one of the most popular sets of dingbats—Microsoft's Webdings—already loaded on your computer, because it ships with most Microsoft products. In addition, visit any font library online and search for "dingbats" to locate more. One of my favorite sites for finding dingbats is www.dingbatpages.com.

► | **QUICK TIP**

Access the font menu in any program and scroll to the bottom to see if you have Webdings loaded on your system. If you don't, you can download a copy of the font from Microsoft by visiting www.microsoft.com/typography/fontpack/default.htm.

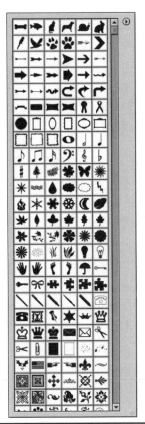

Figure 8-31   Photoshop ships with a wide variety of custom shapes, including these.

TRY IT   To use a dingbat in your design, first make sure the font family of dingbats is loaded on your system. Make sure the Type tool is selected and select the font dingbat's name from the list of available fonts in the Options bar.

Begin typing in an open file to see the dingbats for each letter. The following illustration shows how I typed a capital N using the Webdings font to get this drawing of an eye. To make the icon easier to edit and change as needed, I can convert it from being a bitmap font dingbat into a resolution-independent vector shape.

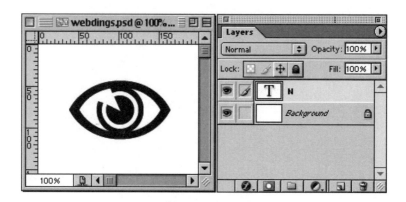

 To convert type to shapes, select the type layer in the Layers palette and choose Layer | Type | Convert To Shapes.

▶ *CAUTION*

You can only create shapes from fonts whose outline data—sometimes referred to as the printer font— is also loaded on your computer. If you try to convert text to outlines but receive an error, return to the source of the font (such as the web site you downloaded it from or the CD you loaded it from) and see if you missed part of the font during the installation. Some fonts, however, were not created with outline data and therefore can't be made into shapes.

CHAPTER 9

Using Favorite Creative Effects

TIPS IN THIS CHAPTER

I f this book is a manual for accomplishment, this chapter is a coloring book and I am giving you license to color outside the lines. This is the chapter in the book where we'll delve into *just* the tip of the tip of the iceberg. There could be volumes written on the creative possibilities that Photoshop offers. Just as each artist is uniquely able to express themselves with different mediums and styles, so is the Photoshop designer equipped to accomplish the same "task."

The bulk of the tips in this chapter access Photoshop's Filter menu. However, given that there are so many filters available in that menu, it's impossible to provide tips for using each and every one in this single chapter. Instead, use these tips as a starting point for your creative journey, and don't be afraid to try new things. In fact, Photoshop gives you so many ways to "fix" your images or return them to previous states, there's no excuse for not trying just a few of these tips on your images.

Before you do so, I'd like to remind you to always save your original document as a Photoshop file (PSD) and utilize your layers. While this is indeed often the part of Photoshop that causes the ooohing and aaahing, chances are good you'll also create things that will also cause you to say "eeew" or "yeck." Unless that's the vibe you are going for, you'll want to make sure you can undo the monster you've created.

▶ **NOTE**

Many of the tips in this chapter use filters from Photoshops's Filter menu. Because of the way in which these filters work, most require you to rasterize any vector data contained on layers to which you want to apply a filter. Rasterized text is no longer editable, and rasterized shapes can no longer be transformed independently of their resolution. If you're worried about this, make a backup copy of the layer before applying the filter.

Another helpful bit of advice to think about before you begin experimenting with filters is to expand the Photoshop memory you have allocated. Applied filters utilize quite a bit of "brain power," so make sure your computer has enough scratch disk (or free disk) space available to grind through all that you are asking it to do. You will also notice that your files increase in size as you continue to add layers to the document, which is yet another reason you want to make sure you have enough space to work freely while utilizing Photoshop.

▶ | **QUICK TIP**

You always have the option to "purge" memory that is being potentially bogged down by information in the "undo" memory, the Clipboard, and the History palette. You'll find the purge options under Edit | Purge. Be careful, though, because once you purge anything, it's gone forever.

Create a Fake Duotone

Creating a true duotone is discussed in Chapter 12 . If your project calls for a limited color palette and you wish to incorporate the use of a duotone image, you should adhere to those guidelines. However, you can also create fake duotones in Photoshop—purely for the sake of creativity and not because of any printing requirements—simply by adjusting the Hue/Saturation of the image. Compare the difference in the photos in Figure 9-1. The one on the left is a true duotone while the one on the right is a fake. To view Figure 9-1 in color, refer to the Creative Effects section of the color insert.

TRY IT   To create a fake duotone, make sure the image you wish to affect is open in Photoshop and select Image | Adjustments | Hue/Saturation. When the dialog box pops up, make sure the Colorize box is checked, and then adjust the sliders to create the color scheme you desire.

▶ **NOTE**

Make sure your image is not in grayscale mode. When creating a true duotone, your image must first be in grayscale mode. To create a fake duotone, your image must be in either RGB or CMYK mode.

Add Noise to an Image

Adding noise to an image is another way to add texture or dimensionality to your image. Sometimes, if the image you are working with is of mediocre quality to begin with, you can add noise to it on purpose, and suddenly your image will look intentionally grainy. Adding noise can also make your image look old or antique.

Figure 9-1   A true duotone created in Photoshop with two specified Pantone colors (left) and a fake duotone (right)

TRY IT   To add noise to an image, make sure the file you wish to affect is open in Photoshop and the layer containing the specific area to affect is active. Then, select Filter | Noise. In the dialog box, adjust the slider or insert the value to increase or decrease the amount of noise you would like added to your image; the greater the value, the "noisier" the image. Compare the two photos in Figure 9-2 to see an example of adding different amounts of noise to an image.

▶ *NOTE*

I recommend selecting the Gaussian method of adding noise. Also, I like to select the option for Monochromatic, to keep all the "noise" in the same hue family.

Add Motion to an Image

Adding motion to an image is a Photoshop specialty: the ability to change a stagnant image into a dynamic one is what makes Photoshop so much fun to work with. Although there are certainly a variety of techniques you can use to add motion to an image, the simplest is to use the Motion Blur filter.

TRY IT   To add motion to an image, make sure the file you wish to affect is open in Photoshop. Open the Layers palette (choose Window | Layers) and select the layer to which you wish to add motion. (If you only want to add motion to a portion of that layer, select that part with a selection tool.)

Figure 9-2   A value of 5 was entered as the percentage of noise added to the image (left), while a value of 20 was entered for the image on the right.

▶ | **QUICK TIP**

It can also be helpful to duplicate the layer, for two reasons. First, you can flip back and forth between the two layers to determine which technique you prefer. Second, you can turn on both layers and reduce the opacity of the top one to alter the effect a bit.

Adjust the opacity of the layer to approximately 60 percent or as desired. Select Filter | Blur | Motion Blur. Enter a value to adjust the angle for the direction you wish the image to appear it is moving in, or click within the circle graphic. Enter a value or move the slider according to the distance you wish the blur to expand. Compare the two images in Figure 9-3 to see how applying a Motion Blur took a simple umbrella and blew it into flight.

Apply a Gaussian Blur to Bring an Object into Focus

Suppose you have a portion of an image that you would like to draw the viewer's attention to. Although there are many ways you could go about creating a focal point in the image, one option is to use the Gaussian Blur feature. Compare the two images in Figure 9-4.

Figure 9-3   An image without the Motion Blur applied (left) and with the Motion Blur applied (right)

Figure 9-4   The image without the Gaussian Blur applied (left) and with the Gaussian Blur applied (right)

TRY IT   To apply a Gaussian Blur to bring an object into focus, first open the image you wish to work with in Photoshop. Use the Marquee tool—I prefer the Elliptical Marquee tool for this technique—and create a selection around the area you wish to focus in on.

Choose Select | Inverse or press SHIFT-CTRL-I (Windows) or SHIFT-CMD-I (Mac) to select the opposite, or in this case, the area you don't want to focus on. Choose Select | Feather or press ALT-CTRL-D (Windows) or OPTION-CMD-D (Mac) to create a gradual transition between the area we'll focus on and that which we won't. Enter a value of approximately 40 in the dialog box: this ensures that the transition between the area that is focused and the area that is blurred is smooth and gradual.

Select Filter | Blur | Gaussian Blur. Enter a value for the desired effect and click OK. The greater the value, the more out-of-focus the peripheral areas will appear. If you're not happy with the results, press CTRL-Z (Windows) or CMD-Z (Mac) to undo and try again.

Use Bitmap Mode to Create Interesting Effects

Generally, when an image is converted to a bitmap, it is for the purpose of creating line art that is placeable in page layout programs. Although this function is useful, converting an image to a bitmap and then converting it back into whatever color mode you are working in can also create savvy creative effects.

TRY IT   To use bitmap mode to create interesting effects, first make sure the file in which you wish to work is open in Photoshop. Use the selection tools or choose Select | All to select an area of an image that you'd like to turn into bitmap mode.

Choose Edit | Copy or press CTRL-C (Windows) or CMD-C (Mac) to copy the selection. Then, choose File | New or press CTRL-N (Windows) or CMD-N (Mac) to create a new document, based on the measurements of the image you have copied into the Clipboard. Give it a name if you wish and click OK.

Choose Edit | Paste or press CTRL-V (Windows) or CMD-V (Mac) to paste the image into the new document. Before you can convert the file to bitmap mode, it must be in grayscale mode. So, choose Image | Mode | Grayscale and click OK when the dialog box pops up to switch to grayscale (an example of which is shown in Figure 9-5).

Next, choose Image | Mode | Bitmap. Enter 600 or higher into the output value and select Halftone Screen as the Method. In the Halftone Screen dialog box, enter a frequency value. If you want a fine screen, enter a value of 60 or higher. If you want the image to look very "dotted" or almost cartoon-like, as shown in Figure 9-6, enter a value of 25 or lower. I recommend leaving the angle at 45 and selecting Round for the shape. Click OK to see the results.

You can now convert the image back into a color mode or save it as a TIFF and place it in another program as a graphic.

▶ *NOTE*

Look at the Creative Effects section of the color insert to see how I colorized the image shown in Figures 9-5 and 9-6.

Figure 9-5   A standard grayscale image

Figure 9-6   Grayscale image converted to a bitmap

Create a Drop Shadow that Will Remain Transparent When Exported into Other Page Layout Programs

Oftentimes a drop shadow is added to an object to create dimensionality. The object appears as if it is free-floating, and the shadow appears as if it is naturally part of it. Once you save your file in an exportable format to bring it into a page layout program, the shadow will not appear transparent against whatever background you have specified in your page layout program.

In other words, in Photoshop, you can tell a shadow how to affect the layer(s) below the shadow. But once the file is saved as a TIFF or EPS, it is then recognized as a placed flat graphic in your page layout program, not a multilayered graphic. Therefore, the graphic will have the same background as that specified in the Photoshop file. Unless you have specified the same background color for both the Photoshop file and the file in your page layout program, the placed image and shadow will not "float" or appear transparent.

The good news is that you can create a drop shadow in Photoshop that will still retain transparent-like qualities once placed in other programs, by treating your drop shadow like a dithered bitmap. That way, when you place it in a page layout program, it will be treated as a bitmapped graphic whose foreground color assignment can be whatever you choose and the background color assignment can be "none" so as to appear transparent against the background.

Remember, though, the shadow must be imported separately from the object. If you create an object in Photoshop and export it with a clipping path, you will have to place that object into the page layout program and then place the shadow behind it in two separate operations. These images are now two separate graphics. This might sound confusing, but it's really a great technique and quite simple if you just follow the steps.

▶ NOTE

If you use Adobe InDesign for your page layouts, you no longer have to use a lengthy technique such as this one to achieve transparent shadows. The reason is that InDesign 2.0 now allows you to apply editable drop shadows and other transparent effects directly within the program, and you can even import layered Photoshop files.

TRY IT Open the layered file in Photoshop and choose Window | Layers to open the Layers palette. Select the layer housing the object for which you wish to create a drop shadow. Choose Select | All and Edit | Copy to copy it. Then, choose File | New and Edit | Paste to paste the contents into a new document, and press CTRL-E (Windows) or CMD-E (Mac) to merge the layers into a flat document.

Use the selection and/or pen tools to make sure just the object for which you wish to make the shadow is selected. Choose Window | Paths to reveal the Paths palette. Right-click (Windows) or OPTION-click (Mac) within the selected area and choose Make Work Path. Leave the Tolerance set to 2.0 and click OK.

> **QUICK TIP**
>
> *If you placed an object into a new file with a white background, it might be easiest to use the Magic Wand tool to select the background and then choose Select | Inverse to quickly select your object.*

Click the small triangle in the top-right corner of the Paths palette and select Save Path. Name the path appropriately and click OK. Then, click the small triangle in the Paths palette again and choose Clipping Path. Make sure the name of the path you just created is selected and click OK. Choose File | Save, and save this file in the EPS file format. Remember, you must have the clipping path named and selected prior to saving, or it will not knock out the background. (You can now place this file into another program and it will appear free-floating with no imported background—but continue reading to add a shadow to the file.)

▶ **NOTE**

Wondering about that option for Flatness when saving a clipping path? In most cases, you can leave that option blank, because it causes the printer to use its default values when printing the file. However, if you encounter printer errors when trying to print a file with a clipping path, refer to the tip "Save Selections as Clipping Paths to Define Transparent Sections of an Image" in Chapter 5 for more information.

In Photoshop, open your object file and immediately save a copy of the file, naming it differently (for example, object_shadow.tif). Make sure the object is selected. In the Layers palette, select Duplicate Layer from the flyout menu in the top-right corner of the Layers palette.

Make sure the duplicate layer is beneath the original object layer in the Layers palette. (You can name it Object Shadow if you like.) Click the background color swatch and select black or a dark color; the darker the color, the denser your shadow will be.

Select the shadow layer and press SHIFT-ALT-BACKSPACE (Windows) or SHIFT-OPTION-DELETE (Mac) to automatically fill the selected area with the current background color. Note, you will not see this layer except in the small preview box of the Layers palette, because it is directly beneath the object layer above it.

Then, select Filter | Blur | Gaussian Blur. The Gaussian Blur dialog box will pop up. Insert the desired value: the greater the value, the softer the shadow; the smaller the value, the more defined the shadow edge will be.

You should now see the shadow behind the object layer. Delete the object layer (because this file is only for the shadow) by dragging its name to the small trash can icon at the bottom of the Layers palette.

Select Image | Mode | Grayscale and click OK when the dialog box asks you if you would like to discard color. Now, select Image | Mode | Bitmap. Under Output, enter 600 and select Diffusion Dither for the Method. If you zoom in to the file, you will see that the shadow is actually a collection of tiny dots that become denser toward the center of the shadow. Make sure the file is saved as a TIFF file (.tif extension).

Import the shadow file into your page layout program. (Make sure you set the background color to None.) You can colorize the shadow in the page layout program, according to the effect you desire to create. Import the object and place it on top of the shadow.

▶ *CAUTION*

In your page layout program, you might notice that the shadow looks clunky (see Figure 9-7) and not at all like the fine dither you see when you open the same file in Photoshop. Some page layout programs do not accurately represent the dithered shadow onscreen. Have no fear: when you go to print your document, the shadow will print beautifully (see Figure 9-8).

Figure 9-7   Shadows often display poorly in some page layout programs, even though they will print fine.

Figure 9-8   Some page layout programs are capable of displaying shadows just as they will look when printed.

Apply Preset Styles for Quick Special Effects

Chapter 8 discussed saving settings for tools as presets in Photoshop, enabling you to access them easily at a later time. In addition to the tool presets you save in Photoshop, the program also ships with several categories of predefined tool presets that can be quite useful for achieving some additional creative effects.

For example, one of the presets saved in the Art History Brush category is called Champagne. I used this tool preset to give an interesting effect to an otherwise unattractive background in a photo of my daughter (see Figure 9-9).

Figure 9-9 The Champagne preset for the Art History Brush helped me quickly reduce the impact of the boring background of this photo.

TRY IT To apply preset styles for quick special effects, open the file in Photoshop that you want to affect. Then, choose Window | Tool Presets to display the Tool Presets palette. Click the triangle in the upper-right corner to access the palette menu, and choose from the four categories of tool presets that ship with Photoshop listed at the bottom of the menu:

- Art History
- Brushes
- Crop & Marquee
- Text

After choosing one of the preceding options, click Append to add the tool presets in those categories to any that currently exist in your Tool Presets palette, or click OK to replace the presets in the palette with those you're loading.

Repeat the preceding steps to add other categories of tool presets to the palette. When you're ready to use one of the presets, click its name in the Tool Presets palette and begin painting or editing your image as desired.

> ### ▶ QUICK TIP
>
> *If you selected an Art History tool preset and are wondering what settings Adobe used to achieve the effect, choose Window | Brushes to open the Brushes palette and take a look. Also, check the Options bar for more settings.*

Remove Blemishes from Human Faces

Give anyone the power of Photoshop and she'll eventually want to know how to "fix" a few blemishes in a personal photo. It's no wonder, because Photoshop is an excellent tool for retouching human faces. In fact, you might think of the new Healing Brush tool as a virtual plastic surgeon's dream.

TRY IT To remove blemishes from photos of human faces, first open the file you want to affect in Photoshop. Choose Window | Layers to reveal the Layers palette and move to the layer containing the person's face.

Then, perform any or all of the following tasks, depending on the type of blemish you're trying to remove:

- Select the Healing Brush tool from the toolbox and an appropriately sized brush tip to "paint" those blemishes away. This works best for blemishes such as crow's feet and wrinkles because Photoshop automatically adjusts the color in the healed areas to match the surroundings.

- Select the Patch tool from the toolbox to "select" the blemishes away by first drawing a selection around an area to be removed, and then dragging it over a "clean" area (the area with which to replace it). This works best for somewhat larger areas of blemishes, such as patches of acne, leftover food, or (as in the next example) spots of paint. However, this tool doesn't work well when the area of the blemish is larger than any other "clean" area within the face. As with the Healing Brush tool, Photoshop automatically adjusts the color in the patched areas to match the surroundings.

- Select the Clone Stamp tool from the toolbox and an appropriately sized brush tip to copy a "clean" area and paste it over a blemish. This works best for irregularly shaped areas, such as patches of acne or uneven skin, where the Patch tool would be difficult to select with. In addition, because you can adjust the opacity of the Clone Stamp tool, you can achieve a more refined cover-up than with either of the Healing Brush or Patch tools.

- Select the Smudge tool from the toolbox and an appropriately sized brush tip to slightly smudge away a tiny blemish such as a spot or freckle.

- Select the Blur tool from the toolbox and an appropriately sized brush tip to blur areas containing harsh color changes or rough patches of skin.

Compare the two images in the following illustration to see how I used the Patch tool to select the paint dab on my daughter's right cheek and cover it with a patch of clean skin from higher up on her cheek.

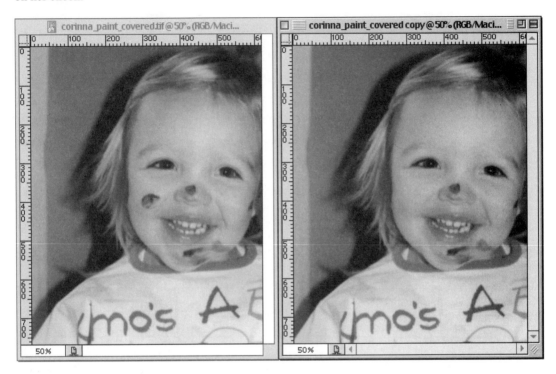

> ### QUICK TIP
>
> *Because the green channel is where the majority of the skin's natural imperfections appear, consider using the Clone Stamp, Smudge, or Blur tools in that channel only. (Choose Windows | Channels and click the Green channel, and then begin editing.) Avoid using the Healing Brush or Patch tools in a single channel, because the color correction performed by those tools works best in the full color (composite) mode.*

Make the Color of Human Faces More Vivid

Because photographs are two-dimensional, human faces in photographs often look flat and washed out. A great way to make the color of someone's face a bit more vivid and three-dimensional is to add a layer overlay of the face using the following technique.

TRY IT   To make the color of a human face more vivid, first make sure the image you want
             to affect is open in Photoshop, and that the layer housing the face you want to edit
is currently active. Then, perform the following steps.

1. Draw a selection around a person's face in an image. Because faces are irregular shapes, I like
   to use the Lasso tool. I usually set the Feather option to about 2 pixels, to soften the edges of
   my selection.

2. Make sure the layer with the face is currently selected in the Layers palette, and choose Layer |
   New | Layer Via Copy or press CTRL-J (Windows) or CMD-J (Mac).

3. With the new layer highlighted in the Layers palette, change the blend mode to Overlay using
   the drop-down menu at the top of the palette.

4. To cause the overlay to blend more with the image below and not look so harsh, reduce the Opacity
   of the layer to between 30% and 60%.

5. If the edges of the overlay are still a bit harsh, you can use the Eraser tool with the Opacity set
   to 50% to slightly erase or soften the edges.

6. Toggle the overlay layer on and off to see the before and after shots. To see how I used this
   technique on a photo of my daughters, see the Creative Effects section of the color insert.

▶ **NOTE**

You can see an example of this effect in action in the Creative Effects section of the color insert.

Quickly Remove Common Color Casts

Photographs that are scanned or brought into Photoshop using a digital camera often take on unwanted
color casts. Alternatively, certain lighting effects can cause a color cast—commonly yellow or blue,
but can be any color—to occur right when the picture is taken. Photoshop contains many ways to
neutralize those color casts, but the quickest way, if you're not concerned about being too precise,
is to use the Auto Color command.

TRY IT   Open a photo that contains a color cast in Photoshop. Choose Image | Adjustments |
             Auto Color, or press CTRL-SHIFT-B (Windows) or CMD-SHIFT-B (Mac) to run the Auto
Color command.

There are no specific options for this command; Photoshop automatically adjusts the color by
neutralizing the midtones and clipping the black and white points to eliminate any extremes in either
the dark or light parts of the image. The amount to which it clips those points can be adjusted in the

Auto Color Corrections Options dialog box. To access that dialog box, choose Image | Adjustments | Levels and click Options.

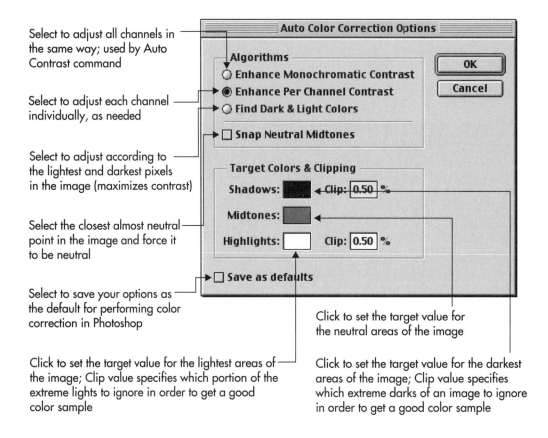

Select to adjust all channels in the same way; used by Auto Contrast command

Select to adjust each channel individually, as needed

Select to adjust according to the lightest and darkest pixels in the image (maximizes contrast)

Select the closest almost neutral point in the image and force it to be neutral

Select to save your options as the default for performing color correction in Photoshop

Click to set the target value for the lightest areas of the image; Clip value specifies which portion of the extreme lights to ignore in order to get a good color sample

Click to set the target value for the neutral areas of the image

Click to set the target value for the darkest areas of the image; Clip value specifies which extreme darks of an image to ignore in order to get a good color sample

If you make changes to anything in the Auto Color Corrections Options box that you want to be used by the Auto Color commands, select Save As Defaults and click OK. These settings are also used by the following commands: Levels, Curves, Auto Level, and Auto Contrast.

Remove Red-Eye from Photographs

Probably the most common request of my family and friends is for me to remove red-eye when I edit their photographs. While there are many different ways of doing this, the following steps outline the way I find to be most effective and precise.

TRY IT To remove red-eye from a photograph, first make sure the photograph is open in Photoshop and the layer containing the eyes of the person is currently active before performing these steps:

1. Select the Elliptical Marquee tool from the toolbox and set the Feather in the Options bar to 2 pixels.

2. Use this tool to draw a circular selection first around the red portion of the left eye.

3. Hold down the SHIFT key and repeat the process with the right eye until you have the red-eye selected from both eyes.

4. Choose Image | Adjustments | Channel Mixer.

5. By default, in an RGB image, the Red channel is selected in the Channel Mixer. Under Source Channels, set the value for Red back to 0 and increase the value of the other two channels (Green and Blue) to equal 100%. I usually set them each to 50%, but you can try other combinations depending on which color to emphasize.

6. Click OK to complete the process.

Create a Perspective Cast Shadow

Photoshop's Drop Shadow layer effect is a great tool for adding simple drop shadows to objects. But how do you achieve a more realistic cast shadow, such as one that falls away from an object in perspective based on the light source, and gets softer and lighter as it fades away? While there isn't a predefined layer effect to create cast shadows, you can create one with a few basic steps.

 To create a perspective cast shadow, first make sure the object to which you want to add the shadow is open and on its own layer in Photoshop. Then, follow these steps:

1. Choose Window | Layers to reveal the Layers palette.

2. Right-click (Windows) or CTRL-click (Mac) the layer in the Layers palette and choose Duplicate Layer. (Alternatively, you could drag the layer over the New Layer button at the bottom of the Layers palette to duplicate it.) If you want, name this layer **shadow**.

3. Make sure black is in the foreground color swatch. If it isn't, press D on your keyboard to make it so.

4. Press SHIFT-ALT-BACKSPACE (Windows) or SHIFT-OPTION-DELETE (Mac) to fill the pixels of the shadow layer with black. (Note that using the SHIFT key in this key combination causes Photoshop to fill only those pixels that currently have color. If you leave out the SHIFT key, Photoshop fills the entire layer.)

5. Press CTRL-[(Windows) or CMD-[(Mac) to move the shadow layer behind the object layer.

6. Press CTRL-T (Windows) or CMD-T (Mac) to access the Free Transform command. Drag the anchor points to change the perspective of the shadow, and press RETURN or ENTER when you're satisfied.

> ▶ **QUICK TIP**
>
> *The Free Transform command gives access to many transformation tools, including Scale, Skew, Distort, and Rotate. To restrict your transformation temporarily, right-click (Windows) or CTRL-click (Mac) inside the Free Transform bounding box and select one of the specific types of transformations from the list. For creating nice cast shadows, I like to use the Distort option.*

7. In the Layers palette, click the first button next to Lock: to lock the transparent pixels in the layer and prevent them from being affected by the next step.

8. Select the Gradient tool from the toolbox and click the gradient sample in the Options bar to select the first gradient, which fills with a gradient between the foreground and background colors. (If you changed your foreground and background colors, press D on your keyboard to return them to black and white. If the background of your image isn't white, click in the background color swatch to change it to match the color in your image's background.)

9. Click with the Gradient tool in the shadow layer, close to your object, and drag away from the object within the shadow. This step fills the shadow with a black that slowly fades to white (or whichever color was in your background color swatch). Repeat as necessary until you achieve the gradient you're looking for.

10. In the Layers palette, click again on the first button next to Lock: to unlock the transparent pixels in the layer and allow them to be edited.

11. Choose Filter | Blur | Gaussian Blur to blur the shadow. Try using a value between 2 and 10 for the Blur Radius until the blurriness of the shadow looks appropriate.

12. To further blur the part of the shadow that is farthest away from the object, use the Marquee or Lasso tool to draw a selection around the farthest 25 percent of the shadow. Choose Select | Feather and feather the selection about 6 pixels. Then, press CTRL-F (Windows) or CMD-F (Mac) to reapply the Gaussian Blur filter with the same settings used in the previous step.

13. To add a slight color to the shadow, click the Layer Styles button at the bottom of the Layers palette and choose Color Overlay. Try Screen as the Blend Mode to begin, and click inside the color sample swatch next to the Blend Mode menu to select the color with which to fill. I like to use the Eyedropper tool to select a color from the shadow parts of the object for which I'm

creating a shadow. So, in the case of the shadow I created for the gift box, I selected a color from the front side of the box that is in shadow.

Change the Color of Someone's Shirt, Shoes, Bag, or Any Other Object in a Photo

Another common task in Photoshop is to change the color of an object within a photograph. For example, my house is currently painted white, and I've been toying with the idea of drastically changing that color. Before I try convincing my husband to spend lots of money and time actually painting it, I prefer to play with the color in Photoshop. (Plus, I can use the enhanced photo to help convince my husband to actually paint it.)

▶ *NOTE*

To see the color I am considering painting my house, take a look in the Creative Effects section of the color insert.

 To change the color of an object in a photograph, first make sure the photo you want to affect is open in Photoshop. Then, follow these steps:

1. Choose Window | Layers to reveal the Layers palette.
2. Click once on the layer containing the object you want to affect.
3. Click the New Layer button at the bottom of the Layers palette to create a new layer above the current one.
4. Select the Brush tool from the toolbox and an appropriately sized brush tip with which to paint.
5. Make sure the color to which you want to change the object is currently visible in the foreground color swatch. If it isn't, click once on the foreground color swatch and select it.
6. Begin painting on the new layer over the area you wish to affect.
7. When the area is covered, change the blending mode for the layer on which you're painting from Normal to another option that helps you achieve the desired affect. I find that Multiple or Overlay works best in most cases, but try several different modes until you find the one that works the best for your particular image. Check the Creative Effects section of the color insert for a full-color example.

▶ *QUICK TIP*

Need to change the color again after you've already painted it? Make sure the new color to which you want to change is visible in the foreground color swatch and the new paint layer is active in the Layers palette. Click the first button next to Lock in the Layers palette to only fill those pixels that already have color. Then, press SHIFT-ALT-BACKSPACE *(Windows) or* SHIFT-OPTION-DELETE *(Mac).*

Add Objects or People to Existing Images

When I was starting out as a digital designer, I did some work for a photographer who specialized in outdoor wedding photography. One of my tasks involved removing extraneous elements (and sometimes people) from shots taken in public (such as a new bride and groom walking along a beach). In other cases, I was asked to actually add people into a photograph if, for example, they weren't able to be in the picture for whatever reason.

More recently, I wanted to give my mom a photo of her three grandkids to use as the desktop background on her computer. The problem was that my two kids live with me in Maine, my nephew lives with my sister in Maryland, and we didn't have any recent photos of the kids together. The solution? I took a photo of my daughters with a digital camera, then scanned a picture of my nephew and used Photoshop to add him to the photo of my daughters.

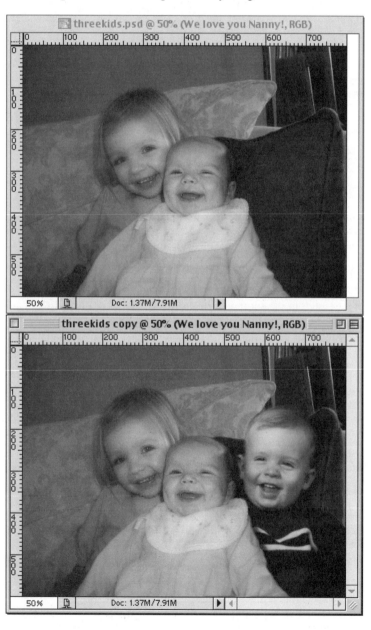

To add an object to an existing image, make sure both files are open in Photoshop. Use one of the following techniques to move the object from its own file into the destination file:

- Use the selection tools to draw a selection around the object. When selecting an element to be placed in another file, I like to add a slight feather to soften the edges a bit. After you make a selection, choose Select | Feather, specify a Radius of 2, and click OK. Choose Edit | Copy to copy the selection, switch to the receiving photo, and then choose Edit | Paste to place the selection on a new layer in the destination file.

► QUICK TIP

If you can see both files on your screen at the same time, you can simply click inside the selection and drag it from one image to the other.

- Use the Extract command to isolate the object. Choose Edit | Copy to copy the selection, switch to the receiving photo, and then choose Edit | Paste to paste the selection on a new layer in the destination file. (See Chapter 5 for details on using the Extract command.)
- Use the Clone Stamp tool to copy and paste the image with an appropriate brush. First, ALT-click (Windows) or OPTION-click (Mac) somewhere in the middle of the object you want to move. Then, switch to the destination file, create a new layer, and begin painting with the Clone Stamp tool to re-create the object in this file. Continue "painting" until you have re-created the entire object.

After you have moved the object from its original file into the destination file, use the Move tool to move it into the precise location where it should reside. Then, click the second button at the bottom of the Layers palette to add a layer mask to the layer containing the moved object.

Select the Brush tool and an appropriately sized brush tip to clean up the edges around the object. When working in a layer mask, painting with black hides the content of the layer, while painting with white reveals it. If you need to make a pasted object appear to be sitting behind another object, as I did with my nephew in the following illustration, hide that portion of the layer by painting it with black.

Then, to add shadows on or behind the object, paint with the Brush tool and an appropriately sized brush tip on a new layer whose blending mode is set to Multiply.

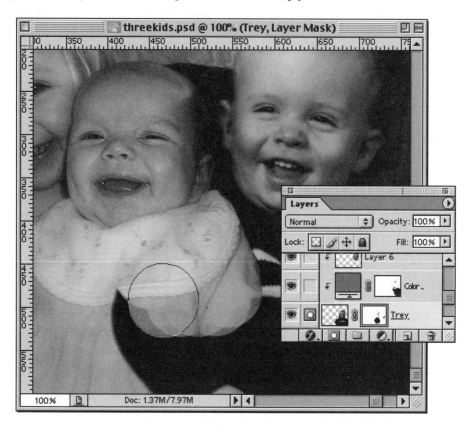

▶ *NOTE*

If you're having trouble getting the pasted object to match the color or tone of its new surroundings, don't miss the next tip.

Adjust the Color of a Pasted Object to Match Its New Surroundings

Whenever I paste an object from one photo into another one, unless both photos were taken under the exact same conditions, I always have to perform some color correction on the pasted object to help it more closely match its new surroundings. Although there are probably countless ways to accomplish this task, adjustment layers do so in a way that offers excellent efficiency and flexibility.

TRY IT To adjust the color of a pasted object to match its new surroundings, make sure the file you want to edit is open in Photoshop and that the layer containing the pasted object or person is currently active in the Layers palette. Use the selection tools to select the portion of the object or face whose color you wish to adjust, and perform one or more of the following tasks, as needed:

- **Match the hue with a Solid Color adjustment layer.** Use the Eyedropper tool to select a neutral color from one of the other faces or objects in the destination image. Then, click the fourth button at the bottom of the Layers palette to add an adjustment layer, and choose Solid Color. To force the color layer to only adjust the hue of the colors beneath it, change the blending mode for the color layer to Hue.

▶ *NOTE*

Whenever you add an adjustment layer while a selection is active, Photoshop automatically adds the adjustment layer above the active layer and masks the adjustment so it only affects the area you have selected. You can alter that mask by clicking it in the Layers palette and painting with an appropriately sized brush tip. Painting in a mask with white reveals areas, while painting with black hides them.

- **Match the tone balance with a Color Balance adjustment layer.** Click the fourth button at the bottom of the Layers palette to add an adjustment layer, and choose Color Balance. Specify whether to alter the tone balance for Shadows, Midtones, or Highlights at the bottom of the dialog box that appears, and then drag the sliders above to the left or right depending on how you want to alter the balance of color. Then, click OK.

▶ *QUICK TIP*

Leave the Preview box checked to preview any changes you're making before actually setting them in place.

- **Match the contrast with a Brightness/Contrast adjustment layer.** Click the fourth button at the bottom of the Layers palette to add an adjustment layer, and choose Brightness/Contrast. Drag the sliders to alter the contrast and brightness independently of each other, and then click OK.

- **Match the black and white levels with a Levels adjustment layer.** Click the fourth button at the bottom of the Layers palette to add an adjustment layer, and choose Levels. By default, Photoshop adjusts all channels at once. To edit the levels for a single channel, first select the channel from the menu at the top of the Levels dialog box. Click the Auto button to allow Photoshop to automatically clip the black and white points in the image, eliminating any extreme darks or lights and creating a more balanced set of values. Alternatively, drag the Input Levels sliders to manually adjust the existing black, neutral, and white points, or use the Output Levels sliders to manually specify new shadow and highlight values. Click OK.

▶ **QUICK TIP**

If you have problems with an adjustment layer affecting not only the layer below it but also any other layers below that one, group the adjustment layer into a clipping group with the layer or layers you want it to affect. See Chapter 7 for more tips on using clipping groups.

Straighten a Crookedly Scanned Image

Even with the best intentions, scanning often results in a crooked photo. Luckily, there's a quick and easy way to fix this in Photoshop.

TRY IT To straighten a crookedly scanned image, first make sure the image you want to fix is open in Photoshop. Select the Measure tool from the toolbox and click along one of the edges of the scanned photo. Drag with the Measure tool for a few seconds, following the edge of the photo, to measure the angle of the crookedness.

After you release the mouse button, the angle (along with other measurements) is displayed in the Options bar at the top of the screen. Immediately choose Image | Rotate Canvas | Arbitrary. Photoshop automatically puts the angle you just measured into the appropriate box in the Rotate Canvas dialog box, so you just have to click OK, and the program does all the work for you! You can then use the Crop tool or Trim command (choose Image | Trim) to crop the straightened photo as needed.

Remove the Dot Grain from a Scanned Image

When you scan an image from a commercially printed book, newspaper, or magazine, the scan often takes on the halftone dot screen used during the printing process. Ideally, your scanner has an option to *descreen* a halftone effect such as this, but that's not always the case. If your scanner doesn't have an option to automatically descreen, you can still minimize the effects of this dot grain in a scanned image.

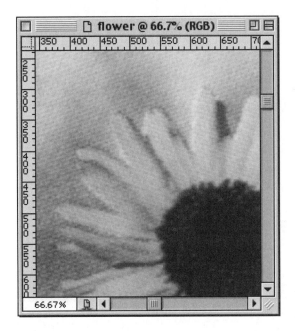

Remember that scanning from a commercially printed item may infringe on the copyright of that item. Check with the author or creator to receive the proper permission before using any copyrighted material in your work.

 If you have access to a scanner, you can make it easier to remove the effects of a halftone screen by scanning the image with the following two things in mind:

- Purposefully place the image on the scanner in a crooked manner.
- Within your scanning software, capture the image at a significantly higher resolution than you plan to use it. In most cases, this will mean scanning the image at approximately 1200 dpi, or however high your scanner is able to scan.

The process of rotating the crooked image and reducing its size will cause the dots to blur and thereby lessen the effect of the halftone screen.

After you scan the image, follow the steps in the preceding tip ("Straighten a Crookedly Scanned Image") to straighten and crop the scan. Then, choose Image I Image Size and reduce the size of the image to be the size at which you intend to use it. Performing these two things—straightening and downsampling an image—does a lot to increase the image's clarity, but there's still a bit more you can do.

To further reduce the effect of the halftone screen on a scanned image, apply a few filters on one or two channels in the image. First, choose Window | Channels to view the Channels palette. Click each of the channels to determine which one contains the majority of the dot grain from that halftone pattern. Then, try applying a Gaussian Blur, with a Radius value of between 1 and 4 (depending on the size of your image) just on the contents of that channel—leave the other two channels untouched to hold the detail of the image.

Another filter that works quite well—if not better in some cases—is the Median filter, because it seeks to remove all noise in an image. Just as with the Gaussian Blur filter, try applying the Median filter (choose Filter | Noise | Median) on the channel that contains the most contrast in the dot grain. If necessary, the filter can also be run on another channel, as long as there is one channel left untouched to retain the image clarity.

Add Color to Black and White Images

Whether you received a black and white photo that you now want to colorize, or you changed a color image into a black and white (or grayscale) image and now want to add some color for a nice creative effect, this tip is for you. You might consider this technique to be similar to painting with watercolor in a coloring book, because although you're adding a "wash" of color, you're not editing the underlying tones that make up the shadows and highlights of the photo.

▶ **NOTE**

For an example of this technique in action, see the Creative Effects section of the color insert.

TRY IT   To add color to a black and white or grayscale image, first make sure the file you want to edit is open in Photoshop. Choose Image | Mode | RGB to switch to a color mode that will allow you to paint with color, even though the photo itself doesn't have any color.

Select the Brush or Pencil tool from the toolbox and an appropriately sized brush tip with which to paint. Choose Window | Layers to display the Layers palette, and click the New Layer button at the bottom of the palette to create a new layer.

Begin painting on this layer with the colors of your choice. Switch the blending mode of the layer to Color to retain the shadows and highlights of the original photo while still adding the new color wash. If the color appears too bright for your taste using the Color blending mode, try switching to Screen.

▶ **QUICK TIP**

When painting skin tones in this fashion, I like to open another photo containing people and use the Eyedropper tool to select actual skin tones from that image.

Quickly Add Clouds to an Image

Earlier in the chapter, I played around with painting my house in Photoshop to see how my siding would look painted blue instead of white. To really convince my husband to do the work, though, I wanted to make my retouched photo look really nice before showing it to him. Because it was taken on an overcast day, the sky looks rather dull and unappealing. Photoshop has a great filter for adding clouds that can really spruce up dull skies like this one.

 To quickly add clouds to an image, first make sure the image you want to add them to is open in Photoshop. Edit the colors in the foreground and background color swatches to be the two colors you want Photoshop to use when creating the clouds. If you're looking to add clouds to a nice spring day, try a medium blue and white. For more ominous rain clouds, try a very dark blue and a medium blue-purple.

Create a new layer by clicking the New Layer button at the bottom of the Layers palette and choose Filter | Render | Clouds. (To restrict your clouds to a specific area of the layer, make a selection before applying the filter.) Photoshop creates a soft cloud pattern based on randomly alternating the values of the colors in the foreground and background color swatches. If you're not happy with the first cloud pattern generated, continue to apply the filter until you're satisfied with the pattern.

▶ | **QUICK TIP**

To force Photoshop to create a cloud pattern with more contrast, press the ALT *(Windows) or* OPTION *(Mac) key when you choose Filter | Render | Clouds. Or to add a cloud pattern with a wild variety of color, try Filter | Render | Difference Clouds.*

Turn Clouds into Water

While the previous tip used the Clouds filter to quickly add clouds to an image, you can apply additional filters to those clouds to give the appearance of rippled water.

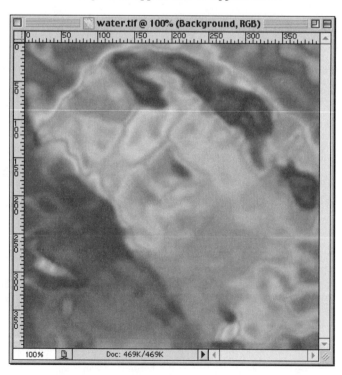

You can then use that "water" in all sorts of other designs, such as this one where I needed to give the appearance that a liquid of some sort filled this chalice.

I copied water from another image and pasted it into a new layer in this file, where I removed the parts I didn't need and reduced the opacity of the layer to achieve the desired look.

TRY IT To turn clouds into water, first choose File | New to create a new file in Photoshop. Specify RGB as the color mode and, for the sake of practice, use a size of 400×400 pixels and 72 ppi.

Make sure the colors currently located in the foreground and background color swatches have a good bit of contrast. If they don't, press D on your keyboard to return them to their default black and white. Then, choose Filter | Render | Clouds to add clouds to the image.

Next, choose Filter | Sketch | Chrome and try using a value between 4 and 7 each for the Detail and Smoothness settings. Click OK. Keep reapplying the filter until you're happy with the results.

To add the appropriate color to the new "water," click once in the foreground color swatch and select a bluish-green (or any other color of your choosing). Choose Image | Adjust | Hue/Saturation and click the Colorize box. This causes Photoshop to colorize the image using the color currently located in the foreground color swatch.

To further customize the appearance of your water, try choosing any or all of the following to apply additional filters to the image:

- Filter | Distort | Glass
- Filter | Distort | Ocean Ripple

- Filter | Blur | Gaussian Blur
- Filter | Blur | Motion Blur

Make Flat Objects Appear Spherical

Suppose you wanted to apply a flat shape to a round object; how would you make the shape look as if it were actually pasted on the object? For example, I had a photo of plain red and green Christmas balls, to which I needed to add some snowflakes. To cause the snowflakes to appear as if they were painted right on the Christmas balls, I applied the Spherize filter to each layer containing a snowflake, and then reduced the opacity of each layer.

▶ *CAUTION*

When you try to apply filters such as this one to layers containing vector artwork (for example, Shape and Type layers), Photoshop warns you it must first rasterize the layer's contents. For Type layers, in particular, this means you can no longer edit text on that layer. If you're concerned about rasterizing a layer, consider making a copy of the layer before applying the filter.

TRY IT   To spherize objects, first open the file you want to work with in Photoshop. If you haven't already done so, create the object you want to spherize, or paste it into the file from another source. For example, when I added the snowflakes to my Christmas balls, I created them with the Custom Shape tool in the file containing the Christmas balls. Make sure to move the object you're spherizing to the center of the "sphere" against which you'll spherize it.

Then, select the Elliptical Marquee from the toolbox and use it to draw a circle around the object you want to spherize. Hold down the SHIFT key while drawing the ellipse to force it to be a perfect circle. The idea here is that you're drawing the sphere against which the object will be spherized. So, in the case of my Christmas balls, I drew a circular selection exactly the same size as the Christmas ball against which I wanted to spherize my snowflake. The object you're going to spherize should fit within the elliptical selection. In fact, it's usually best if the object doesn't entirely fill the selection, so you get a nicer effect. (If it doesn't fit within the selection, the part outside the selection won't be spherized.)

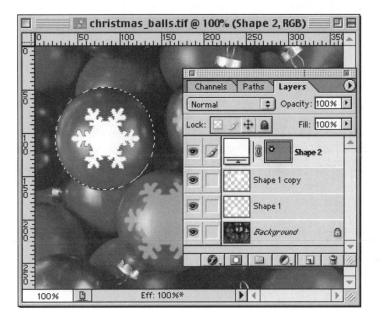

▶ *NOTE*

If you don't draw a selection before applying the Spherize filter, Photoshop applies the filter to the image as if the entire canvas were selected.

After drawing your elliptical selection, you're ready to spherize. Choose Filter | Distort | Spherize. To change the amount of spherization, adjust the slider—negative values cause the effect to appear as if it were receding into the page. To spherize along only the horizontal or vertical axis, change the Mode. Click OK to apply the effect, or click Cancel to go back and edit your selection.

⬐ Transform Objects into Three Dimensions

In the previous tip, I used the Spherize filter to make a snowflake appear to be painted onto a Christmas ball. However, that filter only enabled me to get the snowflake to be painted right on the part of the ball facing us. What if I wanted to make it appear that the snowflake was painted on the underneath side of the snowflake, and only part of it was visible in the photograph? The 3D Transform filter works great for achieving results like that.

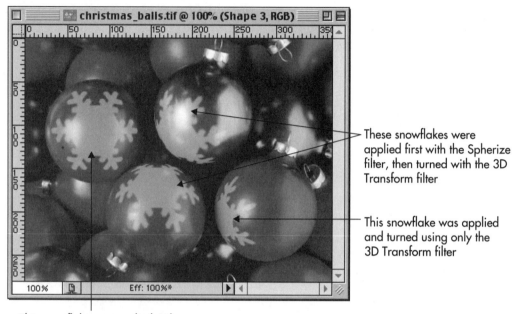

These snowflakes were applied first with the Spherize filter, then turned with the 3D Transform filter

This snowflake was applied and turned using only the 3D Transform filter

This snowflake was applied with the Spherize filter and left unturned

▶ **NOTE**

If you're creating a spherical 3-D object, you don't have to first run the Spherize filter, as I did with some of the snowflakes on my Christmas balls. The 3D Transform filter puts the object on a sphere for you, and also enables you to turn it in three dimensions.

TRY IT ▶ To transform objects into three dimensions, first make sure the object you want to transform is on its own layer in your Photoshop document. In addition, it's a good idea to duplicate the layer by dragging its name over the New Layer button in the Layers palette, just in case you need to easily return to how it looked before applying the filter.

> ▶ **QUICK TIP**
>
> *The preview window in the 3D Transform filter shows you the object in black and white, even if it's in color in your original document. So if your object is white or a light color, as my snowflakes were when applied to the Christmas balls, I suggest temporarily filling the object layer with a darker color. This will enable you to more easily see and manipulate the object in the 3D Transform preview window.*

When you're ready to transform the object, choose Filter I Render I 3D Transform and perform the following steps:

1. Select the Magnifying Glass and zoom in on your object if it's hard to see.

2. Select one of the three wireframe tools—Cube, Sphere, or Cylinder—to map the object to the appropriate shape.

3. Click and drag inside the preview window with your wireframe tool to draw the shape to which you want to map your object.

4. Use the Selection tool (shaped like a filled arrow) to move the wireframe over the object as needed.

5. Use the Direct Selection tool (shaped like an empty arrow) to edit the anchor points and reshape the wireframe as needed. (The Add Anchor Point, Delete Anchor Point, and Convert Anchor Point tools can also be used to reshape wireframes. These tools work similarly to the Pen tools in the Photoshop toolbox.)

6. If you want to delete the current wireframe and start over, use the Selection tool to select it and press BACKSPACE (Windows) or DELETE (Mac) on your keyboard.

7. To move the object with its wireframe on an even plane, use the Pan Camera tool. (This is the same as if you were holding a camera in your hands while moving around an object before photographing it.)

8. To rotate the object within its wireframe (as I did with the snowflake in Figure 9-10), use the Trackball tool and drag around the object.

9. To move the object farther from or closer to you, edit the Dolly Camera value by entering a number between 0 and 99 or dragging the slider.

10. If the transformed object becomes too large or small in the available space, edit the Field Of View value by entering a number between 1 and 130 or dragging the slider (which is displayed when you click the small triangle to the right of the value).

Sphere
wire frame

Cube wire
frame

Cylinder
wire frame

Pan
Camera

Trackball

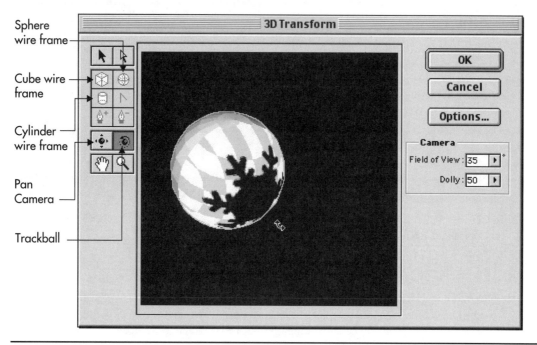

Figure 9-10　I used the 3D Transform filter to rotate my snowflakes on the Christmas balls.

▶ *CAUTION*

If your wireframe turns red at any point in the transformation, Photoshop is warning you that your object is impossible to re-create in three dimensions under the current conditions.

Click the Options button to edit the following settings, and when you're satisfied with the transformation, click OK:

- **Resolution**　Specify the quality of the image after transformation (applies mostly to objects mapped against cylinders and spheres).
- **Anti-aliasing**　Specify the amount of anti-aliasing.
- **Display Background**　Select this option to keep the original object (as it appeared before transformation) on the layer after the transformation is applied. (I recommend making a backup copy of the layer before applying this filter, and then leaving this option *unchecked* for best results.)

▶ *NOTE*

Depending on the object you're transforming, there may be some unavoidable artifacts that appear when the object is transformed. This is caused by the fact that Photoshop is making up the other side of the object you transformed. I usually am able to easily remove these artifacts with the Eraser.

Add Lighting Effects

Whether you're transforming a flat object into three dimensions or simply want to add a new or additional light source to a photograph, Photoshop has a great filter for the job. For example, I added a light source using the settings shown in Figure 9-11 to this image of my nephew, to place the attention more on his face and chest as opposed to the brightly colored grass in the background.

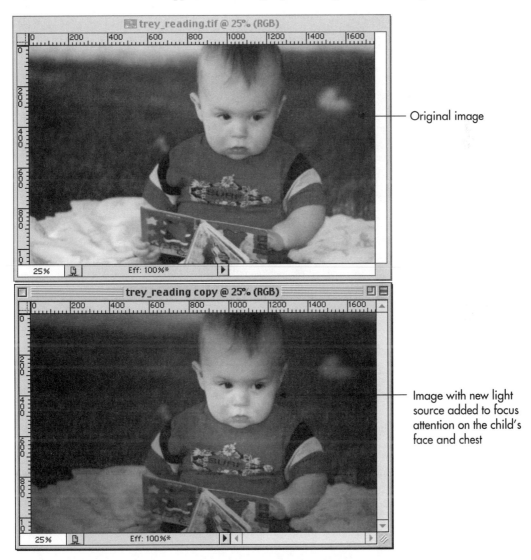

— Original image

— Image with new light source added to focus attention on the child's face and chest

TRY IT   To add a lighting effect to your image, first make sure the image is open in Photoshop and the appropriate layer is active in the Layers palette, and then choose Filter | Render | Lighting Effects.

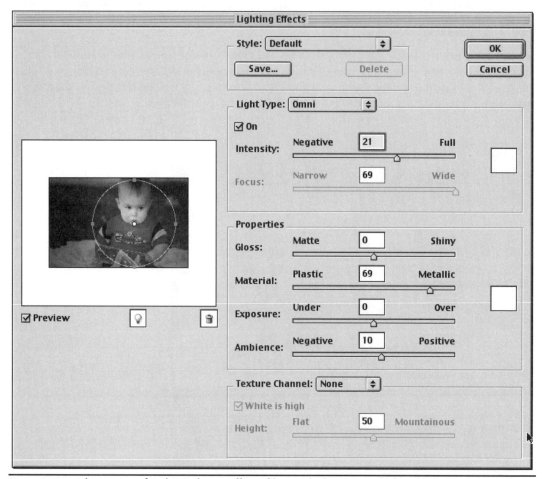

Figure 9-11 The options for the Lighting Effects filter include ways to color the light and adjust its direction.

If you want to try one of the predefined lighting styles Photoshop has provided for you, choose one from the Style menu at the top of the Lighting Effects window. Otherwise, leave the Style set to Default to create your own. Click the top and bottom color samples on the right side of the window to adjust the color of the Light Type and Properties, respectively. Select the Light Type—Directional, Omni, or Spotlight—and adjust the settings as needed.

▶ **QUICK TIP**

To add a second light source, click the small light bulb icon below the preview in the Lighting Effects window, and drag it into your image in the location where you want the light to sit. To remove a light source, drag it to the trash can icon in the preview window.

Retouch an Old Photograph

With the recent resurgence into researching one's family history, people often ask me how to clean up old photographs. While the actual techniques used to retouch old photographs vary greatly according to the particular problems encountered, there are a few tried and true tips I can offer that seem to be useful in the majority of cases. Compare the photos in Figure 9-12 to see how I used these techniques to fix this photo of my husband's aunt.

TRY IT   To retouch one of your old photographs, you need to first inspect it to determine the problem areas, which are listed next. Then, proceed with the appropriate steps, according to the problems you find. If one technique doesn't work for your particular problem, try another until you find something that does work.

> **QUICK TIP**
>
> *If you can, scan the photograph at double the resolution (at least) you intend to use it. This way, any clarity you lose while trying to clean up the image can be gained back (somewhat) by resampling the image down to the required resolution.*

- **Wrinkles or creases in the paper**   Use the Patch tool to draw a selection around the wrinkle or crease and drag it over a clean area of the image.

- **Water spots**   Use the Healing Brush tool and an appropriately sized brush tip to paint them away.

- **Small to medium tears**   Use the Patch tool to draw a selection around the tear and drag it over an intact area of the image.

- **Large tears**   Try to use the Patch tool in the same fashion as you might with smaller tears. However, because larger tears tend to indicate that a portion of the image itself is missing, you may have to use the Clone Stamp tool to copy and paste the missing part back in.

- **A general covering of dust and scratches**   Choose Filter | Noise | Dust And Scratches and increase the Radius until the blemishes are hidden. Then, to gain back some of the clarity lost during that process, choose Filter | Sharpen | Unsharp Mask and use approximately the same Radius as was used during the previous filter.

- **Dust and scratches in only one area of your image**   Instead of applying the Dust And Scratches and Unsharp Mask filters on the entire image, select a specific area first with one of the selection tools. For best results, I recommend feathering your selection. Alternatively, you can apply both filters to the entire image, take a Snapshot in the History palette, and then return to the state in the History palette just before you applied the first filter. Select the History Brush tool and click in the empty box next to the name of the Snapshot you just took to specify that as the state from which you'll paint. Then, "paint" over the dust and scratches as necessary. For best results, lower the Opacity of the History Brush so the transition between the filtered and unfiltered areas of the image isn't stark.

Crease   Spot

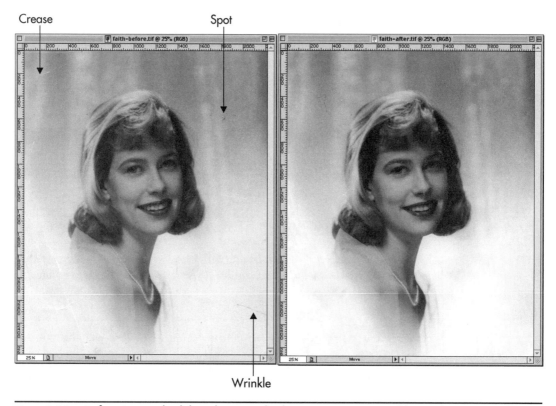

Wrinkle

Figure 9-12   Before I retouched this photograph, there were many wrinkles and creases, a few water spots, and lots of dust and scratches (left). After being retouched, the true beauty of the figure is no longer overshadowed by the defects of the paper (right).

▶ *NOTE*

If you find color casts, see the previous tip in this chapter, "Quickly Remove Common Color Casts."

Add Frames to Photographs

A great way to dress up the otherwise dull edges of a standard rectangular photograph is to add an interesting frame. While you can certainly use the painting tools to hand-paint a frame, a company named Extensis has a tool that makes adding unique frames to photographs a breeze. A demo version

> ▶ | **QUICK TIP**
>
> *If you don't have a copy of PhotoFrame, you can accomplish similar effects on your own. First choose the Elliptical Marquee tool from the toolbox and draw an ellipse over the image you want to frame. Click the New Layer button at the bottom of the Layers palette. Choose Select | Inverse to invert your selection and choose Edit | Fill. Select "White" for the Use, or choose whichever color you want for your frame. Choose Select | Inverse and then Select | Modify | Border, and specify a value of approximately 25, or larger depending on your image. Next, choose a filter from the Filter menu and apply it just to the border pixels that you have selected to achieve some creative frames. If you need some help choosing some filters to start with, try Filter | Distort | Ripple and increase the Amount significantly. Or try, Filter | Pixelate | Fragment.*

of the tool—Extensis PhotoFrame—can be downloaded for free from www.extensis.com/photoframe. Note, you need to have a copy of PhotoFrame installed before trying this technique.

TRY IT   To use PhotoFrame, open the photo in Photoshop to which you want to add a frame. Then, choose Filter | Extensis | PhotoFrame 2.0 to launch the tool. Press F1 to display the Frame palette and click one of the first three buttons to get started:

- Click the Add Frame File button to start with one of the frame files that ship with PhotoFrame. Navigate to one of the three folders in the PhotoFrame directory containing these sample files, or use one of the more than 1,000 frame files on the PhotoFrame CD. (Select a frame and click Open to add that frame to your photo.)

- Click the Add Instant Frame button to start with a simple shape (Ellipse, Rectangle, Polygon, Star, Arrow, or Heart) and begin designing your own custom frame.

You can repeat this process to layer multiple frames on top of each other. They are listed in the Frame palette and can be hidden by unchecking the eyeball, much the same way you hide a layer in Photoshop. To see how I quickly added a frame to a photo of my daughter painting, see Figure 9-13.

Use the additional palettes (Background, Border, Glow, Shadow, Bevel, and Texture) to customize any of the frame files. For example, press F8 to reveal the Shadow palette and click one of the available buttons—Inner Shadow or Outer Shadow—to begin. Then, customize the shadow with the other options that become available after you specify the type of shadow to use (inner or outer).

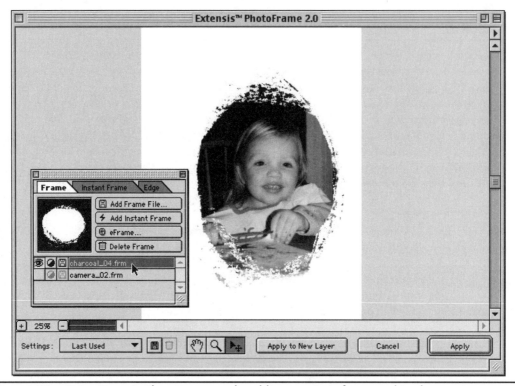

Figure 9-13 Using Extensis PhotoFrame made adding a unique frame to this photo quite easy.

When you're ready to return to Photoshop, click Apply to add the frame right to the same layer as the photograph, or click Apply To New Layer to add the frame to a new layer above the layer containing the photograph.

PART III

Using Photoshop to Produce Web and Print Graphics

CHAPTER 10

Slicing and Optimizing Web Graphics

TIPS IN THIS CHAPTER

I n the first part of this chapter, I discuss the general process used in designing web graphics as well as some terminology and details related to web image file formats. Then, I move on to tips identifying how to define each piece of your mockup and save each in the best file format for the job.

Web Design Process

In Chapter 4, I discussed using Photoshop as a web page layout tool. For professional web designers, this typically involves creating mockups that clients will review before the page is actually "built" and coded. After those mockups have been approved and are ready to be produced, it's time to slice and dice your files—literally. This means you have to translate the various pieces of your mockups into web-readable formats that can be rendered by a web browser.

When slicing and optimizing web graphics, it's important to know which features are available in Photoshop and which are only available in ImageReady (Photoshop's web-specific sister application). In its Help file for Photoshop, Adobe lists the primary differences between Photoshop and ImageReady as the following:

- Photoshop provides tools for creating and manipulating static images for use on the Web. You can divide an image into slices, add links and HTML text, optimize the slices, and save the image as a web page.

- ImageReady provides many of the same image-editing tools as Photoshop. In addition, it includes tools and palettes for advanced web processing and creating dynamic web images like animations and rollovers.

So, when it comes to designing my web pages, I typically use Photoshop. However, when I'm ready to process the web designs and save each piece as a compressed file capable of being displayed in a web browser, I usually switch to ImageReady. Ultimately, the decision is your own, and the only thing for which you definitely *have* to switch to ImageReady is the creation of animation and interactivity like rollovers.

Automatically Generating HTML

When you save web graphics in Photoshop or ImageReady, you have the option to allow the program to automatically generate HTML code according to the design layout. If you don't know HTML, this can be a particularly useful tool. And even if you do know HTML, having Photoshop generate it for you on the fly can save valuable time in getting files on the Web.

As a die-hard HTML coder, I must advise that you use a bit of caution when allowing any application—be it Photoshop, Image Ready, Microsoft Word, or another—to automatically generate HTML for you. Applications that automatically generate code must be programmed to do so, and as such are generally not as flexible as you might be if you were coding the HTML yourself. For example, such applications often overcompensate for the amount of code needed to render a particular page, and can therefore generate significantly larger HTML files than are necessary. This can translate into longer downloads for your users.

My point is that you should inspect any HTML code output by Photoshop to confirm that it serves the needs of your users as well as it can. In addition, I recommend you familiarize yourself with what you can and can't do using HTML (if you haven't already). In fact, I wrote *HTML: A Beginner's Guide* (McGraw-Hill/Osborne) for just that purpose.

When it comes to actually coding your web pages with references to each of the optimized graphics, you have the following options:

- Write your own HTML using a plain-text HTML editor such as Barebones BBEdit (www.bbedit.com) or Macromedia HomeSite (www.macromedia.com/software/homesite/).
- Let Photoshop or ImageReady output the HTML for you based on your design layout and defined slices.
- Integrate the development process with a What You See Is What You Get (WYSIWYG) HTML editor such as Adobe GoLive or Macromedia Dreamweaver.

▶ *NOTE*

Because of the sister relationship between Photoshop/ImageReady and GoLive, there are significant benefits to using layered and sliced Photoshop files with GoLive. Regardless of which method you choose, there are several tips at the end of this chapter that provide more information.

Web Slices

When you save web designs containing slices, the program saves each slice as an independent graphic. This means that although you may start with a single-layered Photoshop file, you'll end up with multiple optimized web graphics. For example, in the case of the following file used to build a basic navigation system for a web site, I ended up with nine files—one logo and eight buttons.

Layer-based slice   User slice

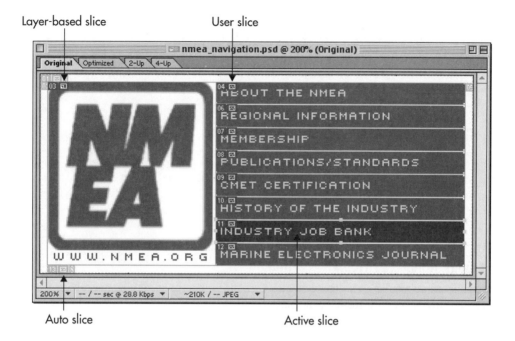

Auto slice   Active slice

In Photoshop and ImageReady, there are three main types of slices, each identified with a different icon:

- **User slices**   Created with the Slice tool
- **Layer-based slices**   Created from layers and based on the contents of the layer; if the size of the layer's contents changes, so will the size of the slice
- **Auto slices**   Created from the leftover space not used by user or layer-based slices

▶ *NOTE*

A fourth and less common type of slice, a subslice, is created any time two or more slices overlap. You can't edit or select a subslice, because it is automatically generated and maintained by the program.

In addition to these slice types, you can further classify each slice by specifying whether it contains an image. This is most useful when you decide to have Photoshop or ImageReady output the HTML code for you. For example, suppose you included sample text in a mockup of a web page you created. That text would need to be entered into the HTML as straight text and not as an image, so you could specify the slice containing that sample text as "No Image" and the program would know not to save the sample text as an image. This is discussed further in the tip "Slice Web Designs According to Page Layout."

Web File Formats

If you try to load a BMP or a PICT into your web page, users see a broken-image symbol. This occurs because graphics in web pages must be in a format understood by the web browser. The most popular graphics file formats recognized by web browsers are GIF and JPEG. A third file format, PNG, is gaining popularity because it's supported by recent versions of the browsers, and a fourth file format, WBMP, is used for optimizing images displayed on mobile computers, such as handhelds and cell phones.

Terminology Related to Web File Formats

Before you dive into working with the actual file formats in the tips and techniques of this chapter, you need to be aware of a few related concepts:

- Compression methods
- Transparency
- Interlacing
- Animation

Compression Methods

Most graphics file formats used on the Web take your original image and compress it to make it smaller for online delivery. Two types of compression methods typically used for web graphics are the following:

- **Lossy**   Requires data to be removed from the image to compress the file and make it smaller. This compression method attempts to remove the least important data first, to minimize the total loss of image quality.
- **Lossless**   Requires no data to be lost when the file is compressed; the actual data looks the same whether it's compressed or uncompressed.

Generally speaking, lossy images tend to be smaller in file size and, thus, load more quickly on the Web. Of course, that isn't true in all cases, and the tips in the later portion of the chapter discuss this in relation to particular file formats.

Transparency

When you view in Photoshop an image that contains transparency, you can see "through" portions. If there is no background "behind" the transparent parts, Photoshop displays a gray and white checkerboard pattern.

When a graphic displayed on a web page contains transparency, the page's background color or background tile shows through in the transparent areas. The issue you need to be aware of is that not all web file formats support transparency. File formats that do support transparency fall into two categories, based on which of the following types of transparency they support:

- **Binary transparency**   Any given pixel is either transparent or opaque.
- **Variable transparency (or alpha channel transparency)**   Allows pixels to be partially transparent or partially opaque and, therefore, is capable of creating subtle gradations.

Interlacing

Have you ever viewed a web page and noticed that a web graphic first appeared blocky or fuzzy before becoming clear and crisp? Interlacing is a process during which the graphic is displayed at multiple levels of clarity, from blurry to clear. An interlaced graphic loads the rows of pixels from top to bottom over several passes, with the graphic appearing more defined with each pass.

Noninterlaced images must be fully loaded before the browser displays them on a page. If you have a large image on a page, users would see only blank space if the graphic takes a while to download. Unfortunately, if the graphic takes too long, users may leave the page before seeing it.

Because interlaced graphics appear more quickly, even if they appear fuzzy, users might be more willing to wait for the page to download fully. Ultimately, the choice of whether to use interlaced or noninterlaced graphics depends on the size and style of the graphics on your page. I generally use interlacing for larger graphics that take up more space on the screen, as opposed to small buttons or icons that load quickly anyway.

Basic Animation

Some web graphic file formats support basic animation as well as still images. These animation files contain two or more individual files called *animation frames*. When the file is played back through the browser, viewers watch the various frames of the animation appear one after the other. The rate at which the frames change can vary between a speedy filmstrip and a slowly blinking button.

 NOTE

Specific tips related to the creation of animation are discussed in Chapter 11.

Slice Web Designs According to Page Layout

In Chapter 4, I discussed how using guides in Photoshop could go a long way toward helping you plan the final web page layout. In particular, Photoshop guides help you slice web designs into the individual graphics referenced in the page's code.

TRY IT   To slice your web designs, first make sure you have the file you want to work with open in Photoshop or ImageReady. In addition, it helps to have guides drawn to indicate where you want to slice the designs. (See the tip "Use Guides to Plan Page Layout" in Chapter 4.) Then, perform any of the following to define your slices:

- Select the Slice tool from the toolbox, or press K on your keyboard. Click and drag to draw boxes around each of the elements and define slice borders.

- Choose Window | Layers to view the Layers palette and click the layer from which you want to create a slice. Then, choose Layer | New Layer Based Slice.

▶ | **QUICK TIP**

Layer-based slices are particularly useful when the content of your slice is tied directly to a single layer. The benefit in using a layer-based slice over a regular hand-drawn slice is that layer-based slices automatically change their size whenever the contents of the layers to which they are tied change.

- If you have guides drawn and want to have the program automatically generate slices based on those guides, in Photoshop select the Slice tool and click Slices From Guides in the Options bar. In ImageReady choose Slices | Create Slices From Guides. (Note, this really only works well if you have just a few guides drawn and any slices you wish to create don't overlap those guides. The reason is that Photoshop creates a slice in every single space outlined by guides, which often means a lot of slice deleting if you didn't need them all.)

After creating your slices, select the Slice Select tool from the toolbox, or press SHIFT-K on your keyboard. Double-click each slice to activate the Slice Options window in Photoshop (see Figure 10-1) or the Slice palette in ImageReady (see Figure 10-2) to specify the following details about your slice:

- Name your slice
- Specify a URL if the slice is a link and you plan to have the program output your HTML code; add a frame or window name next to Target to specify where the link should open
- Specify whether the slice indicates an Image or other web page element (No Image)
- Specify any text to be displayed in the status bar at the bottom of the browser when the user moves the cursor over the image (used if the program outputs the HTML)

- Specify the background type for the slice
- Specify the alternative text to be displayed if the image doesn't (used if the program outputs the HTML)

▶ | **QUICK TIP**

It's important to name each slice. If left unnamed, the program assigns somewhat random names, typically something like mockup_slice_01.jpg. (You can actually customize how those random names are created—see the next two tips for details.)

After your slices are all identified, choose File | Save For Web to optimize each slice, as discussed in the tip "Select the Best File Format for the Job."

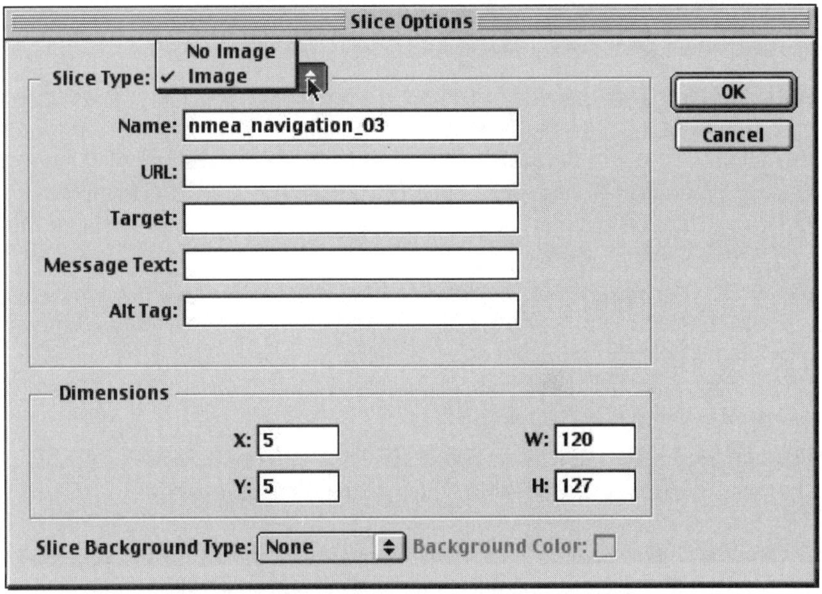

Figure 10-1 Photoshop's Slice Options window

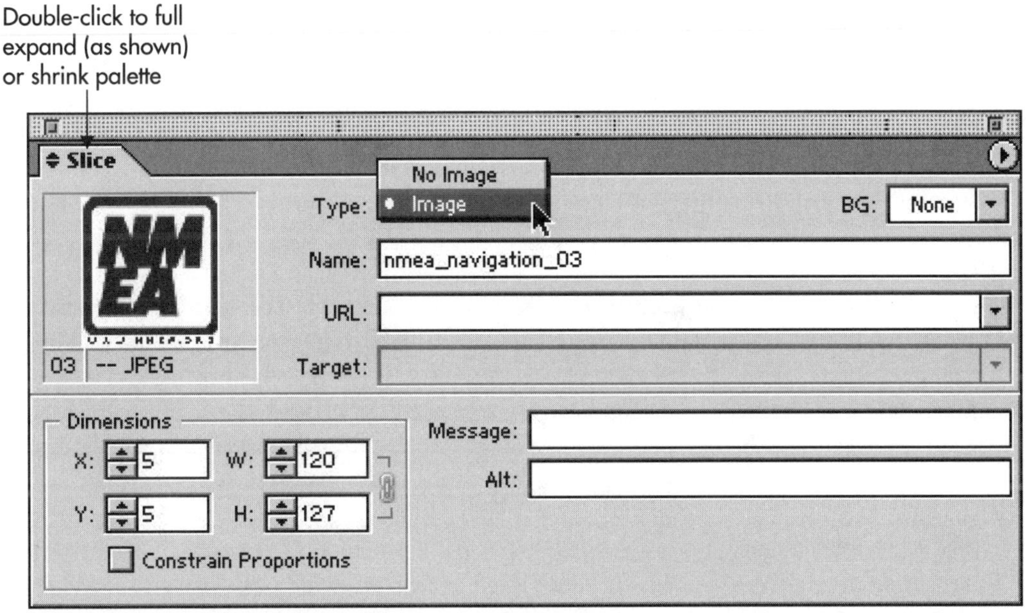

Figure 10-2 ImageReady's Slice palette

Customize Output Settings

Before using the Save For Web function to compress your web graphics, you'll want to customize the output settings according to your specific needs. For example, if you decide to allow Photoshop or ImageReady to automatically generate the HTML code for your web pages, you need to specify whether it should use tables or cascading style sheets (CSS) to lay out the page. Options like this—as well as how slices and files are named and how background images are handled—are set in the Output Settings dialog box.

 To customize the output settings for web graphics, first do one of the following to access the Output Settings dialog box:

- In ImageReady choose File I Output Settings.
- In Photoshop open a file and choose File I Save For Web. In the Save For Web dialog box, click the small triangle next to Settings and choose Edit Output Settings.

After accessing the Output Settings dialog box, choose from the following five options in the second select menu to edit the corresponding aspects of the output settings:

- **HTML** Under "Indent" specify the type of indentation used to help make the HTML more readable; "Tabs" is the most common choice. Under "Line Endings" specify the platform with which your HTML line endings should be compatible: "Win" or "Unix" are most common choices. Because the current HTML specifications require tags and attributes to be lowercase, all attributes to be quoted, all images to contain alt attributes and all tags to be closed, I recommend you specify these settings. Choose "Include Comments" to allow the program to add helpful notes about each section in the code (required by ImageReady in some cases). Select "Include Zero Margins in Body Tag" to remove the default margins at the top of most browsers so your images butt up against the top and left borders of the browser page window. See Figure 10-3 to view these options.

- **Slices** Under Slice Output, specify whether to lay out your web pages with HTML tables (which are less flexible but supported by all current browsers) or cascading style sheets (which are more flexible but are only fully supported by newer browsers, such as Internet Explorer 5+ and Netscape 6+). Under Default Slice Naming, specify how to automatically name slices. (Note that this default slice naming is overridden when you custom-name a slice.)

- **Image Maps** No changes are necessary for the vast majority of cases (used by ImageReady only).

- **Background** Under View Document As choose Image to be able to add another image or a solid color background behind the current image; choose Background if the current image *is* the background of the web page and should be tiled by the browser (only available for nonsliced images). For Background Image, specify the image (if any) to be tiled as a background behind the current image in the browser when the HTML code is written. For BG Color, specify the solid color background (if any) to be placed behind the current image in the browser when the HTML code is written.

- **Saving Files** For File Naming specify how to automatically name files when you don't provide custom names. For Filename Compatibility specify the platform or platforms to which any file names should be compatible. (In Figure 10-4, Mac OS 9 is selected by default because it was the platform I used when I captured the screen; select all options in most cases.) For Optimized Files specify the default folder in which to place the saved images (only used when a file contains slices to be output together). When "Copy Background Image when Saving" is selected, the program automatically saves a copy of any file specified in the Background output settings and with the saved slices in the specified folder. When "Include Copyright" is selected, the program includes copyright information with the image by adding it to the HTML file in the form of comments and metadata (note that copyright information must first be entered by choosing File | File Info). See Figure 10-4 to locate each option.

▶ **QUICK TIP**

Click Save in the Output Settings dialog box to save these customized settings for future use. If you give the file a name and save it in the Presets/Optimized Output Settings folder inside the Photoshop program folder, your customized settings will be available to both Photoshop and ImageReady. Click Load in the Output Settings dialog box to load these settings at a later time.

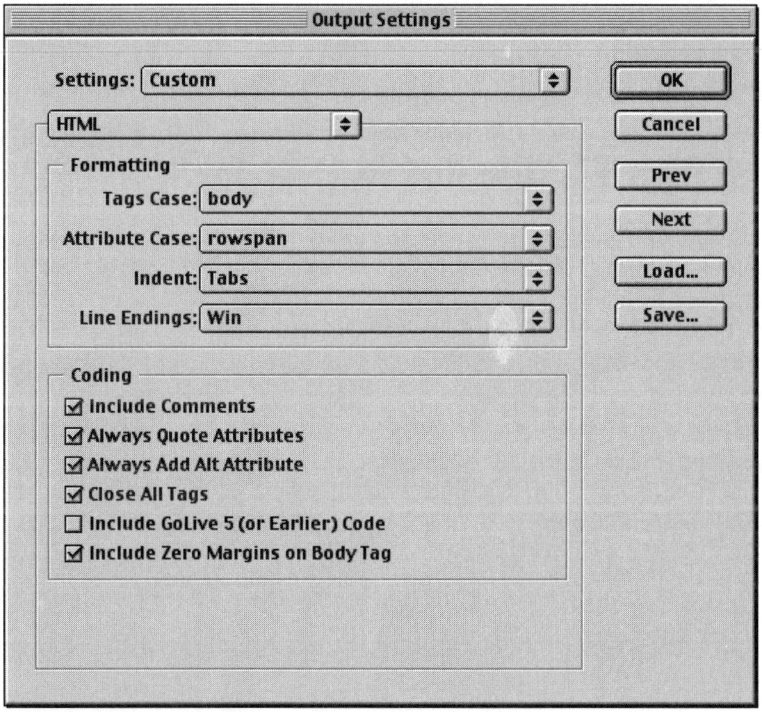

Figure 10-3 Output Settings—HTML

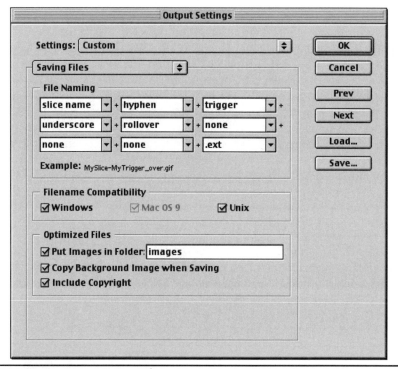

Figure 10-4   Output Settings—Saving Files

Select the Best File Format for the Job

One of the most common things people ask me regarding web design is how to select the best file format for a particular image. While I wish I could give them, and you, a foolproof method, the answer ultimately lies in your own testing.

Fortunately, Photoshop and ImageReady make this testing quite easy by enabling you to compare how a single image (or multiple slices) might look when saved with certain compression settings. In particular, Photoshop offers the Save For Web dialog box, and ImageReady gives us the Optimize palette. Both tools allow us to look at up to four differently compressed versions of the image at once.

 When you're ready to try out different compression settings on your file or slices of a file, do one of the following:

- In Photoshop, choose File | Save For Web. Choose the view type from the tabs at the top of the dialog box.

- In ImageReady, choose the view type from the tabs at the top of the image window. Then, choose Window | Optimize to reveal the Optimize palette.

When selecting a view type, choose Original to view only the original image with no compression. Choose Optimized to view the image with one set of compression settings. Choose 2-Up to view the image with one set of compression settings, next to the original image. Choose 4-Up to view the original image, plus three other shots of that image, each with a different compression setting.

▶ *NOTE*

Even though the program defaults to showing you the original image in the 2-Up and 4-Up views, you can edit the optimization settings for the "original" view as well to end up with two or four differently compressed images, depending on which view you're using.

▶ **QUICK TIP**

If you want to apply the same optimization settings to multiple slices within an image in Photoshop, SHIFT-click the slices with the Slice Select tool before making any changes to the optimization settings. In ImageReady, see the tip "Link Slices to Optimize Multiple Slices at Once" later in the chapter.

Edit each image's optimization settings by first clicking the image and/or slice whose settings you wish to edit in the preview window and then making changes to those settings on the right (Photoshop) or in the Optimize palette (ImageReady). Compare the file sizes printed below each image in the preview window to determine which optimization settings create the smallest file size with the best quality. For details on each file format available (GIF, JPEG, PNG, and WBMP), see the following four tips.

TRY IT When you're finished, in Photoshop click Save to save the slice or file using the selected optimization settings. To save your settings without actually saving the slice or file, click Done to return to the main Photoshop window. In ImageReady choose File | Save Optimized or Save Optimized As. Whether you use ImageReady or Photoshop, the resulting dialog box looks like the one that follows.

Folder where I plan
to save the file

Specify whether to save the images
only, the HTML only, or both

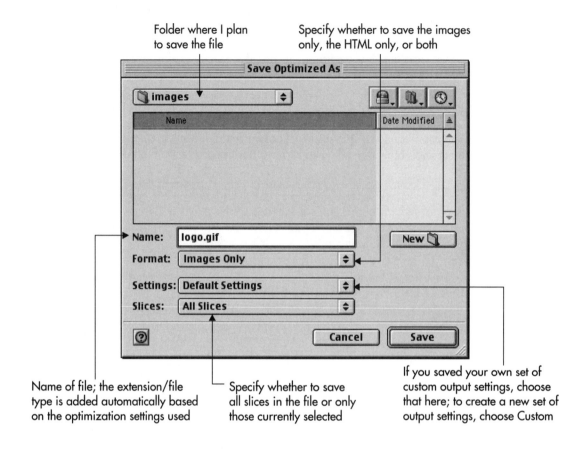

Name of file; the extension/file
type is added automatically based
on the optimization settings used

Specify whether to save
all slices in the file or only
those currently selected

If you saved your own set of
custom output settings, choose
that here; to create a new set of
output settings, choose Custom

QUICK TIP

Annoyed that the program takes a few seconds to automatically regenerate a newly optimized image when you click the Optimized, 2-Up, or 4-Up tab at the top of the file window? In ImageReady, you can uncheck Auto Regenerate from the flyout menu for the Optimize palette to turn this feature off and speed up your work time in ImageReady. This way, you can make changes to the optimization settings first and then click the Generate button in the lower-right corner of the file window as needed. Unfortunately, Photoshop doesn't offer a similar option.

Optimize GIFs

GIF is the acronym for Graphics Interchange Format. Originally designed for online use in the 1980s, GIF uses a compression method that is well suited for certain types of web graphics. This method, called

LZW compression, is lossless and doesn't cause a loss of file data. However, several characteristics restrict the type of files capable of being saved as GIFs. Table 10-1 lists these and other characteristics of the GIF file format.

▶ **NOTE**

According to its creator, GIF is officially pronounced with a soft g. Because the word is an acronym, though, many people pronounce it with a hard g.

Because of the characteristics outlined in Table 10-1, the following types of images lend themselves to being saved as GIFs. In fact, the *G* in GIF gives you a hint about what types of images are best saved as GIFs: graphics. In addition, notice all these types of images tend to have limited color palettes:

- Text
- Line drawings
- Cartoons
- Flat-color graphics

▶ **NOTE**

Images with photographic content shouldn't usually be saved as GIFs unless they're part of an animation or require transparency. In fact, the JPEG file format was created specifically for photographs and therefore does a better job at compressing photographs while keeping them looking good.

Characteristic	Description
Color mode	Restricted to no more than 256 exact colors (8-bit)
Compression method	Lossless by default, although Photoshop allows you to create lossy GIFs
Animation	Supported
Transparency	Supported (binary)
Interlacing	Supported
File type	Bitmap

Table 10-1   GIF File Format Characteristics

To optimize an image as a GIF in Photoshop, perform the following steps:

- In Photoshop, choose File | Save For Web. In ImageReady, choose Window | Optimize to display the Optimize palette.
- Click the 2-Up tab to display your original image on the left (or top) and the optimized file on the right (or bottom).
- If necessary, use the Slice Select tool to select the slice you want to optimize. Otherwise, if no slices exist, continue following these steps to optimize the entire image.
- From the Settings menu, select one of the default GIF settings at the top. To start, I like to choose GIF 32 Dithered, because it's a nice "middle-of-the-road" type of default setting.

After making that selection, the appropriate settings are visible in the space below. For example, if you choose GIF 32 Dithered (as I did in Figure 10-5), the program selects GIF from the File Type menu, Selective from the Color Palette menu, 32 for the number of Colors, and Diffusion as the type of Dithering.

▶ **NOTE**

In the case of Figure 10-5, there were only three colors in the palette even though the default setting I initially used specified 32. This is good—it means the program is not leaving unnecessary colors in the palette, which would inflate the file size. In this image, there are indeed only three colors needed.

If your image looks good with 32 colors, try reducing the number of colors in the color palette as low as you can go without severely compromising the image's quality. If it looks terrible with 32 colors, increase the number of colors a little bit to try and gain back some quality. Don't go too high too quickly, though, because each color you add into the file increases its size. In my experience, few GIF files need more than 32 colors to be successful.

Aside from the number of colors, edit the remaining settings as needed:

- For "Lossy" identify the lossiness level; higher numbers make smaller file sizes but reduce image quality (not available for interlaced GIFs or when Noise or Pattern dithering is used).
- Specify whether to use dithering to reduce banding between colors. (For more information on dithering, see the tip "Use Dithering to Smooth Edges in GIF and PNG-8 Files.") When dithering is used, specify the amount of dither; the higher the percentage, the larger the file size.
- Specify whether the file should be interlaced.
- For "Matte" identify color of web page background when portions of the image will be made transparent.
- For "Web Snap" specify the number of colors you want to force to be web safe.

- Select "Transparency" to specify that the file contains transparent areas. If it does, use the menu below to dither the semi-transparent pixels. (Techniques using the transparency options can be found in the tip "Optimize Transparent Web Graphics.")

- For details on the small circle inside of a rectangle found next to three options in the Settings menu, see "Use Weighted Optimization."

When you're finished, in Photoshop click Save to save the slice or file using the selected optimization settings. (To save your settings without actually saving the slice or file, click Done to return to the main Photoshop window.) In ImageReady choose File | Save Optimized or Save Optimized As.

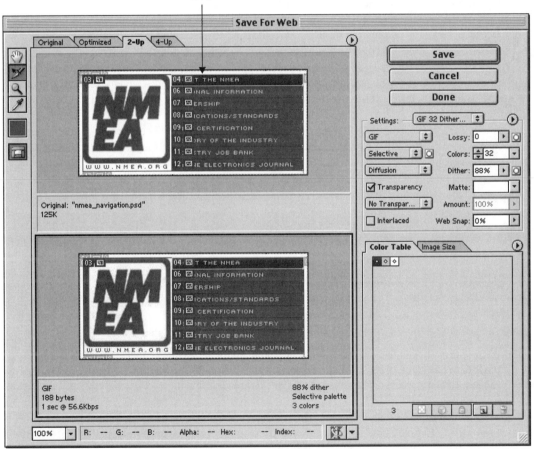

Figure 10-5   When optimizing GIFs, I like to start with the default GIF setting named GIF 32 Dithered.

▶ **NOTE**

See the Web Compression Settings section of the color insert for full-color samples of images with different optimization settings.

Optimize JPEGs

The JPEG file format (pronounced "jay-peg") was created by the Joint Photographic Experts Group, seeking to create a format more suitable for compressing photographic imagery. Table 10-2 shows the characteristics of typical JPEGs.

One major difference between GIFs and JPEGs is that JPEGs don't contain an exact set of colors. When you save a photograph as a JPEG, you might consider all the colors in the file to be recommended only, because the lossy compression might require some colors to be altered. In addition, all web JPEG files must be set in the RGB color mode, as opposed to the print standard—CMYK.

When you save an image as a JPEG, you choose among several different quality levels. The highest-quality JPEG has the least amount of compression and, therefore, the least amount of data removed. The lowest-quality JPEG has the most amount of data removed and often looks a bit blotchy, blurry, and rough.

I usually save JPEG images with a medium to medium-low quality. The decision is made based on how low in quality you can go without compromising the integrity of the file: the lower the quality level, the lower the file size.

 To optimize an image as a JPEG in Photoshop, perform the following steps:

- In Photoshop choose File | Save For Web. In ImageReady choose Window | Optimize to display the Optimize palette.

- Click the 2-Up tab to display your original image on the left (or top) and the optimized file on the right (or bottom).

- If necessary, use the Slice Select tool to select the slice you want to optimize. Otherwise, if no slices exist, continue following these steps to optimize the entire image.

- From the Settings menu, select one of the default JPEG settings at the top. To start, I like to choose JPEG Low, because it's going to give the smallest file size, and I want to quickly see whether I can stand how the image looks at that low quality.

After making that selection, the appropriate settings are visible in the space below. For example, if you choose JPEG Low (as I did in the following illustration of the Optimize palette in ImageReady), the program selects JPEG from the File Type menu, Low from the Quality menu, and 10 (percent) from the Quality percentage slide. Edit additional settings as needed:

- Specify quality level (Low, Medium, High, or Maximum) and further refine it with the percentage slider to the right.

Characteristic	Description
Color mode	Displayed in 24-bit RGB color, also called millions of colors; if the user's monitor isn't set to view 24-bit color, the file is displayed with as many colors as are available
Compression method	Lossy
Animation	Not supported
Transparency	Not supported
Interlacing	Supported (but called progressive JPEG)
File type	Bitmap

Table 10-2   JPEG File Format Characteristics

- When "Optimized" is selected, it creates a slightly smaller file size but causes the file to be unreadable in old browsers. (I recommend you leave it selected because this only affects *very* old browsers.)
- For Blur use higher numbers to blur hard edges in the image (just as the Gaussian Blur filter does) and achieve better file compression.
- If transparent areas exist, select a color from the Matte menu with which to fill them (because the JPEG format doesn't support transparency).
- Select "Progressive" to add interlacing.
- Select "ICC Profile" to save any ICC color profile attached to the image; available only when a profile is attached to the image. (I don't recommend this because most browsers don't currently support this feature, so it wastes file size.)
- Select "Preserve EXIF Metadata" to save any additional information with the file, such as creator; available for pictures downloaded from a digital camera only.

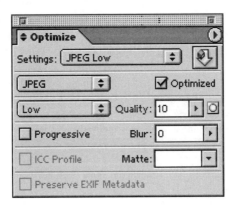

When you're finished, in Photoshop click Save to save the slice or file using the selected optimization settings. (To save your settings without actually saving the slice or file, click Done to return to the main Photoshop window.) In ImageReady choose File | Save Optimized or Save Optimized As.

▶ *NOTE*

See the Web Compression Settings section of the color insert for full-color samples of images with different optimization settings.

Optimize PNGs

PNG, which stands for Portable Network Graphics and is pronounced *ping*, is the newest and most flexible of the three graphics file formats. It was created in response to developers seeking an open-source graphics file format that could be freely developed on the Web. By contrast, for example, each time an online weather station wants to generate a new graphic with the local forecast, it's supposed to buy a license first to develop in the GIF file format. For this reason, PNG was created to replace the GIF file format on the Web.

But after looking at the list of characteristics for PNG, you might think of PNG as being the best of both the GIF and JPEG file formats. Although it isn't intended to replace the JPEG format, it does offer and expand on some of its features.

When saving in Photoshop, you'll notice two types of PNG files: PNG-8 and PNG-24. The key differences are outlined in Tables 10-3 and 10-4.

▶ *NOTE*

Although there is a PNG counterpart that supports animation—MNG (Multiple-image Network Graphics)—it is not supported by most browsers and therefore is not yet a viable alternative to GIF animation.

Because the creators of PNG knew what didn't work in GIFs, they could plan ahead and make what some call a perfect file format. With that in mind, PNG is particularly good in terms of transparency. Unlike GIF, which only supports 1-bit, or 1-color, transparency, PNG can support multiple levels—and multiple colors—of transparency. Keep in mind that while PNGs using 1-bit transparency are smaller in file size than GIFs, those with multilevel transparency are substantially larger.

Characteristic	Description
Color mode	Restricted to no more than 256 exact colors (8-bit)
Compression method	Lossless
Animation	Not supported
Transparency	Supported (binary)
Interlacing	Supported
File type	Bitmap

Table 10-3 PNG-8 File Format Characteristics

Characteristic	Description
Color mode	Displayed in 24-bit RGB color, also called millions of colors; if the user's monitor isn't set to view 24-bit color, the file is displayed with as many colors as are available
Compression method	Lossless
Animation	Not supported
Transparency	Supported (variable)
Interlacing	Supported
File type	Bitmap

Table 10-4   PNG-24 Format Characteristics

An additional benefit of PNG is its gamma correction. The PNG file format has the capability to correct for differences in how computers and monitors interpret color values. While all these characteristics make PNG well suited for almost any type of web graphic, only some of the newest browsers support it. Unfortunately, this means users of older browsers must download a plug-in to view web graphics saved in the PNG format. This might make the format off-limits for many designers until the majority of users have browsers capable of displaying PNGs.

▶ **NOTE**

You can check to see which browsers currently support PNG graphics at www.libpng.org/pub/png/ pngapbr.html.

  To optimize an image as a PNG in Photoshop, perform the following steps:

- In Photoshop choose File | Save For Web. In ImageReady choose Window | Optimize to display the Optimize palette.

- Click the 2-Up tab to display your original image on the left (or top) and the optimized file on the right (or bottom).

- If necessary, use the Slice Select tool to select the slice you want to optimize. Otherwise, if no slices exist, continue following these steps to optimize the entire image.

- From the Settings menu, select one of the default PNG settings at the top. Saving as a PNG-8 uses an exact palette of 256 colors or less. Binary (1-bit) transparency and dithering are available in the PNG-8 setting, just like they are for GIF. PNG-24 offers 24-bit (millions) color mode and multilevel transparency.

- After making that selection, the appropriate settings are visible in the space below. For example, if you choose PNG-24 (as I did in the following illustration of the Optimize palette in ImageReady), three options display—Transparency (selected), Interlaced (not selected), and Matte, which defines the color to blend transparent pixels against.

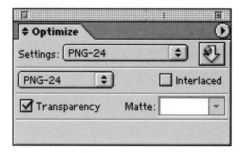

- The options for saving a PNG-8 file are very similar to those available for GIFs. (For details regarding each of these options, see the previous tip, "Optimize GIFs.")

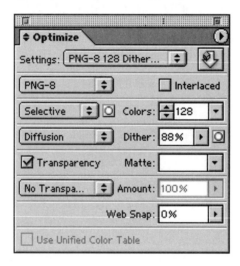

- When you're finished, in Photoshop click Save to save the slice or file using the selected optimization settings. (To save your settings without actually saving the slice or file, click Done to return to the main Photoshop window.) In ImageReady choose File I Save Optimized or Save Optimized As.

► **NOTE**

See the Web Compression Settings section of the color insert for full-color samples of images with different optimization settings.

Optimize WBMPs

If you're going to create any graphics to be viewed on wireless devices, such as a handheld computer or cell phone, you need to use a special file format just for wireless bitmaps, called WBMP. Wireless bitmaps don't offer any type of compression—they don't need it—because files saved as WBMPs are limited to using only black and white. (See other WBMP characteristics in Table 10-5.)

 To optimize an image as a WBMP in Photoshop, perform the following steps:

- In Photoshop choose File | Save For Web. In ImageReady choose Window | Optimize to display the Optimize palette.

- Click the 2-Up tab to display your original image on the left (or top) and the optimized file on the right (or bottom).

- If necessary, use the Slice Select tool to select the slice you want to optimize. Otherwise, if no slices exist, continue following these steps to optimize the entire image.

- From the File Type menu, select WBMP. Because WBMP files only contain two colors (black and white), you don't have any options regarding color. In fact, the only option you have is whether to use dithering in areas that previously had color to simulate a third color in the image.

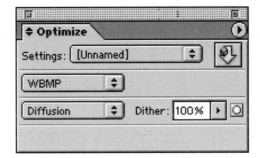

Characteristic	Description
Color mode	1-bit (black and white only)
Compression method	None
Animation	Not supported
Transparency	Not supported
Interlacing	Not supported
File type	Bitmap

Table 10-5   WBMP Format Characteristics

- When you're finished, in Photoshop click Save to save the slice or file using the selected optimization settings. (To save your settings without actually saving the slice or file, click Done to return to the main Photoshop window.) In ImageReady choose File | Save Optimized or Save Optimized As.

▶ **NOTE**

See the Web Compression Settings section of the color insert for full-color samples of images with different optimization settings.

Use Dithering to Smooth Edges in GIF and PNG-8 Files

Dithering is a process in which a color is simulated because it is outside of the currently available color palette. This process causes colors to have a somewhat "spotty" or "speckled" appearance because it often requires two or more similar colors, placed next to each other in a checkerboard-style pattern, to approximate a color.

You can use a type of controlled dithering when optimizing web graphics within Photoshop to specify how to handle colors not found within the active color palette. For example, if you have an image with 256 colors in its palette and you then reduce that color palette to 32 colors, you can specify the type of dithering Photoshop should use when remapping the 224 colors no longer in the color palette.

While dithering can be a good thing, because it may smooth some gradations that might otherwise look rough or blocky, it increases the number of colors used and therefore also increases the final file size of a graphic. If that means users must wait longer to view the file, this is a good reason to avoid dithering.

▶ **NOTE**

When you use a color in your web page that isn't available on the viewer's system, the browser may use dithering to try to approximate the color. This is called a browser dither.

TRY IT   To use dithering to smooth edges in GIF or PNG-8 files, make sure the file you want to compress as a GIF or PNG-8 is open and ready to be processed. In Photoshop choose File | Save For Web. In ImageReady click the Optimized tab at the top of the image window and access the Optimize palette before continuing. (If necessary, use the Slice Select tool to select the specific slice within the image you want to optimize, or SHIFT-select multiple slices to optimize together.)

Select GIF or PNG-8 from the File Type menu. Reduce the number of colors to 32, just to get started. Then, select one of the following from the Dithering menu. (For a visual example, see Figure 10-6.)

- **No Dither**   No dithering is applied; colors are displayed in "bands" around the image.
- **Diffusion**   Colors are randomly "spattered" throughout the image wherever there is a transition between two or more colors; higher dither percentages add more "spatter" to give the appearance of more detail, but also increase file size.

- **Pattern**   Colors are mixed in a halftone-like pattern of squares wherever there is a transition between two or more colors.

- **Noise**   Colors are randomly "spattered" throughout the image, much like the Diffusion method, but without affecting adjacent pixels. This has a similar effect to the Noise filter in Photoshop and can be deliberately used, in cases where the added file size is not prohibitive, for some very creative effects.

No dithering; smallest file size   Diffusion dithering at 88%

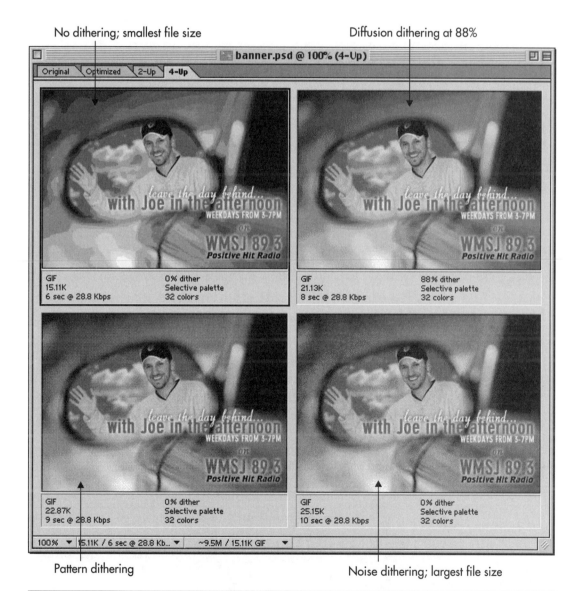

Pattern dithering   Noise dithering; largest file size

Figure 10-6   I used the 4-Up tab to compare the four different dithering options for a single image.

If you select Diffusion, you are also given the option of specifying exactly how much diffusion to use by moving the slider to the right for more diffusion or to the left for less diffusion.

▶ **CAUTION**

If you apply Diffusion dithering to a slice that shares borders with other slices, obvious seams may appear between those slices. To avoid this, see the tip "Link Slices to Optimize Multiple Slices at Once" later in the chapter.

Manipulate the Colors in GIF and PNG-8 Files

Because both GIF and PNG-8 files have limited color palettes (256 colors or less), manipulating those palettes to contain only the colors you deem essential often is necessary, particularly because every color in a GIF or PNG-8 file adds to its size and, in the end, its download time. Both Photoshop and ImageReady give you control over this color palette by allowing you to add, edit, lock, and delete colors in the color tables of GIF and PNG-8 images.

▶ **NOTE**

See the Web Optimization Settings section of the color insert for samples of a few color tables for GIF and PNG-8 images.

TRY IT   To manipulate the colors in a GIF or PNG-8 file, you need to first access the file's color table by performing one of the following:

- In Photoshop choose File | Save For Web. Click the Optimize tab and then select GIF or PNG-8 from the File Type menu on the right. Below that lies the color table.

- In ImageReady click the Optimize tab at the top of the image window and choose Windows | Color Table to display the Color Table palette.

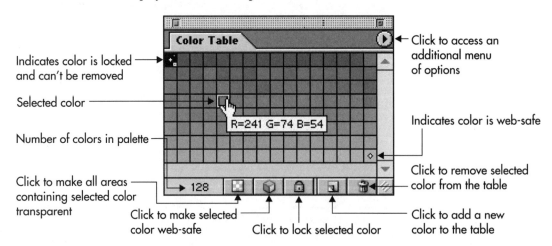

In either case, the color table is filled with the colors in the image, based on the current optimization settings. For example, if you specify there should be 32 colors in the image, there will be 32 colors in the color table. (The only exception is when the program sees that there are fewer than 32 colors actually used in the image, in which case it will only include the colors actually used in the image in the color table.)

Likewise, if you specify that 50 percent of the colors in a color table with 32 colors should be web-safe, the program forces 16 colors into the web-safe palette. You can recognize a web-safe color in the color table because it has a small white circle in the center of it.

To further customize the color table, perform any of the following:

- **Change the display of the color table**   Click the small triangle in the upper-right corner of the table and select from one of the different sorting order options: Unsorted, Sort By Hue, Sort By Luminance, or Sort By Popularity.

- **Add a new color to the color table**   First, make sure there are no colors currently selected in the color table (choose Deselect All Colors from the Color Table palette menu). Then, use the Eyedropper tool to place the color you want to add in the color selection box (in Photoshop's Save For Web dialog box) or the foreground color swatch in the toolbox (in ImageReady's toolbox). Click the New Color button in the Color Table palette to add the currently selected color. (If your color table is restricted to a certain number of colors, such as 128 or 32, the new color will share the space occupied by the color with the closest value to the new color.)

- **Force an existing color to be web-safe**   Click once on the color to select it (from either the image itself or the color table) and click the Web Shift button in the Color Table palette. To force multiple colors to be web-safe, SHIFT-click the colors (if they are next to each other), or CTRL-click (Windows) or CMD-click (Mac) the colors (if they aren't next to each other) and click the Web Shift button. Click the Web Shift button again to reverse the process.

- **Force all non-web-safe colors to be web-safe**   Click the triangle in the upper-right corner of the Color Table palette to access the palette menu and choose Select All Non-Web Safe Colors. Click the Web Shift button at the bottom of the Color Table palette. Alternatively, you can change the Web Snap setting in the Optimize window to 100 percent.

- **Lock a color in the color table, and prevent it from being deleted even if you reduce the number of colors in the palette**   Click once on the color in the color table to select it and click the Lock button at the bottom of the Color Table palette. You can recognize a locked color in the color table because a small white square is displayed in its lower-right corner. To unlock a color, select it and click the Lock button again. (Note that locking a color in Photoshop or ImageReady doesn't guarantee a user will have that color in their system palette when they try to view the image.)

- **Delete a color from the color table**   Select the color in the color table and click the Trash button at the bottom of the palette. After deleting a color, any areas of the image that contained the color change to the color in the palette closest in value to the deleted color.

▶ **QUICK TIP**

In ImageReady click and hold on a color in the color table for a few seconds to see where that color is used in the optimized image. (The areas will be temporarily highlighted.)

Once you've completed manipulating the color table for an image, it may be helpful to save the color table for future use. You can do so by choosing Save Color Table from the Color Table palette menu. Give it an appropriate name (the file extension .act is automatically added) and save it in the Presets/Optimized Colors folder inside the Photoshop program folder. Then, whenever you need to, you can choose Load Color Table from the palette menu to load it.

Optimize Transparent Web Graphics

Two web file formats—GIF and PNG—support transparency. This means you can create web graphics containing areas you can "see through" to whatever is beneath. In most cases, this means you can see the background image or color of the web page in the transparent areas of the graphic.

When you optimize a transparent web graphic, you need to select the format in which to save it. That decision is most commonly made on the basis of how many colors you need to make transparent. While GIF and PNG-8 support binary (or 1-color) transparency, PNG-24 supports variable transparency in much the same way traditional Photoshop files support transparency.

▶ *CAUTION*

Remember that if you choose to use PNG-24 to achieve variable transparency, many users won't be able to see it because their browsers don't yet fully support PNG files. (The latest versions of Internet Explorer and Netscape do support PNG files without plug-ins, but not the variable transparency aspect.) To check out which browsers do support PNG, and to what extent, visit www.libpng.org/pub/ png/pngapbr.html.

TRY IT   To optimize transparent web graphics, make sure you have the file you want to optimize open in Photoshop or ImageReady. If necessary, turn off the Background layer of the file to make the transparent parts of the image visible. Then, in Photoshop choose Save For Web. In ImageReady choose Window | Optimize to view the Optimize palette.

Select GIF, PNG-8, or PNG-24 from the File Type menu depending on which type of transparency and which file format you want to use. Place a check mark in the box next to Transparency and click the color sample box to the right to specify the background color of your web page (against which the image will be placed).

To force a certain color in the image to be transparent, first use the Eyedropper tool to select that color from the image. Then click the first button below the Color Table to "make transparent."

For GIF and PNG-8 you have several additional options related to the dithering of soft edges during the transition to transparency. These are discussed in the following tip.

Use Transparency Dithering When Placing a Transparent GIF or PNG-8 on a Patterned Background

Normally, when you save a GIF or PNG-8 file that has semitransparent pixels in its original image, those pixels are blended with your selected Matte color to become fully opaque. That's how you can "fake" a soft edge with a GIF or PNG-8 file: by using a Matte color that's the same as your web page's background color.

But if your background color isn't solid, such as with a pattern or photographic background, selecting a Matte color can be difficult because the edges become apparent when the transparent graphic is placed on the patterned background. So instead, turn on transparency dithering to dither those partially opaque areas.

TRY IT   To turn on transparency dithering, first follow the steps in the preceding tip to optimize a transparent graphic. Then, change the option in the Transparency Dithering menu from No Transparency Dither to one of the other three options:

- **Diffusion Transparency Dither**   To use a random "spattering" pattern that also affects adjacent pixels to lessen the appearance of the dithering

- **Pattern Transparency Dither**   To use a square, halftone-like pattern

- **Noise Transparency Dither**   To use a random "spattering" pattern that doesn't affect adjacent pixels and may seem more visible

For Diffusion Transparency Dither, specify the amount of dithering in the slider to the right.

▶ NOTE

Dithering is not necessary for PNG-24 because pixels can be semitransparent in PNG-24 files, while they must be either fully transparent or fully opaque in GIF and PNG-8 files. To create the appearance of soft, transparent edges in GIF and PNG-8 files, specify a matte color in Photoshop or ImageReady that is the same as the background color of your web page. See Figure 10-7 for a comparison.

Figure 10-7 For pixels to be partially transparent in this image, it needs to be saved as a PNG-24 (shown left); I can "fake" the soft edge with a GIF or PNG-8 file by using an appropriate Matte color.

Use Weighted Optimization

If you've ever saved JPEG at its lowest quality setting just to get a super-small file size, but wished you could have forced that low quality to only be in certain places of the image, here's your answer: weighted optimization. By deliberately weighting the optimization of certain key settings in Photoshop or ImageReady, you can control where optimization occurs.

For example, in JPEGs you can control where quality is lost. You can also control where dithering occurs in GIF, PNG-8, and WBMP dithering, and which areas of a GIF are more lossy than others. Finally, for GIF and PNG-8 images, you can use weighted optimization to specify which areas of color are most important and therefore shouldn't be dropped from the color table.

Weighted optimization uses masks to tell the program which areas are more important than others. Masks can be derived from outlines around text on type layers, outlines around vector shapes on shape layers, saved selections, or any other mask saved in the Channels palette.

TRY IT To use weighted optimization, make sure the file with which you want to work is open and the mask you want to use is available. In other words, make sure the area you want to designate as being most important is one of the following:

- Text on a type layer
- A shape on a shape layer
- Saved as a mask in the Channels palette

If it is not one of the preceding, then, with the selection tools, make a selection around the area you want to carry the most weight during optimization. Choose Select | Save Selection and give it an appropriate name.

Next, in Photoshop choose File | Save For Web to access the optimization settings for the file. In ImageReady click the Optimized tab and choose Window | Optimize to view the Optimize palette. Select the appropriate file format (GIF, JPEG, PNG-8, PNG-24, or WBMP).

▶ **QUICK TIP**

To quickly draw a selection around the contents of a layer, right-click (Windows) or CTRL-*click (Mac) the layer's preview in the Layers palette and choose Set Selection To Transparency Mask. Then, choose Select | Save Selection to save it as a mask to be used for weighted optimization.*

When an optimization setting can be weighted, a small circle inside a square appears next to it in the Optimize palette. If the circle is filled in, it indicates weighted optimization is currently in use for that setting.

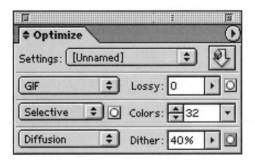

To use weighted optimization, click the icon next to the appropriate setting: Dither, Color Palette, Lossy, or Quality. In the dialog box that appears, specify the use (Text Layers, Vector Shape Layers, or a specified Channel) and adjust the setting below. A preview of the mask is also shown; white areas receive the maximum setting you specify, while black areas receive the minimum amount. Click OK to save or click Cancel to go back without saving.

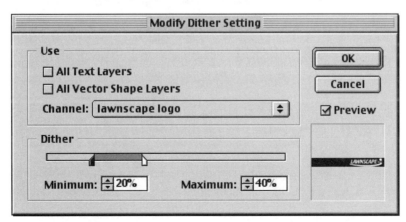

▶ *NOTE*

In the case of using weighted optimization to control the color palette, the colors under the black areas of the mask are removed first during the reduction of colors.

Optimize by File Size

If you have a target file size in mind when optimizing web graphics, you can actually tell Photoshop or ImageReady that file size, and the program will generate an optimized file with the settings required to reach that file size. In fact, if you let it, the program will also choose for you whether the file should be saved as a GIF or JPEG.

TRY IT To optimize by file size, first make sure the file you want to optimize is open in Photoshop or ImageReady. In Photoshop choose Save For Web. In ImageReady click the Optimized tab and choose Window | Optimize to display the Optimize palette. Click the small triangle in the upper-right corner of the Optimize palette (ImageReady) or the Optimize panel in the Save For Web dialog box (Photoshop) and choose Optimize To File Size.

> ▶ *QUICK TIP*
>
> *If you use the 4-Up tab, Photoshop will also generate two additional optimized versions of the image, each with incrementally smaller file sizes than you entered.*

In the dialog box that appears, enter the file size to which you want to optimize the file. To allow the program to choose between GIF or JPEG, click the second button below the file size. Otherwise, leave the first option selected to use the current settings in the Optimize panel (Photoshop) or palette (ImageReady). Click OK to see the results.

Link Slices to Optimize Multiple Slices at Once

Whenever you need to save more than one slice in a file with the same settings, it's best to link those slices together. Not only does linking slices allow you to share optimization settings, it ensures that any dithering applied is done so uniformly across the linked slices to avoid any obvious seams.

▶ *CAUTION*

This is one feature that is only available in ImageReady. To take advantage of this feature with a file in Photoshop, choose File | Jump To | Adobe ImageReady 7.0 to switch to ImageReady.

 TRY IT To link slices, make sure a file with multiple slices is open in ImageReady. SHIFT-click the slices you want to link together and choose Slices | Link Slices. After the slices are linked, an icon appears next to the normal slice icon, indicating the link. Each set of linked slices in a file has different color icons to help you differentiate between them.

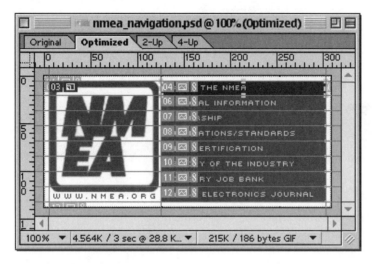

When you select a slice and make changes to that slice's optimization settings, those settings take effect for all the slices in the current link set.

To unlink one slice, select the slice and choose Slices | Unlink Slices. To unlink all the slices in a single set, select one slice from the set and choose Slices | Unlink Set. Choose Slices | Unlink All to unlink all slices in all sets of an image.

Use Photoshop/ImageReady to Preview in a Browser

While Photoshop and ImageReady both do a pretty good job of showing you how an optimized image will likely display in a browser, nothing is better than going to the source. In this case, that means actually previewing your optimized images in any web browser loaded on your computer.

By default, Photoshop and ImageReady set themselves up to preview in any browsers they notice during installation. However, if you have any additional browser(s) on your system, you can specify exactly which one(s) to use for previewing.

 To preview an optimized image in a browser, perform one of the following:

- In Photoshop, choose File | Save For Web and select the browser in which you want to preview the file from the Select Browser menu at the bottom of the window.

- In ImageReady, choose a browser from the Preview In Browser tool near the bottom of the toolbox, or choose File | Preview In and select a browser from the menu.

During the preview, the program shows you the optimized image as well as information such as its dimensions, file size, and format. In addition, the HTML the program would use to display the image (if you asked it to output HTML) is displayed as follows:

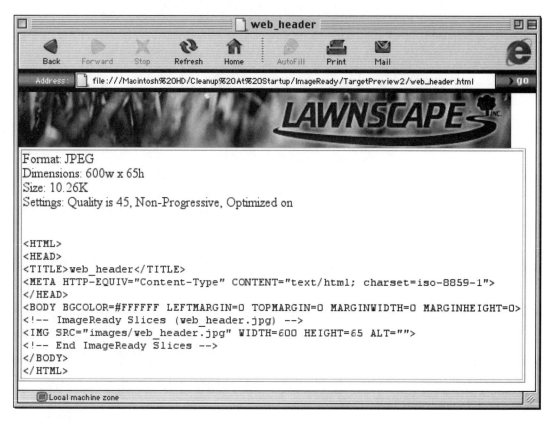

Use Photoshop/ImageReady to Build HTML Code

If you need to quickly translate a Photoshop design into HTML code, Photoshop and ImageReady are capable of doing just that for you. However, before allowing either program to output HTML code for you, keep the following things in mind:

- Name your slices. If you don't, the program generates somewhat random names that may or may not be appropriate in all cases.

- Specify which slices should be saved as images and which should not. If you don't, the program saves all slices as images—even autoslices generated by the program to fill the space around any slices you created.

- Provide alternative text for images, in case they can't be displayed by the browser for whatever reason.

- In areas where you want the program to output text, enter that text (and HTML if necessary).

- Specify the URLs for linked images.

- Specify the background colors (or images) for areas.

To perform each of these tasks, double-click each slice with the Slice Select tool and fill in the appropriate information.

 To automatically build the HTML code for a sliced web design, perform one of the following, according to the program you're using, before continuing:

- In Photoshop choose File | Save For Web. Use the Slice Select tool to select each slice, and adjust the optimization settings on the right accordingly. When you've successfully edited the optimization settings for all slices, click Save.

- In ImageReady choose the Optimize tab at the top of the image window. Use the Slice Select tool to select each slice, and adjust the settings in the Optimize palette. When you've successfully edited the optimization settings for all slices, choose File | Save Optimized As.

> ▶ **QUICK TIP**
>
> *In ImageReady, you can choose File | Update HTML to update the HTML after making changes to a web design file. To accomplish the same task in Photoshop, choose File | Save For Web, click Save, and choose HTML Only as the Format.*

In the Save dialog box, specify the Format. To output all the optimized images as well as the corresponding HTML code, choose HTML And Images. To output only the HTML, choose HTML Only. To customize the type of HTML code the program will write, select Other from the Settings menu and edit the HTML settings as needed.

Import Sliced Photoshop Files into GoLive to Build HTML Code

If you plan to use a visual web development tool (in other words, one that allows you to see how the page looks as you're building it), consider using Adobe GoLive, because it offers many features that fit seamlessly with Photoshop and ImageReady. For instance, after you design a web page in Photoshop or ImageReady, you can drag it into a page layout file in GoLive to have that tool help you optimize the graphics and build the HTML code.

TRY IT To import a sliced Photoshop file into GoLive, first open a copy of Adobe GoLive. If you already have a page to which you want to add the content of your sliced Photoshop file, choose File | Open and select the page to open. Otherwise, choose File | New Page to create a new web page in GoLive.

▶ **NOTE**

Visit http://www.adobe.com to download a free sample of GoLive.

Next, perform one of the following tasks to actually import the sliced Photoshop file into the new web page you created:

- Click once anywhere on the desktop of your computer and double-click the icon for your hard drive's main folder. Navigate through the directory structure until you find the sliced Photoshop file you want to import into GoLive. Click and drag that file into your web page file in GoLive.

- Press CTRL-2 (Windows) or CMD-2 (Mac) to display the Objects palette. Click the second button to display the Smart Objects in the lower portion of the Objects palette. The first button in the Smart Objects set allows you to add a sliced Photoshop file to GoLive, so click and drag it into the web page file. Press CTRL-1 (Windows) or CMD-1 (Mac) to display the Inspector palette. Click the Basic tab, and then click the folder icon next to the Source text field to define which Photoshop file you want to use.

- Right-click (Windows) or CTRL-click (Mac) anywhere in the web page file and choose Insert Object | Smart | Smart Photoshop. Press CTRL-1 (Windows) or CMD-1 (Mac) to display the Inspector palette. Click the Basic tab, and then click the folder icon next to the Source text field to define which Photoshop file you want to use.

After you specify the file to import, GoLive starts the Save For Web dialog box to give you a chance to specify optimization settings for each slice in the image. If you've already saved these settings in Photoshop or ImageReady, you can simply click Save and specify the folder in which GoLive should save the optimized files. Otherwise, select each slice, and make changes to the optimization settings as needed and then click Save.

▶ **NOTE**

If your Photoshop file contains text layers, GoLive gives you a chance to use the topmost text layer as a text variable before optimizing the slices. This means you can change the text on that layer before its slice is optimized. To do so, select the Use option, enter the replacement text in the text box, and then click OK. Otherwise, leave the Use option as is and simply click OK.

When the slices are imported, you can click them and edit settings such as link references and alternative text in the Inspector palette. Because this Photoshop file was imported as a "Smart" object in GoLive, any changes you make to the file in Photoshop will be updated in GoLive as well.

Import Layered Photoshop Files into GoLive to Build DHTML Code

When you import sliced Photoshop files into GoLive using the technique described in the previous tip, the file is placed as if it were a flattened Photoshop file. In other words, the individual layers in Photoshop are ignored. Suppose you wanted to import the text and graphic behind it separately, so they could each be moved independently on the web page in GoLive. To achieve this, you can actually import the layered Photoshop file right into GoLive.

While GoLive typically uses HTML table tags to organize slices from Photoshop files, layered Photoshop files are handled differently. Instead of static HTML table tags, GoLive uses Dynamic HTML (DHTML) to lay out the individual elements, which are called *floating boxes* in GoLive. The benefit of using DHTML is that each element's movements can be dynamically scripted on the page. For example, you could script a section of the page to disappear when a user clicks a certain button.

The drawback in using DHTML to lay out a page is that it's not fully supported by all the browsers your site's visitors may be using. For more information on DHTML and the browsers that support it, visit hotwired.lycos.com/webmonkey/authoring/dynamic_html/ or www.webreference.com/dhtml.

TRY IT   To import a layered Photoshop file into GoLive to build DHTML code, open the page to which you want to add the file in GoLive. Or choose File | New Page to create a new page layout. Choose File | Import | Photoshop Layers To Floating Boxes. Select the layered Photoshop file you want to import and then specify the folder where GoLive should save the optimized files.

Next, GoLive opens the Save For Web dialog box to give you a chance to specify optimization settings for each layer in the image, starting with the lowest layer (usually the Background layer). Make changes to the optimization settings as needed and then click Save. Repeat these steps until all the layers of your file have been optimized and are displayed in GoLive. If you don't want to import one of the layers in your file, click Cancel in the Save For Web dialog box when you see that layer appear. Only that layer will be cancelled, and you can continue optimizing the rest of the layers in the file.

> ### QUICK TIP
>
> *To quickly optimize all remaining layers in a file with the same (current) optimization settings, hold down the* CTRL *key while clicking Save. Likewise, to cancel the optimization of all remaining layers (instead of just the current one),* CTRL-*click the Cancel button.*

Use Photoshop Mockups as Tracing Images When Building Pages in GoLive

If you designed a detailed mockup in Photoshop containing significant portions that are not comprised of graphics, such as the one that includes form elements or large areas of text, it can be particularly useful to have a copy of that mockup in sight when building the code for the web page. GoLive has a feature that not only allows you to have that mockup in sight while you're building the code but also gives you the opportunity to "cut out" portions of that mockup and optimize them as web graphics without having to open Photoshop.

TRY IT To use a Photoshop file as a tracing image when building a web page layout in GoLive, open the file you want to work with in GoLive or choose File | New Page to create a new web page layout. Then, select Window | Tracing Image to display the Tracing Image palette.

Place a check mark in the box next to Source and click the folder icon to locate the file you want to use as a tracing image. By default, GoLive sets the Opacity of the tracing image to 50%. To edit that setting, simply move the slider to the right to increase the opacity or to the left to lessen it.

You can also move the tracing image by first selecting the Move Image tool (shaped like a hand) from the Tracing Image palette. Click and drag the tracing image to reposition it. Or type values into the Position text boxes to more precisely reposition it.

> **QUICK TIP**
>
> *Select Tracing Image from the Change Window Size pop-up menu at the bottom of the document window to shrink the window to match the boundaries of the tracing image.*

To remove a tracing image, uncheck the box next to Source in the Tracing Image palette.

TRY IT To cut out an element from the tracing image and optimize it as a web graphic on the web page, select the Cut Out tool (shaped like Photoshop's Crop tool) in the Tracing Image palette and draw a selection around the section of the tracing image you want to cut out. When you're satisfied with your selection, click the Cut Out button in the Tracing Image palette or double-click the selection to launch the Save For Web dialog box, in which you can optimize the graphic. Or to cancel the Cut Out tool, deselect the tool in the Tracing Image palette.

> **QUICK TIP**
>
> *Cutout images are automatically treated as floating boxes in GoLive, which represent DHTML layers. If you prefer to lay your page out with HTML tables instead, you can convert the floating boxes to layout grids: GoLive's terminology for HTML tables. Choose Window | Floating Boxes to display the Floating Boxes palette. Click the triangle in the upper-right corner to access the palette menu and choose Convert To Layout Grid. GoLive re-creates the page in a new window using HTML tables. (Note that this option is not available if any of your floating boxes overlap.)*

CHAPTER 11

Animated, Interactive, and Data-Driven Graphics

TIPS IN THIS CHAPTER

If you've spent any amount of time on the Web, you know that it's not all flat, static graphics—things are moving and doing things! For example, buttons depress when you move the cursor over them, photos change, music plays, advertisements try to get our attention, navigation bars collapse and expand, and pages otherwise react to our input.

While some of these things are primarily accomplished outside of a graphics program like Photoshop, others can be created and developed almost entirely within Photoshop's sister program, ImageReady, which is customized specifically for web design.

This chapter focuses on providing tips related to other techniques for web design not previously discussed in other chapters. For the most part, these tips fall into three key categories:

- Animation
- Rollovers
- Data-driven graphics

A few other tips relate to more interactive ways to use traditional web graphics, such as with image maps and web galleries. Before I dive into the tips, consider the following overviews of the three key areas discussed in this chapter.

Animation

In its simplest form, animation involves the display of two or more images shown in succession, to give the appearance of motion. Remember those little flip books—the ones that look like a mini-filmstrip if you flip the pages really fast? Those are an example of the most basic form of animation.

At the other end of the spectrum, you might find something like Disney's *The Lion King,* which was a fully animated 90-minute cartoon, complete with music and voice-overs. Even some live-action movies like *Titanic* include forms of animation—such as computer-animated people in crowd scenes—with truly amazing high-tech special effects.

391

Two popular animation formats on the Web are GIF and Flash. While Photoshop is not capable of saving either type of format, two of its sister applications—ImageReady (which ships with Photoshop) and LiveMotion—take care of that problem and integrate quite well with Photoshop files.

GIF Animation

GIF animation is by far the easier type to implement. As such, GIF animation is popular and has been for some time. Lucky for us, Adobe packaged ImageReady—a fully capable GIF animation tool—with Photoshop.

One of the major benefits of GIF animation is its capability to reach the widest possible audience, given that it doesn't require a plug-in or certain version of browser. An animated GIF is saved as a single GIF file, even though it contains two or more frames of animation.

The most common uses of animation GIFs typically involve advertising—albeit somewhat annoying advertising. This is because, for better or worse, movement on an otherwise static page catches our eyes. And advertising on the Web is certainly all about catching the user's eye, as well as their full attention.

▶ | **QUICK TIP**

The final size of a GIF animation file can be as high as the sums of each of the individual frames. This means if you had a file with five frames, each of which optimized to 20KB, your total GIF file could easily top 100KB! To reduce the file size, minimize the movement between each frame so the program doesn't have to redraw every aspect of every frame.

There are a few drawbacks to using GIF animation, the first of which is related to the fact that it is so commonly used for animation. So many users are accustomed to animations being used in banner ads on web sites that most say they don't even look at animation any more because they assume it's trying to sell something. Finally, GIF animation files can't contain sound or any interactivity.

▶ **CAUTION**

"Don't overuse animation….The best animations reinforce the site's goals, tell a story, or aid in navigation. Repeated animations on text-heavy pages distract the eye from the message of the page." Good advice, particularly from a company that sells animation tools: Macromedia.

Flash

After GIF animation, the next most popular type of animation on the Web is Flash animation. The Flash file format was specifically designed to deliver animation and interactivity to web site visitors. In fact, its vector format makes the process much more painless for visitors because its file sizes are significantly smaller than many other similar formats. In addition, its streaming capabilities enable Flash files to be viewed while they're downloading, which is good because users can get to the actual content faster.

The Flash file format, recognized by its .swf file extension, has quickly caught on and can be created from a variety of applications, including Adobe's LiveMotion and Macromedia's Flash. (The term "Flash" can be used to refer to the actual Flash application as well as the file format.) Common uses of Flash include advertisements, navigation systems, movie previews/trailers, cartoons, training programs, and product demonstrations.

With all its benefits, Flash still has a few key drawbacks. First, up until the recent versions of the major browsers, Flash files required a plug-in to be viewed. This meant people had to download an extra add-on component to their browser to view the content of Flash files. Because people typically take some time to upgrade to the latest version of web browsers, portions of your audience using older browsers still need to download the plug-in, if they don't have it already. (The good news is that some studies show between 85 and 98 percent of users have the Flash plug-in installed.)

Another thing to consider is this: not all Flash plug-ins are compatible. This means your users not only must have the Flash plug-in installed, but usually must also have the correct version installed to view your animation.

Finally, the creation of Flash animation is significantly more involved than that of GIF animation. This alone may prevent many people from using it on their web sites.

Rollovers

Rollovers are a form of interactivity that has become extremely popular on the Web. In fact, interactivity is something that's made the Web itself so popular: it enables users to interact with a medium in ways previously impossible. On the Web, users can point and click their way around, forging new paths with each movement.

Content is often delivered specifically according to users' likes and dislikes, as recorded by previous actions and input. Users are always contributing to the flow of information on the Internet. By contrast, television and newspapers are primarily passive, in that users receive information and rarely contribute to it.

Although rollovers don't help deliver customer-specific content, they do help add to the whole interactive experience of browsing a web site. For example, have you ever moved your cursor over a link on a web site and found it changes color or style? This effect is referred to as a rollover or mouseover and makes most users *feel* more interactive with the page.

Rollovers are achieved through a bit of JavaScript code in the HTML file. The good news for ImageReady users is that the program writes the JavaScript for you, so there's no need to learn a scripting language just to add a few rollovers to your web site. (With that said, I must mention that JavaScript is not a difficult language to learn. If you learned or are learning HTML, it's a small step up from that and can easily be learned by practice and experience. Check out *JavaScript: A Beginner's Guide* by John Pollock (McGraw-Hill/Osborne) if you're interested in learning more.)

▶ *NOTE*

Because rollovers use JavaScript, they are only visible in browsers that support JavaScript. While all the recent versions of the popular browsers do support JavaScript, that support can still be turned off by the user in the browser. For this reason, you shouldn't rely on rollovers or JavaScript to transfer important information to the user. Instead, it should be considered an added bonus if the user can see the changes rollovers cause.

Aside from the proper code, you need at least two versions of each image you want to change—one that's present when the page is first viewed, and another for when the cursor is rolled over the image or link—and both of those versions should be the same size. In addition to those two states, you might have another version of the image for when the user actually clicks it, and yet another for images whose links have already been clicked (in other words, visited links).

Data-Driven Graphics

I think any designer who's worked on a large web site with personalized graphics has at some time wished for her own robot to perform the more mundane, repetitive aspects of the job related to that personalization. For example, suppose you are a web designer for a large newspaper. Your tasks include reformatting existing graphics from the printed version of the paper for the online version. Among other things, you are required to adjust the color mode, size, resolution, file format, copyright, and photographer name. Doing these things for a daily newspaper could become a full-time job in itself.

Instead, you can create a template for an image, such as the photo accompanying the lead story of the newspaper, and specify which aspects of the image may change according to the actual photograph being used. (These changeable aspects are called *variables*.) In addition, you identify the different sets of data (such as the photographs and photographer's name) associated with each variable, and you're off and running.

After you finish the template, you can then output the individual graphics using Adobe AlterCast, or by writing a script to process the output. AlterCast is a product that resides on the web server and is capable of creating images on the fly, based on a user's interaction with the web site and/or the variables you specify. (For more information about AlterCast, see www.adobe.com/products/altercast.)

Jump to ImageReady for Animation and Rollovers

While Photoshop is certainly capable of optimizing static web graphics, it is not suited for animation or rollover effects. Therefore, to optimize animated GIFs or save the different states for your rollovers, you'll need to switch over to ImageReady.

TRY IT If you already have a web design open in Photoshop that you want to use for animation or rollover effects in ImageReady, choose File | Jump To | Adobe ImageReady 7.0. Your computer will launch ImageReady (if it wasn't already open) and open another copy of the file in that program.

▶ *NOTE*

If you don't have a file open in Photoshop, you can still choose File | Jump To | Adobe ImageReady 7.0 to open that program and begin a new file.

While you're working in ImageReady, the file appears "grayed out" in Photoshop, indicating you can't access it. If you switch back to working in Photoshop at any time, you'll notice a momentary lag in processing time, while ImageReady sends Photoshop any changes made to the file while you worked in that program.

▶ **QUICK TIP**

The keyboard shortcut for jumping between ImageReady and Photoshop with the active file is CTRL-SHIFT-M *(Windows) or* CMD-SHIFT-M *(Mac).*

If you have any dialog boxes open (such as the Save For Web or Save Optimized As dialog boxes) and you try to jump to the other program, you'll see an alert advising that you must finish editing the document in the original program before you can switch to the new program.

Use Layers to Build Animation

To create GIF animation, you need to design a series of images to serve as the individual frames of the animation. Photoshop's Layers palette can be a great place to start when building these frames, because, by toggling certain layers on and off, you can see your animation take shape.

▶ **NOTE**

I like to use Photoshop when building animation. Even though you can certainly begin right in ImageReady, I find that Photoshop has more tools for actually developing the animation, such as the Scatter option in the new Brushes palette or the Custom Shape tool. So I build my animation in Photoshop and jump to ImageReady for optimization.

TRY IT To use layers to build animation, begin by opening a new file in Photoshop or ImageReady using whichever size your animation needs to be. Because this is a web file, remember to use a resolution of 72 dpi. Next, choose Window | Layers to display the Layers palette.

Begin developing the content of your animation. In other words, if you plan to incorporate a photo of a product, open the photo and drag it into your animation file now. If you want to display text at any point in the animation, type that content now.

Once you have all the content assembled, it's time to begin building the individual "frames" of the animation by arranging your layers so each layer constitutes one frame in the animation.

▶ **QUICK TIP**

To create a standard web ad banner, choose File | New and select 468×60 Web Banner from the Preset Sizes select menu. To specify your own sites to be included in the Preset Sizes select menu, edit the text file called New Doc Sizes.txt located in the Presets folder in the Adobe Photoshop 7 folder. (See the instructions in the file for how to edit it.)

▶ *NOTE*

Alternatively, you can jump to ImageReady at this point and build each frame by turning on the visibility for only the layers needed at each point in the animation. For more hints on using that technique, see the following tip.

For example, to show a bird flying across the screen from left to right and getting bigger as he comes closer, I place the smallest bird to the far left on Layer 1. Then, I make a copy of that layer by dragging its name over the New Layer button in the Layers palette. I move the bird over to the right slightly and use the Free Transform tool (CTRL-T in Windows or CMD-T in Mac) to slightly enlarge him on Layer 2. I repeat this process until the bird finishes his flight across the page.

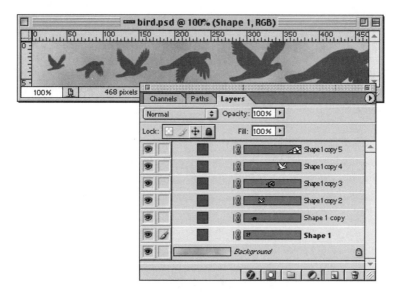

TRY IT After your "frames" have been built in the Layers palette, choose File | Jump To | Adobe ImageReady 7.0 to switch to editing the file in ImageReady. Then, choose Window | Animation to display the Animation palette. From the palette menu (accessible by clicking the small triangle in the upper-right corner of the Animation palette), choose Make Frames From Layers to translate each layer in your Photoshop file into an animation frame—the Background (if present) becomes Frame 1, Layer 1 becomes Frame 2, and so on.

▶ **QUICK TIP**

I created this bird using the Bird Custom Shape tool. I then edited the vector path of the bird to create the alternate version where the wings are flapped down.

▶ **QUICK TIP**

If you need to reverse the order of the frames in the Animation palette, so the contents of Layer 1 are at the end of the animation, click the triangle in the upper-right corner of the Animation palette and choose Reverse Frames from the palette menu.

If you have a Background layer that you now want to be visible in all frames, click inside the first frame in the Animation palette and follow these steps:

1. Click the Background layer in the Layers palette to activate it.

2. Click the triangle in the upper-right corner of the Layers palette and select Match from the palette menu.

3. Under Frames To Match, select Current Animation.

4. Leave all options selected under What To Match, or edit those options as needed.

5. Click OK in the Match dialog box and match how the background appears in Frame 1 to all other frames of the animation.

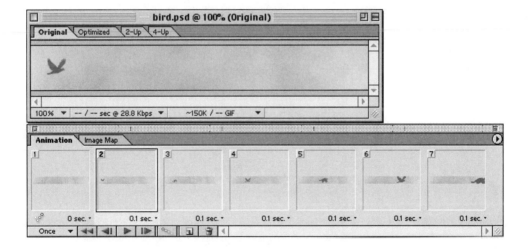

With both the Animation and Layers palettes open, click each frame in the Animation palette and notice how ImageReady turns on the appropriate layer in the Layers palette. To edit a particular frame, click once on its thumbnail in the Animation palette to activate it and then edit the layers in the Layers palette as needed. For more on using the Animation palette, see the next tip. For details on saving the animation, see the tip "Optimize GIF Animations."

Use the Animation Palette to Build Animation

Whereas the preceding tip discussed using layers to build animation, another option is to build the animation from scratch with the Animation palette. In this case, you can import a layered file into ImageReady and turn on the layers that need to be visible in each frame as needed, or you can begin with a new file right in ImageReady. Regardless of whether you import or start a file in ImageReady, the Animation palette is perfectly capable of handing all your GIF animation needs.

TRY IT   To use the Animation palette to build animation, open an existing file in ImageReady, or choose File | New to create a new one. Choose Window | Animation and Window | Layers to display the Layers and Animation palettes, if they're not already visible.

When you begin, there is a single animation frame listed in the Animation palette. The contents of this frame are determined by which layers are visible in the Layers palette. When a layer's visibility is disabled (by clicking the eye icon in the Layers palette next to the layer name), the contents of that layer are no longer visible on the current frame of the animation.

> ### QUICK TIP
>
> *To create a standard web ad banner, choose File | New and select one of the three standard web banner sizes from the Preset Sizes select menu. To specify your own sizes to be included in the Preset Sizes select menu, edit the text file called New Doc Sizes.txt located in the Presets folder in the Adobe Photoshop 7 folder. (See the instructions in the file for how to edit it.)*

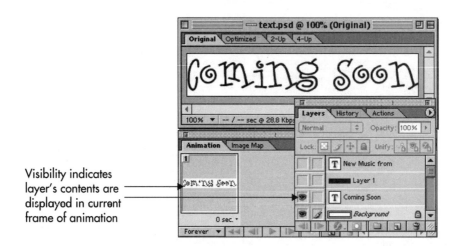

Visibility indicates layer's contents are displayed in current frame of animation

To add a new frame in the animation, click the small triangle in the upper-right corner of the Animation palette and choose New Frame from the palette menu, or click the Duplicate Frame button in the bottom of the Animation palette. In either case, ImageReady ads a new frame based on the contents of the current frame.

Then, to edit the contents of the new frame, make sure it's selected in the Animation palette (if it is, it will have an outline around it) and move to the Layers palette. Toggle the visibility of layers and move or edit the contents of layers as needed to create the desired effect.

In frame 2, the Coming Soon layer is hidden, while both the New Music from and Layer 1 layers are now visible

▶ NOTE

By default, when you add a new layer to a file with animation frames, that layer is visible across all frames. You can select one or more frames in the Animation palette and uncheck the eye icon on a particular layer to make it invisible for the selected layers.

 You can also perform any of the following tasks in the Animation palette to further customize the animation:

1. To move a frame within the sequence of the animation, click once on the frame in the Animation palette and drag it to the new location.

2. To delete a frame, click once on the frame in the Animation palette and drag it over the Trash button at the bottom of the palette.

3. To delete the entire animation, click the triangle in the upper-right corner of the Animation palette and choose Delete Animation from the palette menu.

Continue adding new frames and editing their contents through the Layers palette as needed until you're satisfied with the flow of information in the animation. To save the animation for web use, see the tip "Optimize GIF Animations," later in the chapter.

Copy and Paste the Contents of Frames

In ImageReady, a frame of animation is really like a snapshot of the Layers palette at a specific time in the file's history. For example, Frame 1 might display Layers 2 and 3 but not Layer 1, while Frame 2 might display just Layer 1.

If at any time you want to copy how the layers are displayed in one frame and paste that snapshot into another frame, you can use the copy and paste commands in the Animation palette. You can also use this technique to copy and paste frames between different animation files altogether.

 To copy a frame you will paste elsewhere, follow these steps:

1. Click once on the frame in the Animation palette to select it.

> ▶ | **QUICK TIP**
>
> *To select additional frames, hold down the* SHIFT *key and click in each of the additional frames to select.*

2. Choose Copy Frame(s) from the Animation palette menu (accessible by clicking the small triangle in the upper-right corner of the palette).

3. Select the frame on which or next to which copied files should be pasted.

To paste the selected frame(s), choose Paste Frame(s) from the Animation palette menu, specify the appropriate Paste method (described next), and then click OK:

- Choose Replace Frames to replace the selected frames with those you copied. This doesn't create any new layers in the file (unless you're pasting into a totally different file). Instead, it updates the selected frames to reflect the layer settings from the copied frames.

- Choose Paste Over Selection to add the elements of the copied layers as new layers in the file. So if you use Paste Over Selection in the same file, you end up with double the number of layers. Then, those new layers are only made visible in the frames you selected to paste over.

- Choose Paste Before Selection or Paste After Selection to paste the copied frames before or after the selected frames in the Animation palette. In most cases, this does not add any new layers to your file.

- Choose Link Added Layers to link all pasted layers together, if you're pasting more than one.

Preview an Animation and Adjust the Timing

You don't have to wait until your animation is optimized and saved as a GIF to view it. In fact, you may have noticed a few buttons at the bottom of the Animation palette that look similar to those on your VCR—and they're well suited for the purpose of previewing an animation file.

 TRY IT To preview an animation in ImageReady, make sure the animation is open and choose Window | Animation to display the Animation palette, if it isn't already visible. Click the appropriate button at the bottom of the palette to begin playing the animation.

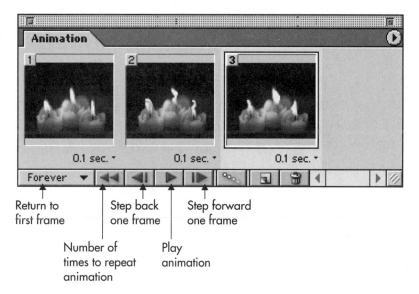

To stop playing, click the Stop button, which (when the file is being played) appears in the same location the Play button previously did.

To adjust the time delay between each frame, click the current time amount (which is "0.0 sec" by default) and select a new time from the list, or choose Other to specify your own duration. When specifying a time delay, you're identifying how long to view the current image before changing to the new one.

Tween Frames for Instant Animation

It is common for animations to include some sort of gradual shift in visibility, placement, color, or other characteristic of an element. For example, in the previous tip, I changed the background color from white to black between Frame 1 and Frame 2. What if I wanted that to be a gradual change instead of such a quick change from solid white to solid black? Or suppose I wanted the text in Frame 2, "New Music from," to drop into the frame from above. In either case, I might have to create many, many new frames and move or edit the contents of those frames by hand to achieve the desired effect. Instead, why not let ImageReady do all that work for you, using the option to Tween Frames?

Tweening is a process where ImageReady looks at two different frames and decides what needs to happen for the elements of the first frame to morph into how they display in the second frame. You can specify how many frames the program should add when tweening to truly customize the gradation of the movement.

TRY IT To tween frames for instant animation, begin with a file in ImageReady containing two frames in the Animation palette. On the first frame, move the elements to the position in which you want them to start. So, in the example where I want to have text "drop" into the frame from above, I need to place that text above the visible area of the frame in Frame 1.

To do so, I click the first frame in the Animation palette, then select the Move tool from the toolbox. After activating the appropriate layer in the Layers palette, I use the Move tool to move the text up above the image area.

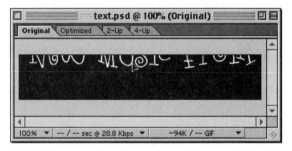

Next, I click the second frame in the Animation palette and again move the text. This time, however, I move it to the location in which I want it to end.

QUICK TIP

If you want to practice tweening in an animation, consider fading an image or text in or out by setting one frame's Opacity to 100% and the other one's to 0%. Another cool effect is to change the angle of an element's drop shadow to give the appearance of a moving light source.

After the beginning and ending frames are set, hold down the SHIFT key and click each frame in the Animation palette to select them. Then, click the Tween button at the bottom of the palette (or choose Tween from the palette menu) to tell ImageReady to create the additional frames *in between* the two selected frames.

Adjust the following options in the Tween dialog box as needed, and then click OK:

- Under Layers, select All Layers to cause the elements of all layers visible on each frame to be tweened. Choose Selected Layer to tween only the elements of the currently selected layer in the Layers palette.

- Under Parameters, identify which aspects of the frames you want to tween. Select Position to tween the difference in the location of any elements on the visible layers. Select Opacity to tween the difference in the opacity of any elements on the visible layers. Select Effects to tween any layer effects used on the visible layers.

- For Frames To Add, specify the number of additional frames to be placed in between the selected layers.

▶ **NOTE**

If your file is set to loop, or repeat, you can select the first and last frames of an animation for tweening, and the new frames will be added after the last frame.

Optimize GIF Animations

Each frame of a GIF animation file has the same characteristics of a GIF, which you learned about in Chapter 10. For example, each frame must have 256 colors or fewer, and can have no more than one transparent color.

Just as with static GIFs, animated GIFs will be much smaller if you keep the number of colors to a bare minimum. I recommend choosing a small color palette and then using only those few colors to create all the frames in your GIF animation. For this reason, drawings, text, and illustrations tend to work better as GIF animations. Photographic and continuous tone imagery don't compress well at all and often cause GIF animations to be much too large in file size—meaning they take so long to download that no one ever gets to watch them all the way through.

Aside from the basic GIF optimization settings discussed in Chapter 10, there are a few additional characteristics you need to know when optimizing GIF animations, as discussed in this technique.

TRY IT To optimize a GIF animation, make sure the file is open in ImageReady. (Remember that Photoshop cannot display or process animation files.) Then, perform the following tasks to prepare for optimization:

- **Set the disposal method.** For each frame, indicate what happens after it's displayed by right-clicking (Windows) or CTRL-clicking (Mac) on the frame in the Animation palette and choosing one of the following options:

  - Choose Do Not Dispose to cause the next frame to be placed on top of this one. (If the next frame contains transparent areas, this frame may then be visible in those areas.)

  - Choose Restore To Background to disable the current frame after it's viewed, so it's not visible if the next frame contains any transparent areas.

- • Choose Automatic to allow ImageReady to select the disposal method it thinks is best.
- • **Adjust the looping.**   Specify how many times the animation repeats. Click the looping option selection box—which is set to Forever by default—and choose Once, Forever, or Other (to specify an exact number of times to repeat).
- • **Adjust the timing.**   For each frame, specify how long the program should wait before displaying the next frame. Click the current delay value below each frame—which is set to 0.0 sec by default—and choose a value from the menu, or choose Other to enter your own value using decimals (for example, 1/2 second should be entered as .5).
- • **Specify the portion of each frame that should be redrawn as each new frame is placed on top of it.**   For example, the program defaults to only redrawing those portions that change from frame to frame, to save in file size. If you need to force the program to redraw the entire screen for every frame, click the triangle in the upper-right corner of the Animation palette and choose Optimize Animation. Then, uncheck Bounding Box and Redundant Pixel Removal. Otherwise, leave them checked for optimal performance.

▶ *CAUTION*

Even though ImageReady allows you to choose JPEG or PNG when optimizing an animation, those formats don't support animation and should be avoided. When optimizing an animation in ImageReady, always use the GIF file format.

Next, choose Window | Optimize to view the Optimize palette, where you can adjust settings such as file format (GIF) and color palette. When selecting a color palette for animation files, try Adaptive, Selective, or Perceptual, because they allow the colors to remain consistent across multiple frames. Click the Optimize tab in the document window to preview how the optimization settings affect the file, and when you're ready to save it, choose File | Save Optimized As. (For more tips on using the Optimize palette to optimize GIFs, refer to Chapter 10.)

Preview Animation in a Browser

After you adjust the appropriate settings, it's a good idea to preview your animation not just in ImageReady but also in a web browser. This is particularly important with animations, because some things, like timing, can only be properly previewed in a browser.

TRY IT   To preview your animation in a web browser, choose Window | Optimize and make sure you've specified the appropriate optimization settings. Then, click the Preview In Browser tool in the toolbox. (Depending on which browser is set up as your system's default browser, the icon on this tool will likely be that of Internet Explorer or Netscape Navigator.) Alternatively, you can choose File | Preview In and select the appropriate browser from the menu.

To replay a nonlooping animation in a browser, click Reload or Refresh in the browser's navigation bar. To stop a looping animation, click Stop in the browser's navigation bar.

Animate with the Liquify Command

The Liquify command is a truly fun filter that can produce amazing animated effects in no time at all. To understand what this command allows you to do, suppose you had a representation of your kid brother created in Play-Doh. Because it's created with such a soft and pliable material, you can easily stretch his ears to the size of Dumbo's, or give him a peanut-shaped head. The Liquify command offers you the same flexibility to stretch, squish, push, and pull any image of your choosing.

In particular, these effects can be animated and saved in ImageReady as part of a GIF animation. Or, the Photoshop file can be dragged and dropped into LiveMotion to be incorporated into a Flash or QuickTime movie.

TRY IT To animate with the Liquify command, open the image you want to affect in Photoshop or ImageReady. In the Layers palette, click and drag the specific layer you want to Liquify over the New Layer button at the bottom of the palette to duplicate this layer. (If you only want to apply the filter to a portion of the layer, use the selection tools to select the portion you want to affect before continuing.)

▶ CAUTION

You must rasterize type or shape layers before applying the Liquify command.

Next, choose Filter | Liquify to launch the Liquify dialog box. If there are any areas of the image that you want to protect from your actions in the Liquify command, choose the Freeze tool (the tenth button down) from the side toolbox and paint over the areas you want to protect. If you need to remove a portion of the image from being protected, use the Thaw tool (the eleventh button in the toolbox) to "unfreeze" that area.

When you're ready to begin distorting the image, make sure you have a few extra hours, because, as I have found, you can easily waste a good chunk of time just playing with this filter. But seriously, to begin the distortions, use any of the first eight tools in the toolbox—Warp, Turbulence, Twirl Clockwise, Twirl Counterclockwise, Pucker, Bloat, Shift Pixels, or Reflection—with an appropriately sized brush. The best advice I can give you in relation to which tool to use is this: try them all. The results vary according to the image, so play around with each tool to see what you can accomplish. The following illustration shows my first step in creating an animation where this birthday cake got sucked into itself.

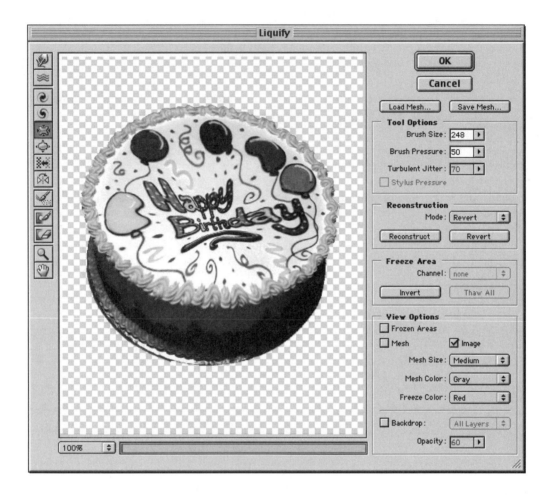

Because this tool uses an underlying "mesh," it's fairly easy to reconstruct that mesh any time you want to return an area to its original view. To do so, select the Reconstruct tool from the toolbox (ninth button) and click-hold or click and drag over the area(s) you want to reconstruct. To reconstruct all nonfrozen areas, choose Revert from the Mode menu under Reconstruction and click Reconstruct. Or, to restore the entire image back to its original view, specify Revert as the Mode under Reconstruction and click Revert.

Under View Options, select Frozen Areas to display all areas that are currently protected from being liquified. Select Mesh to display the underlying mesh for the image, which can be helpful in identifying areas you have not edited. Select Backdrop if you want to see the underlying layers in the file here in the Liquify dialog box.

▶ *NOTE*

Even if you choose to display other layers in the Liquify dialog box, they aren't edited when you edit the active layer.

When you're satisfied with the changes so far, click OK to apply the changes to the active layer. To continue a progression of effects, repeat the entire process (beginning with the duplication of the original layer) as many times as needed. When you're finished, jump to ImageReady if you're in Photoshop. Then, choose Window | Animation to display the Animation palette. From the palette menu, choose Make Frames From Layers to turn each of your liquified layers into a frame in the animation, as I did in Figure 11-1. Refer to previous tips in this chapter for details on editing and optimizing the animation.

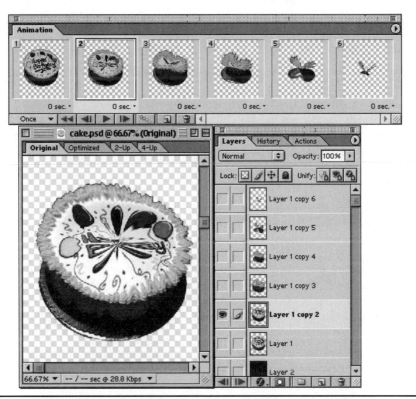

Figure 11-1   I used the Liquify command to distort this birthday cake several times, to give it the appearance of being sucked into itself.

▶ **QUICK TIP**

Need to use the Liquify command on a high-resolution image in Photoshop (as opposed to a screen resolution file in ImageReady)? Doing so can often be quite time-consuming because of how much extra memory is required to edit a large image. To save time, run the Liquify command on a low-resolution copy of the image, then choose Save Mesh in the Liquify dialog box, give it a name, and specify where to save it. Then click Cancel. Now, load your high-resolution image and choose Filter | Liquify. When the dialog box appears, choose Load Mesh and locate the mesh saved from the low-resolution file. Because meshes are resolution-independent, you can now apply the mesh to this image, and all your changes will magically take effect. One word of warning: It may take a little while for the actual rendering to occur.

Place Layered Photoshop Files into LiveMotion when Creating Flash (SFW) or QuickTime (MOV) Content

Just because ImageReady can only handle GIF animations doesn't mean you're limited to only creating content for GIF animations in Photoshop/ImageReady. In fact, the opposite is true. You can create layered files, just like any of the ones shown thus far in the chapter, and place them into Adobe LiveMotion, where the layers can be edited over time and saved as Flash (SWF) or QuickTime (MOV) files.

▶ **NOTE**

Visit www.adobe.com/products/livemotion/ for more information on using LiveMotion.

TRY IT   To place a layered PSD file into LiveMotion, first create or open a file in LiveMotion in which to "drop" the Photoshop file. Then, in LiveMotion, choose File | Place and locate the PSD file you want to import. Next, decide how you want to incorporate the file's layers into the LiveMotion movie. Essentially, you have two options:

1. Convert the layers into a sequence of animation frames, much the same way the Make Frames From Layers command works in ImageReady. To do this, select the object you imported and choose Object | Convert Into | Sequence. (To use the first layer of the file as the background for all frames in the sequence, choose Object | Convert Into | Sequence With Background instead.)

2. Convert the layers into individual objects, which can then be edited and animated in LiveMotion as needed. To do this, select the object you imported and choose Object | Convert Into | Objects. (To group the layers together, choose Object | Convert Into | Group Of Objects instead.)

▶

QUICK TIP

If you've already done all the work of setting up the animation in ImageReady, I recommend choosing the first option and converting the layers into a sequence of animation frames. However, if you only have a layered file, with objects that have not yet been animated, choose the second option to have more control over the animation of individual elements from the placed file.

At any time, you can edit the original file by selecting the object in LiveMotion with the Selection tool and choosing Object | Edit Original. When you save and then close the file in Photoshop, it is automatically updated in LiveMotion.

To edit and animate the placed file in LiveMotion, choose Window | Timeline to display the Timeline. Before you convert a placed file, it is referenced by its filename in the Timeline window. After being converted into a group of objects, it is referenced by the phrase "Group of #

objects," where # represents the number of objects in the group. Files converted into sequences are referenced by the name of the first layer in the file, whereas those converted into sequences with backgrounds are referenced by the phrase "Group of 2 objects," where one object is the background and the other is the animation sequence.

To see the individual frames of a placed file that was converted into an animation sequence (with or without a background), first select the object in the Timeline and then choose Window | Properties to display the Properties palette. Under Index, move the slider to cycle through the individual frames of the animation.

Use the Rollovers Palette to Build Rollovers

When you want to alter the appearance of an image based on the position of the user's cursor, ImageReady has just the tool for you: the Rollovers palette. This palette keeps track of the various different "states" or displays of your images.

TRY IT To use the Rollovers palette to build rollovers, first open the file you wish to edit in ImageReady (Photoshop does not have a Rollovers palette). Edit the layers of the file so the current display shows how you want the image to look in its "normal" state—that is, how it looks when the cursor is not near the image.

Choose Window | Rollovers to access the Rollovers palette. To create a new rollover state, do either of the following:

- Click the Create Rollover State button at the bottom of the Rollovers palette to add a new rollover state to the entire image.

- First use the Slice tool to slice apart the individual images within the larger file. Then, select the appropriate slice in the Rollovers palette before clicking the Create Rollover State button at the bottom of the palette to add a new rollover state just to that slice.

▶ **NOTE**

If you defined slices in your file but don't see them listed in the Rollovers palette, click the small triangle in the upper-right corner of the palette and choose Palette Options from the palette menu. Then, select Include Slices And Image Maps, and click OK.

After adding a new rollover state, notice the actual state you added. In most cases, if this is the first state you're adding to a slice or image, it is considered the Over state. In other words, you're now editing how the area will look when the cursor is placed *over* it.

To change the state to another, right-click (Windows) or CTRL-click (Mac) the slice or image name in the Rollovers palette and select the appropriate state from the pop-up menu. (You don't need to use all of these states in your file. In fact, the most common are simply Normal, Over, and Selected.)

- **Over**   How the area looks when the cursor is placed over it
- **Down**   How the area looks when the user clicks the mouse button while over the area
- **Selected**   How the area looks when the user clicks the mouse button while over the area (the button is pressed and released); this state remains even if the user moves and clicks another button.
- **Out**   How the area looks when the user moves the cursor away from the area
- **Up**   How the area looks when the user releases the mouse button after pressing it while over the area
- **Click**   How the area looks when the user clicks the mouse button on the area (the button is pressed and released) and keeps the cursor over the area
- **Custom**   How the area looks during a custom action (to use this, you must create your own corresponding JavaScript code and place it in the HTML page)
- **None**   No state is attached, and therefore no file will be output when the page is saved out of ImageReady

▶ **QUICK TIP**

To make the Selected state active when the web page is first loaded into the web browser, such as when the user has clicked a link from the home page and is now viewing the corresponding page, double-click the area's name in the Rollovers palette and select Use As Default Selected State below Selected.

When you have additional states visible in the Rollovers palette, it's time to edit how the image looks in each of those states. This process is very similar to adding animation frames—click the state in the

Rollovers palette to activate it and then toggle the layers in the Layers palette on and off, create new layers, and move elements around until you're satisfied with the change from one state to another. (For more tips on editing, previewing, and optimizing rollovers, see the following tips.)

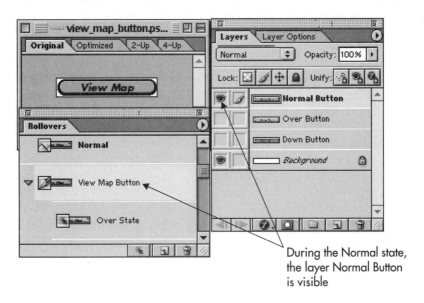

During the Normal state, the layer Normal Button is visible

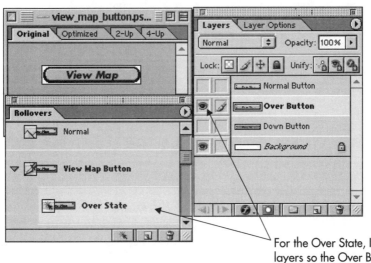

For the Over State, I edited the layers so the Over Button layer is visible (it contains the button in a different color)

Add Layer Styles for Quick and Easy Rollover Effects

In Chapter 6 I discussed using layer styles to add effects such as drop shadows and glows to layers of content. You can do the same thing to create quick and easy rollover effects. For example, you can add a drop shadow to a button so it only appears when the user moves the cursor over the button.

TRY IT To add a layer style as a rollover effect, first follow the steps discussed in the previous tip to prepare your document for rollovers. When you're ready to add the layer style, select the state to which you want to add the style by clicking it in the Rollovers palette. (If you haven't yet created a new rollover state, click the Create Rollover State button in the palette. Right-click [Windows] or CTRL-click [Mac] to specify the exact state to add.)

Next, switch to the Layers palette and select the layer containing the element to which you want to add the style. (If the element is not on its own layer, use the selection tools to select it and choose Layer | New | Layer Via Cut to put it on its own layer.)

Click the Add Layer Style button at the bottom of the Layers palette and select the style you wish to add. In the Layers palette, double-click the name of the layer style you added to customize the effect as needed.

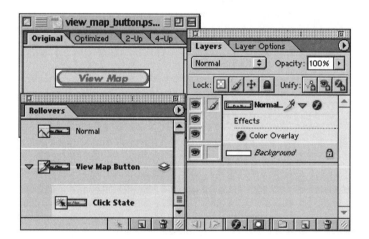

► **QUICK TIP**

You can also use any of the predefined styles that ship with ImageReady. To do so, choose Window | Styles to display the Styles palette. Then, instead of using the Add Layer Style button to add a custom layer style to your image, click any of the styles in the Styles palette. To make things really easy, you can choose one of the rollover styles, which are identified by a small black triangle in the upper-left corner of the style preview. These special styles have predefined rollover states attached to them.

If you ever want to disable the layer style from appearing in a rollover state, click the eye icon next to the name of the layer style in the Layers palette and toggle its visibility off. Or, to delete the layer style altogether, drag its name over the Trash button at the bottom of the Layers palette. To remove all layer styles from a layer, choose Windows | Styles and click the first style button to specify Default Style – None.

Create Rollover Styles to Speed Development of Navigation Systems

When you create navigation systems for web pages, it's common to apply the same rollover effects to multiple icons or buttons in that system. For example, in this navigation system, I have eight buttons, and for each I need to create three states—normal (blue button), over (yellow button), and selected (blue button with yellow outline).

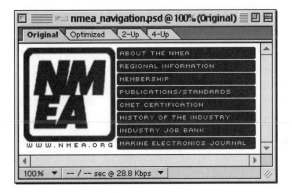

If I were to do this by hand, it would take a little bit of time to create all 24 rollover states. Because each of the things I want to accomplish (changing color and adding an outline) can be achieved with layer styles (Color Overlay and Stroke), I can use the technique discussed in the previous tip to save time.

But to really speed up the process, I can create the three states for a single button and then save those states as a predefined *rollover style* in the Styles palette. After saving my rollover style, I can easily apply it to all of the other seven buttons with a single click.

 NOTE

Because rollover styles are essentially layer styles, you can only create them for layer-based slices. (Different types of slices were discussed in Chapter 10.) For the NMEA navigation shown in the previous illustration, this means each of my buttons must be on its own layer. If you don't want to (or can't) turn your slices into layer-based slices, you can still save time by copying and pasting layer styles (using the Copy and Paste commands in the Layers palette menu) or rollover states (using the Copy and Paste commands in the Rollovers palette menu).

TRY IT To create a predefined rollover style, first make sure the button you want to edit is on its own layer and that the layer is defined as a layer-based slice. If it's not defined as such, right-click (Windows) or CTRL-click (Mac) the layer in the Layers palette and choose New Layer Based Slice before continuing with the following steps.

1. Create the necessary rollover states in the Rollovers palette (as discussed in the previous two tips). For instance, if you want Normal, Over, and Selected states for each of your buttons, select one of the buttons and then add those states to that first button.

2. Add the necessary layer styles to the button to define how the button should look in each of the states you created.

3. When you're ready to save the states and styles as a predefined rollover style, click once on the layer containing that button in the Layers palette to select it.

4. Choose Window | Styles to display the Styles palette if it isn't already visible.

5. Click the Create New Style button at the bottom of the Styles palette, then click the triangle in the upper-right corner and choose New Style from the palette menu.

6. Give the style a name and be sure to select Include Rollover States to make this a rollover style, then click OK.

7. To apply your new rollover style to the other buttons, select each layer in the Layers palette and then click the icon for your rollover style in the Styles palette. When you look in the Rollovers palette, you'll notice each button now contains all the necessary states.

8. To preview how these states react to the placement of the cursor, see the next tip.

Preview Rollovers

The whole idea behind rollovers is that they respond to the placement of the cursor on the screen. However, when you're normally working in ImageReady, these rollovers are not active—that is, the code that makes them work is not yet in place, because that must be output when the HTML file is saved.

However, you can put ImageReady into Preview mode, during which you can get an idea of how the buttons will respond to user input when displayed in the browser. Keep in mind when previewing that all browsers interpret JavaScript a bit differently. To properly test your rollovers, you should view them in several different web browsers before placing them on a live web page.

TRY IT To preview rollovers in ImageReady, press Y on your keyboard or click the Preview Document button in the toolbox. Now, move your cursor over the buttons with rollover states to see how they react. To return to normal view mode, press Y or click the Preview Document button again.

▶ *NOTE*

When in Preview mode, you are limited in what actions you can perform in ImageReady. To return to editing the document, exit rollover Preview mode.

To preview rollovers in a web browser, make sure the appropriate optimization settings are specified in the Optimize palette (see the next tip). Then, click the Preview In Browser tool in the toolbox. (Depending on which browser is set up as your system's default browser, the icon on this tool will likely be that of Internet Explorer or Netscape Navigator.) Alternatively, you can choose File | Preview In and select the appropriate browser from the menu.

Optimize Rollovers

When you output files containing rollovers, two things can occur. First, if you choose to output the images, different optimized files are created for each rollover state in the Rollovers palette. Second, if you choose to output the HTML for the page, ImageReady also writes the corresponding HTML and JavaScript code needed to make the images change according to the location of the cursor.

TRY IT To optimize rollovers, click the Optimize tab at the top of the document window. Use the Slice Select tool to select the slice(s) you want to optimize, and make the necessary changes to the optimization settings in the Optimize palette (choose Window | Optimize to view the palette if it's not already visible).

While optimizing rollovers is essentially the same as optimizing other web graphics (as discussed previously in Chapter 10), there are a few additional elements to consider:

- Typically, rollovers indicate to the user that an image is linked. If you're planning to have ImageReady output your HTML for you, then you need to specify where each image should be linked as well as the alternative text to be displayed if the image doesn't display. To do so, double-click a slice with the Slice Select tool and enter the URL in the Slices palette.

- The various states for a slice are optimized with the same optimization settings for the Normal state.

- Avoid using transparency when you optimize a slice with rollovers unless you want the Normal state to "show through" under each of the states placed above it during a rollover.

▶ | *QUICK TIP*

Name your rollovers so you can recognize which one should be used when. For example, the original link to a section called "school" might be referred to as schoolOff, while the version appearing when the user rolls over it might be called schoolOver.

When you're ready to output the images and/or HTML code, choose File | Save Optimized As. Under Format, specify whether to output the HTML and/or the images. If you want ImageReady to write the JavaScript code necessary to make the rollovers work, you must let it output the HTML. (Otherwise, you'll have to write the code yourself.) Select which output settings to use from the Settings menu, or choose Other to edit those settings. Finally, specify whether to output only the selected slices or all the slices. For more tips on using the Save Optimized As dialog box, refer to Chapter 10.

Combine Animation and Rollovers

Animation doesn't need to occur only when a web page is first loaded. In fact, you can embed animations in rollovers, so that a closed hand opens, for example, when the cursor is placed over it, as shown in Figures 11-2 and 11-3.

▶ **NOTE**

Before proceeding with this tip, review the previous tips in this chapter related to creating animation and rollovers if you aren't already familiar with how to create each.

TRY IT To combine animation and rollovers, open the file with which you want to work in ImageReady (Photoshop cannot display animations or rollover effects). Select the slice you want to use for the rollover and animation and click the Create Rollover State button at the bottom of the Rollovers palette.

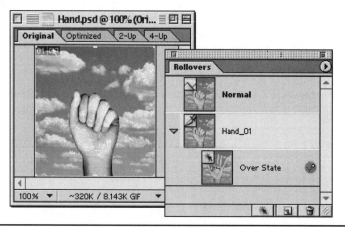

Figure 11-2 The Normal state of this image shows a closed fist.

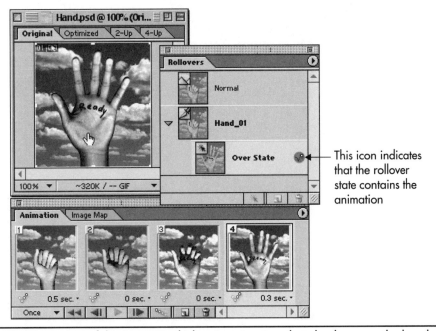

This icon indicates that the rollover state contains the animation

Figure 11-3   The Over state of this image includes an animation that slowly opens the hand and displays the word "Ready" on the palm.

After specifying the exact state (Over, Click, and so on) for the rollover, open the Animation palette and begin adding frames. Edit those frames in the Layers palette until you're satisfied with the progression of the animation. To test the effect, press Y on your keyboard and perform the action necessary to start the animation.

Create an Image Map

So far, the tips in this chapter and the previous one have discussed using slices to break up your web design into individual web graphics. An alternative to slicing a design is to turn it into an image map. When you use an image map, you define *hot spots,* which are similar to slices except they don't get saved as individual graphics. Instead, the file is saved as a single image, and special HTML code is written to let the browser know which pages to load when users click each hot spot.

Image maps are most commonly used when slicing images might be impossible. For example, in the case of this map of Baltimore County, Maryland, in which each region in the county needs to be linked to a separate page, if I tried to slice these irregular shapes, it'd be nearly impossible. But because image map hot spots can be created with rectangles, circles, or polygons, I can save the entire file as a single graphic and identify hot spots for each region within the county.

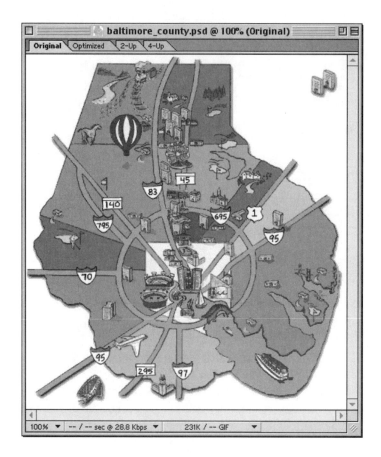

TRY IT   To create an image map, begin by opening the image in ImageReady (you cannot create image maps in Photoshop). Click and hold on the Rectangle Image Map tool in the toolbox and select the shape you want to use to identify your first hot spot: rectangle, circle, or polygon. (Alternatively, you can create image map hot spots based on the contents of layers. To do so, select the layer in the Layers palette and choose Layer | New Layer Based Image Map Area.)

Use the appropriate image map tool to draw a shape around the first hot spot in your image. Choose Window | Image Map or double-click the hot spot to reveal the Image Map palette, where you can edit the size, name, and link. Repeat this process until you've drawn and edited all the hot spots of your image.

If you have any hot spots that overlap, you can click the triangle in the upper-right corner of the Image Map palette to reveal options related to changing the stacking order. (You can also reach these and other options by right-clicking [Windows] or CTRL-clicking [Mac] on a hot spot.) Be aware of the stacking

> **QUICK TIP**
>
> *If you plan to create several hot spots of different shapes, click and hold on the Rectangle Image Map tool and select the tiny triangle at the bottom of the pop-up window. This causes the image map tools to float and gives easy access to all four tools at once.*

order of overlapping hot spots, because the topmost hot spot take precedence when all are linked to different web pages.

You can also use the Image Map palette menu to align hot spots or distribute them evenly along each axis.

Preview and Optimize an Image Map

Essentially, optimizing an image map is the same as optimizing any other web graphic. The important thing to remember is that image maps require extra code in your HTML page to work. Therefore, you should either have ImageReady write that for you or be prepared to write it yourself. If you plan to let ImageReady write that code, be sure to provide all the naming and linking information necessary in the Image Map palette for each hot spot.

 When you're finished editing the image map and ready to preview it, make sure the appropriate optimization settings are specified in the Optimize palette. Then, click the Preview In Browser tool in the toolbox. (Depending on which browser is set up as your system's default browser, the icon on this tool will likely be that of Internet Explorer or Netscape Navigator.) Alternatively, you can choose File | Preview In and select the appropriate browser from the menu.

When you're ready to output the images and/or HTML code, choose File | Save Optimized As. Under Format, specify whether to output the HTML and/or the images. If you want ImageReady to write the special HTML code necessary to make the image map work, you must let it output the HTML. (Otherwise, you'll have to write the code yourself.) Select which output settings to use from the Settings menu, or choose Other to edit those settings. Finally, specify whether to output only the selected slices or all the slices. For more tips on using the Save Optimized As dialog box, refer to Chapter 10.

Combine Image Maps and Rollovers

While a previous tip discussed combining animation and rollovers, you can also add rollovers to hot spots in image maps. So, in the case of my map of Baltimore County, I could display the name of each region when the user activates each hot spot, as shown in Figures 11-4 and 11-5.

▶ **NOTE**

Before proceeding with this tip, review the previous tips in this chapter related to creating image maps and rollovers if you aren't already familiar with how to create each.

 To combine image maps and rollovers, open the file with which you want to work in ImageReady (Photoshop cannot edit image maps or rollover effects). Use the Image Map Select tool to select the hot spot you want to use for the rollover and animation and choose the Create Rollover State button at the bottom of the Rollovers palette.

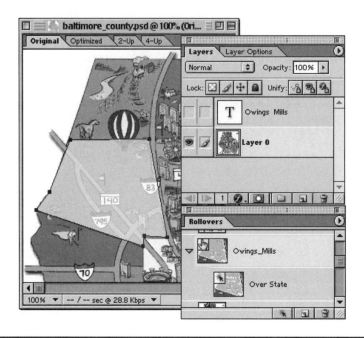

Figure 11-4   The Normal state of this hot spot is visible here.

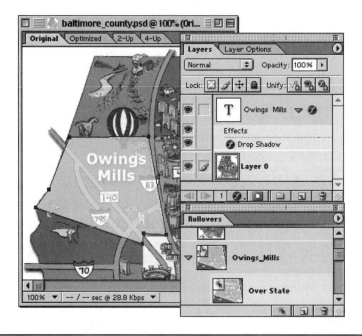

Figure 11-5   The Over state of this hot spot displays the name of the region, "Owings Mills."

After specifying the exact state (Over, Click, and so on) for the rollover, open the Layers palette and begin editing the appropriate layer(s). (If the entire image is on a single layer, and you want to edit only the portion of that layer visible through the hot spot, it may be necessary to select that area with the selection tools and choose Layer | New | Layer Via Copy to first create a new layer with only that area.)

To test the effect, press Y on your keyboard and perform the action necessary to start the animation.

Create a Template Used to Bulk-Produce Multiple Graphics with Adobe AlterCast

ImageReady is capable of helping you prepare to produce large quantities of graphics that are all based on a single template. The idea is that you create your template in Photoshop or ImageReady, and then use ImageReady to identify which aspects of the template may change depending on the actual content used. Finally, you can either output each graphic individually in ImageReady or use AlterCast or a custom script to output them all at once.

▶ **NOTE**

This tip discusses how to create the template for data-driven graphics. To actually bulk-produce the graphics, a custom script or program like Adobe AlterCast is required. For more information, see the Help files for Photoshop.

TRY IT To create a template for bulk-producing multiple graphics with AlterCast or a custom script, first open a sample file in ImageReady. For example, if your template is for the photograph accompanying the lead story of a newspaper, open one such graphic now. Then choose Image | Variables | Define.

Under the Layer menu, select the layer containing the first variable. In the case of the newspaper photo, I'd select the layer containing the actual photograph. Identify which aspects of the image may change—Visibility or Pixel/Text Replacement—and give the variable a name you'll easily recognize:

- **Visibility** Means the layer may need to be hidden in some cases.
- **Pixel Replacement** Means the layer's content may need to be replaced by the contents of another file in some cases. (If you select Pixel Replacement, click the button for Pixel Replacement Options to specify how each new image should be scaled.)
- **Text Replacement** Means the layer's text content may need to be replaced by new text in some cases.

> ▶ **QUICK TIP**
>
> *Need to change the color or style of a layer in some cases? Simply create new layers in your file that take care of all possible scenarios. Then, specify Visibility as the Variable Type for each layer so you can turn them on or off as needed for each graphic to be output.*

Repeat this process with each layer in the Layer menu until all variables are defined.

TRY IT To define the various data sets for each variable—that is, the files to replace each element as needed—click Next in the Variable dialog box (or, if you've left that dialog box, choose Image | Variables | Data Sets). Then perform the steps from the following list that apply to your file.

▶ **NOTE**

If defining data sets for a large quantity of files, it's usually more efficient to perform these tasks in the output program, such as Adobe AlterCast.

- Specify the name of the first data set, in the Data Set menu.
- Select each variable from the Name menu under Variables.
- For Visibility variables, specify a value of "visible" or "invisible."
- For Text Replacement variables, specify the new text.
- For Pixel Replacement variables, click the Choose button to identify the location of the replacement file.

Click the New Data Set button and repeat the process as many times as necessary until all scenarios for the image are created. Then click OK.

TRY IT To optimize each graphic created based on the template, you have several options:

- In ImageReady, choose Image | Preview Document and then select the appropriate data set from the Options bar. Select the appropriate output settings in the Optimize palette and choose File | Save Optimized As to define the filename and location in which it should be saved.
- Save the file as a PSD and import it into Adobe GoLive, where you can assign data sets from a database of content, and then use AlterCast to actually output each individual graphic.
- Use AlterCast or a custom script to output each graphic.

Create a Web Photo Gallery

If you need to quickly create one or more web pages, each containing thumbnail images that are linked to larger copies, Photoshop has a simple way to do it for you. There are even several different templates available—one of which is shown in Figure 11-6—so you even achieve some variety if you need to create more than one web photo gallery.

The greatest benefit of web photo galleries created in Photoshop is that someone who knows little to no HTML can in effect create an entire web site, complete with an e-mail link, to house a portfolio of images. Photoshop even gives you the chance to embed copyright information to prevent the theft of your images.

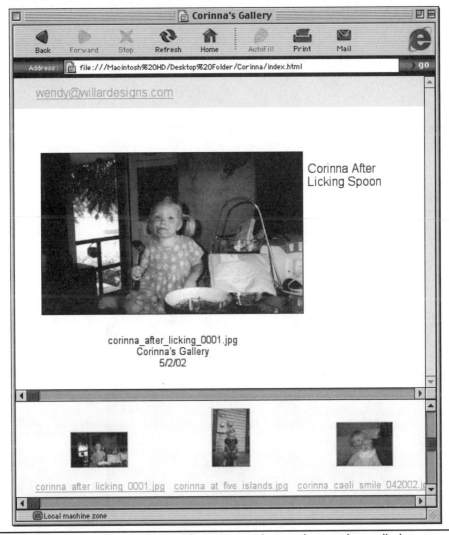

Figure 11-6   This is a quick web photo gallery I created using the template called Horizontal Light.

TRY IT Before you can create a web photo gallery, you need to place all the images you want displayed in the same folder on your computer. Next, make sure the filenames are correct, because they'll be displayed below or next to the image in the gallery. You also need to create another folder, outside of the folder housing the images, where Photoshop can save all the necessary files for the gallery.

Finally, open each file in Photoshop and choose File | File Info to add the following bits of information used in the gallery:

- Title
- Caption
- Copyright
- Credits

When you're ready to have Photoshop create the actual gallery, choose File | Automate | Web Photo Gallery and edit the settings as needed:

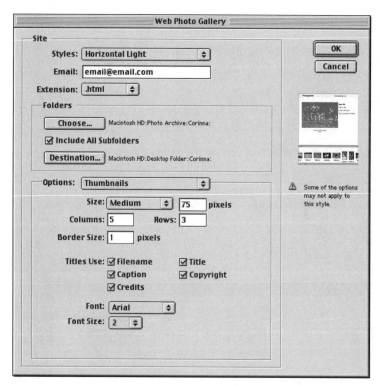

- Enter your e-mail address if you want it to be visible on the web pages.
- Choose from the first menu in the Options section to edit the options for Banner (including the gallery title), Large Images, Thumbnails, Custom Colors, and Security.

- Under Thumbnails and Large Images, specify which of the items you entered in the File Info dialog box to include next to the image in the gallery.

After you click OK, Photoshop goes through the process of creating the various images (at the sizes specified) as well as the necessary HTML files. If you want to, you can then upload the entire folder containing images and HTML to your web server to make the web gallery live.

Create High-Resolution, Web-Friendly Images

While it may seem like the title of this tip is a contradiction in terms, Photoshop 7 includes the capability to export images in the ZoomView format, which is a file format specially designed for delivering high-resolution images to web users. ZoomView images first appear on the page as quickly as JPEGs and in fact look like progressive JPEGs because they come in somewhat blurry and gradually sharpen. Users can then click in the image to zoom in, right-click (Windows) or CTRL-click (Mac) to zoom out, or click and drag to pan. Compare Figures 11-7 (before zooming) and Figure 11-8 (after zooming) to see what I mean.

Figure 11-7   I used this 10MB file on a web page in the ZoomView format, and it first loaded a zoomed-out version like this.

Figure 11-8 After zooming all the way in, I am able to see the petals of the flower with great clarity.

QUICK TIP

Want to see a few ZoomView images in action? Check out the ZoomView Portal Gallery at www.viewpoint.com/zoomview/gallery.html.

There are two potential drawbacks to consider when creating high-resolution images for the Web with ZoomView. First, users need to have the Viewpoint Media Player to view the images. However, this player is free and quick to download from Viewpoint's web site. Second, the owner of the web site on which the high-resolution files will be placed must purchase a license from Viewpoint. (Note, hobbyists and noncommercial users can get a free six-month license.) With that said, if you were working on a web site whose users would enjoy being able to zoom in to an image to see details, those requirements might be a small price to pay.

TRY IT   To create high-resolution web-friendly images with ZoomView, open the high-resolution image you wish to use in Photoshop. Then, choose File | Export | ZoomView to reveal the Viewpoint ZoomView dialog box and follow the steps on the next page.

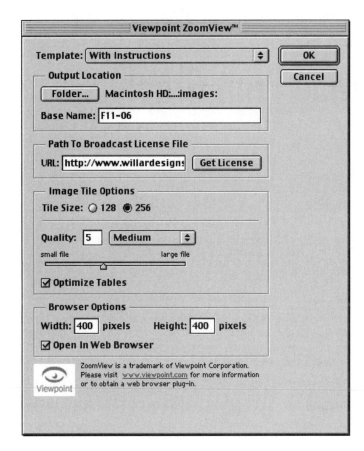

1. At the top of the window, specify whether to include zooming instructions to the user on the image when it's exported. In addition, identify where to save the file, and give it a name.

2. Enter the path to your ZoomView Broadcast license in the URL field, or click Get License if you haven't yet purchased one.

3. For Tile Size, select how many pixels should be included in each tile. In other words, specify how large each tile should be. (It is recommended that you choose 128 for smaller images and 256 for larger images.)

4. For Quality, specify the amount of JPEG compression to be used for each tile—the higher quality the file, the larger the file size.

5. Leave the Optimized Tables option selected, which will create smaller file sizes.

6. Under Browser Options, specify the initial size of the image area on the web page.

7. To automatically launch your web browser and preview the image, leave Open In Web Browser selected.

8. Click OK.

CHAPTER 12

Optimizing Print Graphics

TIPS IN THIS CHAPTER

Print designers have long struggled with how to print their Photoshop files reliably. This means achieving not only consistent color from screen to print, but also consistent quality and layout. In most cases, if you're a print designer, you'll need to be in close contact with the professionals at whichever service bureau or print shop your file will be printed. As discussed in Chapter 2, you need to know how the file will be printed before you can accurately design and optimize the file in Photoshop.

For example, will your file be printed to paper or film? (Film is traditionally used to create a "master plate" when files are printed on mechanical printing presses.) Will you need to create color separations of full-color (CMYK) images? (When CMYK images are printed, you need a "plate" for each color, specifying where that color is placed within the image.) And at what resolution will the file be output?

Another important question to ask is this: "From which platform will the file(s) be outputted?" For example, issues such as fonts can become a big problem when files are printed on a different platform than they were created on. In general, not asking the right questions up front is a common source of much frustration and wasted time by designers.

After you've discussed these and other print options with your service bureau, use the tips and techniques in this chapter to assist in optimizing your print graphics.

▶ **NOTE**

If you plan to print your file directly from Photoshop, either to produce a quick comp or to create camera-ready artwork for reproduction, pay special attention to the two tips at the end of the chapter, "Print Files Directly from Photoshop" and "Specify Accurate Halftone Screen Options."

Make All Adjustments in RGB Mode, then Convert to CMYK

Although virtually all full-color professional presses utilize the CMYK ink mode, it is strongly advisable to do all your Photoshop imaging in RGB mode. Why? RGB images contain a lot more of the original data the image was created with. CMYK deletes information that will not be used on the printing press. Therefore, a designer will have more to work with when altering color and tones in RGB mode. Only when you are ready to finalize an image and prepare it to be imported into its final program environment prior to sending it to press should you then change it to CMYK color mode.

TRY IT When you have completed all of your imaging, select Image | Mode | CMYK Color. You will notice the change in your image and can now save it to be imported into your page-layout program or printed accordingly.

▶ **NOTE**

Sometimes designers are concerned that their images appear less saturated in CMYK mode. Part of that has to do with the fact that your monitor operates in RGB mode, whereas most color files are printed in CMYK. Another reason is simply because there is less information in each of the four ink channels. Most of the time, your prepress professionals are able to "pump up" or "pull back" colors on press to their original saturation. If it is absolutely imperative that a color match perfectly to a prior mockup that your client has seen and signed off on, for instance, talk to your printer about possibly adding in a spot color (a special ink mix) to attain that perfect color. This is a very common practice, and printers are usually very eager to work with you on attaining exact color.

Create a Duotone Image

Duotones are used to increase the visual depth of a grayscale image or for two-color print jobs when spot colors (such as PANTONE inks) are used. Why duotones? A grayscale image printed with only black ink can look significantly flatter than the same image printed with two, three, or four inks, because each individual ink replaces a gray tone with a color shade and significantly increases the image's appearance.

Because duotones use different color inks, they are treated in Photoshop as single-channel, 8-bit, grayscale images. In Duotone mode, you do not have direct access to the individual image channels (as in RGB, CMYK, and Lab modes). Instead, you manipulate the channels through the curves in the Duotone Options dialog box.

▶ NOTE

A swatchbook might just be a print designer's best friend, because it is a reference for how specific inks print and essentially how certain colors end up looking once they are printed. If you plan to do a lot of print design, it's a good idea to have handy a few different swatchbooks—one for each type of color system you use. The most common color system used by U.S. printers is PANTONE.

I recommend always referencing your swatchbook (PANTONE, TOYO, and so forth) as well. When you select specific inks, what appears on your screen might not match what your swatchbook displays, so it's a good idea to have your printer show you sample colors before your file goes to print. Likewise, how a document prints to your desktop printer is not an accurate depiction of how the file will actually separate to plates—your desktop printer usually is only capable of giving you samples of the standard CMYK plates, not special mixes. Always note when an image is a duotone in your file specification, and also provide ink "chips" (samples) to your prepress professional and printer.

▶ QUICK TIP

If your printing specifications don't require limiting your use of color in this manner, you can create "fake" duotones without worrying about specifying inks and so forth. See the tip "Creating Fake Duotones" in Chapter 9 for more information.

 To convert a color image to a duotone, open the image in Photoshop and follow these steps:

1. Select Image | Mode | Grayscale.

2. Click OK when the dialog box asks you if you would like to "Discard Color Information?" (Only 8-bit grayscale images can be converted to duotones.)

3. If you have layers you want to preserve, specify not to flatten when you are prompted.

4. Select Image | Mode | Duotone.

5. In the Duotone Options dialog box, click Preview to view the effects of the duotone settings on the image as you are adjusting it.

6. Click the Type button and select Monotone, Duotone, Tritone, or Quadtone, depending on how many colors you want to use.

7. To specify ink colors, click the color box (the solid square), and the Color Picker automatically pops up.

8. Click Custom to select an ink type. (Unless you and your printer have preselected a "special ink mix," I recommend using only specified ink mixes, not a miscellaneous color from the picker.) Notice that after you select a color and click OK, the ink name automatically appears in the color box next to the ink square.

▶ *CAUTION*

Always specify your ink names! When you import or place your image into your page-layout program, ink names will correspond only if specified correctly (for example, Pantone 113 U). To produce fully saturated colors, make sure that inks are specified in descending order—darkest at the top, lightest at the bottom.

Edit a Duotone Curve

In a duotone image, each ink has a separate curve that specifies how the color is distributed across the shadows and highlights. This curve maps each grayscale value in the original image to a specific ink percentage. The default duotone curve, a straight diagonal line, indicates that the grayscale values in the original image map to equal percentages of ink. At this setting, a 50 percent midtone pixel prints with a 50 percent tint of the ink, a 100 percent shadow is printed in 100 percent color, and so on.

TRY IT To edit the duotone curve, make sure the Duotone dialog box is open, and click the curve box next to the ink color box. Drag a point on the graph. (Usually, eyeballing the effects with the "preview" box selected gives you a good idea of how the percentage values affect your image.) Click Save in the Duotone Curve dialog box to save curves created with this dialog box. Repeat this procedure for each ink color, and click OK.

▶ *NOTE*

The same technique can also be applied to monotones, tritones, and quadtones.

Use Variations to Quickly Alter Color and Tone

The Variations feature of Photoshop is the simplest way to alter color quickly. (It is not, however, the most detailed way to fine-tune your image and is not recommended for precision color management.) The Variations window shows you thumbnails of sample adjustments to color balance, contrast, and saturation of an image. You can quickly select what appears correct and continue to correct within "Variations" or exit the window and see the immediate effects on your image.

TRY IT To use the Variations command, open the image you want to affect in Photoshop and select Image | Adjustments | Variations. As shown in Figure 12-1, the two thumbnails at the top of the Variations dialog box show the "Original" selection and the selection with its "Current" adjustments. When you first open the dialog box, these two images are the same. As you make adjustments, the Current Pick image changes to reflect your choices.

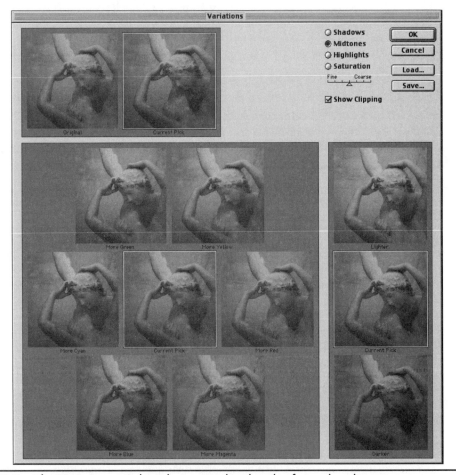

Figure 12-1 The Variations window shows you thumbnails of sample adjustments to color balance, contrast, and saturation of an image.

In the Variations dialog box, make the following adjustments as needed.

- Select Show Clipping if you want to display undesirable color shifts, such as colors knocking out completely to black or white.

- Select the area that you want to alter (Shadows, Midtones, or Highlights).

- Select Saturation to change the intensity of hue in the image.

- Drag the Fine/Coarse slider to determine the degree of adjustment.

- To add a specific color to the image, click the thumbnail that showcases the color you wish to increase within the image.

- To reduce the intensity of a color, click the thumbnail directly across (or opposite) from the color you wish to decrease.

- To adjust brightness, click one of the thumbnails on the right side of the dialog box until you have reached the desired variance.

- Click OK when you are satisfied with the alterations.

▶ *NOTE*

Each time you click a thumbnail, all the other thumbnails change as well. The center thumbnail always reflects the current choice. If at any time you wish to return to the original image, just click the thumbnail at the top labeled "Original."

Use Levels to Correct Color and Tone

The Levels dialog box lets you correct the tonal range and color balance of an image by adjusting intensity levels of the image's shadows, midtones, and highlights. The Levels histogram serves as a visual guide for adjusting the image's key tones. You are also able to preview adjustments as you are moving the "sliders" or by inserting values. You can alter the entire image by selecting Master or individual color channels (for example, CMYK).

▶ *CAUTION*

Although the Auto Levels adjustment option is a viable way for altering color or tone, it is not a recommended feature for high-quality print graphics. It is not precise and should only be used when simple contrast adjustment is required. Auto Levels sometimes overcompensates for tonal variations and will leave an image looking saturated and muddy.

TRY IT   To adjust *color* using levels, open the image you want to affect and select Image | Adjustments | Levels or press CTRL-L (Windows) or CMD-L (Mac). This launches the Levels dialog box, which opens showing what's referred to as an image's histogram.

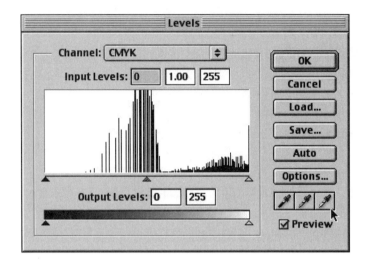

- To adjust overall tones, move sliders below the histogram or insert values in the boxes above.

- To adjust specific colors, select the desired Channel (Cyan, Magenta, Red, or Green, depending on the color mode you are in), and move sliders or insert values according to the desired outcome.

- Click OK when you are satisfied with the alterations.

TRY IT To adjust *tones* using levels, select Image | Adjustments | Levels or press CTRL-L (Windows) or CMD-L (Mac). This launches the Levels dialog box, which opens showing what's referred to as an image's histogram.

- Drag the black slider to the edge of the first group of pixels on the left side of the histogram to increase the darkness of the shadow.

- Drag the white slider to the edge of the first group of pixels on the right side of the histogram to increase the lightness of the highlights.

- Drag the gray slider back and forth between the black and white sliders to alter the intensity of the midtones until you are satisfied with the outcome.

- Click OK when you are satisfied with the alterations.

▶ | **QUICK TIP**

Using the Levels command to alter shadows and highlights is extremely useful when altering a grayscale or black-and-white image. For example, if you have scanned in line art and need to clean up the background, you can use Levels to find your whitest white and your darkest dark and actually come out with fairly clean bitmapped line art. The best way to do this is to not use the sliders at all, but to select the dropper tools on the far right of the Levels dialog box. If you select the "black" dropper tool and click the darkest part of your image, this will redefine that shadow as your darkest dark or "black." Do the same with the "white" dropper tool, and this will redefine the lightest tones of your highlights

Adjust Images for Perfect Skin Tone

Skin tones are a sticky subject in any print job. It's imperative that the "humans" in your images are portrayed with natural-looking flesh tones. Oftentimes, skin tones can tend to print with red overtones. If you request a round of prepress color samples from your printer or prepress professional, they will allow you to point out faulty flesh tones; in most cases, they will also adjust them as you request. There are, however, certain tips to which you as the designer can adhere to make sure your imagery is as accurate as possible.

 To adjust images for perfect skin tone, follow these steps:

1. Make sure you are in RGB mode.

2. Using the Lasso tool, select the flesh tones that you wish to adjust. (Hold down the SHIFT key if you wish to select more than one area.)

3. Feather your selections to allow for a gradual shift from the changed area to the unchanged area. While the areas are still selected (in other words, the ants are still dancing), choose Select | Feather and enter in a low value. If your image is a low-resolution image, you only need to enter a 1-pixel value. For higher-resolution images, enter in at least a 3 or a 5.

4. Choose Image | Adjust | Hue/Saturation. In the Hue/Saturation dialog box, choose Reds in the Edit box and move the Saturation slider to the left; this lowers the amount of red that appears in the skin tone. You can also adjust for other tones that appear "off" in your image by selecting the color tone you wish to adjust in the Edit box.

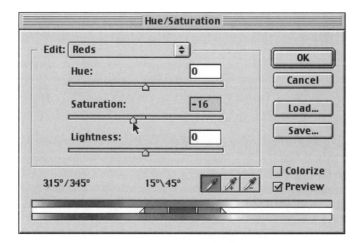

Make Sure Your Whites Are Really White

This tip is particularly helpful if you are scanning line art (such as a logo) to place into another document. Often, your scan might pick up an almost invisible gray tone in the white areas even though it appears white on your screen. With line art that is saved as a grayscale image or in bitmapped mode, it is very important that those white areas are indeed completely clear of any tone at all.

TRY IT To make sure your whites are *really* white, first select the Eyedropper tool from the toolbox and click the white area of your image. Next, choose Window | Info to display the Info palette. Look at the CMYK portion of your Info palette, where all the values should read 0. If they don't, your whites aren't pure.

	R :	252	C :	4%	
	G :	252	M :	2%	
	B :	253	Y :	1%	
			K :	3%	
	X :	3.444	W :		
	Y :	2.028	H :		

To change this, choose Image | Adjust | Levels. In the bottom-right corner of the Levels dialog box, there are three eyedroppers. Click the far-right eyedropper. Now click the area of your image that should be pure white (such as the background portion of a logo). The area that you click becomes your new white-point setting, or the whitest value in your image. Click OK when you are satisfied with your results.

Pay Attention to the Gamut Warning in the Color Picker

Photoshop's Color Picker is chock full of more colors than a designer can imagine. That's the good news. The bad news is that a lot of the very bright super-saturation colors won't reproduce on a full-color press. How can you tell whether your color is out of the CMYK color gamut? This technique shows you.

TRY IT To check for out-of-gamut colors, use the Eyedropper tool and click a color you want to investigate. After the color appears in the Foreground color swatch, click that color swatch to launch the Color Picker.

As shown in the following illustration, the gamut-warning symbol looks like a triangle with an exclamation point. It only appears to the right of the color sample box if the selected color is out of gamut. If it does not appear, your color will most likely appear on press very close to how it appears onscreen. If the gamut warning does appear, notice that directly beneath the symbol is a small rectangle with a similar yet less-saturated color. This is a more accurate representation of how your color will appear when output on a CMYK press.

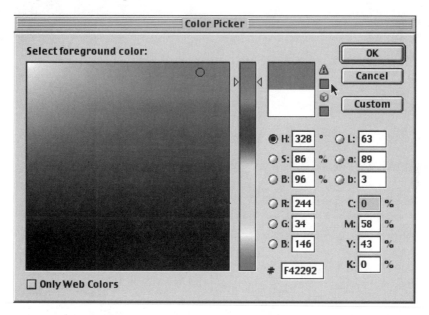

Add Noise to Drop Shadows for Better Results on Press

How imaged shadows appear on a final printout is a dead giveaway to revealing whether your shadows are real or fake. To make your fake shadows appear more realistic in printed designs, use this technique to add a bit of "noise" to them.

TRY IT   To add noise to a drop shadow, open the file you wish to edit in Photoshop and choose Window | Layers to display the Layers palette. Click the Layer Style button at the bottom of the palette and select Drop Shadow to display the Layer Style window.

Under Quality, as shown in the following illustration, move the Noise slider just slightly or enter a small percentage such as 3 or 5. This will give your shadow just enough grain to appear realistic when compared to the "real world."

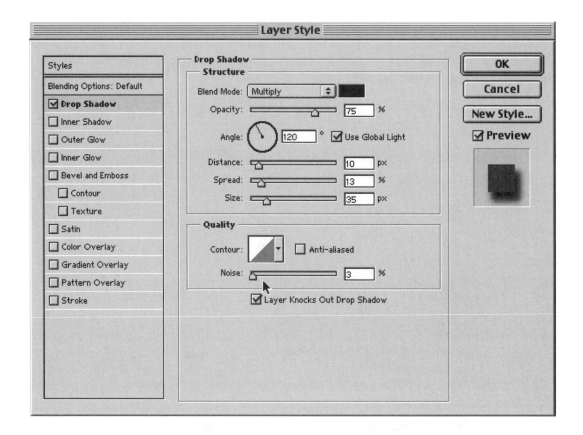

Colorize Grayscale TIFFs in Page-Layout Programs

If your final document is going to be a two-color print job and you have full-color images that you want to use in your document, you need to convert them to grayscale images and then save them as TIFFs. Not only will this give you a better idea of what the images will look like when printed, but it will dramatically cut down the file size of the images.

Although you can assign color to a grayscale image in Photoshop by changing it to a mono- or duotone, it is sometimes more easily accomplished in the resident program in which the final document is being built—particularly because changes to the color can be made without opening and resaving the image file.

▶ *NOTE*

Not all page-layout programs allow you to colorize grayscale images. QuarkXPress and Adobe InDesign both do, but it's best to check the Help files for your particular program before proceeding.

TRY IT To colorize grayscale images in page-layout programs, you must first change the image format in Photoshop. To do so, choose Image | Mode | Grayscale. Photoshop will ask you if you would like to flatten your image. If your intent is to colorize this image in another program, I recommend flattening your image because doing so will make your file smaller and easier for another program to process. If you need those layers, consider saving a copy of the file in Photoshop format before changing the image mode.

After changing the image mode, choose File | Save As and select the TIFF file format.

▶ *CAUTION*

Although this version of Photoshop allows you to save layers with TIFFs, only the latest versions of QuarkXPress and InDesign are able to recognize these enhanced TIFFs. And even if you import a layered TIFF into a page-layout program, typically only the foreground and background will be colorized—not the individual layers. Therefore, I recommend saving your grayscale images without layers if you plan to colorize them in a page-layout program.

Rasterize EPS Files Created in Other Programs in Photoshop

Photoshop will open most documents with the .eps extension. However, not all layers and vector art will appear as they did in the program with which the EPS was created. For example, Adobe Illustrator and Photoshop are quite compatible programs—a lot of the shared features do actually cross over from program to program. You can copy and paste from program to program but layers will not be maintained.

If you open an EPS file in Photoshop, the program rasterizes it, regardless of whether it was created in Illustrator or any other program. In other words, it converts all the information to pixels and not vectors. This is helpful, for instance, if you create a graphic in a vector-based drawing program and you want to incorporate it into an image you are creating in Photoshop.

Another great use of this technique is in referencing an actual page layout (from a program like Illustrator) in a Photoshop design. Screen captures, although extremely helpful, capture information at a resolution (72 dpi) that is not suitable for high-quality print design. Suppose you are working on a catalog and you need to showcase ten various book covers and inside spreads of the books. You can simply save those pages as EPS files from your page-layout program, open them in Photoshop, transform them to be the correct size or alter them as needed, and resave them in the correct file format needed. Voilà—high-resolution "screen captures" of your book covers.

 TRY IT Before you can open a design from a page-layout program, you need to use that program to save a copy of the page as an EPS file:

- In Adobe InDesign, choose File | Export and select EPS as the file type in which to export your file.

- In Adobe Illustrator, choose File | Save As and specify Illustrator EPS as the file type.

- In QuarkXPress, choose File | Save Page As EPS.

Next, open Photoshop and choose File | Open to select that file. As shown in the following illustration, a dialog box appears in which you can verify or change the document size, height, width, and resolution. Photoshop will automatically calculate the size the graphic was last saved in. If you need to change the resolution to match the document you will be using the graphic in, this is where you should enter the correct value.

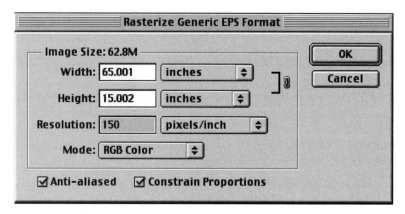

> **NOTE**

Photoshop treats rasterized type as pixels, so type brought in with an EPS file is no longer editable.

Drag and Drop Graphics from Other Programs into Photoshop

Programs created by Adobe are usually quite compatible with each other. For example, suppose you created type on a curve in Adobe Illustrator and wanted to use it in your Photoshop imaging. (Photoshop, as of yet, does not allow you to create type on a curve without a plug-in—see "Creating Text Along a Path" in Chapter 9.) The easiest way to get this—or any vector path drawn in Illustrator—into your Photoshop file is to drag and drop it.

TRY IT   To drag and drop content from another program, such as Illustrator, into Photoshop, first select or highlight the content in the other program. Minimize or shrink that program's document window so you can see both it and your Photoshop file at the same time. (Minimize or shrink the Photoshop window too if needed.)

Once you can see both files at the same time (or at least portions of both), return to the original program and click and drag the selected content from that window into your Photoshop document.

In the case of Illustrator content, you'll notice a brief alert window saying the content is being converted to EPS before it's placed in Photoshop.

▶ *NOTE*

If you are placing vector artwork that needs to be rasterized, you'll be given the chance to resize the artwork in Photoshop before it's turned into pixels.

Drag and Drop Graphics from Photoshop into Other Programs

Whereas the previous tip discussed dragging and dropping files into Photoshop, this one discusses the opposite—dragging and dropping files from Photoshop into other programs. In particular, I find it quite useful to drag and drop print graphics from Photoshop right into Adobe InDesign.

Although you still want to save a copy in a print-ready format such as TIFF or EPS, you can save some time by dragging it into InDesign instead of closing the file in Photoshop and then reopening it in the other program. InDesign treats elements that are dropped into its page layouts as "links" that can be easily updated.

TRY IT To drag and drop content from Photoshop into another program, such as InDesign, first create or open the file in the other program to give yourself a place in which to "drop" the Photoshop image. Minimize or shrink that program's document window so you can see both it and your Photoshop file at the same time. (Minimize or shrink the Photoshop window too if needed.)

Once you can see both files at the same time (or at least portions of both), return to Photoshop and select the Move tool from the toolbox. In the Layers palette, activate the layer containing the content you want to drag. Within the document window, click and drag the image from that window into your document in the other program.

▶ *NOTE*

If you're dropping the file into InDesign, choose Window | Links to view the reference to your original file. If at any time you see a triangle with an exclamation point appear next to your file's name in the Links palette, it means the file has been updated since it was dropped into InDesign. To get the most recent copy of the file into InDesign, click the Update button. If you see a circle with a question mark inside it appear next to your file's name in the Links palette, it means the program can't locate the original file because it's been moved. Double-click the link name to redefine it. Photoshop files smaller than 48K—as well as all text files—are automatically embedded into InDesign files. For this reason, they will not appear in the Links palette.

Save as EPS or TIFF for Placement in Page-Layout Programs

At the beginning of Chapter 2, I mentioned the importance of saving a copy of your file as a layered Photoshop file (PSD). Your Photoshop file should always be your "base" file—you return to it to make all your adjustments. But a PSD file isn't much good outside of Photoshop, because many page-layout programs don't recognize Photoshop files. So how then do you get your work into your page-layout program?

Most page-layout programs require that you import or place your graphic in formats such as TIFF or EPS. Although there are many options for saving your files, these two are most commonly used for print graphics. Adobe's Online Help provides a useful definition of both file formats:

- **TIFF**   Tagged-Image File Format (TIFF) is used to exchange files between applications and computer platforms. TIFF is a flexible bitmap image format supported by virtually all paint, image-editing, and page-layout applications. Also, virtually all desktop scanners can produce TIFF images. TIFF format supports CMYK, RGB, Lab, indexed-color, and grayscale images with alpha channels and Bitmap-mode images without alpha channels. Photoshop can save layers in a TIFF file; however, if you open the file in another application, only the flattened image is visible. Photoshop can also save annotations, transparency, and multiresolution pyramid data in TIFF format.

- **EPS**   Encapsulated PostScript (EPS) language file format can contain both vector and bitmap graphics and is supported by virtually all graphic, illustration, and page-layout programs. EPS format is used to transfer PostScript-language artwork between applications. When you open an EPS file containing vector graphics, Photoshop rasterizes the image, converting the vector graphics to pixels. EPS format supports Lab, CMYK, RGB, Indexed Color, Duotone, Grayscale, and Bitmap color modes, and does not support alpha channels. EPS does support clipping paths. Desktop Color Separations (DCS) format, a version of the standard EPS format, lets you save color separations of CMYK images. You use DCS 2.0 format to export images containing spot channels. To print EPS files, you must use a PostScript printer.

TRY IT   To save your image as a TIFF, select File | Save As or press SHIFT-CTRL-S (Windows) or SHIFT-CMD-S (Mac). Name your file and select TIFF from the Format pop-up menu. Depending on which features your file currently uses (Annotations, Alpha Channels, Spot Colors, or Layers), specify whether to include those in the TIFF version of the file. To embed a color profile, select the appropriate option next to Color before clicking Save to continue and adjust the TIFF options.

▶ CAUTION

Remember that most other programs don't yet support these enhanced features of the TIFF file format, so if you're planning to import this file into another program, you can likely uncheck all boxes and save it As A Copy instead.

In the TIFF Options dialog box, specify whether to compress the image:

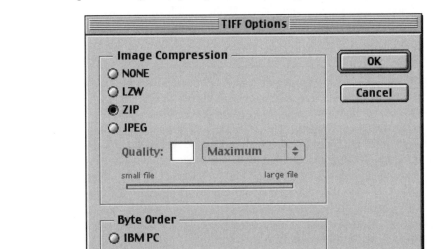

- **LZW** The most common and widely supported; works best for images with large areas of flat color

- **ZIP** Great compression, especially for images with large areas of flat color, but not well supported

- **JPEG** Great compression for photographic imagery, but often produces unreliable results when printed (particularly when color separations need to be made from the image)

► | **QUICK TIP**

Before selecting a compression method, consider why you're using compression in the first place. If it is simply to save space on a disk during transfer to a client or printer, I recommend using no compression (None) at all. If you really need to save space, I find better results in using a program like WinZip or StuffIt to "pack" my files into small suitcases during travel. Then, they "unpack" without any compression adversely affecting the files themselves.

In the second area of the TIFF Options dialog box, specify the Byte Order. Then, if you plan to open this file in Adobe InDesign, for example, check the Save Image Pyramid option to save multiresolution information, allowing the file to be opened at varying resolutions.

▶ **NOTE**

The Save Image Pyramid option currently is not supported by most other programs, so I recommend leaving it unchecked unless you're told otherwise by your output service provider.

If you choose to save your TIFF with layers intact, specify the type of compression to use for those layers at the bottom of the TIFF Options dialog box. If you made a mistake and forgot to choose Save A Copy in the previous window, now's your chance: choose Discard Layers And Save A Copy before clicking OK.

TRY IT To save your image as an EPS, select File | Save As or press SHIFT-CTRL-S (Windows)/ SHIFT-CMD-S (Mac). Name your file and select Photoshop EPS from the Format pop-up menu. If your file contains Layers, Annotations, Alpha Channels, or Spot Colors, Photoshop automatically warns you that the file must be saved as a copy, because the EPS file format doesn't support any of these features. To embed a color profile, select the appropriate option next to Color before clicking Save to continue and adjust the following EPS options.

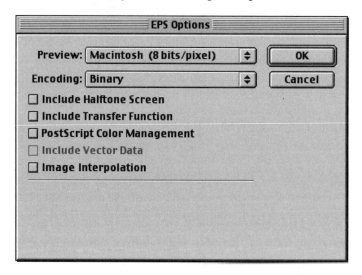

- In the Preview box, select the type of low-resolution image you'd like to use when the file is displayed in page-layout programs that only support low-resolution previews. For cross-platform use, always choose one of the TIFF options—the 8-bit option creates better previews but larger file sizes.

- In the Encoding box, select the way in which the file's data should be transferred to the printer. Although the Binary option typically creates a smaller file size and doesn't edit the original data, it is not supported by all printers. Generally, the ASCII option is recommended for Windows users, while Binary is more commonly used by Mac users. Note that if you use the Binary option and encounter any printing problems, you should switch to ASCII.

- The options for Include Halftone Screen and Include Transfer Function are best left unchecked unless your printer specifies otherwise. To use Adobe's color-management features on the file, check PostScript Color Management. However, if you plan to also use color-management features in the destination file, leave this box unchecked, because the two color-management options could work against each other.

- To keep shapes and type as vectors, select Include Vector Data. Remember this type of content will only be read by other programs supporting vector data, such as Adobe Illustrator.

- Select Image Interpolation to anti-alias the edges of the low-resolution image.

▶ **NOTE**

If your file is in Bitmap mode, you'll also be given the option to display white areas as transparent by selecting Transparent Whites.

▼ Save Your Document as a PDF for Easy File Sharing

Adobe has created a file format called Portable Document Format (PDF), which it describes as "...a flexible, cross-platform, cross-application file format." Some benefits of PDF files include

- Accurately display fonts, even if the user doesn't have the font installed on their system
- Accurately display page layouts, regardless of the platform used for viewing
- Can contain search and navigation features like links

▶ **NOTE**

Photoshop and ImageReady recognize two types of PDF files—Photoshop PDF files and Generic PDF files. Although you can open both types of PDF files in Photoshop, you can only use Photoshop to save images in the Photoshop PDF format. Unlike normal PDF files, Photoshop PDF files can only contain a single page.

PDF files are extremely handy because they are very small and very portable. They can be quickly e-mailed, which is particularly helpful during the proofing process of project development. Even though Photoshop files are generally large, saving a file as a PDF will reduce its size massively without destroying the integrity of what's been created. Furthermore, a designer can share her creation without worrying that it will be altered. Finally, PDF files are flat (without layers) and the type is uneditable (unless you have the full version of Adobe Acrobat, and not just the Acrobat Reader), which makes them very secure for file sharing.

TRY IT   Make sure your document is open. Select File | Save As. In the pop-up menu, choose
Photoshop PDF and name your file with a .pdf file extension. Choose Save to edit the
PDF options.

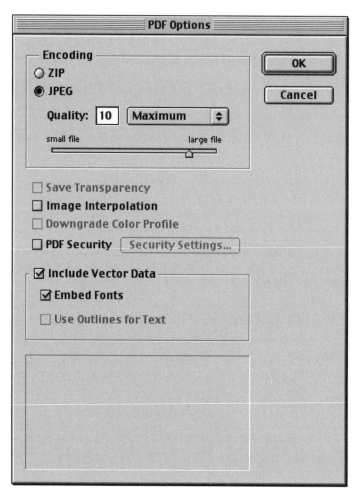

- In the PDF Options dialog box, specify whether to compress the image using ZIP or JPEG
  compression. If your page contains photographic imagery, JPEG will probably do a better job

at compressing the file, whereas ZIP compression works more efficiently on designs with large areas of solid color (such as pages with mostly text content).

- Select Save Transparency to preserve any existing transparent areas, so they will also be transparent when opened in another application besides Photoshop or ImageReady. (Transparency is always visible when the file is reopened in Photoshop or ImageReady.)

- Select Image Interpolation to anti-alias the edges of the low-resolution image.

- Select Downgrade Color Profile if you saved a version 4 color profile with the file (in the Save dialog box) but want the profile to be compatible with applications that don't yet support version 4 profiles.

- Select PDF Security to add a password to the file and restrict access to its content. After checking this option, select Security Settings to specify the level of security.

- Select Include Vector Data to save type and shape information with the file. Check Embed Fonts to save any fonts with the file, if it's important that whomever you're sending the file to sees the content in the same fonts you created it. Otherwise, if you leave this option unchecked and the other person doesn't have one of the fonts you specified, the PDF viewer may substitute that font with another. (The only drawback of embedding fonts is that it increases the file size.) Select Use Outlines For Text to convert the text from editable type to vector shapes. This can be useful if the PDF viewer has a problem reading or printing embedded fonts, but it causes the text to no longer be editable or searchable.

Print Files Directly from Photoshop

As Photoshop's text-handling capabilities increase, so do the number of people using it as a print-layout tool. When you do use Photoshop as a print-layout tool, you'll likely be printing directly from Photoshop, as opposed to the more traditional route of printing from a page-layout program such as Adobe InDesign or QuarkXPress. In cases like this, use Photoshop's Print With Preview command to specify print options before actually sending the file to your printer.

TRY IT To print files directly from Photoshop, ensure the file is ready to be printed and choose File | Print With Preview to access the Print dialog box. At the bottom of that dialog box, select Show More Options to display a window similar to this one, where you can adjust the settings as needed.

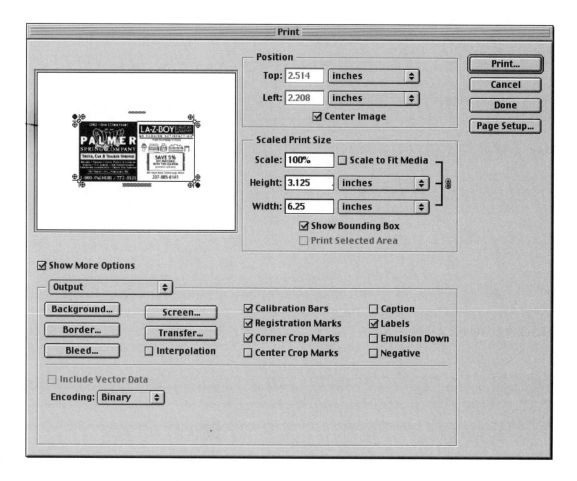

- For Position, place a check mark next to Center Image to center the image in the middle of the available page space.

- For Scaled Print Size, adjust the scale as needed, or select Scale To Fit Media to force Photoshop to scale the design up or down to fit the page size. Alternatively, select Show Bounding Box and then click and drag an edge or corner of the bounding box in the preview window to scale the design dynamically.

- Select Background to add a background color in the space on the paper around your image. (Note, this color will only print up to your paper's margins.)

- Select Border to add a black border around the outer edge of the design when it's printed.

- Select Bleed to print crop marks inside the edges of the image as opposed to outside the edges (which is the default). This option is important if the size of your image was increased to include a bleed amount, and thus your final printout needs to be cut down to a smaller size.

- Select Screen to specify your halftone screen options. (See the next tip for more details on this option.)

- Select Transfer to specify transfer functions used for adjusting the dot gain or loss that sometimes occurs when an image is output to film. In the vast majority of cases, you can leave these options at the default Photoshop values, unless otherwise specified by the professionals at your print shop.

- Select Interpolation to allow the printer to anti-alias the edges of a low-resolution image. If your printer supports this option—most PostScript Level 2 and higher printers do—it can be useful in reducing jagged edges of low-resolution files. However, it may also reduce the clarity of the image when printed.

▶ **NOTE**

All of these settings adjust only the printed file and not how it looks in Photoshop.

- Select Calibration Bars to print a gradation of black from 0 to 100 percent in 10 percent increments below the image, which can be useful in identifying whether the printer prints the full range of blacks in the image. With full-color images, the gradient bar is printed next to each ink in the color separations. (Note, these bars can't print if there isn't enough room around the image on the paper.)
- Select Registration Marks to print marks useful in aligning color separations.
- Select Corner Crop Marks to print helpful crop marks in the corners of the design, which are useful when trimming the image (especially if there's no border).
- Select Center Crop Marks to print helpful crop marks along the center of each edge around the design, which are useful when trimming the image (especially if there's no border).
- Select Caption to print any text entered in the File Info dialog box under Caption. (Note, captions are always printed in 9-point Helvetica text.)
- Select Labels to print the filename above the image.
- Select Emulsion Down to make text readable when the image is printed on film with the emulsion side—the photosensitive side—down.
- Select Negative to print an inverted copy of the entire image, if your service bureau requires it.
- Select Include Vector Data to cause Photoshop to send any vector data in your image to the printer on a separate layer, which allows the vector data to be printed at the full resolution available on the printer.

▶ **QUICK TIP**

If you only want to print a portion of a design, use the Marquee tool to first select the area to be printed, before choosing File | Print With Preview. Then, in the Print dialog box, select Print Selected Area. Or to print only the contents of one layer (or a few layers), turn off any layers containing elements you don't want printed before choosing File | Print With Preview.

- Specify the Encoding method—Binary, ASCII, or JPEG. Binary is the most common and therefore the default. However, some print drivers don't support the binary encoding method. In these cases, ASCII is likely the best alternative. Be forewarned that ASCII files are quite a bit larger and will require more time to process and print. JPEG-encoded files are smaller than both ASCII and binary-encoded files, but the JPEG encoding also decreases image quality and is not supported by PostScript Level 1 printers.

- Select Color Management to specify the source color profile and the print color profile, if different.

▶ **NOTE**

The option Include Vector Data is not available if any of your text layers contain faux formatting, such as Faux Bold.

When you're finished specifying the print options, select Page Setup to adjust the page setup options as needed. Click Print to access the specific print options for your printer. Or hold down the ALT (Windows) or OPTION (Mac) key and click Print One to bypass any other dialog boxes, and just have Photoshop print one copy of the file using the existing settings.

Specify Accurate Halftone Screen Options

Oftentimes, when you're preparing graphics to be printed by professional printers, the print shop will specify the exact halftone screen settings you should use for your files, including the frequency, angle, and dot settings. And even if you're printing the file on your own printer and giving the print shop or service bureau what's considered "camera-ready artwork," it's common for the service bureau to request certain halftone settings in your printed file. This helps ensure the file is reproduced properly on their press.

In traditional printing processes, halftone screens control how much ink is left in each spot of the paper. For example, a screen with large holes leaves more ink, while a screen with smaller holes leaves less ink on the paper. These different amounts of ink are what control how dark or light the color appears on the page. In grayscale images, a single black screen is used. In four-color process printing, four halftone screens are used—one each for cyan, magenta, yellow, and black.

▶ **CAUTION**

Be sure to contact your service bureau for their accurate halftone screen settings before using this technique to change them. If your service bureau doesn't tell you to change them, you can leave the option Use Printer's Screens selected in the Halftone Screens dialog box.

TRY IT   To accurately adjust the halftone screen options of a file, choose File | Print With Preview and select Show More Options at the bottom of the Print With Preview dialog box. Choose Output and click Screen to reveal the Halftone Screen dialog box.

- If you're outputting a grayscale image, use a screen Frequency (between 1 and 999.999) and specify the unit of measurement. Then, enter a screen Angle (between –180 and +180 degrees) according to your service bureau's settings.

- If you're outputting a full-color image, first select the ink color from the pop-up menu and then specify the screen Frequency (between 1 and 999.999), unit of measurement, and screen Angle (between –180 and +180 degrees) according to your service bureau's settings.

▶ **QUICK TIP**

Click Auto to ask Photoshop to generate the screen frequencies and angle it thinks are appropriate for each color in a full-color image. However, if you do use the Auto Screens setting, avoid changing the settings unless directed to do so by your service bureau.

Specify the Shape for your individual dots of ink—Round, Diamond, Ellipse, Line, Square, Cross, or Custom. If you're printing to a PostScript Level 2 (or higher) printer, select Use Accurate Screens to permit Photoshop access to any information needed for high-resolution output.

To save your halftone settings, click Save. Or to turn your settings into the default halftone screen settings, press the ALT (Windows) or OPTION (Mac) key and click the Default button.

Index

INTERNATIONAL CONTACT INFORMATION

AUSTRALIA
McGraw-Hill Book Company Australia Pty. Ltd.
TEL +61-2-9417-9899
FAX +61-2-9417-5687
http://www.mcgraw-hill.com.au
books-it_sydney@mcgraw-hill.com

CANADA
McGraw-Hill Ryerson Ltd.
TEL +905-430-5000
FAX +905-430-5020
http://www.mcgrawhill.ca

**GREECE, MIDDLE EAST,
NORTHERN AFRICA**
McGraw-Hill Hellas
TEL +30-1-656-0990-3-4
FAX +30-1-654-5525

MEXICO (Also serving Latin America)
McGraw-Hill Interamericana Editores S.A. de C.V.
TEL +525-117-1583
FAX +525-117-1589
http://www.mcgraw-hill.com.mx
fernando_castellanos@mcgraw-hill.com

SINGAPORE (Serving Asia)
McGraw-Hill Book Company
TEL +65-863-1580
FAX +65-862-3354
http://www.mcgraw-hill.com.sg
mghasia@mcgraw-hill.com

SOUTH AFRICA
McGraw-Hill South Africa
TEL +27-11-622-7512
FAX +27-11-622-9045
robyn_swanepoel@mcgraw-hill.com

**UNITED KINGDOM & EUROPE
(Excluding Southern Europe)**
McGraw-Hill Education Europe
TEL +44-1-628-502500
FAX +44-1-628-770224
http://www.mcgraw-hill.co.uk
computing_neurope@mcgraw-hill.com

ALL OTHER INQUIRIES Contact:
Osborne/McGraw-Hill
TEL +1-510-549-6600
FAX +1-510-883-7600
http://www.osborne.com
omg_international@mcgraw-hill.com